"*God's Great Story* is an absolute treasure ︙ is a guided journey through the pages of good news each day. I have been using the book with my own family for some time now and see how it helps reduce the intimidation factor that some feel when attempting to read through the Bible on their own. The practical prayer prompts and meditations at the end of each reading are helpful additions, making it easy for students to personally engage with the word of God. But what I like most about *God's Great Story* is that it encourages our teenagers to get into the Scriptures for themselves, and that's where the Holy Spirit does his best work."

Trent Casto, Senior Pastor, Covenant Church of Naples, Florida

"Our teenagers' valuable attention spans are pulled in different directions, and powerful narratives attempt to explain the world to them. However, there is only one story that deserves their thoughtful consideration and assigns meaning and value to everything they can see and everything they can't see. Teens need to know this story and the one who wrote it. In a season of life when time seems to stand still, *God's Great Story* is a devotional that will help teens get to know the one who stands above time."

Gloria Furman, author, *Labor with Hope* and *Missional Motherhood*

"Any devotional worth its salt should motivate readers to understand and read the word of God themselves. I believe that Jon Nielson's book *God's Great Story* does exactly that. This book provides a very helpful structure for daily Bible reading to see how the story fits together to point us to Christ. If you have teenagers in your life, I'd highly encourage you to get this book for them. If you are a teenager, dive in and let this book guide you toward a lifetime of learning to live in this great story."

Chris Bruno, Global Partner, Training Leaders International; author, *The Whole Story of the Bible in 16 Verses* and *The Whole Message of the Bible in 16 Words*

"Devotionals are often either overwhelming or underwhelming. Here is a devotional aimed at young men and women that delivers perfectly. Nielson manages to emphasize the importance of Scripture reading while also informing the reader, pointing to Christ, upholding holiness, and emphasizing grace. This devotional equips theologically and stirs devotionally. As a pastor of a university church, I would be delighted if every one of our students began their day upon their knees with the Bible in one hand and Nielson's devotional in the other hand."

Jason Helopoulos, Senior Pastor, University Reformed Church, East Lansing, Michigan

"The statistics are out there—America's youth are in crisis. Both young men and women are experiencing frightening levels of depression, suicide, drug abuse, and confusion about themselves and the world around them. Worse, many (even those who are seemingly well-adjusted and happy) are drowning in a sea of apathy and ignorance about the only thing that can set their feet on solid spiritual ground: God's word. None too late comes this thrilling book by Jon Nielson. Breaking down God's story into a compelling play of five acts, *God's Great Story* helps our teens (and perhaps their parents) navigate their way through the Bible in a year to see the big picture of redemption—and their place in it. I highly recommend this wonderful, much-needed resource!"

Chris Castaldo, Senior Pastor, New Covenant Church, Naperville, Illinois; author, *The Upside Down Kingdom: Wisdom for Life from the Beatitudes*

God's Great Story

GOD'S GREAT STORY

A Daily Devotional for Teens

JON NIELSON

WHEATON, ILLINOIS

God's Great Story: A Daily Devotional for Teens

Copyright © 2023 by Jon Nielson

Published by Crossway
        1300 Crescent Street
        Wheaton, Illinois 60187

Originally published as *The Story: God's Grand Narrative of Redemption* by P&R Publishing, 2014.

Cover design: Jordan Singer

First printing 2023

Printed in the United States of America

Trade paperback ISBN: 978-1-4335-9033-7
ePub ISBN: 978-1-4335-9035-1
PDF ISBN: 978-1-4335-9034-4

Library of Congress Cataloging-in-Publication Data

Names: Nielson, Jon, 1983- author.

Title: God's great story : a daily devotional for teens / Jon Nielson.

Description: Wheaton, Illinois : Crossway, [2023] | Includes index. | Audience: Ages 10-18

Identifiers: LCCN 2022058958 (print) | LCCN 2022058959 (ebook) | ISBN 9781433590337 (trade paperback) | ISBN 9781433590344 (pdf) | ISBN 9781433590351 (epub)

Subjects: LCSH: Devotional calendars--Juvenile literature. | Christianity--Study and teaching--Juvenile literature.

Classification: LCC BV4810 .N54 2023 (print) | LCC BV4810 (ebook) | DDC 242/.2--dc23/eng/20230418

LC record available at https://lccn.loc.gov/2022058958

LC ebook record available at https://lccn.loc.gov/2022058959

Crossway is a publishing ministry of Good News Publishers.

VP			32	31	30	29	28	27	26	25	24	23
15	14	13	12	11	10	9	8	7	6	5	4	3	2	1

This book is dedicated to my daughters:
Adelyn, Averie, Emilie, and Lucy.
May you grow up reading, loving,
and obeying God's precious word!

Preface

Dear Student,

I've been there. It was the start of a new year. Your church, parent, or youth pastor had challenged you about daily devotions. Maybe you tried to do a "read through the Bible in a year" plan. Maybe you tackled the Old Testament—diving right in at Genesis. Maybe you got bogged down somewhere in the book of Leviticus and wondered when you were going to get out of the part about laws, sacrifices, and infectious skin diseases! Let's face it: reading the Bible—especially reading it every day—is hard work. It takes serious discipline. I think, though, sometimes it's hard for us to read it every day because we forget two important truths about the Bible—truths that make all the difference.

First, we forget that the Bible is not just a book *about* God; the *Bible is God speaking*. The apostle Paul tells Timothy that the Bible is God-breathed, that is, inspired by God (2 Tim. 3:16). There are, of course, many different human authors who wrote the books of the Bible over hundreds of years, but the doctrine of inspiration means that, ultimately, there is one author of the Bible: God himself. The God who made us—and everything else in the universe—made sure that his written word contained exactly what he wanted it to contain. Nothing in the Bible is there by accident! The Bible is God speaking to us, and he says what he says on purpose. This truth has huge implications for how we read, study, and listen to the words of the Bible. We don't read it just to get more knowledge or to get the "right answers" at youth group. We read it to hear God speaking to us! Reading the Bible should be, first and foremost, personal. Do you read the Bible that way? Sometimes I don't. I forget that the Bible is God speaking—to me—today. That fact makes a huge difference in how we approach it.

Second, we forget that the Bible is not just a collection of random books and writings; the Bible is *one story*. This truth comes from the fact that the Bible has one main author: God. If that is true—if God inspired the Bible and is the ultimate author of it—it makes sense that it would all hang together. And it does! The Bible has an incredible unity to it—a unity that would be impossible if God hadn't designed it that way. The Bible is one story. It's a story of God's love and salvation for the people he has created. It has a beginning: creation (Genesis). It has an end: new creation (Revelation). It has a climax: the cross and resurrection. It has a hero: Jesus Christ, God's Son. And the best part is that we are living in the final act of the story. We are living as part of the church of Christ, waiting for Jesus to come back. In a way, we are "Bible characters"!

I've put this devotional together with you in mind. You're a student, between the ages of 15 and 21, and you (like many Christian people your age) have probably had some frustrations trying to get into reading the Bible every day. This devotional will take you through the entire story of the Bible in one year. You won't read every single chapter of the Bible, but you'll read at least portions from every part of the developing story of God's salvation for his people. Each day, you'll read a Scripture passage—usually one chapter or so and sometimes just a few verses. After reading the passage, you'll read an explanation of the passage, which will seek to make the passage clear, remind you of its place in the story, and make an application to your life.

I've called this devotional *God's Great Story* because that's what the Bible is. It is God's story, God's direct communication with us. This devotional has been organized into five acts, just as you would find in a theatrical play. This division comes mainly from Matthew, the Gospel writer, who begins his Gospel with a genealogy of Jesus, divided up into three main sections: Abraham to David, David to the Exile, and the Exile to Jesus. When we add an act on either side (Adam to Abraham and Jesus to the end of the world), we begin to understand that the story of the world can be summarized in this way. We're living in Act 5—we are waiting for Jesus to return!

Before you start, let me say one more thing. Please, please, PLEASE read the Bible passages. Don't just read my devotional thoughts. If you do that, you will have missed the most important and life-giving part of this process: hearing *God* speak to you through his inspired word. The devotional thoughts are meant to help you understand God's word better, not to stand alone as your time with God. If you stick with this thing—every day, with discipline, being consistent—I really do believe that God will speak to you and that you'll come to better understand the Bible as one big story of God's salvation for his people. And it's my prayer that you'll hear God's voice more and more as you get into his word!

In Christ,

Jon

A Bible Study Method

The theological principles that inform our understanding of and approach to God's word lay the groundwork for any Bible study method you choose to use. Your *attitude* toward the Bible is the most important thing; the specific methods are secondary.

But the methods are important! A very simple Bible study method is the observation/interpretation/application model. This method is a helpful one for people who are just beginning to study the Bible. It's easy to remember, and the three "sections" are clearly divided and defined. Here's how it works:

- **Observation.** The basic question in this section is, "What do I *see*?" At this point, you are focused only on making observations about the text. This section is helpful because there are no wrong answers; you can make observations about a biblical text even if it's your first time reading the Bible. Sometimes it can feel as if you're just stating the obvious—but this step is very important. Make sure you don't miss anything that's going on in the passage.

- **Interpretation.** The next move, according to this method, is to begin interpreting the passage. First you asked, "What do I *see*?" Now you are asking, "What does it *mean*?" It's usually helpful to tackle parts of the passage bit by bit, working through the things that it is teaching and communicating. The goal in this section, though, is to settle on the main point that the passage seems to be getting across. You're trying to summarize the "big picture" of the passage in one sentence. Put a sentence together, ironing out a simple and clear summary of your interpretation.

- **Application.** Finally, the last step is to ask the question, "What does this mean for me?" Here you move on from mere interpretation and begin talking about what difference the passage from God's word should make in the way you think and live. This is a very important place to get to, and it can easily lead into prayers that are very focused on the teaching of the Bible passage. Work toward real, practical, and tangible applications of the passage. You can ask questions like, "What does that *really look like* in my life today?" or "How should this affect my mindset as I go about my day *tomorrow*?"

One benefit of this three-step method is that you will very quickly get used to the progression and get better at working through the steps. This method can work very well, especially as you understand the "big story" of the Bible, with the gospel as the center.

ACT 1

Adam to Abraham

And God Said

Imagine your family has a big, strong, beautiful English boxer. Seventy-five pounds of pure muscle, he can jump several feet in the air and sprint much faster than anyone. The dog gets excited when new people come to your house and jumps all over them, pawing at their clothes. Sometimes he wants to play so badly that he'll start trying to bite ankles or shoelaces. He knows how to sit, but when he gets wound up, he doesn't listen to anything you say. In this house—with regard to this dog—words have very little power!

Contrast this with the creation of the world. "In the beginning," we read, "the earth was without form and void, and darkness was over the face of the deep. And the Spirit of God was hovering over the face of the waters" (1:1–2). Then something happens: "And God *said*" (1:3). Have you ever really considered this? When God created the world, he didn't even get his hands dirty. He spoke *words*. The God we worship, know, love, and follow *spoke* an entire universe into existence.

As God created everything in the world, this refrain ("And God said") is echoed by another refrain: "And God saw that it was good." God was pleased with all that he had made; it was good.

Then comes something different. God has a brief "conversation" within the Godhead. The God we worship—one God in three persons (Father, Son, and Holy Spirit)—says, "Let *us* make man in *our* image, after *our* likeness" (1:26). God creates human beings in a completely different way—for a completely different purpose—than anything else in all creation! Human beings alone are created in the image of the eternal, glorious, three-person God. God gives these beings dominion over the earth, and he blesses them and tells them to multiply.

So begins the story of the Bible—the story of the whole world. It begins with God speaking the world and human beings into existence. It begins with God's affirmation of every good thing he had made. And it begins with God's setting apart human beings in a special way for a special purpose. This, to God, is "very good" (1:31).

Take some time to praise God, the marvelous Creator of all things, including you. Marvel at the power of his word. Remember that he made you for his specific purpose. Don't forget to pray about the specific concerns and joys of your day today.

A Day of Rest

The first chapter of Genesis focused on God's work during the six days of creation. God is so powerful that all he had to do was speak and everything came into existence. And God is so powerful that he accomplished everything he had set out to do. Genesis 2:2 tells us, "On the seventh day God finished his work that he had done." Having finished, God did not work on this new day but "rested" (2:2), and through that rest God "blessed the seventh day and made it holy" (2:3).

This passage may only be three verses, but they are verses that introduce a key concept that will echo throughout the whole Bible story: the *rest* of God. This rest of God becomes the foundation for the Sabbath day for God's people—a day for them to celebrate and remember God's rest. Followers of Jesus celebrate this as the Lord's Day until Jesus's return.

I want you to notice something interesting about this short passage. Do you remember the repeated phrase at the end of each of the first six days of creation? "And there was evening and there was morning, the *n*th day." Look at verses 1–3 again. Can you find that phrase after the seventh day? It's not there. The seventh day never ended. In other words, we are living in the seventh day right now! God, enthroned in heaven, is dwelling now in a state of perfect rest. It's not that God has stopped working completely, but he has stopped the work of creation.

Much later in the Bible story, this theme of God's rest comes up again. The author of Hebrews references Genesis 2:1–3 and says these words: "So then, there remains a Sabbath rest for the people of God, for whoever has entered God's rest has also rested from his works as God did from his. Let us therefore strive to enter that rest" (Heb. 4:9–11). What is the rest of God that was ultimately foreshadowed in this passage from Genesis? It is the joyful rest of humans who are saved, not by works, but by grace. Have you entered God's rest—his gracious salvation—through Jesus Christ, who lived and died for you?

Take some time to praise God that he worked magnificently in creation. Think about the fact that now God rests—that we live in the seventh day of creation. Ask him to give you the deepest rest in your soul as you seek to know him more and follow him completely through faith in Jesus Christ, his Son.

Working for God's Glory

Our world sometimes has a warped view of work. People complain about having to work at all, wishing they could quit their jobs and just relax forever. Others make work an idol, viewing it as a way to gain influence, value, and prestige and deceiving themselves into thinking they are like gods because of their success. Sometimes these people desire success in their work so strongly that they neglect to invest in their relationships. In contrast to these views, Genesis 2:4–25 depicts a biblical framework for work.

Note that this passage takes place *before* the fall—before Adam and Eve give in to temptation and disobey the word of God. Therefore, we get a glimpse in Genesis 2 of what God intended for human beings. Here we see that God made the man to work under the authority of God's word in a God-designed, foundational relationship with the woman.

Look at verse 15: "The Lord God took the man and put him in the garden of Eden to *work* it and keep it." Work is not a result of the fall; work is a good thing! Work is a God-given responsibility designed to bring joy, satisfaction, and fulfillment. How is Adam to work? Under the authority and guidance of God's word. In verses 16–17, God gives instructions to Adam about how he should live in the garden; he gives Adam his word to guide his life and work. Finally, we come to the record of God's creation of the woman. This is the perfect, God-designed helper for the man. You can see how fundamental and prominent this relationship is in verse 24. This is the beginning of marriage.

At the outset of the great story of God's work in the world, we find ourselves with a God-designed pattern for man. We were made to work. We were made to live under—and by—the word of our Creator God. And we were made as male and female because God invented the perfect pattern of companionship. Sadly, we'll see in Genesis 3 how human sin horrifically damaged this entire pattern.

Begin today by thanking God for his creative and generous gift of this amazing pattern. Then look at your life. Confess the ways that you do not work for the glory of God. Confess the areas of your life that may not be totally guided by God's word. Pray that God would help you live today with a clear realization that he is your Creator and that you need to be guided by his word every minute.

Attack on God's Word

The famous World War II invasion of the beaches of Normandy (known to most of us now as D-Day) has been immortalized in movies, books, and television shows. It was an amazing battle and one that cost the Allied forces around ten thousand casualties. In any war there are certain arenas—key geographical points—that must be secured to achieve victory. The beaches of Normandy were such a point. The victory there by the Allied forces led to the German army's loss of position in most of France. The battle for the beaches of Normandy was in some ways *the* key battle of the entire war.

There is an epic battle going on in Genesis 3:1–7. The key arena is not a beach; it is God's word. The serpent—Satan himself—chooses the word of God as the key arena for his battle against God and humans. Look at the very first phrase out of the serpent's mouth: "Did God actually say . . . ?" His first strategic move is to question the reliability and truth of what God has said. What should Eve do without hesitation? She should cry out, "Yes, God said it! I believe it! Everything he says is faithful and true, and I will live by and under his word!" But she doesn't. In fact, she attacks God's word in a different way. She adds to it. And Satan, seeing that God's word has already lost its grip on the humans' hearts, seduces them into rebellion against God's word with the promise of knowledge and life.

Men, where is Adam during this whole conversation? Surely if Adam had been there, he would have shut down the smooth arguments of the serpent! Look again at verse 6: "She took of its fruit and ate, and she also gave some to her husband *who was with her.*" Adam is right there. He watches as God's word is attacked by the serpent and doubted by his wife. And he does nothing.

The serpent attacks God's word, Eve begins to doubt the truth of God's word, and Adam does not stand up for God's word. The man and woman rebel, and sin enters the world. This is a very sad day.

Begin today by thanking God for his word. Are you doubting it? Do you add things to it? Do you not stand up for its truth? Pray that today God would help you to listen more carefully to his word.

Run and Hide

One of the scariest phrases an eight-year-old can imagine is when his mother says, "Wait until your father gets home." That phrase, spoken after the boy has done something wrong, is a clear warning—a serious punishment is coming. When that boy hears the door open and his father's footsteps approaching, there is one thing we know he wants to do more than anything else: run and hide!

That's a little, tiny picture of what Adam and Eve are feeling in Genesis 3 after they have blatantly disobeyed the word of God and eaten the fruit that he commanded them not to eat. As soon as they hear God approaching them, they run and hide like scared children. It's not a pretty picture for Adam and Eve when God confronts them either. They begin to play the blame game. "The woman whom *you gave to be with me*," Adam begins, daring to point the finger first at his wife and then even at God himself (3:12). Eve blames it all on the serpent: "The serpent deceived me, and I ate" (3:13). God, of course, knows how it all went down. The serpent—Satan himself—is not without blame. But Adam and Eve must be punished as well. Ultimately they will pay the price with their very lives, and they are sent out from the garden to live and work with toil and struggle until their deaths.

Where's the hope in all this? It's a chapter full of sin, sadness, judgment, and loss of life. It is the very end of paradise! Yet God speaks a word of grace into this seemingly hopeless situation. In the midst of his curse on the serpent, God points forward to the ultimate victory over Satan, sin, and death won by a descendant of Adam and Eve. The offspring of Eve will one day bruise the head of the offspring of the serpent. This promise in verse 15, sometimes called the *protoevangelium* or "first gospel," is God's way of pointing us to his Son, Jesus, even at the darkest point of the story thus far. Jesus, who is God in human flesh, is the one who will one day clean up this mess, conquer death and sin, and finally crush the head of Satan. The war is not lost!

Take some time to think about the wonder of God's grace—that he would promise victory over sin and death even in the midst of human sin and resulting judgment. Praise him for Jesus, who has won the ultimate victory over Satan (and our sin!) by dying on a cross for us and rising from the dead.

A Deadly Cycle

In case we were wondering whether or not the fall of Adam and Eve really did something to the world, we have Genesis 4 as our clear answer. The sin that entered the world through our first parents' rebellion against God's word took immediate effect, even in the lives of their children. Think of sin as a deadly poison; it infects the entire world, dispersing itself to every corner of creation.

Genesis 4 is another sad chapter in the Bible. In verses 5–8, we see an effect of the fall—infectious sin—taking over Cain, the son of Adam and Eve. He evidently does not bring offerings of worship to God in the right way. He gets angry at God. Even after God warns him about the sin that threatens to devour him, Cain deceives his brother Abel, lures him into a field, and murders him in cold blood. This is a terrible day in God's creation.

Amazingly, God shows a measure of grace to Cain. While Cain will be a wanderer in the earth, God nevertheless puts a hedge of protection around Cain and warns to punish any person who might try to hurt him. This is the second time in the Bible that God shows mercy to sinful human beings. Cain is an angry, bitter, selfish man who murders his own brother very intentionally. Does he deserve to die? Absolutely. But God gives him mercy.

Unfortunately the cycle and infestation of sin seems to get worse as the chapter goes on. We are introduced to Lamech, who seems to be a violent, prideful jerk of a man. He brags to his wives about killing a young man and claims that no one should dare come near him to do him harm. Adam and Eve have loosed a plague—an infection—that would creep into every corner of creation. But God is not done. There is a faint glimmer of hope as the chapter closes with the birth of a son named Seth and the beginning of the public worship of God. We have an ugly infestation—and a God who still has a plan for his people.

Look at the world around you. It is not hard to see how sin infects every part of life—government, politics, relationships, and, of course, our own hearts. Remember that God is not done! Think back to that promise that God gave to Adam and Eve in Genesis 3 of the final victory over Satan, sin, and death. Hold on to Jesus today, as the only hope against sin's ugly—but temporary—hold on this world.

Grace amid Evil

When God created Adam and Eve, he gave them a wonderful command: "Be fruitful and multiply and fill the earth" (Gen. 1:28). We see in that command God's gracious intention for the human population to increase and live in the world he had created. But in Genesis 6 we begin to see how the multiplication of the descendants of Adam and Eve led to more and more people—and therefore more and more evil.

When you read the first few verses of Genesis 6, you probably asked yourself, "What in the world is going on here?" We read about sons of God marrying daughters of man and are introduced to a race of creatures called the Nephilim, who were mighty men in those days. Confusing stuff! It seems safe to say that the relationships between these sons of God and daughters of man were forbidden by God—probably because they involved relationships between God's people and people who didn't worship God and most definitely because they involved some kind of sexual perversion. The Nephilim (probably best understood as a race of giants) also seem to be lovers of violence and enemies of God, as they seem to be taking women by force.

One thing emerges clearly from this passage: evil has taken over the earth. We get a brutal summary of human life in the world in verse 5: "Every intention of the thoughts of [man's] heart was only evil continually." This grieves God because God is holy and hates sin. God promises judgment against sin, vowing that he will destroy the earth he has made, along with the people who have rebelled against him so terribly.

The *but* in verse 8 is a beautiful conjunction. In the midst of the evil that has taken over the world, one man emerges who finds favor (or *grace*) with God: Noah. We don't know much about Noah at this point, although we learn later in the story that he is not a perfect man. What does Noah have? Noah has "favor in the eyes of the LORD" (6:8). Because of God's grace to this one man, there will be grace for humanity; God will save some people, even in the midst of his holy judgment against sin.

Are you absolutely sure that you have favor—or grace—with God today? Have you put your faith in his Son, whose sacrificial death for your sins allows you to have favor with God? If so, rest in Jesus today! Thank God that you have favor in his eyes because of Jesus. Ask God for strength to obey his word and follow him, even in the midst of a world that has turned its back on God.

Judgment of Sinners and Rescue of the Righteous

Do you remember singing children's songs about all the animals that paraded onto Noah's ark? They were quite nice—happy sounding and cheerful, with lyrics about the animals' bounding onto the ark two by two. Many of us sang those songs with big smiles on our faces! As nice as those songs are, they are not accurate representations of Genesis 6 and 7 at all! Why? Because the story of Noah and the ark is a story of God's righteous and terrible judgment against human sin.

Genesis 6 tells us that the earth is under the sight of God. God is not blind! He sees the violence and corruption happening in the earth he has created; he doesn't miss anything. And this infinitely holy Creator of all things hates sin. The reality is that human sin against an infinitely holy God must mean judgment and ultimately death. This is what God determines and reveals to Noah: "I have determined to make an end of all flesh, for the earth is filled with violence through them" (6:13). This is an important lesson to learn about God—your Creator. He is holy; he hates sin; our sin against him brings judgment and death.

These chapters in Genesis are filled with death, destruction, and judgment. But what we see in this passage is the beginning of an important pattern for the way that God will work in the world he has made: God, even as he righteously judges sin, always provides gracious rescue for those who fear him and are righteous in his sight. "Noah was a righteous man, blameless in his generation. Noah walked with God" (6:9). Noah was not a perfect man. But he walked with God. He lived under the grace of God. This makes him righteous.

We see in this passage also, for the first time in the Bible, a special word that will come up again and again in the Bible story: *covenant*. God tells Noah, this righteous man who has favor with God, that he will make a covenant with him—a promise to Noah. God promises to save Noah, to rescue him and his family and show him grace.

Think about the holiness of God. God hates sin. God will judge sin. Confess your sins to God today—and be specific! As you confess sin to God, remember that God has shown grace to you. Thank God today for Jesus, whose death in your place rescues you from God's judgment.

God's Covenant with Noah

The great flood that God sent on the earth has finally subsided. This is in many ways a fresh start for human beings. God begins again with Noah and his family, and he even repeats the same command to them that he gave to Adam and Eve hundreds of years earlier: "Be fruitful and multiply and fill the earth" (9:1). You can imagine how grateful to God Noah and his family must be! They alone have been spared from his judgment. They should be excited and ready to begin a new humanity, right?

I'm not so sure. Remember, God has just brought about the death of the vast majority of humanity because of their sin. Noah is a righteous man, yes, but what about his family? What about the children they will have? Who's to say that God won't judge the whole world again by the time Noah's grandchildren get old enough to start killing one another and rebelling against God? If I were one of Noah's sons, I would be terrified!

If you read through the whole Bible, there is one refrain that you will hear again and again: God is gracious and merciful. God shows us this again through the covenant he makes with Noah and his family. What is the covenant—the promise—that God gives to Noah and his family? It's that he will never again send a flood to destroy the earth. God repeats this promise several times, and he even gives them a sign in the sky—a rainbow—that will act as a symbol of his promise to never do this to the earth again. Does God know that Noah's descendants will grow up to sin and rebel against him? Of course he does. But God chooses to show mercy. There will come a day when sin will finally be dealt with permanently; God will finally judge the earth. But God is gracious and patient; he will let human life continue. Be amazed at this God today, who voluntarily makes and perfectly keeps his promises to sinful people—even though he doesn't have to.

Think about how the very life we have on this earth is a gracious gift from God. Thank him for your life! Remember that God is a God who makes promises to people who are sinful and undeserving, promises that he keeps! If you belong to Jesus, God has made a promise to you too. It's a promise that he will forgive you, accept you, guide you, and keep you until you see him face to face.

United by Pride

Think about a time when you did something wrong. Maybe you told a lie to your parents. Maybe you did something that you've never confessed even to God. As you remember that sin, think about what was behind it. My guess is that it could be boiled down to one impulse that began to take over your heart: pride. In a way, pride lies at the root of every sin; it is our sinful desire to make ourselves the god of our lives.

We see that sinful human impulse so clearly in this account. We read in the beginning of the chapter that people everywhere in those days spoke the same language and lived in close proximity. This was the very beginning of civilization; new discoveries were being made every single day. It must have been an incredibly exciting time for the human race! But somewhere along the line, that excitement began to turn into pride. As they looked at their God-given abilities and capacities, the people became dissatisfied with living under God, their Creator. They started wanting to *be* God. Just listen to their words as they begin their plans to construct their great tower: "Let us build ourselves a city and a tower with its top in the heavens, and *let us make a name for ourselves*" (11:4).

In an ironic twist God has to *come down* to see the tower that is supposed to reach into the heavens. Don't read God's words to mean that he is worried that humanity will rise up and overpower him! However, he does recognize the danger in a humanity that is unified not in praise to its Creator but in celebration of its own pride and accomplishment. The people would not destroy God; they would destroy themselves. So God brings judgment on this sinful, prideful, and ultimately laughable attempt of the people to rise into the heavens by their own strength. He disperses them, giving them different languages so that they can't understand each other.

Look carefully at your heart today. Are there ways that you try to make yourself the god of your life? Take some time to confess your pride to God and ask him to help you to want his name to be great in and through your life as you follow his Son, Jesus Christ.

ACT 2

Abraham to Samuel

Great Nation, Great Name, Great Blessing

Genesis 12 begins a story that includes the beginning of the Jewish people, the growth of this new nation, their slavery in Egypt, their wanderings in the desert, and their entry into the promised land. But in this story we will learn much about God our Creator. He is the true hero of the story—remember that! He is a holy God who judges. But he is also a gracious God who does not forsake his people.

It all begins with one man: Abram. We don't know much about this man at the beginning of Genesis 12, other than that his father's name is Terah! Most likely, he was following the religion of the people who lived in his region. We are only told that the Lord speaks to him. And we know what Abram does. He hears God's words to him and *obeys* them. God says to Abram, "Go," and verse 4 says, "So Abram went." Whatever Abram's past was, he responds to God's word with obedience.

Look back for a moment at verses 1–3. God comes to Abram with instructions (to go!), but he also comes to him with a promise, doesn't he? It's a promise—or covenant—with a few different parts. He promises to make Abram into a great nation. He promises to bless Abram and make his name great. He promises to make Abram a blessing and to respond to people on the basis of their responses to Abram. Finally, God promises through Abram to bless *all* the families of the earth. That's a huge promise! God has big plans for Abram—and for all his descendants. He makes big promises to this man, and he makes them unconditionally.

It's good that this promise is unconditional because it doesn't take too long for us to realize that Abram won't be able to keep up his end of the bargain! He's a man who is obedient to God's word, yes, but he's far from perfect. If God's promise had been conditional on Abram's perfect character, this would have been the end of the story. But God is faithful to his unconditional covenant to Abram despite Abram's failures.

We follow a God who makes unconditional promises to undeserving people, even though they are far from perfect! But we still have much to learn from Abram. Pray today that God would help you to respond to his word as Abram did—with immediate, active obedience!

Abram among Kings

When we read passages like this mysterious one, we need to remember that this is not just the Bible story but also *our* story. Everything we read in the Bible relates to us because it all relates to Jesus, and he is our Savior and Lord. We are part of God's people; we just enter the story later than Abram and Lot.

Abram has followed God, left his home country, and brought his nephew Lot with him. Now these two men decide to separate. In Lot's part of the country, a great battle begins between several kings (probably more like tribal chiefs). We see a few of these chiefs getting together to fight a few other chiefs. In the midst of this battle, Lot and his family get captured. As soon as Abram hears the news of his nephew's capture, he gathers his men—an army of more than three hundred—and runs down King Chedorlaomer and his allies.

This king of Sodom comes to meet Abram and makes him the standard offer of the day for coming to a king's rescue: he tells Abram to keep all the possessions recovered in the battle and just let the king have his people back. Abram refuses to take the possessions, probably because he doesn't want to be in any kind of debt to a man like the king of Sodom—presumably a pagan man who was violent and evil.

There is another mysterious character in this chapter: the king of Salem, Melchizedek. In the midst of Abram's return from battle, this king comes out to meet Abram and prepares a meal for him. On top of this, he blesses Abram in verses 19–20. Even more surprisingly, Abram gives Melchizedek a tenth of everything he has!

Notice a few things about this man Melchizedek. First, he is a *king*—the king of Salem. Second, he is a *priest* of God. At this point in the ancient world, there is at least one man who is the king of his people and also their priest, who serves as a kind of mediator between the people and the one true Creator God. In this way Melchizedek foreshadows the great King and Priest to come.

Do you sometimes get lost in the passages of the Old Testament? Pray today that God would show you, even in a new way, that the Bible is your story. It's the story of God's people—and you are part of God's people through faith in Jesus Christ, your great King and Priest!

Faith Counted as Righteousness

Imagine that you are Abram. You've received some great promises from God—promises of blessing, growth, and protection. You want to embrace these promises, but there's that one, tiny little problem that you can't get out of your head: you and Sarai haven't been able to have kids! This is what Abram finally articulates to God in Genesis 15: "O Lord God, what will you give me, for I continue childless. . . . You have given me no offspring" (15:2–3). God, in response, gently reaffirms his promises to Abram. Verse 6 is very important: "He believed the Lord, and he counted it to him as righteousness." First, Abram *believes* God. In other words, he takes God at his word. Second, God counts that belief in his word as *righteousness*.

What happens during the rest of the chapter can be confusing for us. What we see in this strange ceremony is the sign that God gives Abram of this promise—this covenant. In those days when a king or ruler conquered a group of people, he made them perform a particular ritual. The defeated people would make a covenant with that king. As a sign of their promise to serve the king, they would cut animals in half and walk between the severed pieces of the animal. The people who walked between the pieces of the severed animal were essentially saying, "If we break our promises to serve you, King, we deserve to get chopped in half like these animals!" They were swearing *on their very lives* to keep their promise of service.

After Abram chops up the pieces of the animals, we read that "a smoking fire pot and a flaming torch" (15:17)—symbols of God's presence—pass through the pieces. Abram doesn't go between the severed animals—*God* does! In other words, God swears on his own life that he will keep the promise. And God will back this up. One day, many years later, God—in human flesh—would die on a cross in order to keep his promise to bless his people.

How do you hope to be righteous—right and good—in God's sight? Think about the way you respond to God's word, the Bible, which tells us the good news about Jesus, whose death for sin can make sinners righteous. Do you believe it?

A Sign for God's People

The order in which events happen is not always important. Your mom might ask you to help out around the house—to clean your room, take out the trash, and wash the dishes. Does it matter what you do first? Not really, as long as you get it all done. But for other things, the order in which you do them is incredibly important.

We read in Genesis 17 about the covenant of circumcision; it's a sign that God gives to Abram and asks him to fulfill. But the order of events in the story is very, very important here. Abram has already believed God and has been counted righteous in God's sight. Because God has already counted Abram righteous, this circumcision cannot be a condition for Abram's acceptance with God, because it comes *after* God has already accepted him. Circumcision is a *sign*—a sign for God's people that God is their God. It is not a requirement that must be fulfilled in order for God to become their God. Yet it is a very important sign; it sets Abram's family and household apart from the surrounding peoples who worshiped idols and marks them as belonging to God. We know from the New Testament that this sign of the covenant now corresponds to another sign that we Christians practice today: baptism.

As the chapter goes on, we see again that Abram still struggles to fully believe God. We know from chapter 16 that Abram has already tried to make God's promise happen by his own methods rather than God's power by having a baby with his wife's servant. In Genesis 17, it seems that Abram still thinks that Ishmael might be the one whom God will use. But God has something more—something miraculous—in mind for Abram. God says, "Sarah your wife shall bear you a son, and you shall call his name Isaac. I will establish my covenant with him as an everlasting covenant" (17:19). God insists that he will keep his promises to Abram and to the generations that will follow him.

In the Bible, God asks us to do a lot of things, doesn't he? God gave Abram a lot of instructions too. But remember this—God gives these commands to Abram after he has called him, made him his own, and declared him righteous through faith. It's the same with us! Thank God today that "while we were still sinners, Christ died for us" (Rom. 5:8). Pray today that God would help you to obey him with all your heart—not to earn his acceptance but because he has already accepted you through Jesus!

Team Sin or Team Saved

Michael Jordan led the Chicago Bulls to six NBA championships in the 1990s. He was, and is, a beloved hero who achieved great victory for his team and the team's fans. But how do you think other teams thought of him? He was a hated nemesis and a source of great fear. When Michael Jordan came to your town, you knew your team was in trouble. That reality gives us a little picture of the twin truths about God that keep on emerging in Genesis. The same God who saves sinners by his abundant grace also judges sin with great wrath.

In the first few verses of Genesis 18, we find Abraham (whose name was changed from Abram back in chapter 17) being visited by three men. They reveal to him that the Lord has a plan to destroy the cities of Sodom and Gomorrah because of their grave sin against God. Abraham stands before the Lord and essentially begins to bargain with him! Abraham asks God to agree to spare the city on behalf of only ten righteous people who may live there—and God agrees.

We see from what happens in Genesis 19 that not only are there not ten righteous people in the city of Sodom, but there also may only be one: Lot. The men who visit the city are taken in with hospitality and generosity by this righteous man Lot, only to find themselves surrounded by an angry crowd of men from the city, who insist on sexually abusing them. We don't know a lot about this city, but we see all we need to know about the men of the city from this terrible, disgusting account. The city was filled with homosexuality and violence—a place of perversion and unrest. We see one final time in this passage the insistent grace of God; the visiting angels grab Lot and his family and drag them out of the city to safety. Then the reality of God's judgment on the sin of Sodom and Gomorrah is released in the form of sulfur and fire from heaven. Only Lot's family escapes, and even his wife dies as part of God's judgment, as she insists on looking back with longing toward the city full of sin.

Ask yourself how you view sin. Do you hate sin like God does? Do you fight the sin in your own life with fiery passion as you seek to follow and serve your Savior? Thank God today for his grace in your life—for the rescue that he has provided you from his judgment through the sacrificial death of Jesus.

God Is Faithful

Don't you hate infomercials? An obnoxious spokesperson drones on and on about a product you would never want or need, no matter how low the price! There's always that moment near the end where the famous line leads to a climax—you know the line I mean: *"But wait, there's more!* Not only will we sell you this amazing tomato slicer, but we'll also send you these slicer sharpeners absolutely free!"

We see in Genesis 21 a kind of "but wait, there's more" moment that has to do not with a sales pitch, but with the abundant grace of God to keep his promises. First, we see in the birth of Isaac that God has kept his promise to Abraham to give him a son by his wife Sarah. Let's not lose sight of the fact that this is a miraculous birth; Abraham and Sarah had long been unable to have children. But God is gracious and faithful to keep his promises. Verse 1 doesn't let us miss this; listen to the repetition: "The LORD visited Sarah as he had said, and the LORD did to Sarah as he had promised."

Then there's the "but wait, there's more" moment. Abraham—doubting God's promise—had tried to take matters into his own hands and had slept with his wife's servant Hagar. Hagar's son, Ishmael, has now been displaced as the primary son of Abraham; Isaac will be the recipient of all God's promises to him. Yet Abraham surely cared about Ishmael, his son. You can imagine how it broke his heart to be forced by the discord between Sarah and Hagar to send Ishmael away. It is here that God's grace shines brightly. Not only is God faithful to keep his promise to Abraham by giving him a son, but he is also faithful to show protection even to the other son—the one conceived because of Abraham's lack of faith. This child, Ishmael, who existed only because of Abraham's lack of faith, also is a recipient of God's grace and blessing. We know from the rest of the Bible story that the descendants of Ishmael would become—many of them—enemies of God and his people. Still, in this instance, we see clearly again the abounding grace of God to undeserving people.

Our God gives grace to undeserving sinners—and then some. Take some time today to think about God's abundant grace and blessing. Thank him for his rich blessing to you, especially the undeserved blessing of Jesus Christ our Savior.

God Provides a Sacrifice

Genesis 22 is a hugely significant chapter in the Bible—one that could be discussed for a long time. To start, it is best to understand exactly what happens in this passage to see how it demonstrates a great pattern of God: he provides a sacrifice so that his people's lives are spared.

You need to know that many of Abraham's surrounding cultures practiced child sacrifice. They would sacrifice their children to appease the wrath of the gods they worshiped. God had set himself apart from the surrounding idolatrous people groups by *not* demanding that child sacrifice be practiced by his people. So you can imagine Abraham's shock when God appeared to him through an angel and spoke these words: "Take your son, your only son Isaac, whom you love, and go to the land of Moriah, and offer him there as a burnt offering" (22:2). And Abraham went. There is already an application for us at this point in the story, as we observe Abraham's immediate obedience to the word of his God—even as God commands him to do the unthinkable.

You know the climax: just as Abraham is about to bring the knife down to kill his son Isaac, God calls out to him to stop. This is the key point in the story—God *doesn't let* Abraham kill his son! God will not demand child sacrifice from Abraham, although he demands the kind of faith and devotion that would cause Abraham to not withhold an only son from God. At the climax of this story, God does not demand human sacrifice from his people; *he* provides the sacrifice.

In God's sovereignty in putting together his inspired Scripture, this account of Abraham, Isaac, and the almost-sacrifice is designed to point us ahead to another mountain, many years later, and to another Father, who did give up his Son, his only Son, whom he loved. It points us to a cross where God did for us what he would never ask us to do for ourselves. In the end, God keeps this pattern; he does provide the final sacrifice for the sins of his people!

What is God saying to you today through this passage in his word? Maybe you have been reminded in a fresh way of God's love and devotion for you—what he went through in the death of his Son in a way that Abraham didn't have to, so that you could be forgiven and saved. Thank your gracious God for his love and devotion to your forgiveness and salvation!

Every Little Detail

The sixty-seven verses of Genesis 24 form a beautiful—and fascinating—account of Isaac's pursuit of a wife from God's people. We won't be able to summarize the entire story here in just a few words, so we will focus on the foundation for this story, found in the first nine verses.

Abraham is getting old by this point. As he approaches death, he continues to hold on to God's promise to him from years earlier—that God will give the land before him to his many descendants. But Abraham is worried about two things.

First, he is worried that Isaac might marry a Canaanite woman from the land where he is living. That could prove to be very damaging for his son, as the women in the land did not worship God but idols.

Second, he is worried that if Isaac finds a wife from Abraham's people back in their homeland, that wife might convince Isaac to return there—away from the land that God has promised to Abraham's family. So, while Abraham trusts God to keep his promise, he is rightly worried about the effect that Isaac's imminent marriage could have on his descendants.

If we see one lesson emerging clearly from the rest of the account of how Isaac comes to marry Rebekah, it's this: God sovereignly orchestrates every part of this marriage in order to remain completely faithful to his promise to Abraham. God is in control of every detail of this story, even down to the "chance" meeting of Abraham's servant with Rebekah at the well. God puts this all in motion and leads Abraham's servant to the perfect wife for his son Isaac. She is a wife from his own people, yet a wife who is ready and willing to leave her home to join Isaac in the land to which God called him to go. Abraham's descendants will continue to grow and flourish in this promised land of God, because God will make sure of it!

Do you sometimes forget that God is involved in all the details of your life? Pray today, thanking God that he knows every hair on your head and every detail of your day. If you belong to Jesus, you can hold on to his promise to you: that he is working all things "together for good, for those who are called according to his purpose" (Rom. 8:28).

A Tale of Two Brothers

Do you have a brother or a sister? If so, you may notice that two siblings who share the same parents can have very different interests and personalities. One may tend to be intense, high-strung, and self-conscious; the other may be cool, calm, and wonderfully secure in who he is. We get introduced to a situation like this in Genesis 25 as we meet the two sons of Isaac: Jacob and Esau. Abraham has died, and the next chapter in the story of God's people begins with the birth of these twins, who could not be more different!

Even from their birth, these two boys prove to be anything but identical. Esau is red and hairy; Jacob doesn't look like him at all. Esau is a man of the field—a man's man and a hunter. Jacob is more comfortable in the kitchen, hanging with his mother. Their given names are important: Esau's name describes his red and hairy appearance, while Jacob's name describes his behavior—grabbing at his brother's heel during their birth.

We get our first glimpse of the kind of man Jacob is at the end of the chapter. He is a "grabber," or, as his name could also be translated, a "deceiver" and a "cheater." Jacob is sly, cunning, and out to get what he can for himself. Esau, who is physically superior to Jacob, but perhaps not quite so cunning, sells his younger brother his birthright in a moment of weakness. He despises this incredible privilege of being the firstborn son of Isaac because he happens to be very hungry. Esau, we see, is a man of the flesh; he is a slave to his appetites. But what I want you to notice today is that Jacob—this man whom God will choose over his brother Esau—is not much better than his brother! He is a deceitful, cheating, opportunistic, sneaky mama's boy.

While God will ultimately choose to bless this grabber Jacob, it's not because he deserves God's blessing. God chooses him because of who *God* is, not because of who Jacob is. As we'll see, God will do a lot of work on this cheater's heart as the story goes on.

Think about where you were when God first called you to himself. Maybe you were like Esau—basically living for the fulfillment of your own appetites, living for yourself. Maybe you were more like Jacob—living for yourself in a different way, through sneakiness and cheating. Praise God today that he has chosen you—a "bad kid"—and ask him to complete the work that he wants to do in your heart and life!

Jacob the Deceiver

It's very interesting to me that in the Bible a person's name usually tells you a lot about him or her. This chapter takes us deeper into the life of Jacob and shows us what kind of man he really is. In this account, he lives up to his name: he is the deceiver—the grabber.

We begin the chapter with Jacob's mother, Rebekah, eavesdropping on her husband and her son Esau. As she hears Isaac speaking of giving his son his blessing—which would consist of special words of promises from God about Esau's life—she hatches a plan for her son Jacob. While Esau is out hunting, Jacob impersonates his older brother, and his father mistakenly bestows words of God's blessing on him instead of Esau. It is a grand blessing, and it rings of the blessing given to Abraham by God himself: "Cursed be everyone who curses you, and blessed be everyone who blesses you" (27:29). So it's Jacob who receives God's promises to his grandfather Abraham. Esau refrains from killing Jacob but only out of respect for his father, vowing to murder Jacob as soon as Isaac has died. The chapter ends with Jacob's mother sending him away for his own protection.

Do you ever feel bad for God in all this? I do. Look at the people he has to work with! Jacob is a liar, a deceiver, and a grabber. If I were God, I'd regret all the promises I had made to this guy's grandfather. If God is going to keep these wonderful promises—and bless this man Jacob and his descendants—it certainly isn't going to be because Jacob deserves it. Why will God bless Jacob? Because God has decided to keep his promise. What a comforting thing for us to hear today! God is a God who makes promises—and keeps them. We are no more deserving than Jacob, yet God has given us the promise of eternal life through Jesus Christ his Son.

God takes us just the way we are. Jesus died for us "while we were still sinners" (Rom. 5:8). But we'll see as the story of Genesis progresses that while God is faithful to Jacob in spite of his sin, God doesn't intend for Jacob to stay a sinner and a deceiver! To put it another way: God loves you the way you are, but he loves you too much to leave you the way you are. Praise God today that he has chosen to accept you and love you through Jesus. Then ask him to change your heart daily and make you more like Jesus your Savior.

Jacob the Dreamer

Chapter 28 of Genesis begins with yet another picture of the stark contrast between the two brothers, Jacob and Esau. Jacob—the child of the promise—sets off from his home to find a wife for himself from his own people. Esau—the man of physical appetites—takes an additional wife, this time from the clan of Ishmael, in a somewhat misguided attempt to please his father and compete with Jacob.

We stumble upon a lonely scene in verse 10 and following. Jacob is on his own, traveling toward a place called Haran. It gets darker, and he needs to stop for the night. He lies down and takes for a pillow the only thing he sees around him: a stone. In this lonely place in the middle of nowhere, God comes to Jacob. What is going on with this ladder that Jacob sees, with angels of God going up and down on it?

It seems that the best understanding of this is that the ladder represents a connection between heaven and earth. God is demonstrating to Jacob that he will initiate a relationship between human beings and himself. Through God's promise to Abraham and to his descendants, God is establishing an important pattern that he will never completely abandon: God comes near to his people. And so with this vision comes God's restatement of his promise to Abraham, now directed specifically to his grandson Jacob. In the wilderness, God initiates a relationship with this wandering grabber of a man. He reaffirms his promises to Jacob's family, swearing to this lonely man, "I will not leave you until I have done what I have promised you" (28:15).

Don't miss the *response* of Jacob to God's visit. First, Jacob responds in awe to God's words and the dream. Second, he acknowledges God's power and presence. Third, he begins to worship God by setting up an altar and making vows, even swearing to give to God a tenth of all that God gives to him. Jacob—the man who has been living only for himself—is beginning to respond in faith to the God of promise.

Think today about the way that you respond to God's promises and faithfulness to you. Are you in awe of God and amazed that he would draw near to you? Do you regularly respond in worship to God in every area of your life? Respond to God in faith, even as you go about your day today.

A Taste of His Own Medicine

Was there a bully in your class in elementary school? This tends to be a kid who has grown much faster than his or her peers. The amazing thing about life though is that it has a way of bringing such bullies to their knees in humility. You see, no matter how tough, mean, and strong you are, there is always someone out there who is tougher and meaner than you.

Well, life is about to come back at the bully Jacob! Enter Laban, a relative of Jacob's, who is a wealthy and successful man and who has one very beautiful daughter, Rachel. As Jacob approaches Laban's land and sees Rachel for the first time, Jacob has a "love at first sight" kind of moment. He agrees to work for Laban in exchange for the hand of Rachel in marriage. At the long-awaited wedding, Jacob and his bride feast, dance, celebrate, and finally retreat to the tent for their first night together. In the morning, Jacob is given a surprise that is partly comical and also terrible: he thought he had spent the night with Rachel, but he had spent the night with her older sister, Leah! Jacob has met his match in the crafty Laban; the deceiver has been deceived!

The irony of this moment is not lost on the writer of Genesis, as he records Jacob exclaiming to Laban, "Why then have you deceived me?" (29:25). It's reminiscent of Esau's exclamation to his father Isaac after his younger brother deceived him, and perhaps Jacob in that moment saw his estranged brother's face even as he felt the sting of being deceived.

Let's not miss where we are in the larger story of Genesis—and the whole Bible. God is still keeping his promise to undeserving people. Jacob has now taken two wives, marrying Rachel in addition to Leah; God will bless these women with children, who will continue to be bearers of God's promise of blessing to his people. God is utterly determined to bless his people, even though they so often resist his blessing.

We've read about Adam and Eve, Cain and Abel, Noah, Abraham, Isaac, and now Jacob. Think about the common theme that keeps coming up: God's determination to bless his people and keep his promises to them, despite so many of their efforts to the contrary. Thank God today that he insists on blessing you—most greatly in Jesus Christ his Son, your Savior.

Struggling with God

Hopefully, for many of you, the day you first repented of your sins and put your faith in Jesus Christ was a real, climactic turning point in your life. Now we come to an event that is climactic for Jacob. Everything changes for him—and for God's people—after Genesis 32. Knowing Jacob, it's not surprising that this change involves a great struggle!

Jacob has continued to work with Laban and has become wealthy and powerful. God has also blessed Jacob with children by his two wives, Rachel and Leah. But even the growth of his family has not been without struggle. Rachel and Leah—both competing for the affection of their husband—have turned childbearing into a kind of boxing match. One has a child, then the other one has a child to stay even with her sister. They even both convince Jacob to have children with their servant women in order to stay ahead of the other wife. Through Jacob's family's growth, we do see clearly God's determination to bless him, even as this grabber has struggled with God all his life.

In verse 22, Jacob is on his way to meet Esau, scared to death of what his brother might do to get even for Jacob's past injustice to him. As night approaches, Jacob sends everyone else on ahead and remains alone. We then read something very strange: "A man wrestled with him" (32:24). This peculiar fight goes on until morning, when the mysterious man finally releases Jacob, leaving him with a permanent mark—an injury to his hip that leaves him with a lifelong limp.

Jacob refuses to let this man go until the man blesses him. Then Jacob declares that he has seen God face to face. The man who came to wrestle with Jacob in the night was God appearing to Jacob in human form. This struggle represented (in one night) a lifetime of struggle with God. But at the end of the night something shifts in Jacob's heart. He finally sees the need for God's blessing in his life; he begs God for it. And God does what he has been intent on doing all along: he blesses Jacob, even changing his name to Israel, which means "strives with God."

Are you fighting with God today? Is your relationship with him a struggle? The call to the Jewish people in Genesis is essentially the same call to us today: let go, see your need for God, and turn to him alone for blessing. Do that today! Receive his ultimate blessing, which comes only through trusting, loving, and following Jesus Christ.

Worship God with Your Full Heart

Years have passed since Jacob wrestled with God. Jacob and his brother Esau have been reunited, and Esau has spared Jacob's life and forgiven him (33:4). Jacob's family has continued to grow in numbers and strength, and his children are getting older. In these fifteen verses, observe three things.

First, notice Jacob's response to God's call for him to "go up to Bethel" (35:1) and to make an altar to God there. Jacob immediately commands his household to get rid of the idols ("foreign gods") that are in their midst (35:2). It seems that Jacob had not been leading his household faithfully in the worship of the one true God; they had been holding on to idolatry and some of the religious practices of the people around them. Jacob rightly realizes that to follow, serve, and worship God completely, he will need to purge the idols from their midst.

Second, notice God's protection of Jacob and his company; he causes terror to fall on the cities that they pass through in this journey, and he allows no harm to come to them. Throughout the Old Testament, we will find that God is ready and willing to defend his people against all potential enemies; he can preserve the existence of even a small and vulnerable group of people.

Third, notice God's words of blessing and promise to Jacob in verses 11–12. This is a fuller blessing than Jacob has received from God before. It begins with an echo of God's words to Adam and Eve at the creation of the world: "Be fruitful and multiply" (35:11). God is commanding this new people—the nation of Israel—to grow and flourish. Next come God's words concerning the kings that will come from Jacob. This is a promise of great rulers—royal leaders from this nation—which points us many years forward to the monarchy of Israel. Finally, God confirms his promise of the blessing of land to Jacob. Through these promises of blessing, we see God's placing Jacob alongside Abraham and Isaac as a recipient of the promise.

Jacob heard God's call and immediately felt the need to put away all foreign gods and idols in order to fully serve and worship the one true God. Is there anything that you need to put away today, in order to serve God alone, and with your full heart? Pray about these things today, asking God to help you worship Jesus above all else.

Out of the Pit and into Slavery

"It runs in the family." You've heard that phrase, haven't you? Whether competitiveness, humor, or talent, a lot of traits and traditions, strengths and weaknesses, get passed down from generation to generation.

For Jacob's clan, favoritism and sibling strife seem to run in the family. We read at the beginning of Genesis 37 that Jacob loves his son Joseph more than any of his other sons; he even gives Joseph a gift of a very valuable—and very beautiful—coat. Joseph's brothers, not surprisingly, do not like this one bit, and they take their bitterness against their father out on their younger brother Joseph. It doesn't seem that Joseph helps himself out very much, does it? He has dreams that seem to symbolize a day when his whole family will bow down to him in honor, and he tells his brothers all about these dreams!

Finally, a beautiful opportunity to get rid of Joseph seems to fall into the laps of his brothers. Jacob sends Joseph to check on his brothers' work with Jacob's flocks. Joseph's brothers are certainly nasty guys; they want to kill Joseph and toss him into a pit! Reuben convinces them not to kill Joseph, suggesting they just throw him in the pit. (Reuben intends to save Joseph later.) But while Reuben is away, the brothers sell Joseph to a traveling band of Ishmaelites, who carry him down to Egypt. The chapter ends with Joseph's arrival in Egypt as a slave in the house of a man named Potiphar, who is identified as the captain of the guard.

Joseph is now in the lowest place imaginable—in slavery in a foreign land. Yet he will be faithful. More than that, God will be faithful to him. This will be the story of a God who faithfully orchestrates every detail of Joseph's life for his good and for the good of his people.

My guess is that Joseph's day was worse than your worst day! But Joseph does not abandon faith in God, and God does not abandon him. Joseph doesn't know it, but God is using even this terrible day for the ultimate good of Joseph and his people. Ask God to help you trust him that he really is working out all things according to his perfect plan for the ultimate and eternal good of his people (see Rom. 8:28).

Enslaved to Sin

Chapter 37 ended with Joseph in Egypt, serving a guy named Potiphar. We're into the story, and we want to know what happens to Joseph. Then, all of a sudden—wham!—this seedy tale of sex, deception, and sin hits us right in the face. Where is this coming from?

Judah, one of the sons of Jacob, gets married and has some sons. His oldest son, Er, gets married. We don't know much about Er, other than that he is very wicked, so God puts him to death. The custom of the day was that, if an older brother died, the younger brother would marry his widow and have children with her to carry on the name of the older brother. Onan—Judah's next son—marries Tamar (Er's wife), but doesn't let himself get her pregnant, because he doesn't want to pass on the name of his older brother. This selfish, spiteful act leads to his judgment; God puts him to death as well.

At this point, Judah sees that it's not going very well for his sons! So even when his third son Shelah is grown up, he doesn't have him marry Tamar. Tamar, seeing that Judah has not commanded his son to do his duty and marry her, dresses up as a prostitute, deceives Judah into sleeping with her, and becomes pregnant by him. Later Judah, finding out that his daughter-in-law Tamar is pregnant, commands that she be put to death. Tamar, at the last second, reveals to Judah that he is the father of her child; she was the veiled "prostitute" he had slept with. Judah, ashamed, allows her to live, and she gives birth to twin sons: Perez and Zerah. What a sordid tale! Judah's family is wicked in God's sight, and he is no man of high character either.

It seems that the author of Genesis is setting up a key contrast in the story. Think about where we left Joseph: in slavery in a foreign land. Think about where Judah is: a free man in his own land. Two very different situations! But we'll see as the story goes on who is really free and who is really in slavery. More than this, we'll see whom God chooses to be with.

In this passage, we read about a man, Judah, who had the best of circumstances: he was wealthy, free, and successful. Yet his entire family was in slavery to sin. Spend some time in prayer with God today. Ask him to help you draw near to him every day—no matter your circumstances.

God Is with Joseph

When we last left Joseph, he was being delivered as a slave to the household of a man named Potiphar, the captain of the Egyptian guard. As chapter 39 begins, we see that God is not done with Joseph! He is with this young man and blesses him greatly so that he quickly finds his way into the house of Potiphar as his most trusted servant. Think back for a moment to Genesis 38—the sad and sin-stained story of Judah and his sons. What a contrast the situation of Joseph is with that of his older brother back home! God is *with* Joseph, and that is more important than any circumstance.

Joseph, we find, is a handsome man. It doesn't take long before the wife of Potiphar takes notice of this fact and begins repeated attempts to seduce him. Joseph, intent on obeying his God, continues to refuse her advances, and eventually decides to avoid her altogether. Potiphar's wife is not to be denied, though, and she becomes more and more forceful. When Joseph sprints away from her, leaving his coat behind him, the embarrassed woman sees an opportunity to get even with the young man who keeps turning her down. She tells Potiphar, her husband, that Joseph tried to assault her. Potiphar has Joseph thrown in prison for this supposed offense.

Maybe Joseph was now thinking, "Are you kidding me, God?" He's just recently been thrown into a pit by his own brothers and then sold as a slave to a bunch of Ishmaelite traders. Then, just as he's begun to have some success in the household of Potiphar, he's falsely accused and unjustly imprisoned on a bogus assault charge. What terrible luck! Or so it seems.

You see, we find as the chapter closes that God is in charge of this situation too. God has not abandoned Joseph. He begins to give him favor in the prison, so that Joseph is running the show there in no time. God is with this man—even in the depths of prison. And God has great plans to save and bless his people through his faithful servant Joseph.

Have you ever felt like your life is just one bad break after another? Remember this lesson from the book of Genesis: God has great plans to save and bless his people. Ask God to give you faith in him today—even in the midst of difficult things. Praise him for his faithfulness to his people—including you!

The Sovereignty of God

There's a word that describes well the concept that the story of Joseph has been dancing around. It's the word *sovereignty*. When we talk about God being in absolute control, having a plan, being in charge of every detail of Joseph's life, we are talking about God's sovereignty. The Bible is clear, of course, that God's sovereignty over all things does not imply that we do not make real choices. But the story of Genesis doesn't shy away from pointing us to a God who is in utter and complete control of not just the big picture but also of every detail and occurrence in the life of Joseph.

Genesis 40 is no exception. We find Joseph still in prison, where God has begun to give him great favor with the guards. It "so happens" that two of Pharaoh's officials find their way into prison with Joseph: his cupbearer and his baker. God clearly gives Joseph a special gift of discernment and wisdom, as he is miraculously able to interpret the God-given dreams of Pharaoh's servants completely accurately. Just as Joseph said, the baker is put to death, and the cupbearer is restored to his previous position in service to Pharaoh. However, the chapter ends on a sour note. The cupbearer, whom Joseph had asked to bring his cause before Pharaoh, promptly forgets all about his friend in prison once he is out again as a free man.

We should read verse 23, however, as possessing a great amount of irony! The cupbearer has forgotten about Joseph, yes, but we already know from Genesis 39 that *God* has not forgotten about him: "The LORD was with Joseph and showed him steadfast love" (39:21). God still has a plan for him, and in his sovereign control, it is a plan that is far better than Joseph could ever have dreamed. God is still sovereign, even as Joseph sits for yet another two years in a dirty prison, trusting in his Lord to be faithful.

Be comforted that the God who controls and plans all things does have a perfect plan for your life, if you are his child through faith in his Son, Jesus Christ. Even though you may feel like you're sitting in prison, a victim of terrible bad luck, never forget that God is in control. Ask him to help you trust him today.

Wheel of Fortune

The fairy tale of Cinderella, the Will Smith movie *The Pursuit of Happyness*, the life of Johnny Cash—we love rags-to-riches tales. In Genesis 41, we find a rags-to-riches tale that is even more unbelievable than these. It tells the reversal of Joseph's fortunes, perfectly orchestrated by his sovereign God.

Genesis 41 begins with Joseph still seemingly forgotten in prison, a nobody in a foreign land. The chapter ends with him ruling at the right hand of Pharaoh—a man of overwhelming power, fame, and influence. As Pharaoh is tormented by a dream, the forgetful cupbearer's memory is finally jogged, and he tells Pharaoh of the Hebrew man who explained a dream to him two years before. Pharaoh calls Joseph from prison, and Joseph correctly interprets his dream, predicting seven years of abundance in all the land, followed by seven years of famine. Pharaoh, convinced that Joseph has a gift and power from God, not only allows him to stay out of prison but also makes him the second-in-command in Egypt! At thirty years of age, and after years of suffering and seemingly bad luck, Joseph has become a ruler with immense power.

We can't miss what God is doing here. Look at the final verse again: "All the earth came to Egypt to Joseph to buy grain, because the famine was severe over all the earth" (41:57). Earlier in Genesis, God promised to Abraham that all the nations of the earth would be blessed through him. In a small way, God is beginning to fulfill that promise to Abraham through Joseph's blessing of the whole earth through the provision of food. There will be a much greater fulfillment of that promise when Jesus comes many years later, but there is a hint of it here. Also remember who "all the earth" will include: Jacob and all his family! God has put Joseph in a strategic position of power so that, when famine comes, he will provide for God's people. God is remaining faithful to the entirety of his people through his faithfulness to Joseph as an individual.

It is hard to trust God every day, especially when we can't see all the details of his perfect plan. Even at this point in the story, Joseph still doesn't understand what this new position of power will mean for the salvation of his father and brothers back home. But God does. Ask God for faith to trust him, obey him, and follow his Son Jesus—even though you don't know all the details of his plan!

God Meant It for Good

As the seven years of famine begin in the region, other countries begin to suffer from the lack of food—but not Egypt! Joseph, with God's help, has predicted this famine and has led a strategic plan of preparation, so that Egypt has prepared storehouses full of food for survival during this time. People from all over the world start coming to Egypt—and to Joseph—including, eventually, his own brothers. They don't recognize Joseph with all his Egyptian finery, and Joseph takes advantage of this fact. He frames them for theft and even holds their beloved youngest brother, Benjamin, as ransom. Perhaps he is testing his brothers to see if they have any remorse for what they've done, or maybe he is just enjoying the way the tables have turned.

In this chapter, Joseph finally reveals his true identity to his brothers; he "could not control himself" any more (45:1). It is an emotional reunion, and we discover Joseph's true heart. In his new position of power, he easily could have put these Hebrew men to death—these men who had wickedly sold him into slavery so many years before. But Joseph does not. He weeps with them, forgives them, and tells them not to worry. Perhaps the best summary of Joseph's heart and faith comes through the beautiful words that he utters, seeking to tell the story of his own life to his brothers: "As for you, you meant evil against me, but God meant it for good, to bring it about that many people should be kept alive, as they are today" (50:20).

The book of Genesis draws to a close with all God's people—the entire family and household of Jacob—going down to Egypt to live under the care and provision that God has given to them through Joseph. This is God's plan for them—to provide blessing and salvation for them and to prosper and grow them as a people, just as he promised Abraham. This is the end of Genesis, but it is not the end the story of God's people. The very first chapter of Exodus will give us a hint of the trouble that is to come for them.

We serve a God who turns evil on its head like that all the time! God even used the terrible death of Jesus to bring salvation, blessing, forgiveness, and eternal life to all who will repent of their sins and believe in him. Praise God for this today!

New King, Same God

As we begin the book of Exodus, we need to make sure that we do not just breeze through the first few verses, especially verse 7: "But the people of Israel were fruitful and increased greatly; they multiplied and grew exceedingly strong, so that the land was filled with them." Remember how far God's people have come! Not too long ago, God's people were made up of just two individuals: an old, barren couple, Abram and Sarai. Yet just two generations later, here is the evidence that God has kept his promise to his people. The Hebrews have multiplied, increased in number, and even grown "exceedingly strong" in the land of Egypt.

Verse 8, though, is up there with some of the most ominous and foreboding phrases of all time: "Now there arose a new king over Egypt, who did not know Joseph." The Jews' numbers and strength have now become a threat to the Egyptians. And so begins the account of the slavery of God's people in the land of Egypt. They were forced to do all kinds of work for the Egyptians. There were no doubt instances of abuse, beatings, and unfair treatment. God's people had flourished, in accordance with God's promise to Abraham. But what about this? How does this fit into God's plan?

The story in the book of Exodus begins with the slavery of God's people to Pharaoh in the land of Egypt. It will not end there, though! God's plan for his people is for their preservation, salvation, and blessing. In reading the book of Exodus, it becomes clear that God's plan for his people is to bring them out of slavery in Egypt and into worship of him. Even in this first chapter of the book we see the first hint of God's commitment to this plan. Against all odds, and probably at the risk of their lives, the Egyptian midwives defy Pharaoh's orders to kill the male children of the Hebrew people. These women feared God, and God blessed them and used them to preserve the lives of many of his people.

God's big plan for his people in the book of Exodus involves taking them out of slavery and into worship to him. Are you in slavery to anything? Pride? Selfishness? Lust? Sin in general? God's desire for your life is to deliver you through Jesus from slavery and bring you to a place where your whole life is lived in worship to him. Pray today that God would do this in your life!

A Wanderer in the Wilderness

In the Bible, the story of someone's birth is often a very significant indication of what will happen in and through his or her life. Jacob was born grabbing the heel of his brother Esau; he was a grabber and a deceiver for a good portion of his life. And so, when we read of the remarkable events surrounding the birth of Moses, we should be saying to ourselves, "This will be a remarkable man!" Moses will be a remarkable man, because God chooses to work in remarkable ways *through* him for God's people.

From a human standpoint, Moses shouldn't have survived past the age of three months. His mother, knowing that Pharaoh was intent on killing all Hebrew baby boys, essentially gave him up to the mercy of God and sent him floating down a river in a basket! As if by chance, this floating bundle ends up in the hands of Pharaoh's daughter, who decides to adopt the child as her own. In perhaps the most ironic twist of this first part of the chapter, Moses's mother ends up getting paid to take care of her own son.

Moses, evidently something of a hothead as he gets older, gets himself into some serious trouble with Pharaoh. Seeing one of his fellow Hebrews getting beaten by an Egyptian, he kills the Egyptian in anger and hides the body. Pharaoh catches wind of this and puts a price on Moses's head. Moses, though, runs away, and God preserves his life. The section ends with this fugitive on the run in the wilderness.

But the chapter doesn't end there. The slavery and anguish of God's people in Egypt is getting worse, and they begin to cry out to God. We read that God heard their prayer and that he "remembered his covenant with Abraham" (2:24). And, in fact, the entire story of Moses's life proved that God hadn't forgotten his people. God had been at work, preserving the life of this fugitive and preparing to use him to deliver his people from slavery. This Moses—a wanderer in the wilderness—would indeed become the prince and judge over God's people.

In this passage, God was preserving the life of his servant Moses and preparing him to return to Egypt to speak God's words to Pharaoh and lead his people out from slavery. God never stops working out his plan! Ask God to help you remember that today. Ask him to help you trust that he does not sleep or take breaks in working for his people and his plan.

The Burning Bush

There is little doubt that Moses thought he was done with Egypt. He had gotten away with murdering an Egyptian, and he was a wanted man there. His plan was probably to live out his days with his wife in the land of Midian, taking care of the flocks of his father-in-law, Jethro. But this all changed on the day we read about in Exodus 3. It's a normal day, and Moses is guiding the flocks as they graze. All of a sudden, he sees something remarkable: a bush that is on fire, burning with a steady flame without being burned up.

Verse 4 tells us that "God called to him out of the bush." The burning bush—a sign of God's presence—had been placed there by God so that Moses would take notice and listen to God's word to him. He tells Moses that he has heard his people's cries in the midst of their affliction and slavery in Egypt and that he is going to deliver them; he is going to do this through the leadership of this man, Moses. Moses—this fugitive sheepherder—is God's chosen man for a huge mission.

Moses responds to God in the way that we all might respond to a commission like this from God: he expresses a great sense of unworthiness. "Who am I," he says, "that I should go to Pharaoh and bring the children of Israel out of Egypt?" (3:11). Moses was not looking for this kind of responsibility. He knew what he was—a nobody. Moses had no illusions about his own leadership abilities and talents.

Notice, though, how God responds to this humble question from Moses. He doesn't rebuke him. He doesn't try to convince Moses that he's very special and up to the challenge. God reminds Moses of his presence with him in this call: "But I will be with you" (3:12). That is God's answer to Moses's "Who am I?" question. God answers Moses's doubting question with an assurance of his own divine presence with him. That is enough. That is why Moses will succeed in this call: *God* will be with him.

God's promise to you today is that—if you belong to Jesus Christ—he is with you. That is our hope—not that we're strong enough, but that God is with us. He's shown us this through the work of Jesus Christ—Immanuel—"God with us." Trust in him, not yourself, as you follow him today.

God's Control and Human Choice

In Exodus 4–5, God sent Moses and his brother Aaron to Egypt to speak to Pharaoh. Their meeting with Pharaoh didn't go too well; Pharaoh refused to let the Israelites go and made their work much harder by refusing to give them straw to work with. Moses and Aaron, distraught that they brought their fellow Israelites into an even worse situation than before, turned to God for help. In Exodus 6, God again promised the deliverance of his people and sent Moses and Aaron back to Pharaoh, this time with great signs.

What happens in Exodus 7 is quite amazing. There is a magical competition of sorts as Moses and Aaron square off against the magicians of Egypt. By the magicians' dark arts, they are able to turn staffs into serpents. The magicians are even able to match the first great plague performed by God through Moses and Aaron: turning water into blood. These magicians, whose power most likely came from Satan himself, won't be able to keep up long with the almighty power of God! But they do remind us that there is real power in the demonic forces that are at work in our world. Satan and his servants are real and dangerous, although we will see that they are no match for our God.

But what I really want you to notice today is the interesting interplay in this chapter between the obvious sovereign plan of God in all these events and the real human choices made by this king of Egypt, Pharaoh. Look at the way Pharaoh's behavior and attitudes are described in Exodus 7. In verse 3, God says, "I will harden Pharaoh's heart." In verse 4, God tells Moses and Aaron that "Pharaoh will not listen to you." In verses 13, 14, and 22, the text simply tells us that Pharaoh's heart *was* hardened. Both truths—God's sovereign control and real, responsible human choice—are held next to each other in this chapter of Scripture without dissonance. God is always working out his perfect plan in the world, even as human beings continue to make real choices to either follow God or harden their hearts against him!

You serve the God who is working all things according to his plan, and he will let nothing get in the way of that. Thank God today that he—the all-powerful Lord of the universe—has chosen you for himself. Don't harden your heart against him; be ready to listen to his word and obey it!

God's Commitment to Saving His People

These plagues almost seem like something out of a science fiction movie, don't they? Yet these were the first nine plagues that God brought upon the land of Egypt—all because of the hardened, stubborn heart of Pharaoh who would not listen to God's word. God did all this for his people—as a sign to Pharaoh that he was God and that these people belonged to him.

In Exodus 11, God reveals to Moses what his terrible, final plague will be on the Egyptians because of Pharaoh's hard heart. He will visit the Egyptians during the night and take away the lives of all the firstborn in the land—even the firstborn of all the cattle. This will be a terrible, awful, painful sign that God will perform against the Egyptians—and on behalf of his enslaved people. This is a hard chapter to read; we see God doing whatever it takes to save his people from slavery to Pharaoh.

As we think deeply about this chapter, let's notice a few key things that are going on here. First, observe that God is making his chosen servant Moses *great*; God is lifting up his chosen man and making him effective, powerful, and honored in the sight of all the people—both the Israelites and the Egyptians. Second, we see God's insistent plan to bless his people. Verses 2–3 show us the Egyptians' showering the Israelites with goods, so that they become rich on their way out of town. Third, we see the continued awful reality of a heart made hard as stone against God's word. Pharaoh's resistance to God's word, even in the midst of the great suffering of his people, is almost impossible to believe! Yet even today, many people live their lives in continued, intentional resistance to God's truth and God's word. Fourth, though, we get a behind-the-scenes glimpse in this chapter into what God is doing in all this—and *why* God is doing things this way. In verse 9, God tells Moses, "Pharaoh will not listen to you, that *my wonders may be multiplied* in the land of Egypt." God is all about multiplying his wonders—working out all things to the glory of his name.

We serve a God who was willing to do whatever it took to save lost sinners like us—even going so far as to see his own firstborn Son put to death in our place. Thank God today that he is totally committed to your salvation—and your eternal good in him. Pray that he would make you totally committed to the glory of his name in your life.

The Blood of the Lamb

God gives his people very detailed instructions regarding this night of Passover—instructions about how to cook the lamb and how to spread the lamb's blood on the lintel, the crossbeam over the door of each house. These kinds of rituals are pretty foreign to us today. So, how does a chapter like Exodus 12 affect us as Christians?

First, we need to understand its purpose and function in the story of the Bible and its specific place in the book of Exodus. This Passover functions as the ultimate saving picture of God for his people in the book of Exodus, and really, in the entire Old Testament. In the midst of the final tenth plague, God gives his people a way out. God's people have to place themselves under this sign of the Passover. And what is this sign? It is the sign of *blood*. The blood of a lamb. Smeared on the doorway of their homes. It is this sign of blood that will turn away judgment and death from the homes of God's people. We read in two different places in this chapter (12:28, 50) that God's people obeyed his word. They put this sign of lamb's blood on their doors, and they were spared from God's judgment.

As the Bible goes on, this Passover event will become a picture—and a pattern—for the far greater saving event that God performs for his people through the cross, where Jesus, God's Son, dies. Jesus Christ, the second person of the Trinity in human flesh, is called the Lamb of God in many places in the Bible (see John 1:29). That is no accident! That label for Jesus was chosen purposefully by God to direct our memories back to this great saving event in the book of Exodus. God's people have never been perfect, and the Israelites deserved to be judged just as much as the Egyptians did. But God offers his people a way out. He invites them to survive his judgment through the sacrifice of a flawless lamb, whose blood would cover them and save them from death. This is what Christ does for us—in a far greater way!

Thank God that he chose to "pass over" your sins because of Jesus's death. Ask God to help you remember daily that your salvation is because you are under the sign of blood; you are covered because of Jesus. He is our only hope; cling to Jesus, the perfect Lamb of God!

Crossing the Red Sea as on Dry Land

The hardened heart of Pharaoh has finally been broken; he has let God's people go out from the land of Egypt. But he and the people of Egypt begin to say to themselves, "What is this we have done, that we have let Israel go from serving us?" (14:5). God hardens Pharaoh's heart one more time against him and his people, so that this time, no one among the Egyptians will be able to mistake the fact that he alone is the true God.

As we come closer to the main point of this chapter, first notice the attitude—and surprising words—of God's people. Remember, God has only just miraculously delivered them from slavery in Egypt, even sparing their children from death through the sign of the blood of lambs. All it takes, though, is the sight of Pharaoh and his army chasing them for them to immediately turn on Moses and their God in anger, disbelief, and doubt. Listen to their words to Moses again: "Is it because there are no graves in Egypt that you have taken us away to die in the wilderness? What have you done to us in bringing us out of Egypt?" (14:11). Doubt. Anger. Disbelief.

By verse 9, the Israelites are trapped between the armies of Pharaoh behind them and the Red Sea in front of them. God, in the midst of this seemingly impossible situation, speaks these beautiful words to his doubting people: "The LORD will fight for you, and you have only to be silent" (14:14). God, through the hand of his servant Moses, then parts the waters for his people to pass through and brings the waters back together with a rush, consuming Pharaoh and all his forces. God delivers his people in a magnificent way!

God is showing his people that the God who *saved* them from slavery in Egypt is faithful to *keep on saving* them from all their enemies and from all danger. God is not done with his people! He *spared* them from judgment through the sign of the Passover lamb, and he will *sustain* them each day as they follow him, protecting them as he leads them.

God has forgiven your sins, if you have repented and put your faith in Jesus Christ, but he does not stop there! God is with you, protecting your heart and your soul as you live for him. Thank God today for his salvation, and for how he sustains (or keeps) your faith each day.

Gathered to Hear God's Word

Exodus began with the people of God in slavery to Pharaoh in Egypt. As God began to orchestrate their freedom, he had Moses give a very specific message to Pharaoh: "Let my people go, that they may *serve* me" (8:1). Moses repeated this phrase many times to the hard-hearted king of Egypt. God's plan was to take his people out of *slavery* in Egypt and lead them into *service* to him.

God has miraculously taken his people out of the land of Egypt. In the wilderness, God has provided manna from heaven for the people to eat and water from rocks so that they will not die of thirst. God now says to Moses, "Go to the people and consecrate them today and tomorrow. . . . For on the third day the LORD will come down on Mount Sinai in the sight of all the people" (19:10–11). It's finally time! God's people, brought by him out of slavery, are finally going to meet their God and begin worshiping and serving him!

Do they have a great worship service? Do they begin singing songs to God? Does God send his people out on a service project? No. What are the first words of Exodus 20? "And God *spoke* all these words" (20:1). God's people—out of slavery—gather to finally serve him in the wilderness. They gather, prepare, wait, and—finally—God *speaks* to them. Friend, this *is* worship and service to God. It is God's people, prepared and gathered, listening to the word of God with hearts ready to obey.

While we can't go into detail here about all the words God speaks, let's close by understanding an important aspect of the *timing* of these commandments. They are words of law given by God to people that he has already saved and chosen for himself. God could have given these commandments to his people when they were still in the land of Egypt, making his people's obedience a kind of prerequisite for deliverance. But God doesn't do that! He saves them first—then tells them how they can obey him in love and gratitude.

God delivered his people from slavery so that they could serve him by gathering to hear and live under his word. Pray today that God would help you worship and serve him in the way that he wants. Pray that you would be totally committed to listening daily to his word and obeying it.

Burning with Holiness

If you are a teenager, you are part of a generation that tends to value authenticity—being "real"—more than outward appearances. You tend to be more casual because you want to be authentic; you want to be yourself. A problem comes, though, when a *casual* attitude invades our relationship with—and approach to—the almighty and holy God of the universe. Sometimes we can be tempted to forget, in our casual world, that God is frighteningly powerful and awfully holy.

This chapter contains the amazing account of a holy God giving his word to his people through his chosen servant, Moses. God first calls Moses and some of the leaders of the people to himself, and they share in worshiping God together. Then God calls just Moses forward to give him the law, which will be the guide for the people as they follow their God. Moses goes on by himself to the top of the mountain. Listen to the people's perspective of what this is like: "Now the appearance of the glory of the LORD was like a devouring fire on the top of the mountain in the sight of the people of Israel" (24:17). God quite literally *burns* with holiness! For forty days and forty nights, the people are in absolute awe of this sight at the top of the mountain, where a holy God gives his holy word to his chosen servant for all the people to follow and obey. God is scary in his holiness and power. But even though God is powerfully holy, we see his grace in every word of this chapter of Exodus. The infinitely holy God chooses to approach sinful people.

Consider briefly the response of God's people to his word in this chapter. I'll paraphrase what they say: "We've heard your word, God, and we're ready to do whatever you say!" It is a beautiful response to God's word—the right response! And it should be our response to our holy God who has come near to us in Jesus. We should be crying out every day, "Whatever you want from us, God, we'll do it!"

Maybe you need to spend some time today being in awe of the holy God who made you—and who graciously draws near to you through Christ to initiate a relationship with you. That is grace—thank him for it! Ask God to help you respond to him in the way these Israelites did in Exodus 24: "God, we have heard your words, and we will obey them all!"

Pointing Toward the Perfect Priest

God has already made the Israelites his chosen people; then he gives them the law so that they will know how to live as a community that worships God. As you continue to read the Bible story, it will be helpful to keep reminding yourself that God's gift of the law to his people is an incredibly gracious one; God is giving instructions to his people so that they are able to dwell in close proximity to an infinitely holy God. God is teaching his people about his holiness.

In Exodus 32, something terrible happens. Moses is still on the mountain, receiving the law of God on behalf of the people. And the people get impatient. They are sick of waiting for Moses and tired of following this God that they cannot see with their eyes. So they convince Aaron—Moses's brother, the priest—to build for them a calf, made from the gold jewelry that they got from the Egyptian people when they left town. Then they throw a huge party and dance around this calf, singing its praises together.

The people of Israel craved something *tangible* that they could gather around and worship. They grew weary from following an invisible, mysterious God who reigned over them through his word.

Notice a few key things that happen next. First, in verses 25–29 we see immediate judgment on some of the people who have been a part of this sinful idolatry. We are learning an important lesson here, which will be repeated as we go through the Bible: God's holiness is more important than human life. Second, we see Aaron failing as a priest (a worship leader and mediator) for God's people. God's people need a better priest than Aaron! Third and finally, we see Moses fulfilling a very key *mediating* role for God's people; he even offers his own life and soul to God on behalf of the sinful people. While God ultimately doesn't take Moses up on this offer, this exchange does point our eyes forward to one day when God will accept such a request from his own Son.

Pray today that God would lead you to worship him alone, rather than any false idols. Thank him that he has provided you with a perfect priest—his own Son—who laid down his own life so that you wouldn't have to face judgment for the sin and idolatry you have committed.

Someone Greater Than Moses

Exodus 40 includes God's final instructions for Moses and the people concerning the construction of the tabernacle. This tabernacle included a screened-off area that held the ark of the covenant, which was the special symbol of God's holy presence with his people. More than the construction of this tabernacle, though, God gives Moses very detailed instructions for how to consecrate the tabernacle. *Consecrate* means to "set apart" or "make holy to God." After the tabernacle, altar, and even furniture are consecrated, God instructs Moses to wash and consecrate the priests who will serve God, make sacrifices, and help God's people worship him. Verse 33 tells us: "Moses finished the work." Moses led the people in completing all the work God gave them to do. They have prepared themselves through God's stipulations to live, dwell, and worship in close proximity to a holy God. The tabernacle is now ready for God!

But as satisfying as this end to Exodus is in some ways, the last few verses leave us with a sense of emptiness and incompleteness. Yes, the glory of the Lord descends on this tabernacle and fills it. Yes, the people are now ready to worship God as he has instructed. But something surprising—and kind of sad—happens in verse 35: "Moses was *not able to enter* the tent of meeting because the cloud settled on it, and the glory of the LORD filled the tabernacle." Moses, this leader of God's people and chosen servant of God, is ultimately not able to come near to the presence of an infinitely holy God. He too is a sinner; he has to keep his distance from the glory of God. This comment at the end of Exodus leaves us wanting more. God's work with his people is not finished. Their very leader is still not able to be in the holy presence of his Maker; even Moses needs something—or someone—to wash him clean from his sins.

Moses needed the saving work of Jesus in his heart and life. Have you ever thought about that? This great leader of God's people could not come near to God as his glory descended on the tabernacle in Exodus 40. Jesus, who washes us clean from our sins by his death, makes this kind of closeness with God possible for sinners. In Jesus, we will one day live for all eternity in close proximity to our Maker. Thank God for this today, and ask him to continue his changing work in your heart and life.

A Pleasing Aroma?

Leviticus 1 is all about burnt offerings. God calls Moses to himself and gives him some very detailed instructions for these offerings. There are instructions for offerings of animals from the *herd*, like cattle. There are instructions for offerings of animals from the *flock*, like sheep. And, there are instructions for offerings of birds, for those people who couldn't afford to bring larger, more expensive animals to sacrifice. God instructs Moses how to lead the people in properly cutting and cleaning these animals, arranging their body parts on the altar, and even flinging their blood on the sides of the altar.

There is a very interesting phrase, though, that is repeated at the end of each set of instructions. It may have caught your attention as you read. It's the phrase that describes the offering being burnt as giving off "a pleasing aroma to the LORD" (1:9, 13, 17). Let's get real for a moment. Think about hundreds—even thousands—of people bringing cows, sheep, and birds to the tent of meeting and killing them, cutting them up, and having the priests fling their blood on the altar. It would have been an absolutely bloody mess. Animal parts everywhere. Blood spattered all over. And it wouldn't have smelled pleasing. It would have smelled *awful*. Why in the world would God make his people do this? And why in the world would God say that this all would be a pleasing aroma to him?

God is teaching his people an important lesson about his holiness—and our sin. The lesson is this: our sin deserves death. Our sin causes a big, bloody, stinky mess. And, more than this, there has to be *shedding of blood* in order to pay for human sin. Since sin causes death, something has to die in order for the stench of sin to be taken away. The shedding of blood for the sins of his people is the way to favor with their holy God.

As you confess your sin to God, thank him that he does promise forgiveness through the final sacrifice of his Son, Jesus, on the cross. Jesus's cry from the cross—"It is finished" (John 19:30)—tells us that no more bloody sacrifices for sin need to be made.

Sin Offerings

Leviticus 4 is entirely about God's instructions for his people with regard to their sin. The chapter covers instructions for sin offerings—offerings that were given when different people within God's community unintentionally sinned against him by breaking a law, or by not doing something they were supposed to do. The wonderful thing about reading passages of the Bible is that the God who ruled over the Israelites during the time of Moses is the same God who rules over us today; we can learn about our God through the book of Leviticus.

There's an important lesson that is emerging for us from Leviticus 4. It's a lesson about our sin and its effects. You might be asking the questions: Why does God take sin so seriously? Does the sin of God's people really *do* something so terrible? I believe that we find our answer to these questions in the details of the instructions that God gives to Moses. For these sin offerings, God tells Moses to kill the animal before him and then have the high priest do something that may seem strange to us: the high priest is to "dip his finger in the blood and sprinkle part of the blood seven times before the LORD in front of the veil of the sanctuary" (4:6, 17). What is going on here?

Well, the veil of the sanctuary separated this place of holy worship—and God's own presence—from the sinful people of Israel. When God's people sin, they defile the holy presence of God in their midst. They don't just sin against each other; they sin against their holy God, and their objects and place of worship to him become unclean and stained by sin.

Our sin is not just messing up or falling a little short of God's intention for us. Our sin is a dirty offense against an infinitely holy God. This passage also helps us better understand the need for Jesus. You see, just as the Israelites needed the cleansing of blood to make their worship space clean again after it had become defiled by their sin, so we sinners need the cleansing blood of Jesus to have the hope of truly being in a relationship with a holy God.

Our sin against God needs blood and sacrifice to get cleaned up and dealt with. And that's exactly why Jesus, God's Son, came to die! Thank God today again for Jesus, confessing your sin and trusting his forgiveness to you through the cleansing blood of his Son.

A Weighty Ceremony

Have you ever watched a presidential inauguration on television? It's a pretty incredible event. It's a service of great formality, tradition, and weight because of the importance of the office of president. The man being sworn in as the leader of the United States must surely feel the great weight of his responsibility during this service of inauguration.

Leviticus 8 is about a weighty ceremony of preparation—not for a president, but for the priests of God for the people. Aaron and his family have been chosen by God as the ones who will serve as these priests. Priests were called to serve as *mediators* between the people and their God. They were go-betweens—performing sacrifices on behalf of the sinful people in order for them to remain in a right relationship with a holy God. In some ways, the right worship of God by the people of Israel depended on the faithfulness, obedience, and care of their priests.

But we can't help but notice in the passage that the priests—in spite of their weighty role—are no different from the rest of God's people in one important way: they too need to be cleansed by blood in order to be able to serve God faithfully. In fact, that's what this entire chapter is all about! Aaron and his sons are first washed with water. Then they are anointed with oil. After that, a bull is sacrificed for the priests. Then a ram is sacrificed for them. Then *another* ram is killed—a ram of ordination. Finally, Aaron and his sons are sprinkled with oil and blood from the sacrifice one more time. That is a long process of consecration (the process of "setting apart" as holy) for these priests! Yes, they will be servants of God on behalf of the people. Yes, they are called to serve as *mediators* between God and man. But these human priests need the purifying and cleansing blood of sacrifice on their behalf as well, because they too are sinful men.

If there's one thing we learn from this passage, it's that sinful human beings need to be washed by God before they engage in service to God. Before you serve God, make sure that you have been washed by him—forgiven through the death of his Son on the cross for your sins. Take some time today thanking God for cleansing you from sin through Jesus's death, and ask him to help you serve him in response to what he has done for you.

The Goat

Back in Leviticus 10:1–3, you can read about the fiery death of Aaron's two sons, Nadab and Abihu. Unfortunately for these men, they didn't take seriously enough the holiness of their God. They drew near to the Most Holy Place in an unauthorized manner—disrespecting and disregarding the spectacular holiness of God—and they were struck dead on the spot. This frightening event gives us the setting for God's instructions to Moses regarding Aaron's proper role on a very important day for God's people: the Day of Atonement. This was a day for a very special sacrifice that would happen only once a year—a sacrifice that would be offered by the high priest on behalf of the sins of all the people, including the priest himself.

It will help you understand this passage better if you see that the atonement that is happening moves outward; it begins with the priest's sins and moves further outward toward the sins of the people. Aaron begins with a bath and dresses in a very specific manner. He does not come empty-handed, but brings with him several animals—for himself and for the people. Then the sacrifices begin; a bull is killed as a sin offering for Aaron, followed by a goat, as a sin offering for the people. The final part of this special day is different, though, as one sacrificial goat is not killed but sent away into the wilderness. This goat symbolically carries all the sins of God's people far away from where they live, after Aaron has placed his hands on the goat and confessed the people's sin.

So much work has to go into dealing with the sins of fallen people in order for them to be able to live in community with a holy God! We'll find out as the Bible story goes on that atonement for God's people's sin is not only very difficult but impossible. God's people will ultimately need a perfect, final, human, and even divine sacrifice to fully complete a Day of Atonement for them.

The beauty of living as followers of Jesus is that we do not have to work in order to earn our atonement, our forgiveness with God. Jesus has done that for us! He was sent away from God's people (like that "scapegoat") to bear all their guilt. Trust God today that he has accomplished your salvation in Jesus. Then ask him to help you work with all your strength to follow him—because he has already forgiven you and saved you!

Set Apart

In reading the book of Leviticus, we often focus on what we learn about God's holiness and human sinfulness. We have a *vertical* focus. For example, the entire sacrificial system shows us the important reality of the need for cleansing blood in order for sin to be dealt with. In this passage, we see that being set apart for God's people had to do not only with sacrifice but also with everyday life—a *horizontal* focus.

The whole chapter is grounded on a key phrase from God in verse 2: "You shall be holy, for I the Lord your God am holy." First, the holiness of God's people is meant to be demonstrated in their relationships with one another. God calls his people to leave fallen crops and grapes on the ground in their fields in order to provide food for the poor among them, who could come and glean the extra. God's people are instructed against any kind of oppression, deception, hatred, or injustice toward others. In other words, God's call to his people is for all their relationships with the people around them to be characterized by *justice*—fair, righteous, good, godly treatment. Second, the holiness of God's people is meant to be demonstrated in their different behavior compared to the nations around them. Prostitution is to have no place in their community life, and sexual relationships outside marriage are dealt with very seriously. They are not to eat flesh with blood, tattoo themselves, tell fortunes, or even cut their hair in a certain way. God is calling his people to a way of life that is affected in every area by his holiness and his salvation.

Now, we certainly won't apply every single detail of this passage to our lives literally. But the principles in this chapter—about God and his call to his people—are fully applicable to our lives. Because God is holy, he calls his people to live holy, set-apart lives as they respond to his salvation. This must affect the way we treat the people around us, and our lives must look different from the lives of those who don't know Jesus.

God calls us to be set apart for him in the way we live by his Holy Spirit in us. Spend some time today confessing the ways that your relationship with God does not affect your relationships with enough power. Consider how God may be calling you to be more set apart from the world for him.

Remember the Sabbath

Genesis opened with the creation of the world by God. God created all things in six days, and he rested on the seventh day. From that rest of God following creation comes a concept for God's people called the *Sabbath*. God takes this Sabbath day extremely seriously, and his people are commanded to as well; remembering the Sabbath day and keeping it holy is one of the Ten Commandments that God gives to Moses! It is a day reserved for worship to God and a rest from all else.

In Leviticus 25:1-22, we find two surprising instructions from God related to this Sabbath concept: it is applied not only to the people but also to the land and to the entire community of God's people. In verses 1-7, God tells Moses to take a year off every seven years from the farming of the land for crops, harvest, and profit. God's people are to give the *land* a Sabbath year, if you will. Then, in verses 8-22, we find God's establishment of something called the Year of Jubilee. It is to happen once every fifty years, and it includes the return of all property that has been confiscated, liberty for those who have gone into slavery, and another rest for the land from farming and harvesting.

We need to understand that the whole Sabbath concept doesn't make good economic sense. If God's people were only thinking about money and profit, then it would make sense for them to work seven days a week, every week. It's the same with the land and the community; these Sabbaths don't make sense to people who are trying to make money. But God is teaching his people a very important lesson with these commands: God must be greater to his people than anything else. That's why God's people are commanded to drop what they're doing once a week—to take a break—and spend time in worship of their God. That's why God instructs his people to give the land a break every seven years—so they can drop what they're doing and remember that all food and wealth ultimately come from him.

The principle that emerges from this chapter in Leviticus is applicable to us today: we need to always remember that God is more important than anything—any person, any possession, or any job. Take some time today to thank God for all you have, because it all comes from him! Ask him to help you make space in your life to remember his grace and goodness to you, so that you exalt him first in your life.

Man's Highest Good

If Leviticus were a high school paper, chapter 26 would be the beginning of the concluding paragraph. God is wrapping up his commands to his people with some very forceful comments and explanation.

First, there's an extremely important point, which is quite easy to miss, about the reward that God wants to give to his people as they live in obedience to him. What is the great good that God wants to give to his faithful people? Is it land, money, possessions, honor, or fame? The greatest gift—the ultimate good—that God wants to give to his people is . . . God. Look again at verses 11–12; God tells the people, "I will make my dwelling among you, and my soul shall not abhor you. And I will walk among you and will be your God, and you shall be my people." All God's actions for his people, all the laws he gave them, and all his plans for them are ultimately focused on his dwelling with them as their God.

Second, notice that God gives his people a stern warning about what he will do to them if they fail to obey his law and live in accordance with his word. In verses 14–39 he warns the people that, if they disobey, they will experience punishment in the form of disease, famine, defeat by enemies, attacks from wild beasts, exile, and more. God takes sin very seriously!

Third, while God warns his people about the punishment that will come if they disobey, he also reminds them that he will ultimately never forget his covenant with them. In fact, God promises to even remember his covenant promises to his people in the midst of their judgment in exile: "Yet for all that, when they are in the land of their enemies, I will not spurn them, neither will I abhor them so as to destroy them utterly and break my covenant with them, for I am the LORD their God" (26:44). God will judge sin—for he is holy—but he will ultimately never reject his chosen people in a final and permanent way.

How is it that God could judge sin in a final way and yet ultimately keep his covenant to bless his people and never forsake them? One way: it's for God himself—Jesus, the second person of the Godhead—to offer himself in the place of sinners. Jesus takes the judgment that God's people deserve, so that God can fully keep all his promises to them. Praise God today, and thank him for all that he has done for us in Jesus.

War and Worship

God's promises to Abraham and his descendants are still going to come true, and God will continue to be faithful to his people, but it does seem to take a long time. If Genesis was a book about God's *blessing* for his people, and Exodus was a book about God's taking his people from *slavery* to *worship*, and Leviticus was a book about God's *law* for his redeemed people, then Numbers is an "are we there yet?" kind of book. The Israelites spend the entirety of the book of Numbers in the wilderness, failing again and again to have faith in God, and yet continuing to experience God's faithfulness and patience toward them.

Numbers 1 describes the numbering of God's people, especially the men who were twenty years old or more. As the chapter ends, we find that one tribe is not numbered with the rest. It's the tribe of Levi, whose men were set aside by God to handle the care of the tabernacle—the place of worship for God's people. As we reflect on this passage, let's make a couple of observations from this first chapter.

First, notice that all men twenty years old and older in the community of God's people are expected to fight God's battles for God's people. This numbering of God's people is not random; it is for a very specific purpose. God is instructing Moses to determine all who were able to go to war among God's people. To be a man of God in the community of Israel meant to be counted as one who must be ready to fight for God and God's people.

Second, notice that while fighting battles was important, the worship of God by his people is the most important thing to God. Would it have helped the Israelites to count the Levites as part of their fighting men and take them to war with them? Of course; there would have been more people! What does it teach us about God that he would set aside an entire tribe of men—one twelfth of the fighting men—to care for the place of worship? It teaches us that God places great value on the proper and right worship of him by his people.

If we follow Jesus, there is no alternative but to fight for his cause. But God also expects us to take seriously our worship of him. Pray today that God would strengthen you to fight for the cause of the gospel of Jesus Christ and that your worship of your Savior would be the central part of your existence.

Celebrating God's Saving Work

By the time we come to Numbers 9, the people of God have already been out of Egypt for an entire year! Can you imagine that? Living in the wilderness for an entire year—being fed, led, and instructed by an invisible, mysterious God who speaks. But this God remains faithful to his people. He gives them his word—laws by which they are to live in order to stay in community and close proximity with him. He takes care of them—punishing them when they rebel, yet remaining gracious to not abandon them completely. As the one-year anniversary of God's great deliverance approaches, it is time for the people to celebrate—and remember—in the way God intends.

Verses 1–14 describe God's instructions for his people to celebrate the Passover together in the wilderness. God's people obey! The passage tells us, "According to all that the Lord commanded Moses, so the people of Israel did" (9:5). Surprisingly, even the people in the midst of God's people who were unclean—by coming into contact with dead bodies—are allowed by God to take part in this Passover celebration. In fact, the only way that God allows for someone *not* to keep the Passover is if he or she is on a journey far from home and unable to partake in the celebration. What are we learning about God in this passage? We are learning that God places much importance on his people's remembering and celebrating his saving work on their behalf.

The second half of Numbers 9 gives a summary of God's mysterious and gracious presence with his people in the wilderness. His glorious presence, which he represented physically for his people through a cloud that rested over the tabernacle, served as the main guide in their journeys through the wilderness. As long as the cloud rested over the place of worship, the people of Israel stayed put. When it lifted, it was time to move on. While this was a temporary situation for God's people, we see here a beautiful picture of God's people being really and truly led by God.

God always wants his people to take time together to remember his gracious salvation to us through his Son, Jesus Christ. That's why we gather together in the context of the church. That's why we sing, pray, listen to God's word, and teach the Bible to one another. Take some time today to look back. Thank God for saving you through the work of Jesus Christ on the cross for you. Celebrate his salvation today!

Pining after Egyptian Pleasures

As this chapter opens we find the people complaining to God. On the surface, their complaint seems to be about their diet: only this manna from heaven, all the time. They recall the variety of foods that they used to eat in Egypt—the cucumbers, melons, leeks, onions, and garlic. But this is about more than just food; the people are pining after the pleasures—the whole experience—of Egypt rather than trusting God, and his servant Moses, to lead them well and to keep his promises to them.

Here is a challenge for you: find yourself with the people of God and their actions. Think of the times when you—in spite of God's gracious salvation to you—crave the pleasures of the world and complain about the monotony of serving and obeying Jesus day after day. We all do this far too often; we forget to be grateful for God's salvation—and provision—every single day.

While God does bring meat down from heaven, in answer to the complaint of his people, it turns out to be not a tasty gift, but a form of judgment on the people for their rebellious attitudes and words. Verse 33 tells us that "while the meat was yet between their teeth," God brought a great plague against the people, so that many of them died.

Here's what we find from this passage: God reserves the harshest judgment for people who doubt his good promises and reject the leadership of his chosen man. That is exactly what the people were doing. They were rejecting the leadership of Moses and doubting the reality and fulfillment of all that God had promised them; they were longing for the pleasures of Egypt, the land of their slavery. God does not want his people to look back there with longing; he wants them to follow his chosen man and believe that he, God, will keep his promises to them.

Think about the times when you long for the pleasures of the world—for the sins that, apart from Jesus, would keep you in slavery. We are all guilty of this from time to time! Confess this to God today, and ask him to help you follow his chosen leader—Jesus—every day. Ask him to help you believe in his good promises to you. He has promised to save you in Christ, keep you close to him by his Holy Spirit, and give you eternal life and joy in him. Don't chase anything less than this!

Anything You Can Do, We Can Do Better

The people of Israel are still in the midst of their wilderness wanderings and are still led by God's chosen man, Moses. But there is a problem. Aaron and Miriam—Moses's older brother and sister—become angry, envious, and selfish. In Numbers 12, Aaron and Miriam decide to oppose God's chosen leader for his people. They essentially think they can do a better job than Moses, and they begin to say as much. On the surface, they seem to have a problem with the Cushite wife that Moses has taken. This could be referring to Moses's wife Zipporah, or it could refer to a second wife. Regardless, the core issue for Miriam and Aaron seems to be not Moses's wife but Moses's unique role as the leader of God's people. They want more power, authority, honor, and leadership; they feel that God has used them just as much as he has used Moses. Miriam and Aaron have allowed their pride—their selfish ambition—to drive them toward rebelling against Moses, their brother.

There's one big problem that God points out in this passage as he hears Miriam and Aaron speaking in this way against Moses. The problem is this: Moses is not just a leader elected by the people; he is God's chosen leader for his people. God points this out to Aaron and Miriam, noting that he has chosen to set Moses apart from all other people, even in the way that he talks "mouth to mouth" with him (12:8). Rebellion against Moses is rebellion against God. Miriam and Aaron, in their envious attitude toward Moses, have spit in God's face and rejected his rule over them through Moses.

God's judgment on the behavior of Miriam and Aaron is swift, sure, and severe. The writer of Numbers draws our attention to this, first, in verse 4: "*Suddenly* the Lord said to Moses and to Aaron and Miriam." God punishes Miriam by giving her a skin disease called leprosy, which would make her unclean in the community of God's people. It is a tangible, visible, and awful reminder of the infectious power of sin, when people allow it to have power over them.

Every time we sin, we do what Miriam and Aaron did in this passage. We refuse to be led by Jesus, and we insist on selfishly leading ourselves. Take some time confessing to God the ways that you've done that recently. Ask him to help you humbly follow your Leader, Jesus, knowing that he is the Lord of your life and the Savior of your soul.

Big Grapes and Bigger Fear

This chapter begins with God's command to Moses to send men to "spy out the land of Canaan" (13:2). It's an exciting step; this means that the conquest of the land that God has promised to his people is going to begin soon! So the spies set out. They examine the land, watch the people there, and bring back a huge cluster of grapes (which takes two men to carry!) as a demonstration of the fruit of the land. After a forty-day spying expedition, this group of men returns to the people of God. Listen to the words of the spies, or at least most of them: "The people who dwell in the land are strong, and the cities are fortified and very large. And besides, we saw the descendants of Anak there" (13:28).

Predictably, this report has a disastrous effect on the people who hear it. They become terrified. We'll see in Numbers 14 that they start to cry, and they grumble against their leaders. Why are God's people "not there yet" when it comes to entering the promised land? Because they still do not trust God to be faithful to his promises. They doubt his power; they fear human beings more than they trust their God.

This is a sad passage, but there is a bright spot, or rather, two bright spots. Two men—out of the twelve men who went out as spies for the people—stand strong in their courage and trust in God: Joshua and Caleb. We'll learn more about Joshua later; it's Caleb's words that we read in Numbers 13. Listen to this godly man, as he stands up for God to the terrified spies and the weeping people: "Let us go up at once and occupy [the land], for we are well able to overcome it" (13:30). He trusts God! He and Joshua are the only ones who believe that God will be faithful to give them victory and bring them into the land he promised them. Ultimately, Caleb's voice is drowned out in this chapter by the voices of the other cowardly spies, but he does point us to the right, faithful attitude that God's people *should* have in the midst of difficult situations.

We can be so like the spies in Numbers 13—so easily intimidated and scared by our circumstances and so quick to doubt God's power, control, goodness, and sovereignty. Ask God today that he would help you trust him completely. Remember that he has promised to keep you every day as you follow his Son, Jesus. Believe that he will remain faithful to continue his work in your life and heart.

A Mediator for God's People

In chapter 13, the twelve spies had delivered their report on the promised land. Not too surprisingly, the people listen to the majority and begin to weep, grumble, and rebel. Their little speech culminates with a chilling and shockingly sinful phrase: "Let us choose a leader and go back to Egypt" (14:4). That phrase is rebellious and sinful for two reasons. It is a rejection of God's chosen leader—Moses. It is also a rejection of God's salvation for them from the land of slavery. Caleb and Joshua—these courageous, godly men—can't stand to hear such talk from the people. But when Caleb and Joshua insist to the people that God intends to give them the land in spite of the difficulties they may face, the people try to stone them.

What happens next can be a little difficult for us to process. The glory of God appears; God shows up. And it seems that he has decided to punish his people for this rebellion and lack of faith in him. While God's people deserve this kind of punishment, it's not actually going to happen. In this passage, we will ultimately see God respond to his people with mercy through the mediating role of his servant Moses. Moses will step up and stand in the gap for this sinful people, and God will ultimately not finally destroy them. Moses's plea to God culminates with these words: "Please pardon the iniquity of this people, according to the greatness of your steadfast love" (14:19). Moses appeals to God to *forgive* the people in accordance with his *character*. And God does.

Now, the people's actions are not without consequences. God promises to Moses that none of the generation of people who rebelled in this way will enter the promised land, and the spies who brought the bad report back to the people drop dead immediately from a plague. God does punish his people for their sin, but he does not make an end of them completely. He answers Moses's prayer and allows this leader to act as a mediator for this sinful group of people. God will not give up on this stubborn, sinful, rebellious group.

Jesus, in a much more perfect way than Moses, stands in the gap between sinful people and a holy God to plead for God's mercy. If you believe in Jesus as your Savior and Lord, then he is your mediator; God will not finally judge you as your sins deserve. Thank God for sending his Son. Praise Jesus for acting as your perfect and final mediator.

God's Chosen Leaders

Think back for a moment to God's call of Moses—the beginning of Moses's leadership of the people of God. He was a murderer on the run. But what set Moses apart from everyone else? What set Moses apart as the leader was that *God* chose him. God was with him. That's it. That's enough. And that simple reality—God's presence with Moses and his blessing of him—is one that is challenged again in this chapter. We find, in Numbers 16, yet another rebellion from sinful people who want more power, influence, and authority.

The group of 250 men that rises up in Numbers 16 is a group of extremely influential men in the community. At least some of them are priests, as we see from Moses's words to them in verse 9. They serve God's people in the tabernacle, and they lead them in worship of God. But that's not enough for these men; they want more. They want the authority of Aaron the high priest *and* the kind of leadership authority that Moses has. God makes the ground split open to swallow these rebellious men and their families as his judgment on their rebellion. This is a sign of warning to all the Israelites. And it is a clear sign from God that Moses and Aaron are not merely *humanly chosen* leaders, but *divinely appointed* men whom he has handpicked to lead and guide his people.

You may have noticed, in the midst of this intense chapter, that Moses and Aaron tend to be characterized by one main action: falling on their faces. Korah and his friends are puffing out their chests, trying to be bigger, stronger, and more powerful than everyone else. The people, at the end of the chapter, are shaking their fists at Moses and God because of the judgment on their friends. Moses and Aaron just keep falling again and again in humble submission to their holy God. They fall face down because the people's sin makes them mourn. They fall face down to beg God to have mercy on sinful and stubborn people who don't deserve mercy. God hears the prayers of these men, who remain faithful to him in the midst of sin; he even forgives other people for their sake.

When was the last time you—literally or figuratively—fell on your face before God? Do that today (literally or figuratively). Humble yourself before God. Mourn the sin in your own life, and beg him to have mercy on you (and others!) because of Jesus's work on the cross for sins. It is that posture of prayer that God wants from us, his people.

The Sin of a Great Leader

After the rebellion of the people when the spies returned from evaluating the land, God promised to prevent the current generation of Israelite adults to enter the promised land. There will be years of wandering in the wilderness—long years—as this generation dies off. This chapter shows us that even the leaders of God's people are sinful and do not deserve entrance to the land.

The chapter is bookended by the deaths of Miriam and Aaron. While Miriam's death is accompanied by little comment, God reminds Moses before Aaron dies that Aaron rebelled against the Lord. Aaron actually did this more than once, as he had a prominent role in building the golden calf and in rebelling with Miriam against the authority and leadership of Moses. Both of these leaders of the people—Moses's very brother and sister—are found guilty before God, along with all the rest of the Israelite people. Miriam and Aaron cannot enter the promised land.

We've been talking about Moses as God's chosen, faithful leader for his people. Indeed, the people have been judged simply for grumbling against this man. But sadly even Moses is himself not worthy of entering the promised land. What happens in verses 2–13 can be confusing. The people grumble against Moses and Aaron because they are thirsty and want water—that much is clear. But after God instructs Moses to bring water from the rock, Moses seems to do just that: he brings water from the rock for the people. God's response, though, is far from positive.

Is God upset because of what Moses said in verse 10 ("Shall *we* bring water for you . . .")? Is God upset because Moses *struck* the rock rather than speaking to it? Probably both. What we do know is that God sees that Moses has believed neither in him nor held him up as holy in the eyes of the people. Moses succumbs to pride and does not do all he can to hold up God as completely holy before the people. And Moses—this great leader of God's people—receives the same punishment from God as the other Israelites: he will not enter the promised land before his death.

Numbers 20 shows us that any hope we might have in a mere human being to lead God's people is completely misplaced. Do you ever put your ultimate hope in human beings? Let this passage remind you that only Jesus is worthy of your worship, devotion, and praise. Ask God to help you cling to Jesus as your priest and leader every day.

Balaam and the Talking Donkey

There were many other nations around the Israelites, even during their time of wandering in the wilderness. In Numbers 22–24, we come to a strange—and sometimes humorous—account of the king of one of these nations and his failed attempts to curse God's people through an enigmatic prophet named Balaam.

As Numbers 22 begins, it becomes clear to us that God's protection and blessing of his people has not gone unnoticed by the surrounding nations. At least one man—Balak, king of Moab—has noticed it and has become afraid for his own people's safety. So Balak decides to hire a man to curse the Israelites, to set the divine powers against them for their destruction. He sends his messengers to a man named Balaam.

Balaam is an interesting and confusing person. As the story continues, it will become clear that God gives words to this man to repeat; he is not a false prophet in the sense that he speaks lies. But it will also become clear that Balaam, even as he speaks the very words of God, will have no place for a relationship with God or a fear of him. He is out for himself—and especially money for himself.

Now, what happens along the road as Balaam approaches Balak's region is humorous, shocking, and even hard to believe. Balaam's *donkey* speaks to him! As Balaam is going along the road, the donkey sees an angel of God blocking the road, intent on taking Balaam's life. When Balaam continues to beat the donkey mercilessly for not moving, God miraculously touches the donkey's mouth, and the two begin a brief conversation. God is teaching Balaam—and us—a very important lesson. Balaam, as we will find out later, is a proud man who is out for his own gain. He has an inflated view of himself; he thinks that the fact that God speaks through him makes him special, powerful, and worthy of great honor. To that, God says, no. God can use anyone or anything to get his message out and to accomplish his purposes, even a donkey.

God will accomplish his glorious purposes in this world, even if it means speaking his words through the mouth of a dirty animal! But God does want you. He wants to use you to speak his words to people and to accomplish his plan in this world. Pray today that God would make you his humble servant. Remember that you are saved by grace and invited by grace to join God's mission in this world.

God's Unchanging Plan for His People

One definition of insanity is trying the same thing over and over again and hoping for a different result. If there's any truth to that, then Balak is teetering on the brink of insanity! Because Balak fears the Israelites, he is intent on having this "prophet" Balaam curse God's people. This doesn't go very well for him.

This passage in Numbers is meant to be almost humorous to us. Balak gets angrier and angrier as Balaam continues to bless—not curse—God's people. After Balaam's first prophecy about Israel, in which he predicts great flourishing and success for them, Balak comes to him with these frustrated words: "What have you done to me? I took you to curse my enemies, and behold, you have done nothing but bless them" (23:11). Balaam, though not a good man, is bound to speak only the words that God gives to him. He tells Balak, "Must I not take care to speak what the LORD puts in my mouth?" (23:12). The cycle gets more humorous each time, as Balak incorporates different strategies to draw a curse out of Balaam. He tries taking him to a different location. They build some altars. Balaam even faces a different direction—toward the wilderness—when he makes one of his speeches. Finally, after Balaam has spoken four distinct prophecies of great blessing regarding God's people, he and Balak give up and go home at the end of Numbers 24.

Numbers 22–24 teaches us that God's plan for his people has not changed at all since the day he called Abram. As you read Genesis, you saw the repeating pattern that God is intent on blessing his people, although they seem intent on resisting his blessing. God is still fully committed to blessing his people. Numbers shows this as well; the last couple of chapters recount great rebellion from God's people—even from their leaders. God's people certainly don't deserve this insistent blessing of God. But God's purpose for his people has not changed; his stance toward them is one of blessing. Balaam could not curse people that God had not cursed.

If you belong to Jesus today—if he is your Savior and Lord—then you are under God's permanent blessing. Nothing can change that! While Satan, your adversary, would love to make you feel guilty and curse you with accusations, God's word reminds us that, in Christ, we are completely forgiven and washed clean by his death on the cross for our sins. No one can curse people whom God has chosen to bless through his Son!

Called to Be Jealous

God's people are still not there yet, but they are making preparations for when they will enter the land. In Numbers 25 we learn one more important lesson about sinful human beings and about our holy God.

The chapter begins with a sadly familiar theme: Israel is turning away from their God and rebelling against him. They've found a new way to rebel, though; this time they are not pining after their old lives in Egypt, but marrying Moabite women and worshiping their wives' false gods. God's people are breaking the first commandment, which instructed them to have no other gods before the one true God! This makes God angry. It is true that God is love. It is true that God is gracious and merciful. But God is also just, and he *hates* sin. His stern command to Moses (to execute the chiefs of the people), in addition to the plague that he sends on the people as a result of their sin, proves to us that God takes sin extremely seriously. He is a holy God, and he will deal with sin!

What happens next is gruesome, violent, and shocking. Yet in this Old Testament context, it is pleasing in God's sight. As part of the idol worship and marriage to pagan women, one man continues to flaunt his sin in front of God and all the people. He boldly marches a Midianite woman into the camp of the people of God and takes her into his tent to sleep with her. One man has had enough: Phinehas, the grandson of Aaron and part of the priesthood, heads over to this man's tent with a spear and kills both him and the pagan woman. Immediately, the plague stops. Phinehas is commended by God, who says that this man was jealous with God's jealousy.

Today we are not called to engage in holy war against people around us or put to death people that we see living in sexual immorality or idol worship. But we are called to be *jealous* for the holiness of God, especially in our own lives. We are called to hate sin like God does—in the world, and in our own hearts.

We are all idolaters who have—in some sense—broken the first commandment and worshiped gods other than the one true God. The only way that God's wrath can be turned away from us is for blood to be shed and a sacrifice to be made. And Jesus did that for us. He took the spear instead of us. That is grace; thank God for it today!

The Sermon Starts with a Story

The word Deuteronomy means, literally, something like "second law." It is the final book in the Pentateuch—the name given to the books of the law, which make up the first five books of the Bible. Deuteronomy is essentially a long sermon, given by Moses, about the law of God. By the time we come to the end of this book, the era of Moses's leadership will be over, the time of wandering in the wilderness will be drawing to a close, and it will finally be time for God's people to enter the land under the leadership of Moses's successor, Joshua.

The narrator of the book of Deuteronomy gives us a big hint about the subject of Moses's speech that begins in Deuteronomy 1. He introduces the words of Moses in this way: "Beyond the Jordan, in the land of Moab, Moses undertook to *explain this law*" (1:5). That is what Moses wants to do for the people: he wants to explain the law to them. So we might expect that Moses would launch right into a point-by-point lecture, going through the laws of God one by one. But he doesn't do that, although he will repeat many of the laws that we may remember from Leviticus. In Deuteronomy 1—at the beginning of this sermon on God's law—Moses begins by telling the people their own story.

During Deuteronomy 1–3, Moses takes time to remind the people of God of their history (especially all their failures) in order to convince them that their only hope is to trust in God completely. There have been plenty of examples of times that the people tried to do things their own way and many instances when they questioned God's plan for them. There were even multiple points when they wanted to return to slavery in Egypt! Moses doesn't want the people to forget where their pride, sin, and stubbornness got them: it got them forty years of wandering in the desert! Their only hope is to trust God completely, and he *will* keep his promises to them and give them the promised land.

We don't want to dwell in the past, but we do want to learn from our failures that our only hope is to trust in God and follow his Son, Jesus, completely. Thank God that he offers forgiveness and grace for our failures and invites us to follow him and walk with him.

The Joy of Listening and Obeying

You could almost sum up what Moses is saying in this passage in one sentence: "People, listen to God's word, never forget it, and obey it every day!" That is the theme of this section of Moses's sermon. He is calling the people to build their entire lives on the word of God. First, Moses connects obedience to God's word to *life*. Listen to how he begins this section: "And now, O Israel, listen to the statutes and the rules that I am teaching you, and do them, that you may *live*" (4:1). Listening to God's word and obeying it is not just a smart thing for the people to do. Their response to God's word is a life and death issue; listening obedience brings life. And, Moses reminds them, not listening to God's word and not obeying it brings death! The main point of Moses's greatest sermon focuses on the people's response to God's word. To listen and obey means life. To turn away brings death.

Moses also draws the people's attention to the uniqueness and wonder of the God they follow. In other words, the law is not just a sterile, dead rulebook that they have to follow; it comes from the mouth of a deeply personal God, whose relationship with them sets them apart from any other nation on the planet. Listen to Moses's rhetorical question to the people about their amazing God: "For what great nation is there that has a god so near to it as the LORD our God is to us, whenever we call upon him? And what great nation is there, that has statutes and rules so righteous as all this law that I set before you today?" (4:7–8). Moses wants the people to remember that they aren't people who just follow a list of rules—a dead religious system. They are people who have an incredibly close relationship with the holy God of the entire universe! No other nation has a God who comes so near to them, with such grace and love. Moses wants to remind the people that his call to them to hear God's word and obey it is not just a stale command or a burden. It is a privilege, for God has come near to them, and they get to be in a relationship with him!

As you consider this passage, think about the incredible privilege it is to have access to God's word! We have—in our hands and written down—the communication that comes from the holy God of the universe, who created us. Pray to God today; ask him to help you listen to his word and spend your life obeying it.

Such a Heart as This

One of the greatest things for a father of a toddler is the toddler is always excited to see him! When he gets done with work and comes through the door, the toddler greets Daddy with a huge smile! But that delight, unfortunately, does not stay the same forever. Children grow up and sometimes become annoyed with their parents. In these times, that father likely says to himself about his child, "Why couldn't you keep that enthusiasm and excitement about your dad that you had when you were a toddler?"

In Deuteronomy 5, Moses rehearses for God's people the Ten Commandments, but he also reminds them of their initial reaction to God's word, which came to them out of the midst of the fire from the mountain. The people were struck to the core at the power of God's word and at the frightening reality of his glory, greatness, and infinite holiness. Listen to the people's words: "This day we have seen God speak with man, and man still live. Now therefore why should we die? For this great fire will consume us. If we hear the voice of the LORD our God any more, we shall die" (5:24–25). And, in fact, this leads them to cry out for Moses to serve as a *mediator* for them. They beg him to be the one who will draw near to God, hear his word, and come back to pass it along to the people so that they can obey. God says this: "Oh that they had such a heart as this always, to fear me and to keep all my commandments, that it might go well with them and with their descendants forever!" (5:29). It's not unlike the sentiment the father expressed about his child!

God's word and his holiness ought to bring us to our knees in fear, reverence, and obedience. And they ought to make us ask for a mediator—someone to act as a go-between for us and God. We don't deserve to get close to a holy God; we're sinful and we deserve to die because of our sin! But God has always provided a go-between for his people—a mediator who will bring them his word and enable them to obey it and live.

We have a lot to learn from how God's people respond to his word; they begged Moses to serve as their mediator, because they knew they couldn't handle God's glory in the midst of their sinfulness. Thank God today that he has provided the perfect mediator for you—Jesus Christ his Son. Trust Jesus alone for your salvation, forgiveness, and as the only way to a relationship with the Father.

Remember, Remember

You could boil Deuteronomy 6 down and say that it is all about one thing: memory. Moses wants the people of God to *remember* all God's actions for them and all God's words to them. This spiritual memory will be the key to life for God's people; a lack of such memory will bring only judgment.

This idea of a spiritual memory first comes up in verses 4–9. Moses reminds the people of the great foundation of all the laws—that God is one and that the people are to love God with everything they are. After repeating this call to the people, Moses begins telling them how they are to make sure to remember it.

First, they are to make sure to have a *personal* memory of God's word. They are to have it in their hearts—probably implying memorization and a commitment to not just hear the word but also meditate on it regularly. They are even to write these commandments on the doorposts of their homes, so that they can't help but remember them! Moses is calling the people to a committed, personal memory of God's word in their midst.

Second, though, Moses calls the people to a *generational* memory of God's word. He tells them to teach all of it to their children and to talk about God's word all the time in the midst of everyday life. God's people are to remember his word and his salvation—personally and generationally. Moses has called them to a deep, intentional, spiritual memory of all that God has said and all that God has done for them.

In verses 10–19, Moses gives the people a picture of the barriers to this kind of spiritual memory. In other words, spiritual memory for God's people always seems to be very difficult! Moses looks forward to their entrance to the promised land one day; their lives will be filled with good things. They will have cities, cisterns, orchards, and plenty to eat—and their tendency will be to forget that God is responsible for all of it. Moses warns them to remember God in the midst of all that blessing, rather than forgetting him once the promised land has been conquered.

We, like the Israelites, are very good at forgetting things! Pray today that God would help you remember all his words and all his grace toward you. Commit yourself to having a good spiritual memory, so that you don't forget God in the midst of good things in life. They all come from him!

Our God Must Be Wonderful!

I once heard that the biggest difference between dogs and cats can be summarized in their response to human love and kindness. Cats say, "This human loves me, feeds me, bathes me, and gives me a place to sleep; *I* must be wonderful!" Dogs say, "This human loves me, feeds me, bathes me, and gives me a place to sleep; *he* must be wonderful!" Sadly, God's people over the centuries—and up until today—have a bad tendency to respond to his love and grace with the attitude of the cat. We tend to look around at the ways God has blessed us and say, "I must be wonderful!"

Deuteronomy 9 is a reminder from Moses to the people that their entry into the land—and their health and prosperity once they are living there—will not be a direct result of their righteousness. It will be completely an act of God's unmerited favor—his grace to them. Listen to Moses's words, as he anticipates their proud response to blessing: "Do not say in your heart, after the LORD your God has thrust them out before you, 'It is because of my righteousness that the LORD has brought me in to possess this land'" (9:4). Moses knows that this will be the people's temptation, so he sternly cautions them against this response.

Moses goes on to remind them also that *they* can just as easily fall under God's wrath and judgment as the surrounding nations. Not only do the Israelites *not earn* entry to the promised land, but they also have been guilty of sin and have earned God's judgment. Moses reminds them, "Do not forget how you provoked the LORD your God to wrath in the wilderness. . . . You have been rebellious against the LORD. Even at Horeb you provoked the LORD to wrath, and the LORD was so angry with you that he was ready to destroy you" (9:7–8). If it had not been for Moses's mediation on the people's behalf, God would have judged them like the other sinful peoples who currently dwell in the land! Moses's message to the people in this part of his sermon is clear: "You're not getting in because you deserve it; in fact, you deserve quite the opposite!"

We are under God's judgment because of our sin, and yet he shows us unmerited favor—grace unmeasured—by providing his Son, Jesus, to pay for our sins and bring us to life and salvation. Remind yourself that it's not because of your righteousness that you are saved, but because of Christ's righteousness. Let your response to God today, in light of everything he has done for you, be: "Lord, you must be wonderful!"

A Change of Heart

Imagine a high school student named Jake. Jake has a problem—a speeding problem. He likes to drive fast in his car—and it gets him into a lot of trouble in the form of speeding tickets. There are plenty of laws that prohibit speeding, and Jake is aware of those laws. Speed limit signs are posted on every street for every eye to see! But Jake doesn't need more rules. The problem isn't outside him; it is inside him.

It can seem to us that, in Exodus, Leviticus, Numbers, and Deuteronomy, God is just calling his people to follow the rules—to change their behavior. But we see from Deuteronomy 10:12–22 that God was never ultimately after the *behavior modification* of his people through their keeping the rules. God has always been after *heart transformation* in his people as they learn to love him—and are changed from the inside out to follow his word.

Moses's sermon continues with a reminder to the people to fear God, love him, serve him, and keep his commandments, because of who God is and what he has done for them in choosing to save and bless them. Then Moses goes on: "Circumcise therefore the foreskin of your heart, and be no longer stubborn" (10:16). That verse kind of comes out of nowhere, right? Circumcision was the physical sign of God's covenant with his people that was performed on every eight-day-old boy born into the community. Moses now takes that sign and in a metaphorical way applies it to what must happen to the hearts of God's people. They must have circumcised hearts. They must have something happen to them inwardly that is signified by the outward sign of being set apart for God. In other words, at the core of obeying and following God is not *behavior* change but *heart* change. God isn't just after people who keep the rules but people who follow his word *because* they love him completely and have experienced his transforming grace in their lives.

Behavior modification (keeping the rules) comes after—as a result of—heart transformation. Is your heart transformed? Do you find yourself each day wanting what God wants, hating sin more, and desiring to follow his word? Talk to God about this today. Ask him to transform your heart more and more, so that your behavior will be more and more honoring to him.

Jesus, the Perfect Prophet

We've talked a lot about Moses as a mediator for God's people. He helps them worship by instructing them on how they should act and how they should approach God. Although the priestly line begins with Moses's brother Aaron, in this way Moses has a true *priestly* role for God's people. He mediates, goes between, and offers prayers to God on their behalf.

Moses has also been a *prophet* for God's people. A prophet is one who speaks God's word to the world; that is exactly what Moses has done for God's people. In this brief passage, Moses tells the people that this prophetic role is one that the people should expect to always have. Moses looks ahead with these words: "The LORD your God will raise up for you a prophet like me from among you, from your brothers—it is to him you shall listen" (18:15). Moses reminds them of the day when the people were assembled at a place called Horeb, and the people begged Moses to receive God's word for them and bring the message to them, because they couldn't bear to hear God speak and were afraid they were going to die. The people needed a prophet!

This promise of Moses, though, seems to point even further into the future—past even the prophets who speak during the reigns of the future kings of Israel. Moses speaks of *a* prophet—singular—who will come from among the people. This will be a man from the midst of the community of Israel, who will literally and completely have God's words in his mouth. Over the years, the Jewish people began to understand these words of Moses as pointing to one man who would be the perfect fulfillment of this promise—*the* prophet. In fact, in the Gospel of John, John the Baptist is asked several times if he is "the Prophet" (John 1:21, 25). He says, "No!" That prophet—the Prophet—is of course Jesus Christ. The apostle Peter makes this connection in Acts 3:22. Moses's promise here ultimately points us many years forward to one man who would serve as the ultimate prophet for God's people. He would have God's word in his mouth perfectly, because he *is* God—God in human flesh.

Jesus is many things to us—our King, our Savior, our Lord, and our friend. Focus, though, on Jesus as the ultimate prophet. He is the one to whom Moses pointed in this passage—the one who would speak God's perfect word to his people. Pray to God, asking him that he would help you listen to the perfect prophet Jesus.

Careful to Do All His Commandments

When a daughter reaches out her hand to touch a boiling pot of vegetables on the stove, what do you think her father does? It is clear that the pot—bright and bubbling—just looks so appealing to her. But as she reaches out to touch it, her father will grab her hand and say, sternly, "No, that's hot." In the moment, the little girl probably thinks that her dad is being very mean! But of course, he is after her ultimate good: her protection.

Sometimes, as we read law after law in the first five books of the Old Testament, we can begin to see God as an overly strict parent. Does he give laws to his people because he loves lots of rules? Deuteronomy 28 reminds us what God is ultimately after in the lives of his people. His purpose and intention for them hasn't changed since he began to work with them back in the book of Genesis. God is intent on blessing his people. God gives the law to his people because blessing for God's people is attached to living in obedience to his word.

Verses 1–14 lay out the blessings that will come to God's people if they are "careful to do all his commandments" that he gives to them (28:1). They will be blessed in their families, their flocks and herds, their harvests, and their struggles against their enemies. They will be blessed in their establishment by God, who will make them dwell secure and shine forth as a light to the surrounding nations. These blessings will come, Moses says, if the people do not turn aside from God's word and chase after other gods. You read some of the long list of curses that are promised if the people disobey God's word and turn aside from it. Death will come. Plague will wreak havoc in the people's midst. Enemy nations will have their way with Israel. God wants what is best for his people; that is why he gives them the law. He wants to bless them, and he knows that the key to blessing for sinful people is to live under the authority of his word—not turning aside to any other god.

God calls us to live under his word! Obedience to the authority of his word will bring blessing; if we try to get out from under it, curses will come (either now or in eternity). Pray about these things today. Ask God to help you live according to his word—to never turn aside from it to other gods that you might be tempted to worship.

Repentance

The call to Christians is to holiness and obedience, but God provides for their failings as well, through the perfect advocate for sinful people: God's own Son. God demands obedience, but the perfection demanded for our salvation can only ultimately be provided by the perfect God himself. God's people are therefore called to lives of holiness and obedience as they follow God's word and to humble repentance as they realize how short they ultimately fall of his perfect law.

This is the idea that drives this passage from Deuteronomy 30. God *expects* and *anticipates* the disobedience, rebellion, and stubbornness of his people; these things don't surprise him. Verse 1 looks ahead to a day when, because of their rebellion and disobedience, God's people will be driven by him into captivity to foreign nations as punishment. God will not abandon his people, but he will discipline them for their disobedience to his word! But in God's mercy the invitation will continue for them; he invites them to repent and return to him, no matter where they are. A full, humble, heart-and-soul kind of repentance from sin and turning in faith to God will never fall on deaf ears. What an amazing promise from a gracious God! Listen to how Moses describes God's response to this kind of repentance: "The LORD your God will restore your fortunes and have mercy on you, and he will gather you again from all the peoples where the LORD your God has scattered you" (30:3).

There is a hint of something even more as this passage continues. Not only will God accept his people back when they repent, but he will also circumcise their hearts, so that their love will be completely and fully for him. His promise is that he will fix the root problem—the heart problem. We've heard this language before—the language of the circumcision of heart. Now we see a promise from God that he will do this himself! He will fix the hearts of his people, so that they want what he wants and love what he loves.

Do you have a new heart? Are you growing to love God more and changing daily to be more like him—from the inside out? Pray about these things today. Thank God for his never-ending grace to you, and ask him to change your heart more and more so that you can grow to obey him better!

A Leader for the Promised Land

The generation of people who rebelled against the Lord has died, and a new generation is ready to move forward and seize the land. This momentous day will be the topic of the next book in the Bible: Joshua. Before we get there, however, we need to pay careful attention to two things that happen in the final chapter of Deuteronomy.

First, Moses dies. God takes him up to a mountain overlooking the promised land; he shows him the prize that he will faithfully give to his people. But Moses will himself not enter the land. God's punishment for Moses's sin years before will not be reversed. Moses, this great prophet and leader of God's people, is not able to enter the land God is going to give to his people. In case you have forgotten what a great man Moses has been, the final verse of Deuteronomy reminds that "there has not arisen a prophet since in Israel like Moses, whom the LORD knew face to face" (34:10). This great prophet was not perfect; he too needs a Savior.

Second, Joshua takes over. Joshua "was full of the spirit of wisdom, for Moses had laid his hands on him" (34:9). We are introduced to the man who will be worthy and chosen by God to bring his people into the promised land. Moses has already commissioned Joshua to lead God's people and charged him in the sight of God's people to do this with strength and courage. Joshua has been a man of great faith in God's word for years, and now he is poised to step into a great role of leadership for God's people—to lead them by God's word and into the land.

Deuteronomy ends with the people gathered around Joshua—committed to following him and obeying the word of the Lord. They have a new leader, and it is finally time to enter the land. Deuteronomy ends with sadness at Moses's death, but great hope as well for this new generation of God's people led by Joshua.

Remember that Moses himself was disciplined by God for his sin. If this is true for even Moses, how much more do we all need the saving grace of Jesus Christ? Take some time today confessing your sin to God and trusting his forgiveness in Jesus Christ. Second, look at the people's reaction to Joshua: they obey him completely as God and Moses have instructed. Joshua—who will serve as a pointer to Christ, the ultimate leader of God's people—is worthy to be followed. Pray today that you would obey and follow Jesus without hesitation.

Be Strong and Courageous

The climax of the story of the Bible—the life, death, and resurrection of Jesus, God's Son—is still far off. But that doesn't mean that there aren't certain high points in the story of God's people along the way. Joshua 1 is one of those high points! While the death of Moses is a sobering reminder of sin and judgment, the rest of the chapter is full of great anticipation. God is raising up a new leader for his people, and it's *finally* time for them to enter the promised land.

The Lord's call to Joshua includes a well-known phrase that you have probably heard repeated many times: "Be strong and courageous" (1:6, 9). The conquest of the land has not become any less daunting in the past forty years; the land is still filled with fortified cities and strong armies of men. Joshua must be strong and fearless as he leads God's people into the land. But I want you to focus on what comes between those two repeated phrases in verses 6 and 9—the *substance* of what it means for Joshua to be strong and courageous. God calls Joshua to follow the law. The key, or the substance, of Joshua's strength and courage is his faithfulness and obedience to the word of God.

Joshua quickly gathers his leaders and sends them through the midst of the Israelites with the long-anticipated message: "Get ready to go; God is giving us the land he promised." Joshua's quickness to spread this word to the people demonstrates his faith in God's word and God's promises. He immediately responds to God's charge by spreading a message of confidence in God's word to all the people.

Finally, in the last three verses of the chapter, we come to another encouraging moment. God's people respond with faith and loyalty to this new leader that God has chosen for them. They pledge their loyalty to him, promising to obey him as they obeyed Moses. They even end their little speech of loyalty by repeating back to Joshua the words that God spoke to him: "Only be strong and courageous" (1:18).

As you learn about Joshua, let his leadership point you to the ultimate leader of God's people. It is Jesus Christ to whom God said, "You are my beloved Son; with you I am well pleased" (Mark 1:11). It is Jesus Christ who calls all people to follow him. And it is Christ's people who affirm his call as Savior, Lord, and King of the entire world.

Rahab the Outsider

When God first came to Abraham, he promised great blessing—not only to Abraham but to the other nations around him. We have seen this promise beginning to be kept through Joseph, who brought survival to Egypt during a time of famine through the interpretation of dreams given to him by God. Now we will see this promise being kept by God in a different way in Joshua 2. In this story, we find a complete outsider finding her way to God—and receiving the ultimate blessing in him in the midst of his people.

Joshua's first step in this new military campaign to take the land is to again send spies to check it out—this time only two. These men focus in on the key city of Jericho, and they seek to evaluate its strengths and weaknesses to get ready for their invasion. It is in Jericho—this stronghold city for the pagan people—that we are introduced to a woman named Rahab. Rahab is a Gentile, of course, but she is also a prostitute. Is there a less likely candidate for God's blessing at this point in the Bible's story? Probably not. Rahab is an outsider in every possible sense; she is not one of the people of Israel, and she is not living a life according to God's word. Yet it is this woman who will begin to experience the blessing of God—that blessing to the nations that God promised Abraham so many years before.

When Rahab hides and helps the spies, she goes against her own people and her gods. Rahab chooses to place herself with the God of Israel and with his people. Her words tell the whole story: she tells the men of the fear that has come on all the people of Jericho because of the people of Israel and God's hand in their midst. She ends with these powerful words: "For the LORD your God, he is God in the heavens above and on the earth beneath" (2:11). This is a statement of faith in the one true God. Rahab not only fears this God, but she is willing to side with his people and to fight alongside them for God's cause.

In this passage in Joshua, we see a clear picture of one woman—a Gentile prostitute—turning in faith and obedience to God and being spared by his people. Thank God that you, like Rahab, have been accepted by his mercy in Jesus Christ. Then pray that God would give you even more of his heart of mercy toward outsiders, that you would long for lost sinners to be brought into God's family by the grace of Jesus.

Confirm and Affirm

Joshua gets up early in the morning and sets out toward the Jordan River. The ark of the covenant—the symbol of God's presence with the people—leads them as the whole community prepares to pack up and follow Joshua toward the land. In verse 7, God comes to Joshua with an explanation of what he is about to do: "Today I will begin to exalt you in the sight of all Israel, that they may know that, as I was with Moses, so I will be with you." What God is about to do is designed by him to accomplish a very specific purpose: to show the people that he is with Joshua just as he was with Moses. As the community of God's people approaches the Jordan River, Joshua offers up some words of explanation for what's about to happen: "Here is how you shall know that the living God is among you and that he will without fail drive out from before you the Canaanites, the Hittites, the Hivites, the Perizzites, the Girgashites, the Amorites, and the Jebusites" (3:10). The sign that is coming is intended by God to *confirm* Joshua as his chosen leader for his people and to *affirm* to everyone that he will give them the land through this chosen man.

In verses 14–17, we read of a great miracle that God performed for his people. The priests, carrying the ark of the covenant, are leading the people toward the Jordan River in their march into the land. As soon as their feet touch the water, the river is miraculously parted; it shoots apart in two different directions, and the text tells us in verse 16 that the water is piled up in a heap a long way away. Verse 17 tells us that the priests hold the ark of the covenant in the very middle of the river, and while they stand there, holding up the symbol of God's presence with them, the entire community of Israel walks across on dry ground, where just moments before there had been a river. This is an amazing, miraculous sign from the very hand of God!

God's great leader for his people—Jesus Christ, his Son—comes to us with many signs as well, signs that point to him as the promised Messiah of God's people, the one whose life and death are the fulfillment of so many Old Testament prophecies. Do you believe the signs? Ask God to help you see Jesus more clearly and to believe more deeply in the forgiveness, salvation, and eternal blessing that is found only in him.

Signs of the Covenant

As God's people stand on the brink of entering the promised land, there is a problem. They have neglected parts of God's law. They have not been practicing the covenant sign of circumcision, and it seems that they have also neglected the covenant meal of the Passover. Before they enter the land, God will make sure this changes; he will bring his people under the sign and meal of his covenant with them.

First, God commands Joshua to have all men in the community circumcised. This is a sign of the *identity* of God's people and their special relationship with him. We find, in verse 5, that this mark has not been given to all the men in Israel during the years of wandering in the wilderness. God commands Joshua to get the people back under this sign of his covenant by circumcising all the men of the community.

Second, the people celebrate the Passover. It seems that there is a good chance that this covenant meal—along with circumcision—had not been kept regularly by the people during their years in the wilderness. If circumcision was a mark of the people's identity and special relationship with God, the Passover meal was a reminder of God's merciful salvation for them. It looked back to the first Passover in the land of Egypt, when God literally "passed over" the houses of his people that had lambs' blood on the doors and put to death the firstborn sons of the Egyptians.

Under these covenant signs, the people are ready to move into the land. But what about Joshua? The final verses of Joshua 5 describe his encounter with the commander of the Lord's army before the conquest of Jericho. Joshua quickly realizes he is in God's presence and removes his shoes in humility. God confronts the leader of his people and reminds him of the need to worship him, humbly bow before him, and respond to and obey his word. The leader of God's people needs to be led by God.

God brings his people under his appointed covenant signs. For us, as New Testament Christians, these signs are baptism and the Lord's Supper. Baptism marks us as belonging to God's people; it is the new covenant sign for believers in the church. The Lord's Supper is the Passover Feast that allows us to remember the saving work of Jesus Christ on the cross; it is the new covenant meal for the church of Jesus Christ. Ask God today that you would understand these sacraments in a new way!

The "Battle" of Jericho

Joshua didn't really fight the battle of Jericho. Neither did the people of Israel. In fact, the battle of Jericho wasn't much of a battle at all. God fought this "battle" for Joshua and the people, and it was a pretty one-sided fight.

If you don't believe this, start by looking at the first few verses of Joshua 6. It's there that God gives to Joshua one of the strangest battle plans in military history. He commands Joshua to march around the city of Jericho for six days straight, with the priests walking with the people, holding trumpets and carrying the ark. On the seventh day, the Israelite army is to circle the city seven times, after which the priests will blow the trumpets, the people will shout, and the walls of the city of Jericho will collapse before them. No military strategy. No careful plan for the invasion of the city. Just walking around it thirteen times, blowing some trumpets, and shouting. What's God doing here? God is showing the people that he, and he alone, will fight for his people to bring them into the promised land. That's how God begins his instructional speech to Joshua: "See, *I* have given Jericho into your hand" (6:2).

Everything happens just as God said it would. The people, led by Joshua, obey God's instructions. They circle the city for six days, then seven times on the seventh day. The trumpets are blown, the people shout, and the walls crash to the ground. From there, it's just a mop-up job for the Israelites; they just walk right in and meet with little resistance as they take control of the city. The writer of Joshua is careful to point out, though, what happens to one woman and her family, whose fate is different from all the rest of the inhabitants of Jericho. Rahab—that onetime prostitute who placed herself with God's people in the fear of him—is saved by God's people and becomes a part of God's community. God shows his grace to this woman, even in the midst of the judgment that he brings on the enemies of his people.

We sometimes forget that we serve a God who doesn't need our help. We are tempted to try to "help" him along in different ways. But God—now and always—wants to fight for his people. He wants to lead us, guide us, empower us—and save us by his gracious action in Christ. Pray today that you would trust God to take care of you completely. Trust him to fight your battles—including your greatest battle against sin and death.

Achan's Sin

Joshua 7 begins on an ominous note: one man, Achan, is guilty of taking some treasure from Jericho for himself, rather than giving it to the treasury of the Lord. This is blatant sin against the command of God given through Joshua; we know that this will not bode well for Achan. What we may not expect is that this will not bode well for the entire people of God.

As they prepare for the next battle in their conquest of the land, you can imagine that their hopes are high, and their spirits are soaring. The invasion of Ai would surely go just as smoothly as the invasion of Jericho, right? Wrong. The people are beaten by the army of Ai and chased out of their land. Joshua is dumbfounded and has no better response than to fall on his face before God. God comes to Joshua and makes it clear to him what has happened: a member of the community has disobeyed his word. God guides Joshua in narrowing down the possible culprits, and Achan's sin becomes apparent: he has stolen a cloak, some silver, and some gold and has hidden these treasures under his tent. The punishment is swift, decisive, and comprehensive; Achan and his entire family are stoned and burned because of this sin.

This is a difficult passage, and it can be a hard one for us to swallow. What can we learn from God's word in Joshua 7? First, we need to see that sin by one member of the community of God always affects the whole community. God punished Achan, yes, but the entire community of Israel felt the consequences of one man's sin, as their men died in a failed invasion attempt against Ai. Sin is never completely localized or isolated; it always has communal affects.

Second, we need to see that God takes sin deathly seriously, often more seriously than we expect. Achan is put to death for his sin and so is his family. Why? Because God's holiness is more important even than human life. There is no room in the community of God for greed, selfishness, and the rejection of his word. God wants people who will obey him and value him above all other earthly things.

We know that God provides grace for us in Jesus Christ; apart from him all of us would share the fate of Achan! Pray today that God's grace would motivate you to take sin even more seriously every day. Ask him to help you see that sin affects not just you but also your whole community of faith—your family, your friends, and your church.

Renewing the Covenant

The specific verses in this passage take place after the battle of Ai. They depict a service of covenant renewal, as is indicated by the title of this section in your Bible. Now, this is a passage that we could easily just skip over, seeing it as some meaningless ritual that is almost random. But it is so much more! Here are two brief observations about what happens in this passage.

First, this service of covenant renewal is a direct instruction from God to the people through the mouth of Moses. Turn back for just a moment to Deuteronomy 27:1-8. You can read about Moses's instructions for this very ceremony. Joshua, the leader of God's people, is obeying the words of God and of his servant Moses by leading the people in this ceremony.

Second, draw your attention to two striking parts of this ceremony, which may be lost on us if we read through this section too quickly. To begin with, Joshua leads the people in covering stones with plaster and writing the words of the law of Moses on the stones. Then the people split up according to their tribes and go to two different mountains. So half of the people are on one mountain, Mount Gerizim, and half of the people are on another adjacent mountain, Mount Ebal, with a valley separating them. From there, the people shout back and forth to each other the words of the law—one group shouting the curses for disobedience and the other group shouting back the blessings for obedience. What a scene—thousands of people, standing on two different mountains, shouting God's law at each other. Even as the people enter the promised land, Joshua leads them into an immediate commitment to live under God's word—etching it into stone and even shouting it back and forth at one another!

This ceremony can be a great lesson to us as God's people today. Are we etching God's word into our lives with every day, with every step, and with every great accomplishment? Are we involving ourselves in communities with other believers where we hear God's word—and even speak the truths of God's word into each other's lives? Pray today that you would get back under God's word at every turn in your life. Ask him to lead you by Scripture every day. Pray that you would speak his word faithfully into the lives of the people around you and that you would listen to biblical truth from them as well.

Unfinished Business

The writer of Joshua lists the accomplishments of Joshua: the kings in the land that he has defeated. And it is quite a legacy! All in all, Joshua has led the people of God into victorious battle over thirty-one kings, who are all listed by name in Joshua 12. Joshua was the right man to lead God's people in this time; he had great military success as he strongly and courageously led the people and followed the word of God.

God comes to him and says, "You are old and advanced in years, and there remains yet very much land to possess" (13:1). The work is not yet done for God's people; there are still many enemy nations in different parts of the land. Yet even though there is work to be done in the continued conquest of the promised land, God instructs Joshua to go ahead and divide the land— even the unconquered land—among the twelve tribes of the people. God promises that he will continue to fight the battles for the people against the inhabitants of the land: "I myself will drive them out from before the people of Israel" (13:6).

The next chapter in this story should be a happy one, shouldn't it? It should be about more military victories, continuing until the entire land is rid of God's enemies and cleared completely for God's people to worship him alone in peace. That should be the next chapter! But it's not. Listen to Joshua 13:13: "Yet the people of Israel did not drive out the Geshurites or the Maacathites." This verse could be looking back to the time of Moses, but it continues: "Geshur and Maacath dwell in the midst of Israel to this day." The writer of Joshua, looking back on the time of Joshua, gives us a future perspective on the conquest that was commanded by God. It was never fully completed. God's people didn't drive *all* the peoples out of the land. In fact, sinful and idolatrous people were allowed to dwell in the midst of God's people.

The total conquest of the land was about purging sin from the people's midst and setting themselves apart to worship God alone. That principle holds true in our lives today. Jesus's death on the cross wins the ultimate battle against sin, and all who follow him are called to put sin completely to death. We have been forgiven, so we are not to let sin dwell in our midst any longer. Pray today that God would help you be vigilant to fight and completely destroy the sin that plagues you, by the power of his Holy Spirit in you!

Cling to the Lord Your God

When someone gives a speech near the end of his or her life—with death fast approaching—we usually expect that he or she will talk about something important! Final speeches have a way of revealing what is near and dear to a person's heart. Joshua 23 records such a speech from Joshua, the great leader of God's people.

While Joshua will call the people to do certain things, the first thing he does is remind them of what God has done for them. Joshua wants the people to remember that God has done the fighting for the people as they have entered the land. All Joshua's other instructions begin with this foundational reminder: God has fought on his people's behalf and given them great victory and inheritance.

As Joshua begins to instruct the people, his main concern is one heard many times before, but obviously something that is at the forefront of Joshua's mind and heart. Joshua urges the people to keep the law and obey closely God's word. The emphasis is on sticking closely to this word—not turning aside from it in any way. At the end of his life, during his final speech to the people of God, Joshua focuses on their obedience and adherence to the *word*. That is his chief concern! Why? God's word, according to Joshua, is what sets God's people apart from the surrounding pagan nations and protects them from sin and idolatry. Joshua urges them to keep God's word "that you may not mix with these nations remaining among you"—it is their faithfulness to God's word that will protect them from sinful mixing (23:7).

Joshua's speech carries with it a serious warning. If they do not keep God's word—and if they mix with the idolatrous nations that surround them—God's punishment will come to them, and the very nations that tempted them will bring serious trouble and suffering on them. There is only one way forward for God's people: to walk according to the word of the one true God without turning aside in any way.

Joshua's command could well be given to us as God's people today! God has saved us; he has done the miraculous saving work for us through Christ. We are called to respond by building our lives—every day—on his perfect word. Pray today to God about this. Ask him to give you strength to follow hard after him—walking straight according to his word without turning at all.

Serve Him in Sincerity and Faithfulness

Joshua is saying his goodbyes to the people of God. He has served them well, and he has led them faithfully according to God's word. As he approaches death, Joshua now leads the people in responding to God with a covenant of their own—a promise of faithfulness and obedience to God.

In a way that was similar to many treaties of the day, this covenant ceremony begins with a lengthy recounting of God's gracious and faithful dealings with his people over the years. Joshua tells the story to the people of God's saving work on their behalf. He means to establish the obvious pattern of God's faithful work on the behalf of his people; he intends to jog the memory of the Israelites and to lay out for them the irrefutable evidence of God's goodness and grace in their lives.

Like other treaties of the time, the necessary call to obedience on the part of the people follows this lengthy recounting of God's goodness and faithfulness. The obedience of the people is to be done in light of God's gracious dealings with them; it is the right response to their God. What is the response? It is to serve the Lord with "sincerity and in faithfulness" (24:14). It is to put away all foreign gods and worship God alone. The people promise to do this!

Interestingly, Joshua challenges this covenant promise made by the people. "You are not able to serve the Lord," he says, citing God's jealousy and the people's inability to turn from their sin (24:19). When they swear their allegiance even more solemnly, Joshua accepts their promise this time but notes that they are now witnesses against themselves that they are responsible to keep their promises to God.

So God's people finally enter the promised land, under the faithful leadership of a man who lives under God's word. The land is divided up, and a new era has begun for God's people. Yet a question lurks as we move forward: What will happen to the next generation? The book of Judges answers that question.

We ought to—like the people of God—make our covenant with God, to always obey him, love him, and worship him alone. Yet we must remember that we can never fully hold up our side of the bargain. The same grace that God gives for our salvation is necessary for life in him. Pray today that God would continue his faithful, gracious work in your life, even enabling you to keep your covenant with him.

But the People Did Not

The book of Judges starts off with a bang! The people of Israel seem to be obeying Joshua and completing the full conquest of the land. They win a great battle against the Canaanites and the Perizzites, and they capture Jerusalem and the peoples who surrounded the city. Then comes the big conjunction. It's the conjunctions in Scripture that often are key; they direct our attention to something important that's happening in a passage. It's the *ifs*, *and*s, and *but*s that often clue us in to a very important lesson that God's word has for us.

Judges 1:21 is the first big *but* in the passage: "*But* the people of Benjamin did not drive out the Jebusites who lived in Jerusalem." This is bad news for God's people, and there's more to come: "When Israel grew strong, they put the Canaanites to forced labor, but did not drive them out completely" (1:28). But wait, there's more: the tribe of Ephraim doesn't drive out the Canaanites from their region, the tribe of Zebulun doesn't drive out all the pagan inhabitants from theirs, and Asher and Naphtali also fail to complete the conquest of the land. The people of God do not completely drive out the nations of the promised land.

You may know that these nations did not worship the one true God; they worshiped idols and were therefore enemies of God and his people. Many of them were guilty of violence, unnecessary bloodshed, and terrible religious rituals. Most of all, they were a menace, a snare, and a temptation to God's people, the Israelites. Remember, God is a jealous God. He demands that his people give him their total allegiance and their worship. The command to complete the conquest of the land is a command to rid the region of all idolatry, sinful practices, and potential temptations for God's people. This command is about the glory and holiness of God and the purity of God's people as they prepare to live in total worship to their jealous God. When this command is not obeyed, you can probably guess the sad results that will follow.

Allowing sin to continue to dwell in our midst will only lead to disaster in our lives and hearts. Pray to God today for strength to clear out—and even put to death—the sin in your life. Thank him for saving you by the grace of Jesus, his Son, who died for your sin on the cross. Ask him to help you as you follow him in holiness, obedience, and hatred of the sin for which Jesus died.

Cycling through Judges

What will come of the failure of God's people to complete the conquest? In a word, what will come will be a series of repeating cycles for God's people. That's what characterizes the book of Judges more than anything else—cycles.

Judges 2 begins with a stern rebuke from the angel of the Lord to the people for not completing the conquest and for failing to break down the pagan altars in their midst. The people weep with regret and make sacrifices to God. Immediately after this, Joshua's death is recorded, along with a sad comment about the next generation that rose up after his death: "And there arose another generation after them who did not know the LORD or the work that he had done for Israel" (2:10). In the very next verse the first part of the Judges cycle begins: the people turn from serving and worshiping God and begin worshiping idols.

Verses 11–23 serve as a summary of the cycle that will play itself out many times throughout the book. It happens in a series of steps.

Step 1: God's people turn away from obedience to him and begin to worship the pagan idols and false gods of the surrounding peoples.
Step 2: God disciplines his people by giving them up to their enemies in battle.
Step 3: The people cry out to God for mercy, and he raises up a judge who delivers the people from the enemy nation. There is then peace for God's people as long as that specific judge is alive.

Then the judge dies—and the cycle begins again with Step 1! It's a story of habitual sin. God's people can't break the cycle! But it's also a story of God's repeated merciful saving acts. God keeps delivering them from their enemies through sending judges, even though the people's obedience doesn't stick.

Judges is a sad book, as you'll see, although each tale about each specific judge brings glimpses of hope—and often amazing stories. The judges, though, are only faint glimmers of what is really needed for God's people. They can't keep cycling through judges again and again, only to fall back into sin and idolatry. God's people need a king.

As you read through passages from Judges, ask God to help you see yourself in the stubborn Israelite people. Thank him that he kept mercifully saving his people through judges. Thank him, even more, that he has offered to us the ultimate Judge— the only one who could finally break the power of sin and its hold on our lives!

Ehud, a Man with a Plan

The cycle has begun. The people have sinned and turned away from loyalty, worship, and obedience to God, so he has given them into service to King Eglon of Moab for eighteen years. The people cry out to the Lord, and he sends them a judge named Ehud. Ehud is a crafty, courageous man—a man with a plan. He's also left-handed, which seems like a random detail at first. We read that he makes himself a sword with two edges (probably meaning that it's sharpened on both sides of the blade) and shows up to present the tribute to King Eglon. It would have been customary for the king's guards to check for weapons on the person who brought the tribute to the king. But since most people are right-handed, they would have probably only patted down the left side of Ehud, the side on which a right-handed man would carry his weapon.

After delivering the tribute, Ehud turns back toward King Eglon, telling him that he has a special message for him. As the king stands to hear what Ehud has to say (a message from God!), Ehud steps quickly toward him, stabs him in the stomach with his double-sharp sword, and escapes from the palace off the balcony. The guards can't figure out what's taking their king so long, and there's a foul odor coming from the room, so they think Eglon is going to the bathroom! When they finally go inside, they find their king dead on the floor. The assassination triggers a great military advance for God's people, and they slaughter the Moabite army and win freedom for eighty years.

It seems that, in this narrative, we are confronted with an extremely—almost disgustingly—vivid portrayal of the reality of sin through the person of King Eglon. The writer of Judges goes out of his way to tell us about Eglon's weight—he was a very fat man. His death is disgusting. Ehud stabs him, and his intestines and waste pour out of him. This is the vivid, disgusting picture of the sin—and death—of those enemies of God who oppose his people. Eglon, and all Moab, had gotten "fat" by oppressing and enslaving God's people. The punishment for this will be severe, and their disgusting sin is ultimately and embarrassingly revealed as God's judge triumphs over them.

Remember that Jesus has triumphed over your sin, filth, and guilt on the cross, cleansing you by his blood. Pray that God would help you trust him as the perfect, holy judge of sin, as you cling to Christ your Savior.

Gideon and the Real Hero

The story of Gideon is a story of an unlikely hero who was probably one of the last people that the Israelites would have expected to deliver them from their enemies. Gideon, when the angel of the Lord appears to him, says as much: "Please, Lord, how can I save Israel? Behold, my clan is the weakest in Manasseh, and I am the least in my father's house" (6:15). There is nothing special about this man, Gideon; he was not even a leader in his own family, much less in the community of Israel. Not only that, as the story continues in this chapter, we see that he's not exactly a man of exceptional courage or faith either! He demands a sign that will somehow prove to him that the messenger comes from God.

After the miraculous sign occurs before his eyes, Gideon is still too afraid to knock down the altar of Baal in the town during the day; he does it secretly at night, when nobody can see him. When he's discovered as the culprit, he's bailed out by his dad, who argues on behalf of the independence of Baal not to have his son put to death. Finally, even after Gideon has begun to gather people together to follow him as the leader, he still isn't fully convinced that God will save Israel by his hand; he demands yet another sign from God (which God, in his merciful patience, again provides).

Why does God choose this man? If the story of Gideon teaches us anything, it's that God ultimately is the one who must get things done for his people. Gideon is the judge that God will use, but Gideon is not the hero of this story; God is. God will deliver his people from their enemies, and in this instance, he will go out of his way to choose the most unlikely judge in order to remind his people that they must trust in him—and him alone.

God can use anyone, at any time, to accomplish his wonderful purposes in this world. Our response—our role—is to believe him, trust him, and love and worship his Son Jesus. Pray today that God would hold his rightful place as the hero of your story. Pray that God would give you humility to see your weakness—and your complete dependence upon him. Ask him to accomplish great things through you—and even in spite of you—for his glory!

A Puny Army

Has there ever been a time in your life when something good happened to you—something for which you *knew* you could take none of the credit? Obviously, there is one ultimate example—a thing for which none of us can take any credit: our forgiveness and salvation in Christ. It's this undeserved gift to which Judges 7 points, a gift that is so clearly an act of God that we could never dream of taking credit for it!

God makes his intentions clear to Gideon: "The people with you are too many for me to give the Midianites into their hand, lest Israel boast over me, saying, 'My own hand has saved me'" (7:2). Everything that will happen next is motivated by this; God does not want the people of Israel, led by Gideon, to have any opportunity to pridefully assume that they won the battle against the Midianites because of their own numbers or military strength. God knows that the best thing for the people is to have no choice but to acknowledge his hand in their salvation.

So the strange battle preparations begin! First, Gideon sends home everyone who is afraid; more than two-thirds of the army immediately disperses, leaving ten thousand men. Then comes the real elimination. Gideon takes the army down to a body of water and divides them based on how they get drinks of water! So with three hundred men—a puny army—Gideon is finally ready (in God's eyes) to fight the Midianites.

Knowing Gideon's fearful nature well, God sends him down into the Midianite camp to encourage him. Gideon hears one man recounting a dream to the man with him, followed by the man with him naming Gideon and declaring that he will conquer the Midianites in battle. Gideon takes heart and leads the men into battle. Surrounding the army of Midian, they take them by surprise in the middle of the night, and God throws the Midianites into confusion as Gideon and his army break clay jars and shout! The rest of the battle is a mop-up job, because the Midianites are so disoriented that they start killing each other. This is a great day for God's people—under Gideon and under God.

Pray today that you would be reminded again of God's overwhelming and totally undeserved salvation. Ask him to amaze you again with the wonder of grace—that undeserving sinners like you and me receive forgiveness through Jesus Christ and his death on the cross. Give the credit to God in prayer today!

The King They Want but Not the One They Need

Gideon had led the way in a truly miraculous fashion. So we shouldn't be surprised at the sentiment expressed by the people of Israel: they want to make Gideon their king. Listen to their words to Gideon: "Rule over us, you and your son and your grandson also, for you have saved us from the hand of Midian" (8:22). The men of Israel are going beyond accepting Gideon as a temporary judge; they are proposing a kingly line built on his descendants! Is this finally someone who can—as the king of God's people—stop the repeating cycle of sin and judgment by faithfully beginning a line of kings to rule?

It doesn't take long to find out the answer to this question. Gideon is *not* the king that the people of God need. Two problems immediately emerge in this passage. First, Gideon responds to the invitation of the people to rule over them by asking for their gold and constructing an ephod (or idol) of it. This ephod became a snare to the people—and to Gideon's own family—as they began to worship it instead of the God who gave such a miraculous victory to them through Gideon! Gideon failed at what would have been the most important role for the king of God's people: to lead them in worship and obedience to the one true God. Second, we find out another disappointing fact about Gideon: he took many wives for himself.

Sadly, we are left with temporary peace as long as Gideon lives but a return to the Judges sin cycle after he dies. In fact, the writer of Judges seems to hint at Gideon's failure as a leader by mentioning specifically that the people turned away from God in worship to idols "as soon as Gideon died" (8:33). They didn't wait very long; as soon as their judge was in the ground, they went back to their sinful ways and forgot everything God had done for them!

Before you move too quickly to judge the people of Israel, put yourself in their shoes. It would have been very difficult for the everyday Israelite to stand strong against the tide of popular opinion to say no to Gideon's ephod! As you pray, start by thanking God that he has given you his Son—the perfect, faithful Leader for us, God's people. Pray that he would keep you close to him, following his example, his teaching, and his word, so that you can stand strong against every sinful pressure you face!

A Surprise Leader and a Foolish Vow

When we are introduced to Jephthah in Judges 11, Robin Hood may come to mind! He was an outcast, sent away from his family because he was the son of a prostitute. Yet Jephthah became a mighty warrior, and he attracted other outcasts—"worthless fellows" (11:3)—who gathered around him like Robin Hood's band of outlaws. You may have wondered if there would be a less likely hero for God's people than Gideon, after reading his story. Well, here he is!

The people of Israel have (again!) turned away from God and sinned by worshiping idols rather than him. As punishment, God allows the Ammonites, a wicked enemy people, to gather against Israel in battle. This great Ammonite invasion is what looms over God's people as Judges 11 begins; the people are desperate to find a warrior who can lead them against this powerful foe. So they turn to the man they don't respect, but need desperately: the outcast, Jephthah. After making them swear to make him their leader if he defeats the Ammonites, Jephthah agrees to lead the battle. God then uses this outcast to deliver his people from their enemies!

This story, even with such great victory for God's people, ends in a terribly bitter way. Jephthah makes a very foolish vow before the battle against the Ammonites—he swears to sacrifice to God whatever comes out of his house first, if God gives him victory. As Jephthah approaches his home after the battle, *his daughter* runs out to him from the house. Jephthah keeps this foolish vow and puts his own daughter to death as a sacrifice. This "savior" of God's people is no better than the surrounding pagan nations, who were sometimes guilty of child sacrifice in order to appease their gods. Jephthah is used by God for the good of his people, but he doesn't seem to really know and love God. The rest of his brief judgment of Israel is plagued by civil war.

God can use anything—and anyone—to accomplish his purposes! In this passage, we saw him use a misfit—an outcast—to deliver his people from a terrible enemy. Friend, God will use you for his purposes. My prayer is that you know him and love him and find yourself not only used by God, but loved and accepted as God's child. Pray today that you would truly love and follow Jesus and be used by God for his people and also belong to his people!

Samson

Samson will not be the final, ultimate judge for God's people, but his story will point us forward in significant ways to the great leaders of God's people to come—Samuel, John the Baptist, Jesus Christ. Why is this?

First, Samson's birth is marked by the barrenness of a woman, which God miraculously turns into a pregnancy. Samson's mother, the wife of a man named Manoah, was unable to have children. This theme should already be a familiar one to us; it was the struggle of Abraham and Sarah, who were unable to have any children of their own until God miraculously gave their son Isaac to them. The greatest judge of God's people in the Old Testament—Samuel—will be born to a mother who thought she was unable to bear children. Elizabeth—the mother of John the Baptist—was barren until God miraculously gave her a son in her old age. You see, this is a pattern—the pattern of God turning barrenness into fruitfulness for the sake of his work in and through his people.

Second, Samson's birth is announced by an angel from God. Again, we should read that and immediately be aware that something big is going to happen through the life of this baby that will be born. When God gives great leaders to his people, angels announce their births.

Third, Samson's entrance on the scene comes with a promise of salvation for God's people from their enemies. Listen to the angel's words to Samson's parents: "The child shall be a Nazirite to God from the womb, and he shall begin to save Israel from the hand of the Philistines" (13:5).

Samson gives God's people many great victories over the enemy Philistines. He is their "savior" in this way. But Samson will prove to be no different from the rest of the judges we've seen so far. He is fatally flawed and corrupted by sin. He is certainly not the one to rule over God's people in a final way. God's people still need a greater and eternal judge. They need someone who will be born into a sinful world and announced by rejoicing angelic hosts—someone who will save God's people, not from an enemy army but from their sins.

God simply will not give up on his people! Thank God for this today. Thank him that, though we deserve to have him give up on us, he doesn't! He didn't stop, in fact, until his own Son hung on a cross to provide a final and ultimate way for salvation for the people he loves. Thank God for his commitment to us, even though we don't deserve it.

Greatly Gifted and Sinfully Flawed

In some ways, Samson epitomizes the judge figure in the book of Judges. He is the most physically—and supernaturally—strong and deadly. Samson, because of God's great gift to him, is an absolute beast of a man; he is the ultimate judge! But he epitomizes the role of judge not only because of his incredible strength but also because of the glaring weaknesses in his character. Samson is proud, singing often about his accomplishments without giving praise to God (see 15:16). He is angry and impulsive, getting himself into dangerous situations, and retaliating in the heat of the moment (see 15:4–5). Most of all, as we see in Judges 16, Samson has a big weakness for women—and specifically foreign women, who do not fear the Lord.

Samson gets himself into a bad situation because of his sexual appetites: he falls in love with a Philistine woman named Delilah. Not only is Delilah's loyalty not with God, but her loyalty isn't even with Samson! She is commissioned by the Philistines to get secret information from Samson, and he eventually gives into her prodding and tells her the secret to his strength. Perhaps he had begun to think that he didn't need God—that even without keeping the Nazirite vow he would remain strong and powerful. Samson gives in to this temptress Delilah, loses his strength, and is taken into slavery by the enemy Philistines. They gouge out his eyes and put him to work grinding in a mill in a prison.

But God is not yet done with Samson! At a great feast of worship to the false god Dagon, the Philistines decide to bring Samson out as entertainment. Samson, leaning against the pillars of the great house, sees his opportunity to take his revenge. He pushes with all his might and literally brings down the house, crushing thousands of Philistines, killing "more than those whom he had killed during his life" (16:30).

It's not quite a satisfying ending, is it? Samson is strong and mighty, and he brought great victory to God's people in a temporary fashion. Yet he is terribly and sinfully flawed and does not possess the character needed to reign over God's people in a final way.

Are you greatly gifted in some way? Perhaps in music, athletics, academics, drama, or leadership? Guard your heart! Pray that God would make you reliant on him! Pray that he would help you use your gifts for the glory of Jesus, your Savior, not to fulfill your own appetites.

Return to God

The first line of the book of Ruth does not fill us with very much hope. It begins: "In the days when the judges ruled" (1:1). There is still no king—no one to rule over God's people to help them follow, worship, and obey him. Is there any hope that the story of Ruth will be a happy one, taking place during this time of danger, sin, and unrest?

The story of Ruth begins with a bad decision. A man named Elimelech, his wife Naomi, and their two sons leave the promised land during the time of a famine. Why is this a bad decision? In the midst of a difficult situation, this man decides to take his family *away* from God's people and *away* from the land of promise. To make matters worse, he takes them to the land of Moab—a land filled with God's enemies, as well as sinful idolatrous practices. And it gets even worse than this! Elimelech's sons, Mahlon and Chilion, both marry Moabite women: Orpah and Ruth. An Israelite takes his family away from God's people and God's place, even allowing his sons to take foreign wives. Can it get any worse?

For Naomi, it did. While sojourning in the land of Moab, Naomi lost her husband and both of her sons to death. It's no wonder that Naomi declares later in the chapter that "the hand of the LORD has gone out against me" (1:13). But then comes the greatest surprise of the passage. After Orpah accepts Naomi's plea for her to return to Moab to find a new husband while Naomi heads back to Israel, Ruth *refuses!* Ruth clings to Naomi, speaking these remarkable words: "For where you go I will go, and where you lodge I will lodge. Your people shall be my people, and your God my God. Where you die I will die, and there will I be buried" (1:16–17). Ruth even refers to God in verse 17 not with a general word for a god, but with the Israelite name for God—Yahweh. This Moabite woman—from a people outside God's covenant community—has come to fear and know God.

We serve a God who makes a habit of bringing hope out of hopeless situations, if his people will only return to him. As Naomi finally turned back to God's people and God's place, we are called to turn back to God in repentance, trust, faith, and obedience—and he will be faithful to forgive and bring great hope. Pray today that you would cling closely to God. If you need to return to him, do that today!

A Worthy Man Is Hard to Find

Let's zoom in on Boaz. The text tells us that he is a worthy man. To find a worthy man during the time of the judges was probably pretty rare. So, what is it about Boaz that shows us his worthiness in this passage?

Boaz, we see, is a man who continues to obey God's word during a time of chaos, unrest, and disobedience. Boaz obeys and supports the practice of *gleaning*, commanded by God in the law. Gleaning was basically a farmer's form of charity; he would command his workers to leave the crops that had fallen on the ground during the harvest so that poverty-stricken people could pick up the scraps and be fed. Boaz also is a man who respects and protects women in the midst of a culture that was not doing this. Boaz speaks kindly to Ruth in verses 8–9, and commands his workers not to bother her at all. We can see from Naomi's words in verse 22 that it wouldn't have been unexpected for Ruth to be mistreated, or even assaulted, in the midst of gleaning. Boaz is a different kind of man—different from most of the men of his day. He lives his life under God's word, even with no king on the throne to force him to do this.

The chapter ends with another important development in the story: we find that Boaz is a relative of Naomi's—a redeemer. We'll learn more about what that means in the next chapter, but you can bet that's a good thing for Ruth! As we close, I want to draw your attention to a phrase back at the beginning of the chapter, one that you may have read over quickly. Look back to verse 3. When Ruth went out to glean, the text tells us that she "happened to come" to the field of Boaz. That phrase "happened to come" could also be translated "as if by chance." It's meant to be incredibly ironic. In other words, we are supposed to laugh, and say, "It's not by chance! God has a hand in this." God will be faithful to Ruth, and he will start by putting her in contact with a man who is worthy.

We can learn from Boaz. This man was worthy—obeying God's word and protecting defenseless women—even in the midst of a culture that was doing neither of those things. Pray today that as you follow Jesus Christ and his word, you would have the courage to be worthy in this way, standing up for God's word in the midst of a generation that may turn away from him completely.

Boaz the Redeemer

A few things in this story are specific to this ancient culture—they strike us as strange but would have been normal for Ruth and Boaz. Uncovering a man's feet in the middle of the night and crawling into bed with him is not one of those things! That would have been scandalous then just as it would be now. Naomi instructs Ruth to do something that sends a clear message to Boaz: "I want to be your wife." This would have been shocking and probably even humorous for the original Jewish readers of the book of Ruth. Nothing sexual happens in this scene, but it would have been considered inappropriate behavior. Ruth is completely putting herself out there, asking Boaz to take care of her and love her.

What Ruth says about Boaz being a redeemer does need to be explained a bit. According to the law, if a man died and left behind a wife or a family, his brother was responsible for marrying his wife, caring for his children, and protecting the heritage and estate of his dead brother. If the man who died had no brother, his uncle would care for his family. After that, the duty would go to a cousin, and so on. Ruth is saying to Boaz, "You're a relative of ours, my husband is dead, and you can 'redeem' me through marriage." Boaz, knowing that he is not the closest relative of the family Ruth has married into, tells Ruth that he will work it out by bringing the issue to the closest related kinsman redeemer. If that doesn't work out, Boaz promises to redeem Ruth himself through marriage. Ruth goes away from this covert meeting with a promise from Boaz, and Naomi too is confident that Boaz will take care of the rest.

Think how far Naomi and Ruth have come! They started out far away from God's *place* (Naomi because of a move, and Ruth because she is a Moabite) and far from God's *people*. Now, by turning back together, they have come back to God's place, and have taken steps to become connected with God's people—through a righteous man named Boaz.

Ruth's pursuit of Boaz is a model for our pursuit of Christ. Ruth found the person who was capable of redeeming her entire situation, family, and life, and she went after him, willing to do whatever it took. Pray today that your attitude toward the pursuit of Jesus Christ would be that committed. He is the one true Redeemer—the only one capable of bringing forgiveness, eternal life, and true joy and satisfaction. Go after him—whatever it takes!

From Bitter to Blessed

Ruth 4 brings us to the conclusion of this wonderful love story. Boaz again steps up to the plate as he fulfills the role of redeemer for Ruth and makes her his wife. But we realize something as he works out the details of this marriage: the actions of Boaz are actions of sacrifice. Boaz is doing the right thing in claiming Ruth as his wife, but he is not doing the *easy* thing. Boaz, the worthy man, steps to the plate. He is not selfish or worried about the sacrifice; he does what is right.

Naomi—the one who renamed herself "Bitter"—is now recognized by the women around her as "Blessed" (4:14). She becomes the nurse of the child of Boaz and Ruth, and she is finally happy again—surrounded by family and filled with God's blessing. This love story could truly end with the words: "And they lived happily ever after."

But there's one big surprise that wraps up the book of Ruth—hopefully you didn't miss it! Obed, the son of Boaz and Ruth, is the grandfather of David, *King David.* You see, God was doing some wonderful things for individuals in this book. He was taking care of Naomi, bringing her from emptiness and bitterness to fullness and delight in his blessing. He was taking care of Ruth, bringing her from the pagan land of Moab into the people of Israel and to the worship of him as the one true God. But God was also using his work in the lives of these individuals to contribute to the ultimate blessing of his people. He was preparing this family to one day bring forth a king to rule over his people.

God is faithful to us—even in the small details of our lives. But he is weaving our individual stories into the tapestry of his big, beautiful plan for all of history. Ruth—a Moabite nobody—became not only an accepted member of God's people, but also the great-grandmother of King David. God was faithful to her, and also faithful to his people, who needed a king to one day help them break the sin cycle during the time of the judges.

As you trust and follow the perfect King—Jesus Christ—remember that your story is part of God's great plan for all his people for all time. You are part of the big story, and God wants you to play your role. Pray that he would help you to be faithful, living according to his word every day, that you would be able to point others to the perfect King and Savior.

Samuel Is Born

As 1 Samuel begins, we wonder if the king has finally come to God's people. An important biblical pattern is repeated again: a barren woman, a vow, and a miraculous God-given birth of a child. The very birth narrative of Samuel shouts to us, "This will be an important man!"

Hannah, a godly woman of Israel, is unable to have a child, no matter how much she prays and begs God. There's a humorous moment in the story when the priest, Eli, observes Hannah praying so fervently in the temple that he thinks she must be drunk! Recognizing the genuine and godly heart of this woman, Eli sends her away with a word of blessing, and before long, God has answered Hannah's prayer: Samuel is born. Hannah, who has vowed to give her child up for the service of the Lord in the temple, keeps her promise. She and her husband bring the boy Samuel to Eli and give him to the service of the Lord. And so, Samuel comes into the service of the Lord—but as a priest, not a king.

Samuel will not be a king, but he will be the greatest judge God's people have ever seen. He will give them victory over their enemies, like Gideon, Jephthah, and Samson. He will bring peace to the nation, like the many judges before him. But he will not carry with him the common sinful flaws. Samuel, unlike any of the judges before him, will be marked by an unhesitating obedience to God's word. He will, in fact, carry with his leadership of God's people many different elements of leadership—*priestly* elements, *kingly* elements, and *prophetic* elements. He will be a mediator for God's people (their priest). He will rule over God's people as their leader and warrior (their king). He will speak God's word faithfully and truly to God's people (their prophet). In this way, Samuel will foreshadow, like no judge before him, this threefold reign of Jesus Christ over God's people—the perfect prophet, priest, and king.

Think about Hannah for a moment—sad, downcast, and desperate for children. God answered this woman's prayer! And he chose to do it in a way that blessed not only her but also the entire nation of Israel. Her son became a great and godly ruler for the people! God cares about the details of your life; thank him for that today, and pray to him about all your fears, struggles, and doubts. Then ask him to make your story part of his great story. Ask him to use your life to bless those around you and to lead them to faith in the great King: Jesus.

Corrupt Leaders

There is perhaps no place that corruption in leadership hurts and shocks us more than in the church. Our pastors and spiritual leaders are supposed to be godly men of integrity, character, and humility. Unfortunately for Eli the priest, his two sons were spiritual leaders who fit the corruption bill at every level. These priests had become absolutely filthy, and God wasn't going to put up with it much longer.

What was so wrong with the behavior of Hophni and Phineas, Eli's sons? First, they disobeyed God's instructions concerning how the priests were to make sacrifices for the people. God's law had set aside a way for the priests to take food for themselves from the animal sacrifices that were brought to them. But there were very strict instructions for this: the priests were allowed to take meat for themselves from the breast and the right thigh of the animal. What were these priests doing? They were plunging a three-pronged fork into the pot of boiling meat and taking whatever meat happened to come out as their share (in other words, *not* just the breast and the right thigh!). Hophni and Phineas were abusing the sacrifices of God's people and stealing from them in the midst of worship. Second, these worthless priests were sleeping with the "women who were serving at the entrance to the tent of meeting" (2:22).

Put yourself in the shoes of an Israelite during this time. You come to the place of worship, bringing an animal to sacrifice to God for your sin in accordance with his law. You get to the place of offering, and the priest takes more than his share and doesn't let you offer your full sacrifice to God! You find that your mediator—the man who is supposed to go between you and your God—is filthy, corrupt, and completely unfit for the priestly position. You would ask yourself, "Can *this* worthless man really mediate between me and a holy God?" This passage tells us that God's people need a *faithful* priest. In the midst of this terrible account of worthless leaders, we find this verse of stark contrast: "Now the boy Samuel continued to grow both in stature and in favor with the LORD and also with man" (2:26). God's faithful priest is coming.

If you are in any position of spiritual leadership, even just in your group of friends, pray that God would help you use that position well! As you pray, remember that you do have a perfect mediator—Jesus, the ultimate priest. You can find forgiveness through his ministry on your behalf.

Speak, for Your Servant Hears

First Samuel 3 is the kind of passage that leaves an impression. This chapter opens by telling us that the "word of the LORD was rare in those days" (1 Sam. 3:1), and so we should be surprised by what comes next! God does speak, yet he speaks not to the priest, Eli, but instead to the boy, Samuel. And God has to call out three times before Samuel learns it is the Lord who has spoken, and only then can Samuel respond accordingly.

Samuel's response to God, in fact, is characteristic of the entire life and ministry he has ahead of him. After finally realizing that the voice he hears is not Eli's but God's, Samuel goes back to bed. When he hears the voice calling him again, his response is, "Speak, for your servant hears" (3:10). You could not better sum up the ministry and leadership of Samuel than with those words! Samuel is marked by being a man of God's word, living under it, and speaking it faithfully to God's people.

The message that God gives to Samuel is not necessarily a happy one, is it? It's a word of judgment, specifically against Eli's worthless sons. Yet this is the first word God calls Samuel to bring to his people, and Samuel faithfully passes it on to Eli, who accepts it as God's will.

This is God's call of Samuel as his prophet to his people—the one who will faithfully lead them by speaking God's word to them. As the chapter draws to a close, we see the power and influence of Samuel beginning to grow: "The LORD was with him and let none of his words fall to the ground" (3:19). He becomes known by all God's people as a great prophet—not because of his great personality, military strength, or leadership charisma, but because people recognized that he truly spoke God's word. That word will be the power and force behind Samuel's ministry and leadership.

As you consider the attitude of your own heart toward God's word—the Bible— ask yourself these questions: What is my posture toward the Bible when I read it and hear it taught or preached? Am I bored by it? Am I critical of it? Or do I, like Samuel, come to God's written word every time saying to God, "Speak, I'm listening, and ready to obey"? God uses people who adopt that kind of attitude toward his word. Pray today that you would be ready to listen to God's word and willing to obey.

God Will Not Be Used

The writer of 1 Samuel doesn't allow us to wait too long, wondering whether God's word through Samuel is going to come true! Following the call of Samuel, we immediately plunge into a battle scene in 1 Samuel 4. We see the Israelites against their archrivals, the Philistines. The first skirmish doesn't go very well for the Israelites. The people wonder why God has allowed the wicked Philistines to defeat them in battle. They do not know that this is all happening in accordance with God's word—spoken through Samuel—about his judgment on the wicked sons of Eli.

The priests and people decide to bring out the ark of the covenant and march it in front of them into battle so that they will achieve victory. Now you may know that the ark of the covenant was the symbol of God's presence with his people; it was located in the holy place of worship. But the ark was just that—a *symbol*. God's people, as we can see from this action, have decided to use the ark of the covenant as a kind of good luck charm for battle. They are, essentially, seeking to use God, rather than live in submission and worship to him.

Marching out this symbol of God's presence did not change the fact that the real God behind the ark was intent on judging his people for the grievous sin of their priests, Hophni and Phineas. The chapter ends with great sadness as Eli dies, essentially from shock, when he hears the news of the death of his sons and the Philistine's capture of the ark.

The Israelites needed to be reminded that God did not live in the ark! God cannot be contained by any religious charm or symbol, and he will not be wheeled out by his people for their own personal use. God is holy, mighty, and just, and he demands obedience, repentance, and holiness from his people. No religious ritual could deter God's righteous anger against the sin of these wicked men who had abused their position, damaged God's people, and rebelled against his word.

Are there religious rituals or "good luck charms"—prayers, church attendance, devotions—that you privately think will help you get in good with God? Friend, God will not be used. He doesn't want us to use him for our purposes; he wants us to repent of our sins, turn to him, and follow him and his good purposes. Pray today that you would not use God, but that you would humbly make yourself totally available to him and obedient to his good purposes for you in Christ.

The God of the Entire World

When the Philistines defeated the Israelites in battle, they took the ark of the covenant. They set the ark up in their temple alongside their god, Dagon. They had, from their perspective, defeated the God of the Israelites, along with the people; the Israelites' God would now come to live with their victorious god, Dagon.

God had other plans. Even though the ark of the covenant was not where God lived, it was nevertheless linked to the one true God of Israel—the God of the entire world. It was a big mistake for the Philistines to assume that this God didn't have any power outside Israel and that he would stand to be set in subjection to their god Dagon. The first morning after setting the ark beside Dagon, they find Dagon lying flat down on his face in "worship" to the ark of the covenant. The Philistines set poor Dagon back in his place. But the next morning, it's even worse; this time, Dagon is again face down, but he is missing his head and his hands. Because of the presence of the stolen ark in their land, the people are struck with a terrible plague of tumors, and they are in great anguish. This continues in each city where they move the ark as well.

God is teaching the Philistines that he will not share his glory with any other so-called god. God won't share his space with Dagon! God demands his own space; he is the only true God of the universe. He is also teaching his people that he does not need us to fight his battles for him. God didn't need to be in the land of Israel to assert his dominance over other gods, powers, and nations, and he didn't need an army of Israelites to bring the Philistines into submission. God fights his own battles; he doesn't need us! Finally, though, God is showing his people that he has not abandoned them; he is not done with his people. He judged them for their sin, yes, but he will not allow his enemies to have the final triumph over him or his people.

Remember that the God who created you, loves you, and saved you is a God who will not share his space with other gods in your life. He demands your worship, loyalty—your all! Pray for God to help you to give him total reign over your life, and that you would not share him with other idols that might get in the way.

Wanting to Be Like Everyone Else

As Samuel nears the end of his life, the people realize that his sons are poised to potentially take his place of judgment over them. It is because of this, and because of other motivating factors that we'll also discuss, that the people come to Samuel with a shocking request: they want a king.

Why is this a shocking request? Because it has been the fact that the Israelites didn't have a human king that set them apart from every other pagan nation surrounding them. They didn't have a human king because God himself was their King; he ruled personally over them. Now, while Samuel probably contributed to this request for a king by setting his wicked sons up as judges, there was one great motivating factor for the people in making this request: they want to be "like all the nations" (8:5). In fact, even after Samuel has warned them about their request, they repeat this very same request in an even stronger way: "No! But there shall be a king over us, that we also may be like all the nations, and that our king may judge us and go out before us and fight our battles" (8:19–20). It is clear—from God's own words—that this is a rejection of God himself. *He* has been the one fighting the battles of the people, and he is far better than any human king! The people, though, want to be like everybody else.

Now, it's true that God's law had allowed for a king to someday rule over his people; there were instructions given for Israelite kings in Deuteronomy 17. And it's true that God ultimately decides to not punish his people for this request but to grant it and use it for his good and perfect purposes in the lives of his people. God is faithful to bring good—even eternal good—from a sinful request like this. But it is still sinful. This was an act of rejection by God's people. They were rejecting God as their great King and following an impulse that many of us struggle with today: wanting to be like everybody else.

I still feel the temptation, as I'm sure you do, to try to fit in—to be like everybody else. To talk like they talk, to do what they do, to tolerate sin the way they tolerate sin. Pray today that God would help you not allow that impulse to be the primary motivating factor in your life! Ask him to help you follow him as your King above all else, with his word as your guide. If you are saved and forgiven by Jesus, you are set apart for him!

Head and Shoulders above the Rest

In 1 Samuel 10, we see God giving the people what they want—*exactly* what they want. They wanted to be like all the other nations around them. They wanted a king to serve as their figurehead, to represent them well to the surrounding people groups. God gives them Saul.

Saul is, in every way, the king that the people would choose. He just looks like a king! We've learned earlier in the story that Saul stands a full head and shoulders taller than the majority of the people of Israel. Humanly speaking, God could not have given his people a more kingly king. And you can see from their response to Saul in 1 Samuel 10 that they agree with this assessment. In verse 24 Samuel announces Saul before the people and says, perhaps with a twinge of cynicism, "Do you see him whom the Lord has chosen? There is none like him among all the people." The people respond with shouts: "Long live the king!" They finally have their human king, like all the other nations.

Some promising signs accompany the rise of Saul. He has a strong experience with God in verse 9 and a significant change of heart. If you glance ahead to 1 Samuel 11, you'll see that his first military exploit results in a great victory. Also, right at the end of 1 Samuel 10, we see that Saul refrains from taking revenge on the people who grumble at his being king. Still, we can't help feeling a sense of dread as Saul assumes the throne. Samuel's words about Saul—"There is none like him"—remind us that the Israelites *already had* a divine King, whose rule set them apart from every other nation. The strange drama of Saul's coronation—when Saul has to be dragged out from his hiding place among the baggage—leaves us with certain questions about Saul's courage, bravery, and character. Most of all, we should be a bit worried by how the writer goes out of his way to describe Saul's physical appearance. It's as if he is shouting at us, "This guy *looks* like a king!" But a question emerges in the back of our minds: "Does he have the *heart* of a king?"

We focus on looks, popularity, fame—and often we even make choices based on those things. Pray today that God would help you see past people's looks, whether you find them attractive or unattractive. Pray that he would help you see people as he sees them: his infinitely valuable creatures, who need the saving grace of Jesus Christ to follow and love their God.

Under Pressure

In 1 Samuel 13, we find Saul in the first pressure-filled situation of his reign. He is at war with the Philistines—the enemies of God's people who continually plague the Israelites. Saul's son Jonathan achieves a great victory over part of the Philistine army: their garrison of soldiers at Geba. In response to this, the Philistines call out their entire army to fight against the Israelites. Saul is in a tough place, to say the least! On top of being vastly outnumbered, some of his men are starting to hide in caves, and some begin to run away to the surrounding regions.

Samuel had given Saul a very important command: he was to go ahead to Gilgal, where Samuel would eventually join him to offer sacrifices to God. Saul was to wait a full seven days for Samuel to get there; Samuel was the priest, and only he was authorized to lead the people in sacrifice and offerings to God. As the pressure builds, Saul begins to crack. Finally, he decides to do something about it. Saul calls for the animals and the wood for the offering, and offers the burnt offering himself. Right after he finishes it, Samuel shows up! And Samuel is not happy with Saul. In fact, he takes this action extremely seriously, saying that because Saul has done this, God will not allow his kingdom to continue but will choose another man to be king over his people—"a man after his own heart" (13:14).

It doesn't seem too hard to understand why Saul might just take care of the sacrifice by himself! Yet God had determined in his law that *only priests* would conduct sacrifices on behalf of his people. Saul—a king, but not a priest—was not allowed to do what he did. It was a slap in the face of God and a blatant disregard for the command of Samuel and the word of the Lord. More than that, it shows us what was in Saul's heart. In a situation of pressure, tension, and danger, he proudly tried to take care of things himself instead of waiting for God.

Saul couldn't have two roles! He was only a man—and a sinful man at that. He needed a priest to make sacrifices for him, and the fact that he tried to do this himself revealed a heart of pride. Pray today about any pride that you might have in your heart. Confess your sin to God. Ask him to forgive you for the ways that you sometimes act like you don't need him—as Savior or even to get through every day.

To Obey Is Better Than Sacrifice

Soon after Saul takes the throne, God sends Samuel with an important message for him: destroy the Amalekites. Why the Amalekites? Because hundreds of years ago, they had attacked the Israelites in the wilderness after they left Egypt. God hasn't forgotten this! He had made a promise to his people back then that he would be in perpetual war against the Amalekites. This command that God gives to the newly enthroned King Saul is a command to keep his promise to his people concerning the total destruction of their enemies.

With this clear command from God, Saul goes to war against the Amalekites and their king, Agag—and he has a great victory. He destroys the army and the people. Then comes a big *but* in verse 9. Saul and the people spare the king and all that is good. God's command was for the total destruction of God's enemies. Saul simply does not do this.

When Samuel shows up, Saul really begins a downward spiral. He claims that he has completely obeyed God's command to him. He blames the people for the sparing of the Amalekite king and animals, rather than taking responsibility as their leader. He finally confesses, but quickly, hoping for a quick fix to his disobedience. Even at the end of his interaction with Samuel, Saul seems to be motivated more by what he will look like in front of his men than by where he stands with God. Samuel again confirms that because of Saul's disobedient heart and rejection of God's word, God will give the kingdom to someone else—someone with a heart that is given to God.

At the heart of this chapter we find a kind of poem that Samuel speaks to Saul—a poem in verses 22–23 that summarizes well what God is looking for from his people. God wants *obedience*, not *sacrifice*. He wants people who listen to his word, not people who just go through the motions. Ultimately, God wants people who give him their hearts. That is what Saul never seems to do! And that is what will set David apart as God's chosen king to lead his people.

Pray today that God would help you—by his Holy Spirit—put to death the sin in your life! Don't let sin hang around, leaving some parts of your life untouched by God's presence. Peace with God through Christ means war with sin—fight it with the intent of completely destroying it!

The King No One Expected

We love to see unlikely heroes go from anonymity to fame—fueled by their humility, integrity, and often a good bit of luck. The story of David captures us in this way. If Saul was the obvious choice for king, then David was the least likely king one could imagine! Last in his own family. Tending the sheep. Living in the shadow of his strong and handsome older brothers. Yet called by God to lead his people.

As 1 Samuel 16 begins to unfold, we see that even Samuel was guilty of falling into the thinking of the people at some points. God calls him to go anoint a new king from the sons of Jesse. When Samuel gets there, he is immediately taken by the outward appearance of Jesse's sons. He sees Eliab and says to himself, "Surely the LORD's anointed is before him" (16:6). This is what the people said about King Saul! He looked like a king. He was handsome, tall, and strong. He was the *people's* choice for a king. But he did not have the kind of heart that God was looking for. God makes a gentle rebuke to his faithful servant Samuel: "Do not look on his appearance or on the height of his stature, because I have rejected him. For the LORD sees not as man sees: man looks on the outward appearance, but the LORD looks on the heart" (16:7). Even Samuel needed to be reminded that God sees past outward appearances to the heart.

After Samuel anoints David—much to the surprise of Jesse and his other sons—David immediately begins to grow and flourish, with the enablement of God's Spirit. The rest of the chapter lays the groundwork for the rise to prominence of this young man, David. He is taken into the service of King Saul, who has clearly continued a downward spiral into sin and now madness and rage. David plays the harp so beautifully that his music is the only comfort for the tormented mind and heart of Saul. David began the chapter in a field, with a bunch of sheep. By the end of 1 Samuel 16, he is in the court of the king. God has chosen his king for his people—the king that no one expected.

Remember today that God looks at people's hearts, not only their outward appearance. Remember that he wants you to be a person who obeys his word and follows his Son inwardly, and in a way that shows in your life. Thank him that he looks at your heart, not your outward appearance. Then pray that you would see others the way that he sees them.

In Need of a Champion

Where are you in this story? Where can you find your main application for this passage? With what characters do you identify? You see, throughout our childhood years in Sunday school classes, we were taught to find ourselves with David. We are taught to be brave like David, to trust God like David, to not be afraid of the "giants" in our lives like David. We have failed to find ourselves in the right place in the story.

Consider, first, where we are in the big story of the Bible. God's people (the Israelites) are now in God's place (the land of Israel) under God's rule (human kings, guided by God's word). So, where *would* we be, if we lived during the time of David and Goliath? We would have been living lives as pretty normal, everyday Israelites. A good question to ask—especially in Old Testament passages—is this: What was the normal Israelite doing? That is where we find ourselves in the story of David and Goliath.

The people are terrified. Verse 11 tells us that when Goliath, the champion of the Philistines, stood before Israel, Saul and all the people were greatly afraid. They stand by and watch while David steps up to fight their great enemy. David comes to Saul and begs him for the opportunity to fight Goliath. He goes into battle alone, with nothing in his hand but his sling and some stones. He marches boldly to Goliath, the giant of a man, and boldly declares that he will defeat him in God's name. God gives David victory over Goliath, and he kills him, then cuts off his head. After Goliath is already defeated, the people rise up with a shout and join in the battle that is essentially already over.

We are not the David figure in this story—Jesus is! We're the terrified and helpless people of Israel, lost in our sin and in need of a champion, a Savior. Jesus is the champion for God's people. He defeats sin, Satan, and death, while we stand by and watch him die on the cross and rise from the dead. Then, in his great love for us, our champion invites us to join in his cause—his glorious mission in the world.

Thank Jesus that he is our champion. Like David, he fought the battle in the place of helpless and terrified people, and we are called to join his cause, so that others will know about the salvation and forgiveness that is found in Christ alone.

Biblical Friendship

If anyone had the right to be viciously envious, it was King Saul's son Jonathan! As heir to the throne, Jonathan saw firsthand the failure of his father and the rise of David, the man who would one day rule the kingdom instead of him. Many of us would have reacted much differently than Jonathan to this attack on his inheritance. We would have been angry at David, envied God's blessing on him, and perhaps hoped for his downfall. Instead Jonathan encourages, supports, and defends David.

How does Jonathan model true biblical friendship for us? First, he loves David sacrificially. The writer of 1 Samuel uses very strong language to describe Jonathan's commitment to David; he repeats two times the fact that Jonathan loved David "as his own soul" (18:1, 3). He demonstrates this love for David by giving him his armor, his robe, his sword—things that would have been symbols of his royal position as the son of the king. Jonathan loved David without any self-serving agenda. Second, Jonathan loves David because he supports God's plan for his life and for God's people. Jonathan recognizes that his father does not have a heart after God's heart and that David does. Jonathan recognizes and submits to God's will in the transfer of kingship from the line of Saul to the line of David. In befriending and supporting David, he submits to the will of his God for his people.

The people of Israel are attracted to this young warrior who serves God and fights on their behalf. They even sing a song in his honor: "Saul has struck down his thousands, and David his ten thousands" (18:7). Saul of course begins to notice this, and his response is predictably not like the response of his faithful son Jonathan. Saul begins to be tormented by envy; he hates David, and even attempts to kill him with a spear in a fit of wild rage. But David is blessed by God and chosen by him to lead his people as their king one day. Saul lives in envy, bitterness, and fear of this young man who has the approval of God and the people. While his own son embraces God's plan for David, Saul continues to spiral downward—further and further into anger, hatred, and sin.

Pray today that God would make you a friend who loves sacrificially and who encourages the work of God in the lives of your friends. Pray that the reign of the true King—Jesus—would be the central motivation in all your friendships.

Anointed but Not Yet King

David is in a very interesting—and precarious—situation. He has been anointed by Samuel as the rightful king of Israel, with God's full blessing and approval. But there is still a king sitting on the throne. And that king—Saul—is none too happy about David's anointing by God and his incredible popularity with the people of Israel.

In the midst of all this, the friendship between Jonathan and David stays incredibly strong. It is probably the strength of Jonathan's love for David that makes him incredulous at the thought that his own father is out to kill David. David, however, insists that this is the case. They agree that Jonathan will secretly investigate the true intentions of Saul regarding David by evaluating his reaction to David missing a dinner celebration in the king's palace. It is an understatement to say that Saul's actions betray his intentions for David! Not only does Saul confirm that he wishes David dead, but he also tries to spear his own son out of anger for his support of David.

In the middle of this dinner investigation, the stark contrast between Saul and his son Jonathan is truly revealed. We've already discussed Jonathan's selfless love for David; Jonathan loves David not because of any hidden agenda, but because Jonathan genuinely wishes the best for David and trusts God's plan for both of their lives and for the people of Israel. This kind of selfless love is unfathomable to Saul, a man who has only ever known pride, self-interest, and personal ambition. His words betray this; he cries out to Jonathan, "As long as the son of Jesse lives on the earth, neither you nor your kingdom shall be established. Therefore . . . he shall surely die" (20:31). Saul has no category for Jonathan's ability to look past his own interests and support the will of God for establishing the kingdom of someone else. Saul is blinded by his own pride and hatred and put to shame by the humility and sacrifice of his godly son.

Jonathan is an example of a true Christian friend. But he is more than that. He is a man who overlooks his own ambitions for the sake of the rightful king of God's people. Pray that God would help you sacrifice your own selfish ambitions and pursuits for the sake of the glory of his King, Jesus. Just as Jonathan got out of the way for David, so we are to get out of the way as we point others to our Savior and King.

The Hunter Becomes the Hunted

By the time the events of 1 Samuel 24 take place, it has been many years since Samuel's covert anointing of David as the king of Israel. David—wanted by King Saul—is a man on the run. Surely there were times when David was tempted to hurry things up a bit in terms of God's plans for him. If ever there was a chance—and seemingly a God-given chance—for David to bump off Saul and take over the kingdom, it was now!

Saul is again after David, with the intent to kill him. In fact, he has brought out three thousand men with the sole purpose of hunting David down. David, now well used to the wilderness terrain from being an experienced outlaw, nevertheless allows Saul to come close to his hiding place. The passage tells us that Saul actually goes into the cave where David and his men were hiding, to go to the bathroom! There he was—Saul, David's enemy—alone and relieving himself in a dark cave. If ever there was a chance to end the reign of this stubborn and envious king, it was now. David—the man who will be king—refuses to take the crown by his own strength, apart from the will of his God.

Even after merely cutting a bit off Saul's robe, in fact, David is stricken with remorse. He wishes he could take back even that small action—that tiny affront to the king who had been once anointed by God through the prophet Samuel. *This* David is the rightful king, the man after God's own heart, the man who will not grab for himself the crown but will wait for his God to deliver it to him in God's time and in God's way.

As David reveals this foregone opportunity to kill Saul after Saul leaves the cave, Saul is overcome with shame. Again, this complicated king feels remorse for his actions—but not the kind that will bring lasting change. Even though he affirms David's future as king and admits that his attempts to kill David have been evil, it won't be long until Saul is on the hunt for David again.

Pray today that your heart would be like David's heart. Pray that you would trust God to work his will in your life, in his time and way. Pray that you would work with all your strength for the cause of Jesus Christ, trusting that his power will accomplish his purposes as he has planned it.

Don't Miss the Forest for the Trees

The Old Testament contains many amazing stories. As you read these wonderful stories about individuals, you should also recognize that all these smaller stories are part of a much bigger, ongoing story: God's big story. A lot of the characters along the way don't get what God is doing! They are focused on their own little stories and filled with pride, selfishness, and rebellion. But the people who receive God's blessing are the ones who see the big story—the ones who submit to God's word and God's rule.

Nabal is a very rich man who is shearing his sheep in Carmel. David, who has been in that area with his men for some time, sends a message to this man requesting food and gifts. Nabal responds as only a fool could: he denies the humble request of David with strong words and treats him like a nobody. Infuriated, David gets his men ready for battle; he is ready to return evil for evil and destroy Nabal and all his family, men, and goods.

Abigail is a woman who sees the big picture—God's big story. She knows her husband is a terrible fool and has acted stupidly by inciting the wrath of a great warrior like David. But she also knows that David—the future king of God's people—must be stopped from killing Nabal and his men in retaliation. So Abigail comes to David, loaded with gifts and with very wise words. She begs him to overlook Nabal's fault, reminding him of his future as the anointed king of God's people: "The LORD will certainly make my lord a sure house, because my lord is fighting the battles of the LORD, and evil shall not be found in you so long as you live" (25:28).

God does ultimately take care of the fool Nabal; he dies just days after his foolish and harsh words to David. David doesn't miss this opportunity: he takes this wise and godly woman as his wife! What could have been a great massacre by David becomes a marriage that was ordained by God. All because a wise and godly woman kept her eyes on God's big story and God's plan for his chosen king.

Ask God to help you keep his big story in your view. It's this story that reminds us that we are children of God through the death of his Son on the cross—children who have his Spirit within us, guaranteeing that we are destined for eternal life and reign with him!

Sin Brings Forth Death

Saul's reign had begun with such promise! The people had cheered him, for he had the look of a king. But Saul's reign—and life—comes to an end with a great sense of sadness and loss. First, he is defeated by the enemies of God's people—the Philistines. Second, he dies by his own hand. Instead of fighting until the end, Saul turns to his armor-bearer and asks him to kill him to put him out of his misery. When the man refuses, Saul falls on his own sword in order to end his life before the Philistines overtake him. Third, Saul is mocked and mistreated by his enemies even after death. When the Philistines find him, they desecrate his body by cutting off his head and hanging his body on the wall in one of their temples.

This is the end that was coming for Saul—the minute he chose to reject the word of God and to refuse to obey him. First Samuel 31—this end of the road for Saul—is where unrepentant sin against God ultimately leads. To defeat. To despair. To shame. Remember who else dies in this battle: Jonathan. Saul's sinful rebellion against the word of God has ended not only in his own destruction, but also the death of his son, the faithful man Jonathan.

In the midst of this terrible defeat for the Israelites, and this sad ending for Saul, David has continued to survive in the wilderness with his band of men. It will soon finally be time for the king to take the throne. This king—the king with a heart like God's heart—will be different from Saul. And yet even David will leave us looking for something more. No merely human king will be enough to both *lead* God's people and *save* them from their sins.

More than anything else, a passage like 1 Samuel 31 ought to fill us with humility; it ought to serve as a serious warning to us all. Pray today that you will submit your heart completely to God through repentance and faith in his Son, Jesus Christ. Ask him to keep you faithful in obedience to his word. Ask him—as young as you may be now—to keep you faithful to the end.

David to Exile

Love Your Enemies

You can understand the motivation of the young man who comes to David with a story in 2 Samuel 1. He claims to have been the one who put Saul out of his misery, at Saul's request. We know this is a lie; the narrator of 1 Samuel 31 told us that Saul took his own life. This man is trying to get in good with the next king of Israel, whom he assumes will be happy that his rival has been murdered. He's hoping for some kind of reward from David, or perhaps even a high-ranking position in his service.

Unfortunately for this young Amalekite, he has vastly underestimated the next king of Israel. This David is no grabber for power. He is not the kind of man who will reward someone for killing Saul—even though Saul has many times tried to kill him! The punishment for the lying man comes quickly and decisively; David commands one of his young men to put him to death for killing the man that God had once anointed as king over his people. David has refused time after time to oppose the man God has put in place over his people, and he will defend (even after Saul's death) the very man who had hunted him and made him a fugitive. David—the next king of God's people—has refused to trade evil for evil.

David's respect for the anointing of God on Saul goes even further: he composes a lament in honor of both Saul and Jonathan, a lament that he teaches to all the people of Israel! It's a beautifully composed song. Even after Saul's death, David leads the people in respecting their king—the king God had set over them. David, on the cusp of finally taking the throne, ends honorably in his dealings with Saul, loving his enemy even to his death and teaching God's people to do the same.

What keeps David from hating Saul and celebrating his death? It is his deep fear of God and his respect for God's king. That fear of God transforms his feelings toward Saul and even enables him to genuinely mourn Saul's death and exalt him in the eyes of the people of Israel. Pray today that your fear and love for God would truly motivate you to love even your enemies (or people who hurt and mistreat you). After all, we are people who once were enemies of God because of our sin; we were loved by God through Jesus's death for our sins—while we were still his enemies!

War and Sovereignty

After the death of Saul and his mighty warrior son, Jonathan, the people of Israel are left with a void in leadership. It is finally time for David to step up and take the throne. So, as a man after God's heart, David inquires of the Lord and is told by God to go up to Hebron. The men of Judah (the southern part of the kingdom) immediately anoint David king there over the house of Judah.

Abner, the commander of Saul's army, has other plans. He has survived the battle against the Philistines, and he decides to take another of Saul's sons—Ish-bosheth—and set him up as the king of Israel (the northern part of the kingdom). There are now two competing kings over God's people. The people of Judah follow David, trusting that he is the king that God has chosen for his people. The people of Israel follow Ish-bosheth, as they cling to the fading dynasty of Saul.

This situation, almost a civil war, leads to much violence and bloodshed. Joab, the leader of the army of David, leads his forces against Saul's general, Abner. These are men of violence and war; you can tell by the war game that they stage near the pool of Gibeon before they begin the real battle. After this deadly game, the battle begins, and Abner's army is badly beaten by the army of Joab. You read about the deadly chase that happens after this battle, as Abner flees from the scene; Joab's brother Asahel is killed by Abner (a fact that Joab will not forget).

As we read passages like this, we need to recognize that God is completely sovereign over these events. It is a different time from ours, yes, but God reigns and rules in the details of even these brutal battles and bloody conflicts. We see too that David emerges blameless of any personal vengeance, pride, or brutality in these conflicts. He has mourned the death of Saul and rewarded the men who gave him a proper burial. In the next chapters, David removes himself from the revenge killings that occur and even punishes the men who commit them (see 3:28–34 and 4:8–12). This is a man who is guided by God's word.

Even in the violence, God was in control and was faithfully setting up his chosen king. Pray today that even in times of unrest, chaos, and hardship in your life, you would trust that King Jesus is reigning at the right hand of God! Pray that God would help you trust him today—and know that the King is in place over all nations and people.

Finally!

Years before the events of 2 Samuel 5, Samuel had made his way to the home of Jesse, and secretly anointed a teenager named David as the next king of Israel. Now, many years later—after long wanderings in the wilderness, sojourns in foreign lands, and many near-death experiences—the time has come for David to take complete control of the kingdom. Second Samuel 5 is a chapter filled with joy and with a great sense of arrival. We read of David's establishment as king, the full support of the people for his rule, and the consolidation of his kingly power as he defeats the enemies of God and his people.

There is simply no good explanation for the rise to power of a shepherd boy like David, except that it is the sovereign plan of a powerful God at work. David was a nobody, the youngest and last son of his father. Now he is reigning over all God's people. David's greatness and power are tied to God's hand in his life; there is no other explanation. We also need to recognize that, while this is not the end of the Bible story, it is nevertheless one of the great high points. We have reached a wonderful fullness in the development of God's kingdom: his people (the Israelites) are in his place (Jerusalem) under his rule (the rule of his chosen king, David). We see the people, led by their elders, gathered around David, acknowledging his rightful place as king: "Behold, we are your bone and flesh. . . . And the LORD said to you, 'You shall be shepherd of my people Israel, and you shall be prince over Israel'" (5:1–2). The people of God—with one unified voice—set up God's king, affirming him with God's words to him and pledging their allegiance to him. This is a great moment for the people of God—a true high point here in the Bible's story!

Just as the people gathered around David in unity, affirming his God-given role as their leader, so we ought to rally around our great leader. Jesus is the one who fights our battles for us. He is the one who brings true unity to God's people. He is the true hero of God's people—the unlikely hero who conquered our enemy (sin, Satan, death) by his own sacrificial death on the cross and his resurrection three days later.

Pray today that you would have total and complete loyalty to your Savior and King. Ask God to make you fully committed to serving his cause—his purpose—in this world. Pray that your identity would be grounded in your relationship with Jesus.

Israel's King Worships the King

The celebration continues as chapter 6 opens. David—the newly anointed king of God's people—has been established over both Judah and Israel. The people are unified in their support of him. God is giving him victory in battle over the enemy Philistines. The next step is to bring the ark of the covenant back to its place in Jerusalem, the central city of David's rule. Second Samuel 6 should be *only* a celebration. But as it turns out, two different individuals bring a somber tone to the chapter and teach us two very important lessons.

The first character that jumps out at us is a man named Uzzah who is helping to oversee the transportation of the ark. As the ark is on its way to Jerusalem, the oxen in the procession stumble. Without thinking, Uzzah reaches out for the ark in order to steady it. His action was in direct violation of the law of God, which instructed that no one should touch the ark. Because of this, Uzzah is struck dead by God on the spot. Even David is shaken up by this—and struck with a deep fear of God. What is God doing here? He is reminding David and the people that his holiness is the most important thing—even more important than human life. God is the true King of his people—the King who rules King David as well. And this King is infinitely and terribly holy.

Second, we are introduced in this chapter to David's wife Michal, who is a daughter of Saul. As the ark of the covenant is finally brought into Jerusalem, we get a wonderful glimpse into the humble and worshipful heart of David. Excited at the prospect of the ark returning to God's people in Jerusalem, David is "leaping and dancing before the LORD" (6:16). The people love him for this; it shows his total lack of pretension and his genuine joy in the Lord and love for his people. Michal, however, is not happy! She comes to David with harsh words, telling him that he has acted like "one of the vulgar fellows [who] shamelessly uncovers himself" (6:20). For Michal, the daughter of Saul, a king should act kingly and serious. For David, a man after God's own heart, a king of God's people should be known by his vibrant worship for the one true King.

We serve a God who would be completely justified in striking us all dead right now—like Uzzah beside the ark. Yet this is a God who has chosen to show us mercy and grace, by allowing his own Son to be struck dead in the place of sinful people! Praise God for that today, with great joy.

A Forever Kingdom

Certain passages in the Bible serve as markers along the way—major sign-posts that remind us what God is doing in the big picture of things. Some of these signposts take the form of covenants—promises that God makes with his people. In 2 Samuel 7, in the midst of the rise of the nation of Israel, God comes to King David with another great covenant.

The passage begins with David's desire, in light of the peaceful kingdom God has given him, to build a house—a temple—for the worship of God. But he will not be the king to build a temple for God; his son will do it. Nathan tells David the words of God to him: "When your days are fulfilled and you lie down with your fathers, I will raise up your offspring after you, who shall come from your body, and I will establish his kingdom. He shall build a house for my name" (7:12–13).

Yet as the passage continues, God's words to David through the prophet Nathan seem to go several steps further than the reign of David's literal son Solomon: "I will establish the throne of his kingdom forever. . . . Your throne shall be established forever" (7:13–16). That *forever* language should strike you as a bit much—even for the wonderful reigns of David and his son Solomon. You see, as marvelous as the kingdom of Israel was under David and Solomon, things didn't stay that way for long. In fact, just two generations after David, things begin to go terribly wrong with God's people and God's king.

Since no human king could ever establish a reign that would last *forever*, this king would have to be more than merely human! This promise of God to David is ultimately about God's Son, Jesus, who would come to earth as a human descendant of David! In fact, when God sends the angel Gabriel to Mary, he informs her about this using the language of David: "And behold, you will conceive in your womb and bear a son, and you shall call his name Jesus. He will be great and will be called the Son of the Most High. And the Lord God will give to him the throne of his father David, and he will reign over the house of Jacob forever, and of his kingdom there will be no end" (Luke 1:31–33).

God's forever King for his people is Jesus! His kingdom is "not of this world" (John 18:36), and the path into it is through the King's death on the cross for the sins of his people. Have you entered God's kingdom through the sacrificial death of the forever King? Pray about this today.

Seeing, Sinning, Scheming

David is a lover of God—a humble man who, unlike Saul, lives not for selfish gain but for God's glory and the good of God's people. The events of 2 Samuel 11 shock us every time we read them! The kingdom is secure. God's chosen king is on the throne. And the man after God's own heart falls prey to sin.

This passage begins with a subtle narrative comment that speaks volumes; the events that are described take place "in the spring of the year, the time when *kings go out to battle*" (11:1). While David has a well-trained army that is equipped to fight the country's battles for him, *he* should still be the one leading them out into battle.

While the passage doesn't go into too much detail about what happened between David *seeing* Bathsheba and *sending* for her, we can imagine that it all began with a look. That look led to a longer look. That gaze became sexual lust. And before long, David was overcome by his own desire. He—being the king—sent for Bathsheba, and she became pregnant.

What David does next is what we all are tempted to do when we sin: he *schemes and plots* in order to get away with it. His initial thought for a cover-up is not for murder but for calling Bathsheba's husband back from battle. His hope is that, while at home, Uriah will sleep with his wife, so that he will be assumed to be the father of Bathsheba's unborn child. But David didn't plan for the godly character of Uriah! This godly man refuses to sleep with his wife in the midst of wartime when all his other fellow soldiers are not at home with their wives. David's scheming finally turns deadly. He arranges for Uriah to be left alone during a point in the next battle, so that the enemy troops will vastly outnumber him, and he will be killed.

The passage ends with an incredibly ominous phrase: "But the thing that David had done displeased the LORD" (11:27). No one ever gets away with sin, even though it may seem that way for a time.

Pray today that God would help you not relax in your walk with him. Ask him to keep you from sin and to protect your heart from the attacks of Satan's temptation. We will not reach perfection in this life; we know that! But by the power of the Holy Spirit in us, we need to keep pursuing Christ our Savior and holiness in him.

You Are the Man!

David has done a terrible thing—many terrible things, in fact! He has lusted after another man's wife, committed an adulterous affair, schemed and plotted to cover it all up, and finally killed the innocent man whose wife he had taken. Quite a nasty list for David! But time has gone by, and David appears to have gotten away with it. Bathsheba has become pregnant, and a son has been born to David.

After some time, God sends a prophet named Nathan to David. He employs an interesting strategy to demonstrate to David the heinousness of his sin, telling him a heart-wrenching story about a wealthy man with many flocks of sheep who takes a pet lamb by force from a poor man so he can have it for dinner. David is immediately enflamed with anger and calls for the death of this evil rich man. David is not prepared for what happens next. Nathan turns to him with words that cut right to the heart: "*You* are the man!" (12:7). This story illustrates what David has done in abusing his power and taking advantage of Uriah!

It is David's response to this rebuke from God's prophet that reminds us that, while he has done a terrible thing, he is still a man after God's own heart. He could have had Nathan killed on the spot. He could have thrown him out of the palace and rejected his words. After all, he was the king; he could do what he wanted! David doesn't do this. He submits himself to God's word and to Nathan's rebuke with these simple words: "I have sinned against the LORD" (12:13).

There will be consequences for David's actions; Nathan tells him that the son that has been born to Bathsheba will die. While this brings great grief to David, David ultimately accepts God's discipline for his sin, realizing that God has mercifully chosen to spare him and show him eternal forgiveness. As the chapter ends, we see God beginning to restore his favor to David. He gives him victory over the Ammonites, and another son is born to Bathsheba. God shows his grace in this birth especially; this son will be a very special son to David and to God's people. His name is Solomon.

Turn to Psalm 51 and read it as a prayer to God. As you read, consider David's repentant heart. Note how seriously he takes sin. Learn from his desire for God's mercy. Use this psalm to guide your repentance when you fail to obey God completely.

Facing the Consequences

God truly forgave David for what he had done. But 2 Samuel 13 leads us to an important realization as we consider the mess in David's family. While God forgives sin immediately, that does not mean that sinful behavior will not have lasting consequences in this life. David's sin with Bathsheba—the sin for which God forgives him—causes terrible violence, chaos, and rebellion among his own children. Sin always has devastating consequences, even though God forgives sinners who repent.

You may remember that Nathan told David this would happen. Second Samuel 12 focused on the loss of David's child as the punishment of God for his sin. But Nathan said something else to him as well: "Thus says the Lord, 'Behold, I will raise up evil against you out of your own house'" (12:11). Second Samuel 13 is the terrible, disgusting, and sad fulfillment of these words. Amnon, one of David's sons, becomes lustfully obsessed with his half-sister Tamar. His friend Jonadab helps him lure her into his bedroom by pretending to be sick. When she comes to help him, he rapes her and then sends her away in disgust.

The story gets worse. Tamar's brother Absalom, another son of David, is rightfully furious about what Amnon has done. But instead of dealing with the situation in a godly way, he waits for the opportunity to take his revenge. Finally, the time comes. Two years after the rape—two years with hate and revenge flooding Absalom's heart—he convinces his father to send Amnon out to the wilderness with his sheepherders. He gets Amnon drunk and has his servants put him to death on the spot.

Lust, rape, hatred, revenge, plotting, murder. All these awful things plagued David's family—and that's only in chapter 13! Sin always has devastating and far-reaching consequences; we must not forget this. David was forgiven by God, but that does not mean that his sinful behavior will not have a terrible effect on his family.

Spend some time today confessing your sin to God and trusting that he has completely forgiven you through Jesus's death on the cross for you. Be honest and open about what sins you are currently struggling with; God's grace is sufficient for you! As you seek to follow Christ today, remember that sin is never merely personal; it always has devastating and far-reaching effects. Let that fact—along with your love for your Savior—motivate you toward holiness today!

King on the Run

Unfortunately for David—and for the kingdom of Israel—Absalom is not done with his violence and rebellion. Sin breeds more sin. Absalom has taken after his father, at least in terms of David's pursuit of sin and deception as demonstrated in his adulterous affair with Bathsheba and the murder of her husband. However, he has not learned from David the true and humble spirit of repentance.

Absalom's evil intentions become immediately clear as the chapter begins: he wants the kingdom for himself, and he is willing to do whatever it takes to get it. He begins by seeking to win the hearts of the people through kind words, flattery, and his good looks. His plan works wonderfully; we are told by the narrator that he "stole the hearts of the men of Israel" (15:6). By the time David realizes what is going on, it is almost too late! Absalom's conspiracy begins to gain traction, and he gathers a notable group of men around him. David and his leaders are forced to flee Jerusalem; his entire household goes out with him as they fear for their lives in light of Absalom's rebellion. It is a sad scene: the great king of God's people fleeing the city of Jerusalem with weeping and mourning.

How did we get here? The once-high king of God's people, who had the united support of everyone in Israel, is now on the run—fleeing for his life from his own son! If this passage is teaching us anything, it is this: sin leads to more sin—which leads to more sin! David's sin is still creating devastating consequences for him, even years after it happened. His son Absalom has imitated his father; he is seeking to take what he wants when he wants it. But he has not learned from his father the humble heart of a man after God's own heart. There was never any repentance in Absalom's life for the murder of his brother Amnon. His father's embrace and acceptance of him was not what he needed; Absalom needed the punishment of a just father!

First, consider the seriousness—the terrible destructive power—of sin. Let that encourage you to be vigilant against the sin that tempts you daily! Second, wonder anew at the glorious power of Jesus—the one who once for all broke the power of sin and death on the cross for his people. What an amazing Savior we have! Thank God today that sin will not breed forever. Thank him that his own Son conquered sin and death forever.

Absalom, Absalom!

As we read a passage like 2 Samuel 18, we can't help but acknowledge the *reality* of this story. We are reading about real people—with real struggles, temptations, and desires. Let's home in on three different characters as we consider this passage.

First, consider David's men. They are characterized, more than anything else, by their intense loyalty to David, God's king. When David attempts to go out with his army to fight the army of Absalom, his men sternly forbid him. Listen to their words of loyalty and reverence for their king: "You shall not go out. . . . If half of us die, they will not care about us. But you are worth ten thousand of us" (18:3). David's loyal men are with him to the death. They fight on behalf of David and achieve a great victory in defense of his kingdom.

Second, let's consider Absalom and the lessons that we can learn from him. Absalom teaches us that rebellion, treachery, and sin against God's chosen king will always end in tragedy and destruction. Ultimately, God will not allow this young brash upstart to dethrone the anointed king of his people; sinful attempts to claim the throne will result in defeat and death. In an ironic twist, it is Absalom's very prized characteristic—his long-flowing hair—that contributes to his downfall. He is left hanging in a tree by his hair, defenseless against David's men. It's almost a pathetic ending to the handsome man who had won the hearts of the people and brought danger so close to his father David's doorstep.

At the close of the chapter, we find David not congratulating and thanking his loyal men but weeping bitterly by himself at the loss of his son Absalom. David is still experiencing the effects of sin in his life and family, and this results in confusion, agony, and deep personal conflict. While David does eventually emerge from his mourning and greet his loyal people, he is nevertheless pictured in this chapter as a broken and conflicted man—weeping over the son who has followed his path of personal sin but has lacked true repentance and a fear of God.

Pray to God that you would follow Jesus with the fierce, devoted, and humble loyalty of David's men. Ask him to give you strength to never oppose—but always support—the cause of Jesus in this world. Following him will not always be easy, but it will be eternally valuable and glorious.

King of the Hill

It's tough to get to the top; it's even tougher to stay there. David's reign as the king of God's people was blessed and protected by God, to be sure. But it wasn't always easy; there was always someone trying to knock God's king off the throne.

Not long after the rebellion led by David's son Absalom dies down, another upstart rises to prominence in an attempt to steal the throne—and the allegiance of God's people—from David. This man's name is Sheba—a "worthless man" (20:1). You read in this passage about his rebellion against David. He is obviously something of a charismatic leader; he gets a decent following of people from Israel, the northern part of the kingdom.

Even though the men of Judah stick close to David, their king, the security of the kingdom is again in jeopardy because of Sheba's rebellion, although the rebellion ultimately comes to nothing. Joab and his brother Abishai lead a full-out pursuit of Sheba that ends at a city called Abel, where Sheba has hidden himself. Joab—intent on taking down the entire city for the sake of the hidden Sheba—wisely listens to the words of one woman in the city, who is loyal to God's people and God's king. The people of the city decide that it's not worth it to harbor a fugitive, and they cut off Sheba's head and throw it out to Joab. Just like that, the rebellion is over, and everybody goes home.

What do we learn from a passage like this—a story filled with violence, betrayal, rebellion, and lots and lots of bloodshed? We need to get above the details, at least at some level, and realize that while God doesn't condone all the actions that David's servants are performing, he is nevertheless sovereignly protecting and preserving the reign of his chosen king for his people. Lots of people will take shots at God's king; Sheba is not the only one! But God will not allow David to be taken down. God is in control, and he will be faithful to David to keep his reign and the kingdom intact during David's lifetime.

While we ought to courageously stand up for Jesus, we don't need to fight his battles for him! We need to keep believing in him, keep holding fast to his word, and keep trusting that he is ultimately on the throne—at the right hand of God the Father. Pray today that you would be found faithful and loyal to him when he comes.

The Lord Is My Rock

Many sports teams like to sing Queen's "We Are the Champions" after a big win. For King David, a similar claim would not have been far from the truth. By this point in 2 Samuel David has become the champion of his part of the world. The kingdom is completely under his control; Saul's family and all David's other rivals for the throne are dead. The Philistines and the other enemy nations of God's people have been defeated by David and his armies. So he too sings a song—not a song about his own power and glory but a song exalting the name of the Lord whom he holds responsible for his blessing and success.

David gives God all the credit for the blessing in his life and the victory he has had over his enemies. He begins with a summary statement:

The LORD is my rock and my fortress and my deliverer, my God, my rock, in whom I take refuge, my shield, and the horn of my salvation, my stronghold and my refuge, my savior; you save me from violence. (22:2–3)

David portrays God as his true source of strength; he is the defender of his life and the one who saves him from all danger.

David recognizes the cosmic power of God behind the circumstances of his life. In verses 8–16, David uses a *theophany*—a cosmic and magnificent appearance of God. God "bowed the heavens and came down," and he "thundered from heaven" (22:10, 14). David describes God as waging war on his enemies, and he recognizes that the divine hand of the almighty God has been behind every victory that he has achieved.

Finally, David acknowledges that God has dealt with him on the basis of his faithfulness to God. Listen to David's words about himself, which seem almost prideful to us at first glance: "The LORD dealt with me according to my righteousness; according to the cleanness of my hands he rewarded me" (22:21). Is David claiming perfection? We should certainly hope not; we know what he did with Bathsheba and her husband Uriah! Still, David is affirming that he has lived a life characterized mainly by faithfulness to God and obedience to his word, which includes heartfelt repentance when sin does happen (see Psalm 51).

As you pray to God today, sing this song of deliverance to him. Those of us who have faith in Jesus have experienced God's eternal victory and salvation in our lives. In him, and through the death and resurrection of his Son, Jesus, we have been given victory over Satan, sin, and death.

A Costly Cup of Water

The movie *Gladiator* tells of a shamed Roman general, Maximus, who fights his way back into influence through amazing bravery in the Colosseum. *Braveheart* presents us with a Hollywood version of William Wallace, the Scotsman who led his men against occupying British forces. The men described in 2 Samuel 23 far outshine Maximus and William Wallace. These men zealously battle for the cause of their worthy king.

These exploits are amazing! Josheb-basshebeth kills eight hundred men at one time with a spear. Shammah takes a stand against the Philistines during a battle that has his colleagues fleeing in the other direction; he defends his land and defeats a great number of the enemy Philistines. Benaiah (who also killed a lion in a pit) fights a spear-carrying Egyptian with nothing but his staff; he merely grabs the spear out of the Egyptian's hand and kills him with it. Why do these men do battle in this brave way? Because they are intensely loyal to David, God's king. They are committed to fighting his battles, whatever the cost and against any odds.

What is it that points us to David's worthiness in this passage? It's the record of the three men who broke into the Philistine camp—risking their lives—just to get David a drink of water. David's response to their brave and selfless act is humility and honor for the lives of his men. He refuses to drink the water, pouring it out in praise to God and referring to it as the blood of the men who have obtained it for him at the cost of their lives. David values the lives of the men who serve him.

While this passage is largely a positive picture of devotion to a king, it nevertheless ends on a sour note. The narrator doesn't want us to miss something. Who brings up the rear in the list of David's mighty men? It's *Uriah the Hittite*. The man whose wife David stole, the man David murdered. David, the worthy king of God's people, killed one of his own loyal mighty men. David is not God's forever King. At this point in the story, we're still looking forward to a King from David's line who will not betray his followers but will offer his own life for their eternal salvation.

Pray today that you would bravely—and daily—serve the cause of Jesus in this world. Ask God to give you strength to be a mighty follower of him, strong against sin, brave for his truth, and devoted to him at any cost.

The Sinful Census

This chapter begins with these strange words: "Again the anger of the LORD was kindled against Israel, and *he incited David against them*" (24:1). It's worth, in this case, taking a look at the parallel version of this passage, which you can find in 1 Chronicles 21. There you'll see that Satan—not God—is given the credit for inciting David to the evil decision he makes. While we don't have time in this context to explore all the subtleties of this seeming contradiction, we'll say for now that God, in his sovereign plan, sometimes does use even evil for his glorious purposes in this world.

David's sin may not strike us today as so terrible; he makes the decision to number the people that he rules. Why is this wrong? It's wrong because it demonstrates that the king of God's people is moving away from complete trust in God alone to defend his people and defeat their enemies. Joab gets this; he begs David not to go ahead with the census. But David, in a stubborn attitude of sin, goes ahead with it.

After the census is completed, we are again reminded why David is a man after God's own heart: he is struck with guilt because of his sin and repents and confesses it to God. While the repentance is real, there will again be consequences for David's sin—this time against God's people as well. God sends a plague on the people of Israel, which stops just short of doing destructive damage on the city of Jerusalem.

As the chapter—and the book of 2 Samuel—draws to a close, we read in verses 20–25 about a seemingly random business transaction between David and a man named Araunah the Jebusite. It's not random, though. On this piece of land, David's son Solomon will one day build the temple of God—a house for God's name. The writer is pointing us forward, even in this story, to God's big plan for his people to worship him in his place. God is working even through the sin of David to accomplish his purposes for his people and to lay the foundation for the great reign of Solomon.

If the story of David shows us anything, it's God's faithfulness. God's faithfulness to David—to forgive him of sin and bless his reign. God's faithfulness to his people—to provide them with a faithful king and to protect and bless them through him. Praise God today for his faithfulness to his people, then and now. Thank him that you follow the great Son of David, Jesus Christ, the fulfillment of all God's promises to his people.

Crowning Oneself King

As David grows old and weak, another one of his sons sees an opportunity to seize the throne by force. Adonijah was the son born after Absalom, and he has learned much from his older brother! He is young, brash, and ambitious. While he probably knows that Solomon is next in line for the throne, he proudly attempts to crown himself. But that's not how it works! People don't crown themselves, and it never works out for those who try it. Adonijah is *not* the right king for God's people, and his attitude and grab for the throne only confirm this fact.

In Samuel 2:12, Nathan the prophet stepped in and confronted David about his sin with Bathsheba. And he shows up again here, along with Bathsheba, the mother of Solomon and David's wife. Nathan now comes to David again with wise words—this time concerning Solomon, the right king for God's people. He and Bathsheba both recognize that, without the public establishment by David of his son Solomon as the king, David's sons will almost surely create a civil war after his death as they battle for the throne. David has made a promise to Bathsheba that Solomon will reign after him; she and Nathan now urge him to make good on that promise. David wisely does so; he sends men throughout the land to anoint Solomon and announce his imminent reign to the people. The news is greeted with great shouting and unified rejoicing from the people. God's king—the son of David—is ready to reign.

Almost immediately, we see that David's choice of Solomon is a good one; Solomon's character emerges as he deals with Adonijah. Hearing the celebration over Solomon's anointing, Adonijah realizes that he is in big trouble! So he runs away—fleeing to the place of worship and grabbing the horns of the altar. It's an ill-advised attempt to find refuge in a holy place; the nature of Adonijah's rebellion means that he deserves to die, even if he hides by the altar! Nevertheless, the new king over God's people shows mercy to his enemy. Solomon does not put Adonijah to death but allows him to return to him and fall in loyalty at his feet.

As you pray today, remember that we—in our sin and rebellion—are all like Adonijah. We try to crown ourselves. We oppose God's King, Jesus. Yet if we repent and return to him, he shows mercy. Take time today to bow your knee in repentance, praise, and loyalty to Jesus the King.

David's Deathbed Speech

Death brings a deep seriousness; words become more meaningful. So as King David lies on his deathbed, we can imagine that he will choose his words carefully as he speaks one final time to his son Solomon.

David begins by speaking on a subject that will be very familiar to us: the importance of holding fast to God's word. That is, in fact, the true duty of a king over God's people and, for David, that's what it means to be a man. Listen to his words: "Be strong, and show yourself a man, and keep the charge of the LORD your God, walking in his ways and keeping his statutes" (2:2–3). The first deathbed words that David speaks to his son concern his obedience to God's word. David then reminds Solomon of God's promise to him about the reign of his descendants and urges him to walk closely with God in light of that promise.

Then this deathbed speech goes in a different direction—one that can be confusing to us. David instructs his son Solomon to kill two enemies and dangerous men and to treat loyal servants well. While there's been some personal insult to David by both men, these commands are less about personal vendettas and more about the security and peace of the kingdom under Solomon. Joab, who had murdered two Israel army commanders, had brought great guilt and shame on David's house because of his actions. David instructs Solomon to punish Joab for these cold-blooded murders so that no one in the kingdom can hold them against Solomon and his followers. Shimei, who had cursed David, must also be held accountable for his actions, lest his continued presence in the kingdom create strife and danger for the son of the king Shimei had cursed. The central purpose is for Solomon to take the necessary steps to safely and securely establish his kingdom and rule over God's people.

That is exactly what happens; the chapter concludes with the beginning of a new era for God's people. The son of David sits on the throne, and he enjoys complete control of a unified kingdom.

David lived under God's word and wanted more than anything else for his son to do the same. How about you? Do you live under—and according to—God's written word at every turn? Pray today that the heartbeat of your life would be loving Jesus and living according to his word. That will lead to a legacy that is worth passing on.

The Wise King

In the Old Testament, almost no one comes off completely without fault. The kings and leaders of God's people—even the good ones—fail at some points. This points us to the need for a ruler for God's people who will be free from the sinful complexities of fallen human beings—toward a Savior who will live perfectly, die sacrificially, and reign eternally.

While the moral complexities of Solomon only get more pronounced as his life continues, they show up at some level right from the start! First Kings 3 begins with the account of Solomon's marriage to the daughter of Pharaoh—part of an alliance that he made with this king of Egypt. This action in and of itself brings into question the character of Solomon. God's people were not to intermarry with the surrounding nations, in order to stay completely focused on the worship of the one true God.

Even with these failures, Solomon is presented to us in 1 Kings 3 as a godly and faithful king for God's people. The central interaction of this passage points us to this fact. It's nighttime, and we see a dream conversation between God and Solomon. God comes to the king, asking him to make a request of him—any request! Solomon resists any temptation to make a selfish or proud request; he asks humbly for God's wisdom, requesting that God give him an "understanding mind" to lead his people well (3:9). God is pleased with this request and promises to give Solomon not only wisdom but also riches and honor beyond imagination.

The well-known story of the two women fighting over one baby follows closely on the heels of the nighttime conversation with God. Solomon wisely finds a way to determine the true mother of the fought-over child. Judgments like these soon become public knowledge to the nation of Israel, and Solomon's fame and reputation grow day by day, as the people stand in awe of their king.

We know this picture of the rule of the wise king can't last, but it does give us a glimpse of what God is ultimately after for his people—living under the perfect and wise rule of Jesus, who will reign forever. As you spend some time with God in prayer today, consider this picture of Solomon's reign. Ask that God would make you content to live under the rule of Jesus now. Pray that he would help you live with great hope at the prospect of living under the perfect reign of King Jesus forever.

God Kept His Promise

In Genesis 12:2–3, God made this promise to Abram: "I will make of you a great nation, and I will bless you and make your name great, so that you will be a blessing. . . . In you all the families of the earth shall be blessed." God has been faithful to his people and his promise. He has established them in his place, Jerusalem. He rules over them through his chosen, wise king, Solomon.

The first nineteen verses of the chapter list the *people* who are in service to King Solomon. He has put in place high officials over parts of his kingdom: secretaries, recorders, commanders of the army, and men in charge of palace affairs and forced labor. He has also developed a system where twelve officers serve as his representatives across the nation, overseeing a system of taxation and also providing food for the king and his royal household. Solomon, with his God-given wisdom, has put in place an incredibly well-organized system of government.

The rest of the chapter describes the incredible *wealth*, *riches*, and *influence* of King Solomon. His kingdom stretched farther than it ever had before, or ever would in the future. The amount of possessions and animals he had was truly remarkable! More than that, he had become rich in his wisdom; he composed proverbs and songs and blessed the people with his teaching. It's not only the people of Israel who are blessed by the king's wisdom, though; "people *of all nations* came to hear the wisdom of Solomon," even other kings (4:34).

Think of the average Israelites during the reign of Solomon. What is their experience? The passage tells us the answer to this in three ways. The people "ate and drank and were happy" (4:20). The people "lived in safety . . . all the days of Solomon" (4:25). The people "came to hear the wisdom of Solomon" (4:34). What a time for God's people!

If you've read the Bible before, you know that this human monarchy won't last forever; it will become clear that God's people need an eternal King—one who will save his people, not just from the Philistines, but from their own sins. But for today let this picture of Solomon's reign encourage your faith in God as you spend some time in prayer. Thank him for his faithfulness to his promises to Abram and to his people—promises that once seemed so unlikely.

The Temple

After years of wandering in the wilderness, many years of the rise and fall of various judges over God's people, and the establishment of the Davidic monarchy, the time is finally right for Solomon to build a house for the worship of God—the temple. Today we'll make a few observations about this magnificent building, as well as the king who constructed it.

First, it's important to note that Solomon builds the temple with careful attention to God's law. *All* the building plans and the appropriate materials for the temple's construction had been laid out for God's people many years before. Exodus 20:25, for example, includes God's command to his people that any altar built must not make use of stones that have been cut with any metal tool. You can see—from 1 Kings 6:7—that Solomon paid careful attention to such commands from God's word.

Second, we need to remember that this temple was a symbol of God's presence with his people. It was, in many ways, the meeting place for God and the people of Israel—a place of worship, word, and sacrifice. In fact, God comes to Solomon with a great promise, in light of his construction of this temple: "Concerning this house that you are building, if you will walk in my statutes and obey my rules and keep all my commandments and walk in them, then I will establish my word with you . . . and will not forsake my people Israel" (6:12–13). While God's presence with his people is not *dependent* on a great temple, this temple will nevertheless serve as a great reminder to the people of God's presence with them.

But the passage in view extends until 1 Kings 7:1 for a reason; that verse tells us that Solomon took thirteen years to build his own palace, compared to seven years for the temple of God. Yes, Solomon built a wonderful temple for the people's worship of God, *but* he also spent a lot more time on his own palace. We seem to be getting another hint of a problem with King Solomon—a problem that may affect his ability to give his entire, undivided heart in worship to the one true God.

This marvelous temple that Solomon built served an important purpose for God's people, but it still ultimately pointed forward to a far greater meeting place between God and sinful people: the body of Jesus Christ. Consider your own heart in light of Solomon's apparent obsession with his own house. Ask God to show you if you have a divided heart, or if you are totally devoted to his service, praise, and worship in your life.

A Word Fitly Spoken

Abraham Lincoln's Gettysburg Address. Martin Luther King Jr.'s "I Have a Dream" speech. John F. Kennedy's famous comments following the moon landing. These speeches were given at key moments in the history of our nation when thousands of people were focusing on a key leader. First Kings 8 records such a key moment in the history of the nation of Israel.

Solomon's prayer is beautiful—rich, humble, and moving. But it also gives us key insights regarding the temple and its function—and limitations. First, Solomon's prayer reminds us that he recognizes the symbolic nature of this house for God. Listen to his words: "Will God indeed dwell on the earth? Behold, heaven and the highest heaven cannot contain you; how much less this house that I have built!" (8:27). Solomon acknowledges that no building could ever *contain* the God of the universe. God will not "live" in the temple in some permanent or limiting way. The people of Israel will begin to forget this over the years. They will begin to attach significance to the temple itself, rather than to the God whom they met with and worshiped in the temple. While the temple was a beautiful place of worship, and its construction by Solomon was blessed by God, God would never ultimately and only attach himself to a building.

A second key insight that we gain from Solomon's prayer regards the reality of God's grace and mercy toward his sinful people. God's people were called to obedience to his word—we know that. Solomon and the people are still commanded to keep the law! Yet Solomon's prayer points us to the reality of the people's inability to perfectly obey God's word. Anticipating the day when they do fail, Solomon prays for God's mercy and grace to overwhelm even their sin:

"If they sin against you—for there is no one who does not sin—and you are angry with them and give them to an enemy . . . if they repent with all their heart and with all their soul in the land of their enemies . . . then hear in heaven . . . and forgive your people who have sinned against you" (8:46–50). Solomon looks forward to the way God ultimately will deal in grace with his people—even people who stand guilty as lawbreakers, but who repent and return to him.

Pray today that you would respond every day in joyful obedience to the God who came near to sinful people. Thank him for sending Jesus, Immanuel—"God with us"—to serve as the perfect and final "meeting place" between God and sinners.

Blessing to All the Nations

If there is a high point to the Old Testament—a peak in the story of the Israelite people—we come to it in 1 Kings 10. This passage contains the climax of the monarchy in Israel and the height of the fulfillment of God's promise to Abraham, at least humanly speaking. God's promise to Abraham was a promise about blessing—not only to Abraham's family but to all the nations of the earth.

As Solomon's kingdom has increased in wealth, power, and influence, his reputation has spread as well. Eventually, the Queen of Sheba hears of Solomon's wealth and wisdom and decides to make a long journey to see this king of Israel. Armed with difficult questions, this Queen of Sheba is ready to put King Solomon to shame, although she comes bearing great gifts—"spices and very much gold and precious stones" (10:2).

It seems that the queen desires to test Solomon's wisdom; she inquires about many different subjects and comes prepared with lots of questions for him. To her amazement, King Solomon "answered all her questions; there was nothing hidden from the king that he could not explain to her" (10:3). The passage goes on to tell us that after her conversation with Solomon, and after seeing all his possessions, servants, and wealth, "there was no more breath in her" (10:5).

While we don't know whether the queen's exclamation of blessing for Solomon is an expression of personal faith in the God of Israel, it is still a beautiful summary of the blessing that God has given to his people in and through the reign of King Solomon: "Happy are your men! Happy are your servants, who continually stand before you and hear your wisdom! Blessed be the LORD your God, who has delighted in you and set you on the throne of Israel" (10:8–9). King Solomon and God's people have arrived, and even the great Queen of Sheba acknowledges it and is blessed by it. God has established his people in his place under his rule, so that even distant monarchs come to experience the great blessing of God.

God's kingdom—established through the death and resurrection of his Son—is one of great blessing and one that attracts and blesses people from all nations. People from every tribe, tongue, and nation are invited to gather around Jesus, the true King, and experience salvation and blessing through him. First Kings 10 is a picture of what is to come. Pray that God will give you eyes to see his true kingdom—Jesus's kingdom.

Pride Comes before a Fall

I'm sure you've heard the phrase "pride comes before a fall." For the people of Israel and their monarchy, the very height of the kingdom under Solomon—the glory and wonder seen in 1 Kings 10:1–13—immediately precedes its downfall. It's not exactly a mystery as to why this downfall happens. In the verses immediately following the passage about the Queen of Sheba, we see how even the great Solomon fell terribly short of God's ideal for a king.

Turn back in your Bible to Deuteronomy 17. You'll see that, in the second part of that chapter, Moses lays out for God's people instructions concerning the king who would one day rule over them. Now look at verses 16–17 of that chapter. You'll see that, for a king who came to power over God's people, three specific commands were given. The king was, first, not to take many horses and, second, not to take many foreign wives and, third, not to amass too much gold and silver for himself.

What do we learn about Solomon in this passage? We find that, in spite of all the good he accomplished for God's people, he explicitly disobeyed these three commands from God's law regarding the king of his people. He gathered thousands of horses for himself. He amassed unbelievable amounts of silver, gold, and wealth. Most troubling of all, he took one thousand total wives—many of them foreign women, who turned his heart away from completely devoted worship to God alone. Solomon didn't keep God's word perfectly and fully.

You see, the account of Solomon in the Bible shows us that no human king can provide perfect rule and leadership for God's people. Even at the very height of the monarchy of Israel—when everything is going so well—Solomon fails in three distinct ways to lead God's people according to God's word. God's people need a king who is even greater than Solomon. God will provide this King for his people, but it will get much worse before it gets better.

We all have the tendency to justify sin and keep selfish areas of our lives from the rule of Jesus. Ask God to help you give over everything to him. God wants us to be ruled by his King—Jesus. He is the Savior of sinners, and he demands that saved sinners give up every sin and selfish tendency to follow him.

A Divided Heart → A Divided Kingdom

Imagine a girl named Michelle, who doesn't like the sandwiches that her mother makes for her to take to school. As she packs her backpack each morning in her bedroom, she decides to throw her sandwiches out her window! Unfortunately for her, the neighbors eventually notice the growing pile of discarded sandwiches, which is outside their window as well! She thought she would get away with it, but she was mistaken.

Sometimes we can be tempted to almost believe that undiscovered sin won't catch up with us. While Solomon's sin didn't catch up to God's people during his lifetime, it did during the lifetime of his son, Rehoboam, whom we read about in this passage.

After the death of Solomon, Rehoboam takes over in chapter 11. Almost immediately, the people come to him with a fairly reasonable request: they want him to lighten the load that his father Solomon had put on them. Rehoboam chooses to reject the wise counsel of the older men of Israel and to follow the counsel of his young buddies. They tell him to be tough—to show the people who's boss! Jeroboam, who had opposed Rehoboam's father Solomon as well, sees his opportunity to gather disgruntled people as his followers. The people of Israel—the northern part of the kingdom—follow Jeroboam in his revolt against Rehoboam. The people of Judah—the southern part of the kingdom—remain with Rehoboam. This almost leads to a terrible battle, when Rehoboam calls out one hundred eighty thousand "chosen warriors" to fight against Jeroboam and the forces of Israel (12:21). But at the last minute, God sends a prophet to call Rehoboam back from this civil war. God's place—and God's people—have been divided.

Desperate to keep his people unified in the northern region, Jeroboam decides to put a stop to all religious journeys to Jerusalem and constructs places of worship for the people in Bethel and Dan. What begins as an attempt toward unification of his kingdom turns into full-fledged idolatry. The two calves of gold that he makes become sin for God's people, who travel to bow down before them.

What happened to Solomon's own divided heart now happens to the kingdom! Pray that God would protect you from a divided heart—a heart that is pulled in different directions by Satan and this world. Ask God to help you worship him in everything and with everything in your life.

Rehoboam and Jeroboam

While Rehoboam and Jeroboam were on opposite sides of a bitter rivalry, they had much in common. These rulers of opposing halves of the kingdom are brought together by one common trait: a rejection of God's word and a heart of disobedience to him.

Before wrapping up the account of the life and reign of Jeroboam, the writer of 1 Kings gives us a brief story about him, which explains a lot. His son has gotten sick, so he sends his wife to the prophet Ahijah. The fact that he sends her in disguise gives us a good indication of his reputation with the prophets of God! The message that he gets from Ahijah is not a positive one; it is a word of judgment against him and his house. Because Jeroboam has not followed God's word like David did, God promises to bring harm upon his house, even swearing to make an end of every man associated with him. On top of this, Jeroboam's son—the one member of his family that is pleasing to God—dies as soon as Jeroboam's wife returns to Jeroboam with the message from the prophet. This seems extremely harsh, doesn't it? We've said this before, but this passage forces us to affirm this truth again: God takes sin extremely seriously. God will not be mocked. Jeroboam not only sinned against God in his personal commitment to idolatry, but he also "made Israel to sin" through his sinful leadership of God's people (14:16).

Jeroboam's rival, Rehoboam, does not come off much better; here is the summary of his reign: "And Judah did what was evil in the sight of the LORD, and they provoked him to jealousy with their sins that they committed, more than all that their fathers had done" (14:22). Rehoboam is a serious step backward from his father Solomon, especially when it comes to spiritual leadership of God's people. The effects of the people's sin under him begin to show immediately as Shishak, king of Egypt, wars against Jerusalem and takes away much of the treasure that Solomon had gathered. Rehoboam dies while ruling over a divided kingdom that has far less wealth and security than it did under his father.

As this story develops, let's make sure that we find ourselves—our own attitudes and behavior—in the descriptions of God's people and their kings. We tend to follow the wrong leaders. We tend to want to worship other things than God. We need a Savior. Take some time in prayer and confession to God about these things.

Walk the Path Less Traveled

In this passage, we begin to see a pattern: the kings of God's people are judged based on the extent to which they walk in the ways of David. Before you start feeling too badly for these kings who followed David, make sure you don't overestimate the standard to which they were being held. The demand from God for these kings was not total perfection but faithfulness to his word personally, as well as in their leadership of God's people. David was not perfect! Still, the pattern of David's life was a steady obedience to God and heartfelt repentance whenever he fell into sin.

First, we read about Abijam, the son of Rehoboam. He takes over when Rehoboam dies, and his reign over Judah does not last long—only three years! While we aren't told much about his life and reign, we know the most important fact: "He walked in all the sins that his father did before him, and his heart was not wholly true to the Lord his God" (15:3). While God did not take away the kingship from his line, his reign was plagued by war with the northern kingdom, and he was soon dead and gone.

Second, we read about a contrasting king: Asa, the son of the wicked king Abijam. Asa "did what was right in the eyes of the Lord, as David his father had done" (15:11). For him, this meant working to rid the land of idols and prostitutes, not to mention a wicked and manipulative queen mother. Even though Asa did not completely get rid of the high places of worship—where much idolatry occurred—he is remembered as a king who was faithful to God and walked in the pattern of King David before him.

The book of 1 Kings will continue with these summaries of the reigns of the kings who would follow David and Solomon in both Israel and Judah. Some accounts are lengthy, with accounts of battles, interactions with prophets, and important leadership decisions. Some kings are summarized with little more than a sentence—their reigns summed up with either a word of praise or condemnation. While there will still be some good kings to come in Judah, the downward trajectory of God's divided kingdom has already begun. There will not be another David for God's people, at least humanly speaking.

Perfection is impossible; salvation comes only through God's grace by faith in the sacrifice of Christ for sin. Still, faithfulness to Jesus should summarize our lives. Consider the summary of your life thus far. Are you walking with Jesus? Is your life a pattern of faithfulness to him?

Judgment Is Coming

Hanging over the story is a dark and heavy sense that God's people, and certainly the northern kingdom's kings, are going to get what's coming to them. It's only a matter of time before God's judgment against sin and idolatry comes on them with fury.

We know that judgment is coming because of what we've learned so far about God. He is perfectly holy; he will not allow sin against his holy name to go unpunished. The prophet Ahijah, in the midst of the sin of Jeroboam, lifts up his eyes and looks forward to a day when the northern kingdom of Israel will be judged through exile in a foreign land. Because of their idolatry, and because their kings led the people into sin against God, they will be defeated and taken out of the land by enemies who do not love God.

While we don't see this exile judgment in this passage, we do see the continued downward progression of the wicked kings of Israel. First, we read about Baasha. He, like Jeroboam, leads the people of Israel into sin—so much so that he invokes a word against him by the prophet Jehu. After Baasha's reign ends, his son Elah takes over. He too is an evil man! After only two years of his reign, a man named Zimri plots against him, kills him and the people in his house, and takes the throne for himself. While Zimri's plot takes a bad man off the throne, his reign is short-lived—only seven days! His end is awful; when the people close in on him, he burns the king's house down around him and dies in the blaze. Finally, we come to Omri, who takes over the kingdom after Zimri's conspiracy fails. He too does what is evil in God's sight, sinning against God's word and leading the people in "provoking the Lord . . . to anger by their idols" (16:26).

Baasha. Elah. Zimri. Omri. The kings of Israel, and therefore the people of Israel, are spiraling further and further into sin and rebellion. God will not wait forever; judgment is coming soon.

As you pray, spend some time thanking God for his patience. Thank him that, while he is just, he is also merciful and patient, giving time for people to repent and put their faith in Jesus Christ. Judgment is coming for Israel—and for this world too. Thank God for the refuge from judgment that is found in Jesus Christ alone.

Ahab and the Prophet

For the northern kingdom of Israel, it seems like it can't get any worse; their leadership has descended as far as possible into sin, right? Wrong. Enter King Ahab, son of Omri. Even with all the evil of the kings of Israel who have come before him, Ahab finds a way to become the worst king yet! Listen again to the description of his reign: "And Ahab the son of Omri did evil in the sight of the LORD, more than all who were before him. And as if it had been a light thing for him to walk in the sins of Jeroboam the son of Nebat, he took for his wife Jezebel . . . and went and served Baal and worshiped him" (16:30–31). King Ahab not only allows the people to continue worshiping idols; he also leads the way in a personal commitment to idolatry and the worship of Baal. And he somehow finds a way to locate a wife who is even more evil than he is!

Yet at the darkest point for the monarchy of God's people, God sends them a ray of light: the prophet Elijah. First Kings 17 begins with the entry of this man—the prophet who will serve as the foil to the evil King Ahab. His first word to Ahab is a word of judgment and punishment for the king and the land: there will be a drought for two years. Elijah, after prophesying this drought, runs for his life and hides from Ahab. His word comes to pass, though, proving the reality of his calling as a true prophet of God. God is establishing Elijah as a true prophet; he is identifying himself with this man. God is demonstrating that Elijah speaks true *words of God* by allowing him to perform mighty *signs from God.*

So at the darkest point of Israel's history—a point when the king of Israel has descended into unimaginable sin and idolatry—God raises up a true prophet for his people. Elijah will speak God's words into the situation. God will allow this nobody to speak and act powerfully in the face of even the mighty King Ahab. In other words, God is not silent. He is not ignoring the sins of the leaders of his people. He is faithful to keep speaking his word into the situation, and he will do this through his faithful prophet Elijah.

Thank God today that he does not abandon his people. He does not abandon you and me! He has spoken his word into the darkness of this sinful world, most powerfully through the word made flesh: Jesus, his Son. Thank God today as you consider these things.

A Fatal Duel

Elijah, up to this point in the story, has been working in private, speaking God's word to the people, but staying hidden from King Ahab. Now, though, it is time for Elijah to go public. He will go before Ahab in the name of God with one clear purpose: to remind the king and the people of the power and identity of the one true God of Israel.

Before we get to the battle on Mount Carmel, though, let's take a moment to focus on this amazing man Obadiah. As the ruler over the household of the evil King Ahab, this man had nevertheless continued to fear God and reject the idolatry of the nation. He had even proved his faithfulness to God by hiding one hundred prophets of God from Jezebel, who was trying to slaughter them. Obadiah stayed faithful to God in a time of idolatry and sin, and at the risk of his own life.

Ahab probably thought that this "prophets' duel" would be an opportunity for Elijah (and God) to publicly fail before the people; the day might even end with the long-awaited execution of his enemy Elijah! They gather together on Mount Carmel, and Elijah puts forth the challenge: whichever god answers his prophets by sending fire to consume the animals on their altar has proved himself as the true and most powerful deity. The prophets of Baal cry out to their god for hours, even cutting themselves with knives as part of their religious rituals. No fire comes from heaven. Elijah is up next, and he stacks the deck against himself, drenching the altar with jars of water! Fire rushes down from heaven, consuming not only the offering but also the altar, wood, stones, and water in the trench. The passage ends with the people falling on their faces and obeying Elijah as he commands the execution of the priests of Baal.

God's people should have remembered that God was the one who had brought them out of slavery in Egypt, sustained them in the wilderness, brought them into the promised land, and set King David over them. But God's people are good at forgetting. And so, in this passage, we see God remind them—with fiery heavenly power—that he alone sits enthroned in the heavens. His people are to worship and fear him alone.

Pray that God would remind you that he is utterly unique—merciful, just, powerful, holy, loving—and the only one worthy of your worship. Ask him to help you give your life and heart to nothing less than him.

Prophet on the Run

The health and wealth gospel. Definition: the message that if you follow and obey God, your life will get easier, safer, and more comfortable. Problem: nothing in Scripture gives us any indication that anything resembling the health and wealth gospel is the usual experience of the followers of God! We might expect that Elijah, God's faithful prophet to his people during the days of the wicked King Ahab and Queen Jezebel, would experience great earthly blessing, success, and fame. That is simply not what happens! Here's what this passage tells us.

First, it may get worse before it gets better. Elijah had defeated the prophets of Baal and escaped from the hand of Ahab, but it turned out Ahab wasn't his most dangerous enemy. It was his wife, Jezebel! All of a sudden, Elijah is on the run—fleeing into the wilderness for his very life. Elijah's struggles are not over; they are just beginning!

Second, we will not always understand what God is doing during every situation in our lives. We see, in this passage, a very human Elijah. Listen to some of his exclamations to God: "It is enough; now, O LORD, take away my life, for I am no better than my fathers" (19:4). He complains a bit to God, "reminding" him that he has been very faithful to the Lord—and look where it has taken him! Elijah—the great prophet of God—was in a very dark place. He was questioning God's plan for his life.

Third, God always remains faithful to those who serve him. God first sends his angel to strengthen him with some food and drink. More than this, though, God draws near to Elijah with his very presence and his word. In this great scene, God sends several natural signs to Elijah—a great wind, an earthquake, and a fire—indications of God's power and might, like he had demonstrated on Mount Carmel with the priests of Baal. Yet God chooses to visit his prophet in the sound of a "low whisper" (19:12). He reminds Elijah of his plan. Then he calls him to anoint the man who will minister with him and take over when he is gone: Elisha. God has not left his servant alone.

While we may not understand every hard thing in our lives, we can be confident that God will be faithful to his people. He will not abandon us but will always draw near to us with his presence and his word. Ask God to remind you of these things. Ask him to give you strength and perspective to put your hope in him, not in health and wealth.

God's Great Mercy

You've probably heard someone say at some point that the God of the Old Testament is a God of wrath and judgment, while the God of the New Testament is a God of love, mercy, and grace. There are lots of problems with a statement like that, not least of which is the suggestion that either there is more than one God or that God somehow drastically changed his personality! But when you read the Bible carefully, you realize that it's just not *true*. First Kings 21 proves this.

Ahab, the king of Israel, sees something that he wants: a vineyard, owned by a man named Naboth. When Naboth refuses to sell it to him because it's part of his family's inheritance, Ahab pouts around like a big baby. Ahab's wife—who, we discover, is far more evil and cunning even than wicked Ahab—tells him that she'll take care of the situation. She sets Naboth in a public place and gets some "worthless men" to bring false charges against him in front of all the people (21:10). The plan works perfectly; Naboth is convicted of speaking words against God, and he is dragged out of the city and stoned to death.

God is not happy with Ahab's actions, to say the least! He sends our faithful friend Elijah to speak to the king, and his words are not happy ones. Because of the sin of Ahab, Elijah declares that death will come to him and his house, and that dogs will lick up the blood of both Ahab and Jezebel when they are killed.

But then comes the shocking grace moment in the passage! Ahab, after hearing God's word through the prophet Elijah, tears his clothes, fasts from food, and walks around with an attitude of mourning. God takes notice of this and tells Elijah that because of Ahab's repentance, he will not completely wipe out Ahab's house during the days of his reign. Was Ahab's repentance real and lasting? Maybe, but probably not. It seems that it was a short-lived response to God's promised judgment against his sin. Still, God shows mercy—even to Ahab!

God extends to sinners the opportunity for repentance, forgiveness, and salvation. That is the glory of the cross of Jesus—the place where sin was dealt with forever for those who repent and put their faith in him. Thank God today that he shows mercy to you. Ask him to help you respond to him today with repentance that lasts, so that you can walk with him every day in obedience to his word.

Ahab, Jehoshaphat, and Ahaziah

It's one of the rare times when Judah and Israel—the southern and northern parts of the kingdom—are fighting along *with* each other and not *against* each other. Ahab, king of Israel, and Jehoshaphat, king of Judah, ride into battle together against the king of Syria and his army. Before the battle, the prophet Micaiah had made a chilling prediction to Ahab: he would lose the battle and would be killed in the process. Ahab, though, thinks he's smarter than the prophet—and God. He goes out into battle in disguise. But in the midst of the fighting, someone draws his bow at random and hits Ahab with a death blow. The story of Ahab ends with a gruesome detail: as the servants of the king wash his blood from the chariot where he was shot, the stray dogs of the city gather around to "help." This was the very prediction the prophet Elijah had made about Ahab years before.

As 1 Kings draws to a close, we learn about two more kings: Jehoshaphat of Judah and Ahaziah of Israel. They couldn't be more different! Jehoshaphat, despite his friendship with Ahab, does "what was right in the sight of the LORD" (22:43). While he doesn't remove all the high places of worship, he clears the land of a nasty problem of prostitution, which had plagued Judah during the days of his father. But everything Jehoshaphat is, Ahaziah is not. In fact, he turns out to be a lot like his father, Ahab. He does evil before God, worships the idol Baal, leads the people of Israel into sin, and basically makes God angry "in every way that his father had done" (22:53).

You can probably guess that Israel—the northern kingdom—is headed downhill fast! It won't be long before we see God's judgment come against them in the form of exile. Judah will hold on a little longer, but its kings will ultimately fail as well. Second Kings will continue this sad, sinful, downward slope toward exile and punishment for God's people. A human monarchy *must* not be the final answer for God's people. God must have a far greater— and more permanent—plan to bring his people *forever* into his place and under his rule.

We need a heavenly, perfect, and divine King to lead us, guide us and, yes, save us. Spend some time praying to God today, remembering that he is your true King. Ask him to be enthroned in your heart and life. Confess to him the ways that you fail to trust him completely as your ruler.

Elisha

In the midst of both good and evil kings and reigns in both Israel and Judah, God's prophets ministered as representatives of the one true King of God's people: God himself. Second Kings 2 describes a kind of "changing of the guard" between two of these prophets: Elijah and Elisha. Elijah, who had spoken God's word boldly to King Ahab (among other kings), was nearing the end of his life and ministry. Elisha, his apprentice, was ready to carry on the mantle. Three important things happen in this passage—things we shouldn't miss.

First, we see that Elisha receives from God the spirit-filled prophetic ministry of Elijah. Elisha asks his mentor, "Please let there be a double portion of your spirit on me" (2:9). Elijah lets him know if Elisha sees him as he is taken away, then that will be the sign that God has granted his request. Elisha does see Elijah being carried away, and his parting of the water with Elijah's cloak as he leaves confirms that the powerful ministry of Elijah as God's prophet has truly been passed to him.

Second, we see that Elisha receives from God the power of a true prophet. The men of Jericho come to Elisha, as he spends some time in their city, with a big problem: the water supply is dirty, undrinkable, and ineffective for sustaining life. Elisha—filled with the power of God—miraculously heals the water for the people. God is confirming through powerful signs that Elisha is his man—a true prophet for God's people.

Third and finally, we see that Elisha receives from God the authority of judgment as God's prophet. After being jeered at and mocked by some young people near Bethel, Elisha calls down two bears to maul forty-two boys! Did he mess up? Is this prophet losing it already? No. These young men—from a region known for its idolatry—mocked the prophet of God and, therefore, God himself. God extends authority to his prophet to execute judgment on his behalf. It's a frightening and shocking passage, but one that once again reminds us of the seriousness of sin and the reality of judgment by an infinitely holy God.

Men like Elisha point to the great prophet to come—Jesus himself—who will not only speak God's word to his people but actually be God's Word in human flesh for sinful people who need salvation. Thank God for his tireless faithfulness to his people. He keeps sending his word through his men—and he won't stop until he sends his own Son to earth.

People from All Nations

Second Kings 5 is one of those sporadic accounts in the Old Testament that reminds us that the God of Israel is the God of the entire world. He is the God of Israel, and he does have a specific place for them in his plan; they are his treasured possession among all the nations. Yet he is also the Creator of the universe—and of every single human being. His is a vision for people from all nations to know him and worship him.

In 2 Kings 5, during the ministry of the prophet Elisha, we suddenly find ourselves taken out of Israel and into the land of Syria. We are introduced to a powerful man named Naaman, the "commander of the army of the king of Syria" (5:1). While Naaman's military exploits were widely known, he had been no match for one formidable foe: a terrible skin disease known as leprosy. In God's sovereignty, a servant girl in Naaman's household (who was an Israelite, captured by Naaman in a battle against God's people) tells him about the great prophet of Israel: Elisha. So off he goes to Israel. Naaman, after balking briefly at Elisha's strange command to bathe in the dirty Jordan river, finally obeys his instructions—and is miraculously healed of his leprosy!

Naaman is not a Jew, remember; he is a Gentile! Yet he is miraculously healed of his disease by the prophet of God's people. But there's even more than that here. Naaman is not only healed *physically*; he is also healed *spiritually*. Because of Elisha's miracle, Naaman puts his faith in the one true God. Listen to his words: "Behold, I know that there is no God in all the earth but in Israel" (5:15). God is making a statement here! Blessing, healing, and saving faith are not just things to be experienced by those who are ethnically Jewish; they are available to all people—of any race—who put their faith in the Creator God. In fact, years later, Jesus will make this very point to the Jewish religious leaders of his day—men who were very proud of their ethnic Jewish heritage. Jesus offends the Pharisees by pointing out that God—even in the Old Testament—has a concern for all nations and all peoples.

Ask God to help you have a vision for his work in this world. Pray that he would help you long for the day when people from every tongue, tribe, and nation gather around his throne in heaven and sing praises to Jesus—the Lamb who was slain to save sinners.

Seeing with an Eternal Perspective

In this passage, God gives a brief behind-the-scenes glance to the servant of Elisha. God pulls back the curtain on a seemingly daunting situation and shows this man what's going on. And that makes all the difference.

As the passage begins, we see that the relationship between Israel and Syria has again moved into war. The king of Syria keeps advancing in battle against Israel, but he runs into a big problem: the army of Israel always seems to anticipate his every move. At first, the king of Syria thinks he has a traitor in the camp, but it is ultimately revealed to him that Elisha—the prophet of God—is the key to the Israelites' great battle plans. With God's help, Elisha has been warning the king of Israel about the strategy of the Syrian forces. So the king of Syria decides to deal with this problem prophet; he brings his entire army to go after Elisha!

Imagine that you are asleep in your house. You hear a noise and wake up to find that you have been completely surrounded by a gigantic army, sent out with the sole purpose of taking you down. That's essentially what happens to Elisha and his servant. The Syrian army surrounds their city, and the servant of Elisha looks out on the sight of what will be sure death for the both of them. Elisha, though, is calm. He says to his servant, "Those who are with us are more than those who are with them" (6:16). When his servant still fears greatly, Elisha prays that God would "pull back the curtain" and give him a behind-the-scenes look into the right perspective on the situation. The servant looks out again, but this time sees the mighty, yet invisible, forces of God—in all their might. Horses everywhere. Chariots, not of iron, but of fire. God's prophet is not outnumbered at all!

Elisha's servant needed a fresh perspective. He needed to be taught to see every situation through God's eyes—with an eternal perspective. God was gracious to him, taking him behind-the-scenes to see the invisible, but still very real, realities of God's control that were around him all the time.

We are intimidated and fearful because of seemingly hopeless situations, and we forget that God is always working—always active behind the scenes. Pray today that God would help you remember that. Pray that he would give you trust in him to guard your heart and your mind in Christ Jesus, your Savior.

Jehu's Judgment

Judgment. It's a theme that has come up again and again as we have walked through the story of the Bible. The holy God of the universe will punish sin and rebellion against his perfect word. God had promised as much—through his prophets—to the household of the wicked King Ahab years before. How does God accomplish this judgment against Ahab's house? Through one man: Jehu.

By the time we get to this passage, Jehu has already killed Jezebel, the evil wife of Ahab. Then he moves on to Ahab's sons, as he has them executed by the men of Jezreel. Jehu continues on his journey of judgment, stopping to execute some of the relatives of the former King Ahaziah. Finally, he turns his eyes to the prophets of Baal who remain in the land of Israel. He devises a nasty trick, luring them into the house of Baal under the pretense of wanting to do a worship service to the idol. Once they're there, Jehu has his men slaughter the priests of Baal, destroy the idols and the house, and turn the whole place into a public restroom! God's judgment against sin does come against the house of the wicked kings of God's people.

At first, we are hopeful about King Jehu, aren't we? It seems that he is motivated in his actions by a desire for God's will to be done. He seems to be a defender of God's holiness and obedient to God's word. Is Jehu doing God's work of judgment because he loves and worships God alone? Sadly, no. Jehu becomes an example of one whose *work* accomplishes the holy judgment of God, even while his *personal life* and heart are not given over completely to God in worship. Verse 29 gives us the sad refrain: "Jehu did not turn aside from the sins of Jeroboam the son of Nebat, which he made Israel to sin." While Jehu seems to be passionate for God's holiness and violent against sin, his own heart is never completely given over to God in obedience. This should be a warning to us all! God can use people for his purposes; he can use anyone. Being used by God for great things does not guarantee faithfulness to him. We need to be personally given to God in faith, repentance, obedience, and love.

Good deeds are no substitute for a heart that is personally given to God through repentance and faith in Jesus Christ. Pray today that God wouldn't let you miss this. Ask him to help you do great things for him and also to know and love him with all your heart.

Jehoash and Jehoiada

For the people of God, life had been pretty stressful lately! Good kings were rare, and many of them—even in Judah—had not led the people well in the worship of God. War was common, and the average Israelite lived with the very real threat of foreign invasion looming over them. In this kind of situation for God's people, it's not surprising (though it's still sad) that the temple of God had fallen into disrepair.

Enter Jehoash, king of Judah. Crowned at only seven years old, Jehoash had one very important thing going for him: a priest named Jehoiada. Jehoash was not a perfect king; he did not completely clear Israel of the high places of idol worship where the people made sinful sacrifices. Still, he committed himself from a young age to listening to the instruction of this faithful priest, who spoke God's word to him. Out of this relationship his desire to repair the temple emerges. Jehoash evidently realizes that as the leader of God's people, he is responsible for repairing the temple of God. He needs to help God's people worship him!

So Jehoash decides to go all out to make these repairs happen. He takes a chest, bores a hole in the top of it, and sets it at the entrance to the temple. He has the priests gather all the money that comes into the temple, and they set it all aside for the necessary repairs to the temple. The temple becomes full of bustling activity and work, as carpenters and builders are hired and timber and stone are carried in. Jehoash has taken seriously his role as a leader; he has attached value to the worship of God by taking care of God's house.

Still, as this passage winds down, we are reminded that God's judgment will still come. Although Jehoash reigns as a faithful king of God's people, the Israelites' trend of idol worship, disobedience, and rebellion continues. Second Kings 10 shows how God began to cut off parts of the *land* of Israel. In this passage, we see God begin to take away the *wealth* of Israel. To avoid a full-scale invasion by the Syrians, Jehoash gives their king a tremendous amount of wealth from the royal dedicated gifts.

Pray that God would give you strength and energy to put in time and effort to know him better and to grow in love for him. Ask him to help you grow and maintain your relationship with Jesus, by his grace. Don't let your heart and soul fall into disrepair!

Drums of Judgment and Exile

In J. R. R. Tolkien's *Fellowship of the Ring*, the Fellowship stands deep in the Mines of Moria, reading the account of a battle fought many years before on that very spot. The account records the approaching enemy's drums getting closer and closer; the battle is coming. It's a bit like what we're experiencing as we read about the downward decline of the monarchy in Israel. We hear the drums of judgment and exile approaching—first far away, but now getting closer and closer. God's punishment for sin is coming, and this monarchy will not go on forever. Yet even as this downward march continues, we see signs of God's grace in all of it. Even in judgment, God will not permanently abandon his people!

The great prophet Elisha has died, and the cycle of kings has continued. Jeroboam II takes the throne in Israel and, not surprisingly, he is yet another king in Israel who neither fears nor obeys God. The narrator summarizes his reign with familiar words: "He did what was evil in the sight of the LORD. He did not depart from all the sins of Jeroboam the son of Nebat, which he made Israel to sin" (14:24).

Despite the sin and failure of Jeroboam II, the passage tells us that he "restored the border of Israel . . . according to the word of the LORD, the God of Israel" (14:25). God actually allowed the kingdom of Israel to *grow* for a time under this terrible king! The passage tells us that, first, he saw the affliction of his people, which was very bitter. More than that, though, we find that God is being faithful to his own promise and love for his people—a promise that does not involve blotting them completely out of the earth. God's plan for his people—even in judgment—is not to wipe them out entirely. God will punish sin, yes! But as the story of the Bible goes on, we will begin to hear more and more about God's preservation of a faithful remnant of his people, even in the midst of exile, punishment, and judgment.

Thank God that, although he would have been justified in giving up on you, he sent his Son Jesus to accomplish perfect and eternal salvation for you: forgiveness from sin and eternal life. Praise God for his grace today.

Carried Out of the Land

We've been expecting this for a long time now: judgment. In this passage, judgment finally comes for God's people. It comes in the form of exile; they are carried *out* of the land God had promised them. It is God essentially saying to his people, "If you will continue to refuse to live under my rule, then I will take you out of my place." For Israel, the northern kingdom, the capture and exile come at the hands of the wicked Assyrians and their king. They conquer God's people and carry them away to their country to keep them there as slaves and servants. God's people, because of their sin, have become a people without a home.

In case we've forgotten the reason for this severe judgment, the narrator does us the favor of reminding us! God's people have been asking for this for years. According to the writer of 2 Kings, the people of Israel "had sinned against the LORD their God, who had brought them up out of the land of Egypt" (17:7). They had rebelled against the very God who had delivered them from slavery, given them land, and made them into a great nation. Rather than obeying him, loving him, and serving him only, they had been influenced by the surrounding nations and had turned to false gods, idols, and sinful practices. After listing the offenses that the people have committed against their God, the writer of 2 Kings adds one more key witness against them: the *warnings* of God. It's not as if God has been silent during this sin and rebellion; he has warned his people again and again through his word and through prophets who spoke his word! These prophets proclaimed a consistent message: "Turn from your evil ways and keep my commandments and my statutes" (17:13). Still, the people have not listened. Israel goes away into exile, and only Judah—the southern part of the kingdom—remains intact.

Judah won't get off the hook, though. The narrator tells us, "Judah also did not keep the commandments of the LORD their God" (17:19). Judgment comes sooner for Israel, but it is on its way for Judah as well. They too have failed to obey and worship their God faithfully, and their sin will not go unpunished.

Thank God today that he does send his own Son to save his people from their greatest exile—the exile of sin and eternal death. Take some time today confessing your sins to God in light of this passage and asking for his forgiveness and grace through Jesus Christ, his Son.

King Hezekiah

The good King Hezekiah and God's people find themselves in a deadly and dangerous predicament. The Assyrian armies have invaded their land, much like they had invaded the northern part of the kingdom. The messengers of the king of Assyria openly mock God and seek to intimidate the people into surrender by telling them how badly they will beat them. The people are frightened, but they wait for their king to lead them. King Hezekiah needs to respond. But what will this godly king do?

It is through Hezekiah's response to this Assyrian threat that we discover the true heart of this king. He doesn't turn to idols, or even some brilliant military strategy. He turns in humility to God in prayer. Hezekiah knows that God is his and the people's only hope; he knows that God alone must be his rock and his fortress. He acknowledges God as Lord over all creation—the Creator of all things. Then he calls God's attention to the mocking words of the Assyrians and the plight of God's people in light of their invasion. Finally, he calls out to God for salvation from his enemies. Notice how he ends the prayer as well; it is all about the glory and fame of God's name, not his. He concludes: "So now, O LORD our God, save us, please, from his hand, that all the kingdoms of the earth may know that you, O LORD, are God alone" (19:19). Hezekiah trusts God to fight the battles of the people. He wants God to get the glory.

God, in his mercy, answers Hezekiah's prayer! We are introduced, in this chapter, to a prophet of God from whom we'll hear much more later: Isaiah. This man of God brings to Hezekiah God's response to his prayer of faith. God acknowledges the evil of Assyria and his plan for his people. And he makes this promise to the forces of Assyria: "I will turn you back on the way by which you came" (19:28). God makes good on this promise. In the night, while the armies of Assyria lie camped outside Jerusalem, God sends his angel to put to death 185,000 of their troops. The Assyrians and their king wake up in the morning to dead bodies everywhere; they have nothing else to do but turn back toward their homeland. The battle has been won for God's people—and they didn't even have to lift a sword!

Pray that God would show you where you are tempted to trust in things of this world for your security and salvation. Ask him to help you trust him alone for your salvation and your daily health and growth in him.

King Josiah

We can learn a few important lessons through studying the kings. First, we learn a human king is not the final answer for God's people. They need a "forever King" to rule over them—and to save them from themselves! Second, despite God's judgment, he does have a lasting plan for his people that he will not forsake. Even though exile will come for Judah too, God has a plan that goes beyond that judgment to lasting salvation for his people. God is gracious, and he will not destroy them forever!

When Josiah takes the throne, we are surprised to read that he "walked in all the way of David his father, and he did not turn aside to the right or to the left" (22:2). Josiah steps up to serve, follow, and obey God, and in doing so, he breaks the pattern of the previous two kings. Pretty impressive, especially when you consider that Josiah took the throne when he was only *eight* years old!

The first thing we read about Josiah happens during the eighteenth year of his reign. As in times past, the temple of God has fallen into disrepair. So Josiah gathers money to fix it up. As the workers repair the temple, they discover a copy of the book of the Law that has been lost for years. They bring it to the king, and Josiah listens as God's word is read out loud before him. As he listens, he begins to realize the great sin of God's people. They have not kept God's law faithfully. They have not been paying attention to his word. Josiah tears his clothes in repentance and mourning over the sin of God's people.

Josiah *listens* to God's word and *responds* in repentance and faith. That is the behavior of a true follower of God! He takes action too; you can read in 2 Kings 23 all about the reforms Josiah puts in place in Judah, getting rid of idolatrous practices and attempting to reestablish the worship of God for God's people. While Josiah's actions don't change God's plan to judge his people for their sin, God is pleased with Josiah's leadership and promises to not bring disaster during his reign.

Do you tremble at God's word and respond to it in repentance and faith? Do you make reforms in your heart and life according to what the Bible says? Pray today that God would give you a humble heart like that of King Josiah. Ask him to help you understand, listen to, and obey his word.

King Nebuchadnezzar & King Zedekiah

There may have been some people in Judah who thought this day would never come, even with all God's warnings of judgment and his messages through his prophets. God would never really allow his people to be taken out of the land, would he? And even if the Israelites were conquered in battle, God wouldn't allow the *temple*—the place set aside for his worship—to be touched, would he? Second Kings 24–25 answers these questions with a resounding, yet sad, yes. The holy God of Israel is *this serious* about the sin of his people.

By the time 2 Kings 25 begins, King Nebuchadnezzar of Babylon has defeated Judah and taken thousands away into exile. He did leave some people behind in Judah but only the "poorest people of the land" (24:14). Over these, he placed a king named Zedekiah; Nebuchadnezzar had already taken away Jehoiachin, who had been king over Judah. Zedekiah, even in the midst of God's judgment of his people through the exile, still chooses to do what is evil in God's sight. More than that, he chooses to rebel against the king of Babylon. So the Babylonians come back to Judah.

This time, Nebuchadnezzar comes for more than a battle. He besieges the city of Jerusalem so that the people begin to starve. His army captures King Zedekiah, and they slaughter his sons, gouge out his eyes, and take him as a slave to Babylon. Then they do the unthinkable: the Babylonians burn down the temple of God—the place of worship for God's people. They carry away all the riches and treasures of the temple as well and take them to Babylon. When they get there, Nebuchadnezzar has several leaders of Judah—including two priests—put to death. The defeat and exile of God's people is now complete.

God has been warning his people about this for years! Yet they—and their kings—have continued to worship idols rather than the one true God. They have repeatedly chosen sin and selfishness instead of obedience to God's word. The exile reminds us that God truly hates sin; sin brings judgment and death. Yet even this is not the end of the story!

Take some time today to confess your sins to God. Consider the ways that you set up idols to worship instead of him. Think about your tendencies toward sin and selfishness rather than wholehearted obedience to his word. Most importantly, thank him that Jesus Christ, his Son, paid the full penalty for your sin and rebellion on the cross.

Obeying God Carefully and Joyfully

We won't be spending too much time in the books of 1 and 2 Chronicles, because they record many of the same events and accounts that we find in 1 and 2 Samuel. But we will take a quick dip into each book—and we'll go backward in the timeline of the Bible's story as we do this.

Just two chapters earlier, 1 Chronicles 13 contains a very different scene involving the transportation of the ark of the covenant under David's supervision. For one thing, the ark was not transported in accordance with the specifications in the Levitical law (people placed the ark on a "cart," rather than having it carried by the Levites; 1 Chron. 13:7). And, when the oxen stumbled and Uzzah reached out his hand to touch and steady the ark, God struck him dead on the spot. It was not a good day for David and the people of God!

Here in 1 Chronicles 15, though, David has learned his lesson. David summons the priests, admitting his previous mistakes, and tasks them to carry the ark of God "on their shoulders with the poles, as Moses had commanded according to the word of the LORD" (15:15). Accompanying the procession of the ark are musical instruments and Levitical singers, offering joyful praise to God along the way (15:16–24). God blesses and protects this procession; the people go forward with joy—and they offer sacrifices of thanksgiving to God as well (15:25–28). This is a beautiful account of God's forgiveness and restoration toward his people, as he grants them favor and comes yet again to dwell in their midst. It's also a story of King David humbly learning from his mistakes—and turning once again to carefully follow God's word to the letter.

At the end of the passage, though, we find a bitter note: Michal, David's wife (and daughter of King Saul), despises David "in her heart" as she watches him dancing, worshiping, and singing praises to God publicly (15:29). It's a reminder to us that the worship of God will not be embraced by everyone. David is willing to worship his gracious God publicly—with reckless abandon. To Michal, in her bitterness, this demonstration of praise is foolishness and an embarrassment.

1 Chronicles 13 shows the danger of failing to obey God carefully—particularly in how we worship him and enter his holy presence. Here in 1 Chronicles 15, though, we find the joy and grace that comes when we approach our God rightly—according to his word. Today, pray that you would approach God as he intends: in repentance and joyful faith in his Son!

Abandoning the Law of the Lord

Far too often—just when we feel most secure—we are most prone to pride, temptation, and turning away from our God. Such was the case for Rehoboam, son of Solomon and king of Judah. Second Chronicles 12 opens with these words: "When the rule of Rehoboam was established and he was strong, he abandoned the law of the LORD, and all Israel with him" (12:1). At the height of his strength and security this man turned from the very God who had granted him this success and power.

The result of this turn to sinful pride is immediate and disastrous for Rehoboam and the people of God, who follow him into sin. King Shishak of Egypt—helped by soldiers from other nations as well—invades Jerusalem and plunders much of the treasures of the royal palace and the temple. A prophet named Shemaiah leaves no doubt as to the cause of this invasion: it is God's abandonment of Rehoboam, because Rehoboam has abandoned God (12:5). We see clearly the justice of God, who will indeed punish sin, and who will not ignore those who abandon his word.

Even so, God shows grace to his sinful people in this passage. Rehoboam and the people repent, turning to God with sorrow and begging for his mercy (12:6–7). While God allows the invasion of Jerusalem and the plundering of treasure, he relents of complete disaster, refusing to allow his people to be utterly destroyed (12:8, 12). On top of this, God allows good conditions to continue in Judah, even despite the people's sin and rebellion.

Sadly, Rehoboam never learns his lesson, despite God's mercy to him (12:13–14). He continues in evil, refusing to humble himself before God and worship him alone. He dies—a man who experiences God's grace and mercy, but who is never changed by it. It's a warning for all of us to see the grace of God to us—sinners, all of us—and respond with faith, humility, and obedience!

The gracious character of God is written all over this chapter, even as he brings just punishment to Rehoboam and the people because of their sin. Today, pray that God would give you a softer and more humble heart than Rehoboam. Ask him to remind you of the grace and mercy he has shown you through his Son— and to give you strength to respond with faith, obedience, and heartfelt worship.

ACT 4

Exile to Jesus

He Will Never Leave You Nor Forsake You

Have you ever wondered if God will give up on you? Maybe you've felt, at times, that you're a hopeless case, not deserving God's continued love and care in your life. I've felt that way before! Friend, if the book of Ezra tells us anything, it's that God does not give up on his people. He will keep his promises to them, and he will remain faithful.

The very fact that the Bible story continues after 2 Kings and 2 Chronicles is a sign of this wonderful truth. God could have ended his work with his people with the exile, and he would have been completely justified in doing so. After all, God's people had sinned terribly. King after king had turned to the worship of idols—and all the sins that accompanied idol worship—and the people had followed their kings into this disobedience. But the story doesn't end with exile; God is not done with his people.

We'll focus on the central point of Ezra 1: God's sovereign and gracious care for his people, even during and after exile. You might have been a bit confused to read about Cyrus, king of Persia, in the opening verse of Ezra. Yes, Judah was taken captive by Nebuchadnezzar, king of Babylon, but the Persians conquered Babylon shortly before the events of the book of Ezra occurred. One of the first acts of this King Cyrus is to issue a proclamation declaring that the Israelites in exile are permitted to return to the land of Israel to help in rebuilding the temple in Jerusalem. The narrator, of course, lets us know that this is not merely an inclination of Cyrus's own heart; it is part of God's sovereign plan for his people. God's exiled people are returning to God's place.

While the book of Ezra will ultimately show us that a return to a physical land and a tangible temple is not the final answer for God's people, this is still a story of great hope for those of us who trust in God. The exile is not the end! God does judge sin, but this story reminds us that he will never permanently abandon those who are truly his people.

Remember that if you belong to Jesus Christ, God will not give up on you. He will accomplish his good purposes for you and complete the work he has begun in you. Pray that God would do that. It may begin with repentance of sin, if you've been going down a sinful path. It may involve returning, in prayer, to the cross and remembering that your sins have truly been paid for through Jesus's death.

Hope amid Rubble

Hope amid rubble. It's an encouraging thought, isn't it? Even after great suffering and destruction, there is room for new beginnings, a fresh start. The exiles have returned to Jerusalem from Babylon, and it is time to begin rebuilding the temple—and their way of life.

The fresh start begins with the keeping of the Feast of Booths, which was commanded in the law of God and most likely had been neglected by the Israelites in years past, under the reign of many wicked kings. Offerings are again made to God, in accordance with God's word, even before the rebuilding of the temple begins. Finally, under the leadership of a man named Zerubbabel, the great project starts: the people of God begin work on the new temple. The exile is ending; God's people are rebuilding what has been torn down by God's enemies. The temple will be rebuilt, and the worship of God will again have a place in the land. After judgment comes mercy—and a new beginning.

But in verse 12 comes a gigantic surprise. When the foundation of the temple is laid, not everyone is happy. Not everyone shouts with joy. Some people weep instead. Who? The oldest generation. Why? Because they are the only ones who remember the splendor and grandeur of the first temple—the one built by Solomon. They can tell just by looking at the foundation that this new temple will not come close to comparing to the first one. And so they weep. They realize that Solomon's temple will never again be matched. They have returned to the land, yes, but they can never go back to the glorious days of King Solomon.

In the midst of this passage of great hope for God's people, we are beginning to see that a *physical* temple and an *earthly* kingdom will never be the final answer for God's people. This temple will not be a place for God's people to perfectly worship him forever; it won't even compare to the first temple! God's people need a greater temple, an eternal kingdom, a perfect King. Ezra 3 points us to something much greater that God has in store for his people: salvation through his own Son.

God will not stop moving his people toward this truth. He will even give them the ultimate new beginning—forgiveness of sins through the death of his Son on a cross. Is your hope in Jesus, more than any earthly thing? Is he the King of your life and the hope of your heart? Consider these questions as you approach God in prayer today.

Meet Ezra

The events of Ezra 7 and following happen fifty-seven years after the dedication of the temple whose foundation was laid in the last chapter we read! The temple has been rebuilt in Jerusalem. The Passover has been celebrated. The people are back. And it's finally time for us to meet Ezra.

The most important thing the writer of the book wants us to know about Ezra is that he is a *priest*. His lineage, in fact, is traced all the way back to Aaron, the chief priest during the time of Moses. And this Ezra is not just any priest. He is "skilled in the Law of Moses" (7:6). More than this, the "hand of the LORD his God was on him" (7:6). The narrator tells us that Ezra "had set his heart to study the Law of the LORD, and to do it and to teach his statutes and rules in Israel" (7:10). Ezra loves God's word and has been diligent to study it carefully in order to teach others. God's people are back in the land and again have a temple. Now, also, they have a leader: a priest who knows and loves God's word and can lead them in the right worship and service of their God.

Yet again, a pagan king (this time, Artaxerxes of Persia) does something that is clearly part of God's plan for his people: he sends Ezra back to the land of Judah, along with a decree allowing all exiled Jews to return with him. This is clearly God's hand at work, giving favor with the king to Ezra and bringing his people back out of exile. Again, we are reminded that God has not finally given up on his people!

As you read more about Ezra the priest throughout the book, consider his life, leadership, and love for God. Ezra is passionate about God's word—and passionate about the right worship of God by God's people! In all this, Ezra points us forward to a far greater priest who will one day come. The one who will *be* God's Word made flesh. The one who will enable the right worship of God by God's people through his great sacrifice for sin on the cross.

Would people say that you have "set your heart" on studying God's word, living by it, and telling others about it? Ask God today to help you have this kind of commitment to him. Pray that you would commit yourself more passionately to knowing and living by his word, so that you can better tell others about the love and grace of Jesus Christ, his Son.

Sinister Sin

Up until Ezra 9, things appear to be going pretty well for God's people. All is well—at least from a distance. Think of a neglected carton of strawberries in the fridge. At first glance they may look bright, red, juicy, and ready to eat, but, looking closer, you see it: mold has grown and dirtied the fruit. Here in Ezra 9, the temple has been rebuilt, worship of God has been reestablished, and Ezra the priest is leading the people according to God's word. But something is lurking beneath the surface that is about to be exposed. Sin has crept into the lives of God's people, infecting the entire group.

What is this sin specifically? It's the sin of intermarriage with people who do not worship the one true God. Instead of remaining distinct as God's chosen people, intermarriage with pagan people caused God's people to intermingle with sinful practices and cultures; this almost always led to rampant idolatry, sin, and perversion. What is perhaps most striking about this sin in this passage, though, is the individuals who are most guilty: the *leaders* of God's people. Listen to the report that is brought to Ezra the priest: "And in this faithlessness the hand of the officials and chief men has been foremost" (9:2).

We can picture the sorrow and agony on Ezra's face as we read about his response to this report. He tears his clothes in anguish. He rips out hair from his head and his beard. Ezra spiritually and physically hurts at this sin in the midst of God's people! His prayer to God (recorded by Ezra in the first person) gives us insight into his heart for the holy God too. "O my God," he prays, "I am ashamed and blush to lift my face to you, my God, for our iniquities have risen higher than our heads, and our guilt has mounted up to the heavens" (9:6). Ezra—while he himself is not guilty of the sin of intermarriage—is broken and in anguish at the way that sin has affected the community of God. He acknowledges the sin. He owns it. He confesses it before God. He pours out his heart in genuine sorrow for the offense that this sin has brought against the holy God of Israel.

Pray today that you would have a heart like Ezra's, specifically in your response to sin in the midst of God's people. Ask God for a heart that mourns and grieves over sin, knowing that Jesus died to make an end of such sin.

Drastic Measures

Ezra was certainly sorry for the sin of God's people! As Ezra 10 begins, we see that the men of Israel are sorry too. One man, Shecaniah, speaks for all the people as he confesses the sin openly before Ezra and before God: "We have broken faith with our God and have married foreign women from the peoples of the land" (10:2). They all feel bad about their sin! That's a good thing. It means that they recognize the seriousness of sin and the holiness of God. But sometimes being sorry isn't enough. As we see from Ezra 10, repentance must involve more than feeling sorry for sin; it must include a dramatic turning away from sin.

Shecaniah goes on in his public confession of sin: "Therefore let us make a covenant with our God to put away all these wives and their children, according to the counsel of my lord and of those who tremble at the commandment of our God, and let it be done according to the Law" (10:3). This seems extreme to us today! After all, some of God's people had gotten married to these foreign people and even had children with them. To then put them away seems cruel, harsh, and even wrong. We need to understand, though, that for this particular time in the history of God's people, this was what true repentance for God's people demanded.

The book of Ezra ends on a sober note, as those guilty of intermarriage are called out by name and brought out before the people. Even some priests of God have committed this sin; they too repent and commit to put away their foreign wives. The names are right there—written out for everyone throughout history to read.

The book of Ezra records a time of great hope for God's people. The exile is over; God is not done working with his people for their salvation and for his glory in the world! But he will demand their total devotion to him. There must not be sin in their midst. They must not sacrifice their unique identity as God's people by compromising themselves and their worship of him. And so this book of hope ends with drastic repentance by God's people for this sin.

Are you still living in sin today, even though you've confessed Jesus as your Savior? Or have you truly repented—asked him to forgive you and turned 180 degrees away from your sin to follow him? Pray about these things today. Ask God to make you a person of true repentance, humility, and total commitment to Christ.

Meet Nehemiah

Nehemiah is the sequel to Ezra. The book of Ezra described the ministry of the faithful priest who led God's people in right worship and real repentance from sin. The book of Nehemiah describes Nehemiah, the cupbearer to King Artaxerxes, who becomes passionate about the rebuilding of the Jerusalem walls and the faithfulness of God's people to God after the exile. Both books show us the faithfulness of God to his people. He will reestablish them in the land—even after the punishment of the exile—by providing them with faithful leaders.

The book begins approximately thirteen years after Ezra has come to Jerusalem. Nehemiah, an exiled Jew, has done well for himself in exile: he has come into the high position of cupbearer to the king of Persia. As Nehemiah goes about his daily work in the service of Artaxerxes, he receives a message from one of his Jewish brothers who has been back to Jerusalem. The people are experiencing "great trouble and shame" (1:3). More than this, the rebuilding projects that the people have attempted are terribly incomplete; the wall of Jerusalem is broken down. Jerusalem stands in ruins—shamed and defenseless.

Nehemiah, even given his royal position in Persia, has not lost his love for God and his people. His heart breaks at this news, and he responds with an emotional plea to God. He begins with heartfelt repentance; God's people have sinned against him by disobeying his word. But he also claims God's promises to his people. God had promised judgment for sin, but he had always told them, "But if you return to me and keep my commandments and do them, though your outcasts are in the uttermost parts of heaven, from there I will gather them and bring them to the place that I have chosen" (1:9).

Nehemiah has a plan, as we'll see in chapter 2. So as Nehemiah 1 ends, we are left with questions: What will God do? Will he answer Nehemiah's prayer? Will the walls of Jerusalem be rebuilt? On a larger scale, what will become of God's people in Jerusalem?

As you spend some time in prayer today, ask God that he would give you a heart that is faithful to him in an ever-changing and unstable world. Pray that he would help you love him and his people above all things—whether you endure great suffering or experience great success. Ask him to keep your heart and your life anchored in him.

The Man of the Hour

After beseeching God for his hand to be with Jerusalem and its ruined walls, Nehemiah discovers that *he* is God's man for the hour! We'll look briefly at three aspects of Nehemiah, this great leader.

First, consider Nehemiah's heart. Although he is employed by the king of Persia, he cannot help but be dejected when he considers the plight of God's people and God's place. Nehemiah's heart is with God's people, although he personally is prospering. Even the king notices it. When he asks what is wrong, Nehemiah's answer reveals his heart: "Why should not my face be sad, when the city . . . lies in ruins, and its gates have been destroyed by fire?" (2:3). Nehemiah is incapable of joy as long as the city of God lies in ruins. His heart is always with God's people and God's place.

Second, observe Nehemiah's commitment. After boldly asking the permission of King Artaxerxes to return to Jerusalem to oversee the rebuilding of the wall, he gets to work scoping out the project, keeping it quiet until the time is right to gather men to help him. He goes out by night to begin an inspection of the wall, trusting only a few men to go with him. At last Nehemiah makes his announcement to the men of Jerusalem: "Let us build the wall of Jerusalem, that we may no longer suffer derision" (2:17). They rise up to help him. Nehemiah's enthusiasm is contagious!

Finally, though, note Nehemiah's opposition. Almost no valuable work for God comes without significant trials and opposition; this work is no exception. We get a hint of what will come later in the book when we are introduced to two evil troublemakers—Sanballat the Horonite and Tobiah the Ammonite. Sanballat could very well be an Israelite who judged in Samaria; he perhaps opposes Nehemiah's work because he is power hungry and jealous. Tobiah is an Ammonite—a Gentile—and his agenda is not completely clear. Whatever their motivation, we know that these men oppose this work of Nehemiah and the returned Jewish exiles. They will fight the project to which Nehemiah has been called by God!

God uses people who, like Nehemiah, love his people and his purpose in this world, who prize the cause of the gospel of Jesus Christ above all earthly things. Pray today that God would give you a heart that is completely committed to the cause of Jesus Christ. Ask him to help you pursue Christ and the good of his people, even in the midst of opposition.

Building Opposition

In many parts of the world, believers in Jesus face opposition—sometimes even the threat of death—because of their commitment to the God of the Bible. We also ought to be firming up our commitment to Christ and the advance of the gospel, knowing that we too may someday face opposition and persecution for our faith.

Nehemiah had gathered men in support of his call from God to rebuild, and here we see them working hard to build the wall. At this point, the opposition comes. Remember Sanballat and Tobiah from Nehemiah 2? They begin with simple mockery, taunting Nehemiah and the builders, saying that a small fox could even knock down the newly constructed walls of Jerusalem. Before long, though, the mockery has turned into full attack. Sanballat and Tobiah gather together with other men who hate God's people, and they plan an attack on Nehemiah and his men.

Nehemiah's response to Sanballat and Tobiah should guide us as we deal with opposition today and, someday perhaps, persecution. First, he prays. In verse 4, Nehemiah calls out for God to "hear" and to "turn back their taunt on their own heads." As the attack on the city becomes imminent, Nehemiah prays again for God's protection over the men and the wall. Yet while Nehemiah prays to God, he doesn't stop there. He commits himself to protect the city and the people. The work in Jerusalem continues, but not without a guard now posted—men with swords, spears, and bows located around the city to watch and defend.

The attack from Sanballat, Tobiah, and their men never comes. It could be that they got scared away by the bolstered security of Jerusalem; we don't know. Whatever their reason, we do know that God was faithful to Nehemiah and his people; he protected and guarded the work to which Nehemiah had been called. As this project goes on through the rest of chapter 4, we are left with a beautiful picture of the Christian life: God's people, hard at work in labor for him, telling others about God's blessing and salvation, advancing God's kingdom by God's power—yet all the while remaining vigilant against sin and the schemes of the devil.

Are you dedicated to helping others know and love Jesus Christ more? As you commit yourself to his cause, are you on guard against Satan's attacks on your heart and soul? Pray about these things as you spend time with God responding to this passage of his word.

Life under God's Word

Against opposition and threats, Nehemiah has led God's people in this great initiative. The walls of Jerusalem stand again; the city is once more secure. Or is it? You see, the returned exiles need more than just *physical walls* to reestablish them in God's place under God's rule. They need to return to life under God's *word*. The walls are back up, but the people need to get back under God's rule.

After the returned exiles are counted and organized (see Nehemiah 7), all the people gather together. We are then introduced to a familiar character: Ezra the great priest for God's returned people, who brings out the book of the Law before all the people. In one of the greatest worship services found in the Old Testament, he reads out loud from God's word—all morning! And the people stand, in worship, listening to God's word. Some preaching goes on too! Some of the priests go throughout the crowd to help explain the word that is being read: "They gave the sense, so that the people understood the reading" (8:8). This was a great return to God's word for God's people—back in God's place. Ezra and Nehemiah know that a return to the land—even the rebuilding of the temple and the Jerusalem walls—is not enough. God's people need to return to hearing, obeying, and living under God's word.

The people respond to this worship service in a couple different ways. First, they weep—probably from a realization that they have broken the commands of God's word and need to repent and come back to him. While this is a right response by the people, Nehemiah and Ezra don't let the people stay in that grieving state for too long! This is a day of celebration and holiness. They instruct the people to eat, drink, and rejoice in the God who has brought them back to the land and who will again lead them by his word. The second response by the people goes beyond merely listening to God's word read aloud; they actually begin obeying it—bringing back the customs that had been commanded by God. They are back in the land, surrounded by rebuilt walls and once again living under the word of their mighty God.

The only true security for God's people—then and now—comes as they live under his word. Pray about this today. Ask God to help you find your security in living according to his word—trusting Jesus, following him, worshiping him by listening to him, and doing all he asks.

Opposing Every Evil Practice

Everything seems to be going well! Yet Nehemiah's work is not yet done. Nehemiah 13 shows us that God's people are a mess; many reforms must still be made. As Nehemiah exposes sinful practices in God's community, we see a powerful example of the right response to evil—in our own lives and in the midst of God's people.

Nehemiah wants God's people to live faithfully under his word, and so he opposes every practice that does not fit with what God commands.

- After hearing God's word concerning foreigners in the midst of Israel, the people go about separating all the people of foreign descent, according to God's law.
- The priest Eliashib has given a special room in the temple to Tobiah—the enemy of God's people who opposed the rebuilding of the walls! Nehemiah throws out him and his stuff.
- The priests haven't been well cared for by the people, in accordance with the law. Nehemiah makes sure this happens.
- Many of the people are not respecting the Sabbath day; they are working, hauling things around, and selling goods. Nehemiah shuts everything down the night before the Sabbath to help the people focus on getting ready for a day of rest and worship.
- Nehemiah discovers that there are Jewish children, born to one non-Jewish parent, who can't speak the Jewish language (and therefore can't understand God's word!). Nehemiah gets pretty fired up about this one, pulling out the hair of people who have intermarried and making the people promise not to do this again!

While Nehemiah is a hopeful book, with God's people resuming life and worship under his word in the land after exile, it ends with a reminder that we're not there yet. God's people are still a mess. As passionate as Nehemiah is about reforming them and purging sin from the community, it is obvious that much work still needs to be done for them to live in holiness and obedience to him. They need a Savior.

Pray that your faith in Jesus Christ would lead you to an intense, zealous commitment to holiness and obedience. Ask God to give you a heart like his as you follow the Savior who died to free you from sin's power.

Esther in Exile

It's easy to have a sense of confusion as we begin to read the book of Esther. Why is this book even here? It's a story about a king and a queen in Persia. We've never heard of them before. It doesn't seem to have anything to do with the continuing story of God's people in God's place under God's rule. Why are we all of a sudden reading about the royal happenings of King Ahasuerus in Persia? Because *God's people* are in exile in Persia. This story is the story of God's people; it will involve them! And, so, it is part of our story.

In this chapter, you won't get to the Jewish people's involvement yet; the passage is setting the stage for what is to come. The king of Persia, Ahasuerus, has become extremely angry with his queen, Vashti. In the midst of a great celebratory feast, he had called her forward to march her around to show off her beauty—and she had refused his request. At the suggestion of his advisors, Ahasuerus sends Queen Vashti away from his presence permanently to make an example of her for the entire kingdom. So at the end of Esther 1, we are left with a king of Persia and no queen. The stage is set for our main character—Esther—to enter the scene. We'll read more in Esther 2 about what this all means for God's people!

In the book of Esther, we have gone backward in history from Ezra and Nehemiah. We are getting a glimpse of life in exile for God's people, and we'll see his preservation and protection of them during the entire time. Amazingly, the book of Esther does not even mention the name of God one time! And yet it is a story about God. He is active and in control—even from behind the scenes. And so, Esther is a book for you—for us. It is a book for every Christian who feels like God is silent, distant, or far away. The book of Esther reminds us that, even when God seems nowhere to be found, he is always there—working, protecting, caring for the people he loves.

Take some time in prayer today, asking God to teach you about his powerful and perfect care for his people. Ask him to remind you that he is always working and always in control. Pray that you would come to trust him even more as you follow, love, and serve Jesus.

Queen Esther

Throughout *Great Expectations*, the novel by Charles Dickens, one of the recurring themes of the plot is the mysterious benefactor. Pip, the main character and narrator, continues to find that he is cared for—mysteriously and secretly—by an unknown person. This person had remained anonymous, but had been there—helping and giving—all the time. In the book of Esther, God is a bit like a mysterious benefactor; the name of God is not even mentioned specifically in the book of Esther. Yet this book has the secret hand of God written all over it.

Not surprisingly, it isn't long before King Ahasuerus begins looking for a new queen. His advisors come up with a plan that only a king could pull off: they gather women from all around the kingdom and bring them one by one to the king as a kind of ancient dating competition. The plan will be for Ahasuerus to select a wife for himself from the women who are paraded before him. The king likes this plan, so the competition begins.

In the midst of the women who get taken away for the king is a Jewish exile named Esther. She is being raised by a man named Mordecai, a Jew who is old enough to remember being carried away into exile by Nebuchadnezzar. We are told that Esther is beautiful, so it's no wonder that she is immediately chosen for this wife competition. What is amazing is that Esther—this Jewish exile—wins the heart of King Ahasuerus. Esther—one of God's people—now sits on the throne of Persia with a crown on her head next to the mighty King Ahasuerus. But there is one problem lurking in the background: Esther hasn't told anyone that she is a Jew. We're left wondering if that will create any problems for Esther if her heritage is discovered.

An exiled Jew has taken the throne; God's secret hand is at work even in the love life of the king of Persia. We don't know yet *why* the timing of Esther's rule will be important, but we can be sure that God is up to something. And, whatever it is, it will have to do with his gracious protection of his people.

If you belong to Jesus, God's plan for you is for your eternal good—and for the good of his people through your life. Pray today that you would trust God and all that he has planned for you. Ask him to grant you faith, even when you don't understand what he's doing!

Hateful Haman Hatches a Plan

There's always a bad guy. Throughout the story of the Bible, we see again and again people who actively oppose God and his people: The serpent in the garden, questioning God's word and tempting Adam and Eve into sin. Pharaoh, brutally enslaving God's people and seeking to prevent their worship of their God. God's work in this world will always meet with opposition.

Haman, a powerful man in Persia, has just been promoted to a position of great power by King Ahasuerus. With this position comes great honor, prestige, and respect from the people; they even bow down to him in worship. Mordecai, a worshiper of the one true God, refuses to take part. He won't bow down, and he boldly explains that his refusal is because of his Jewish heritage. Haman's response shows that his heart is captured by sinful ambition, self-absorption, and dangerous insecurity. Because of this one perceived slight, Haman hatches a plan to destroy every single Jewish person in the land of Persia.

Haman sells the idea to the king in a cunning way, explaining that the Jewish people scattered throughout Persia have different laws, customs, and practices, and do not respect the king. There's money involved too: Haman promises to donate a large sum from his personal bank account to the king's treasury if Ahasuerus allows him to go ahead with the slaughter. The king is convinced. He signs an edict, and preparations for a massive day of murder begin. The city is thrown into confusion as the exiled Jews begin to panic. With the vengeful intention of one egomaniac, the future of God's people has been put in jeopardy.

Humanly speaking, it looks like the end of God's people. Yet there is one thing that Haman does not know: there is a Jewish woman sitting next to King Ahasuerus on the throne. She has been placed there by God—intentionally, quietly, and secretly. We begin to wonder what Esther's role will be in this story and how God will use her in the preservation and protection of the people he loves. This villain Haman will be no match for the sovereign God of the universe. He's not done with his people yet.

As you see opposition to God and his gracious work, ask him that you would recognize and remember his sovereign hand in all things. Pray that he would help you trust his plan; his gracious purpose involves you too.

If I Perish, I Perish

It seems that a queen should be able to go make a request of the king, even to twist the arm of her husband a bit! But that was not Esther's situation. The king obviously had an incredible amount of power and authority, even over his wife. He was so much in charge, in fact, that Esther feared for her very life if she dared enter the king's presence without being officially summoned by the king. She tells Mordecai as much: "If any man or woman goes to the king inside the inner court without being called, there is but one law—to be put to death, except the one to whom the king holds out the golden scepter so that he may live" (4:11). On top of this, Esther still hasn't revealed to King Ahasuerus the most dangerous fact of all: she is a Jew! She belongs to the race of people who are about to be slaughtered by *his* edict.

It is in Mordecai's response to Esther in this passage that we come closest in the book to seeing a reference to God, although his name is not specifically mentioned. Mordecai's words—famous words—call Esther's attention to the sovereign plan of God for his people and the potential part that Esther's life and reign may be designed to play in God's work. Mordecai's rhetorical question to Esther is what finally urges Esther to spring into action: "And who knows whether you have not come to the kingdom for such a time as this?" (4:14). Mordecai understands that God's hidden hand may indeed have placed Esther in a place of influence to use her in mighty ways for the protection and preservation of the people he loves.

Esther's ultimate response to Mordecai's plea is one of faith—and one that we should seek to emulate as we stand strong for Jesus Christ and his people in this world. She prepares to take her life in her hands and enter the presence of the king. Her words prove it: "I will go to the king, though it is against the law, and if I perish, I perish" (4:16). Esther has embraced her royal position, not as a selfish enjoyment, but as an opportunity given to her by God, as part of his sovereign plan.

Esther took her life in her hands, recognizing that her royal position had been given to her by God so that she could use it for God's people. Pray today that your success—your positions of influence—would be, for you, opportunities to glorify God and tell others about his love and grace in Jesus Christ.

Reversal of Fortune

Esther has thrown a private party for her king and invited Haman. She hasn't revealed her great request to the king yet, but in Esther 5 she promised to do so at the next day of the feast. That night, as the king tosses and turns in his bedroom, unable to sleep, he calls for the book of the chronicles to be brought to him—the book that contains the stories and deeds surrounding his reign. As his servants read it to him, he discovers something: Mordecai, Esther's uncle (though the king is not aware of this fact), had discovered and foiled a plot against the king's life some years before. Realizing that Mordecai has never been sufficiently thanked for this loyal deed, the king calls Haman to him to ask his opinion on how to honor one of his men.

We know that Haman—because of his hatred for Mordecai—has put a plan in motion to slaughter every single Jewish person in the Persian empire. He is full of murderous hatred for God's people. But his response to the question from the king gives us another insight into his sinful heart: he is a man consumed by proud self-absorption. He can't imagine that the king could be talking about anyone other than him! So he designs the thank-you package that he would most enjoy: being paraded around the city, clothed in fine garments, with someone shouting out his greatness in the sight of the king. Unfortunately for Haman, the king gives this treatment to the man Haman hates most: Mordecai!

As the feast begins again the next day, Esther braces herself to act on her promise to Mordecai and to God's people. She reveals Haman's plot to the king. More than that, she finally admits that *she* is a member of the Jewish people—the very people that Haman intends to slaughter mercilessly. The king, already angry, becomes furious when he mistakes Haman's plea to Esther for his life as sexual assault; if Haman's fate wasn't already sealed before, it certainly is now! In an ironic twist, Haman is marched out and hung from the very gallows that he had been preparing for Mordecai.

The story is not over yet; the edict of the king still hangs over the nation of Persia, commanding that all Jewish people be killed. We'll see in Esther 9 how the preservation of God's people is accomplished.

Pray today that God would reveal to you the sinful attitudes that still may be lurking in your heart. Ask him to help you recognize these sins, confess them, turn from them, and become more like Jesus, your Savior.

Feast of Purim

In Esther 9, we discover a very important reason for the story of Esther in the lives of the Jewish people. It was recorded—and told over and over again—to help them remember the meaning and purpose of the Jewish Feast of Purim.

As this chapter opens, we see how Ahasuerus has responded to the plight of the Jews and his own wife. In Esther 8 he gave them full authority to defend themselves against all who tried to hurt them. In this passage, a great battle rages all over Persia. Exiled Jews rise up to defend their lives, and God gives them a great victory over their enemies. They kill five hundred men in Susa, the capital city, and seventy-five thousand in total. King Ahasuerus also has the sons of Haman—the great enemy of God's people—put to death. This is a great day of victory for God's people! On the day when Mordecai and Esther thought they might be wiped out completely, they end up defeating all who oppose them in Persia and securing for themselves safety and security, even in exile. God has saved the lives of his people—and then some.

In the second half of the chapter, we see the Purim feast inaugurated. Mordecai, now a great ruler in Persia, establishes the feast for the people, and Queen Esther confirms it with her royal stamp of approval. The name comes from the word *pur*, meaning "to cast lots." Haman had cast lots for the destruction of the Jewish people, so the name of the feast reminds the people of its foundation. For many years to come, Jews would celebrate the Feast of Purim. When children asked their parents what the feast was all about, the parents would reply, "It is to remember and celebrate God's preservation of his people through the hand of Queen Esther." This very biblical book is there to help them remember.

And so, we come to the end of the book—the story of Esther, reminding us of God's faithfulness to his people even while in exile. This book, without even one mention of God's name, has his faithful and sovereign handwriting all over it. He will not forever abandon his people to destruction. His salvation will prevail.

Pray today that you would actively remember God's work in your life. Ask him to help you more intentionally look back to his hand of faithfulness to you—especially the day of your greatest deliverance and salvation, at the cross, where Jesus died for you.

The Lord Gives and Takes Away

Why do bad things happen to good people? When something bad happens to me, does it mean that God is punishing me for some reason? If God loves me, then why is he letting me go through this? Have you ever asked any of these questions? If you have—or if you are right now—then Job is a great book for you to read.

With the book of Job, we come to a new portion of the Bible: Wisdom Literature. Wisdom books contain much poetry, vivid imagery, and lyrical language. They are intended to give God's redeemed people instruction for wise living. We don't know who wrote the book of Job, but it is a masterpiece of literature with much to show us about our great God.

The first thing we learn about Job is that he is "blameless and upright" (1:1). Job fears God and says no to sin. He is also greatly blessed by God—wealthy beyond most of our imaginations! Yet Job has remained a humble worshiper of God in the midst of all this material blessing. We even see him making sacrifices on behalf of his children, praying to God for forgiveness and mercy toward them.

Job's godliness and success do not go unnoticed. Satan—the enemy of God and the accuser of God's people—comes before God to challenge him concerning Job. (God, of course, has pointed out to Satan his faithful servant.) Take away Job's material blessings, Satan suggests, and "he will curse [God] to [his] face" (1:11). What happens next is shocking to us: God allows Satan to attack Job.

First, Job's oxen and donkeys are taken by raiders. Then his sheep and servants are burned up by fire. After some more animals are lost, the greatest blow comes down: Job's children are killed in a house collapse. There has perhaps been no man who has experienced this much tragedy and loss in the space of one day. Yet much to Satan's chagrin, Job's response—amazingly—is one of faith in his God: "The LORD gave, and the LORD has taken away; blessed be the name of the LORD" (1:21). Job chooses to keep praising God; he worships him not because of circumstances or blessings but because of who God is.

Pray today that you (like Job) would be a person who loves God for God's sake alone—not just because of what God can give you. Ask him to show you the beauty and the value of Jesus, his Son, so that you need him alone, not any earthly or material blessing.

Circumstances Don't Change God

Satan is not done with Job yet. He comes to God with yet another challenge. "Skin for skin," he says (2:4), meaning that a personal attack on Job's physical body is what has been missing. Intense physical suffering, Satan thinks, will finally expose a lack of faith in God that lurks beneath the surface of Job's heart. And so, again, God grants Satan permission to go after Job, denying him only the ability to take away Job's life.

Satan's design for Job involves incredibly painful sores; we are told they cover his body from "the sole of his foot to the crown of his head" (2:7). His only available comfort is sitting in a pile of ashes, scraping the itching and burning sores with a piece of broken pottery. To make matters much worse, this new trial becomes too much for even his wife to handle. She begins to lose faith in the goodness of God and begins to urge Job to do the same. "Curse God and die," she begs her husband (2:9). It is in Job's response—even as his own wife turns away from God—that we see his true heart of faith revealed. Job continues to affirm God's sovereign control, submitting to receive even evil from his hand.

How many of us have faced even a fraction of the suffering and personal tragedy that Job endured? I can imagine loss of possessions; the loss of my family would be unspeakably painful. But if those closest to me began to abandon faith in God in the midst of suffering, counseling me to "curse God and die," that would be a dark and devastating place. It is from that dark place that Job's faith in God grows, thrives, and remains. He continues to affirm God's good plan for him, even in the midst of great suffering. He refuses to let his *circumstances* change his belief in the *character* of his God.

But there's more to this story. Enter Job's three friends—Eliphaz, Bildad, and Zophar. They've heard about his tragedy and suffering, and they've come a long distance to comfort him. We'll soon learn, though, that they're not great comforters! And it will become quickly apparent that they do not have a good explanation for a God who would allow suffering and tragedy for people who love and serve him faithfully.

Pray that God would give us hearts like Job—hearts that respond in praise to him because of who he is and not because of what our circumstances look like on any given day. God has saved us through the death and resurrection of his Son; that will never change, and neither will he!

The Struggle Is Real

In Job 3, a new part of the book begins. It contains a series of dialogues between Job and his friends—the "comforters." This continuing conversation spans forty entire chapters; Job's friends have a lot to say! This passage focuses in on Job's first extended speech—a cry of lament in the midst of terrible personal suffering.

You can feel the anguish in Job's words as you read this chapter. Remember, he's been sitting with his three friends in silence for seven whole days, as he continues to scrape himself in agony with a piece of broken pottery. Finally, he opens his mouth—and utter grief and bitterness pour out. He begins by cursing the day of his birth, essentially wishing that he had never been born. Job's words expose us to a man whose life circumstances have gone so wrong that he at least feels like it would have been better for him never to have existed. There's even a part of him that wants to die. For Job, nothing is left that brings him joy in his life. He summarizes his situation with these cold and sad words: "For my sighing comes instead of my bread, and my groanings are poured out like water. . . . I have no rest, but trouble comes" (3:24–26). These are the words of a man whose life has become pure pain.

God's word at this point is showing us real, honest suffering and struggle from someone we know to be righteous, godly, and faithful. Job does not waste time with religious platitudes, Christian clichés, or "everything will be fine"-type lines. Job honestly pours out his anguish with his words before his friends and before God. Remember, Job is a man who loves and worships God, and God finds him faithful. Yet Job does not shy away from describing clearly, vividly, and emotionally what suffering and pain feel like! He cries out from the pain and expresses his anguish clearly to God. Still, what we don't see in Job's words is a questioning of the character of God. While his suffering brings him great pain, this pain does not turn into bitterness toward God. Job—a godly and faithful man—responds honestly and openly to pain, while refusing to abandon his faith in his holy God and Savior.

Pray today that God would make you an authentic follower of him—honest about your struggles and yet faithful to Jesus in every situation. Ask him to give you strength and faith to cling to him and his word, even through great pain and suffering.

What'd You Do, Job?

The first speech from Job's friend Eliphaz today is a good summary of the stance of all three of Job's companions. The main point? Job *must* have done something to make God angry or all these tragic things never would have happened to him. Eliphaz begins by speaking from his experience; he's never seen such bad things happen to good people. "Remember," he says, "who that was innocent ever perished?" (4:7). Even though Eliphaz has observed the righteous life of Job, as we see in verses 3–6, he is confident that some hidden sin in Job's life has brought this on him. He concludes with a convincing rhetorical question: "Can a man be pure before his Maker?" (4:17). Even Job, Eliphaz insists, cannot be completely pure and right before God.

Of course, in his final point, Eliphaz is right. No human apart from Christ can ever be perfectly right and pure before an infinitely holy God. But Eliphaz is dead wrong in his assertion that Job must have done something to make God angry, that God must surely be punishing him for some secret sin. We know, as Eliphaz does not, that Job is not being punished by God for rebelling against him. In fact, it's quite the opposite. What drew Satan to Job was his incredible faithfulness and obedience to God. Job's suffering comes *because* he has been righteous and upright, not because he has failed in some way. Eliphaz, then, is an example of a person who is incredibly shortsighted. He thinks he knows how God will act every time.

For those of us who know and love Jesus, and are suffering greatly, we should be encouraged by the fact that Eliphaz is wrong about the necessary meaning of our suffering! For Job, suffering entered the life of a faithful man who loved God, and God was not punishing him in any way. There is also a warning here, though, as we look at the closed-minded response of Eliphaz to Job's suffering. He tries to play God by interpreting Job's circumstances. And he's absolutely wrong! Eliphaz—and Job's other friends—remind us that we need to be very careful about interpreting God's purposes. His ways are much higher than our ways; we need to let him be God.

Pray today that you would trust God's perfect plan for your life. Ask him to help you stay faithful to Jesus, even through suffering. Remember that he is a God who has eternally good plans for you, even though that may mean difficult things now.

Misdiagnosed

In Job 13, Job defends himself against the barrage of speeches from his friends, all of which have a common theme as their main point: Job is suffering because God is punishing him for his sins. Job is not afraid to respond to these friends, who feel too comfortable speaking on God's behalf: "You are giving me a wrong diagnosis for my suffering." Job is not perfect; he knows that. Yet he rightly defends both his faithfulness to God and God's higher purpose in his suffering. Job's words to his friends are somewhat harsh, as he rejects their counsel and "comfort." "As for you," he says, "you whitewash with lies; worthless physicians are you all" (13:4). These "doctors" are no good for Job's illness; they are stuck on a wrong diagnosis. What Job needs is not people playing God and pointing fingers at some secret sin that doesn't really exist; he needs people helping him trust God's sovereign plan even through suffering.

It is worthwhile to contrast the friends' assuming that they knew the mind of God with the depiction of Jesus given in Philippians 2: "Though he was in the form of God, [he] did not count equality with God a thing to be grasped" (Phil. 2:6). It was due to this humility that Jesus was able to become our ultimate physician and healer, as Jesus "emptied himself, by taking the form of a servant, being born in the likeness of men" (Phil. 2:7). With their judgment Job's friends assumed the place of God, but with his humility Jesus took on the likeness of men. Job's friends were not sympathetic to his distress, but in Jesus we have a "high priest" who is able to "sympathize with our weaknesses" (Heb. 4:15).

It is clear that Job's friends were off the mark. And in Job 13:20, Job shifts suddenly from talking to his friends to talking to God in prayer. While he has affirmed his faithfulness to God before his friends, he invites God to show him his sin—if there is sin to be brought into the light. Job is open to God's diagnosis, even if he has finally rejected the diagnosis of his friends! Job is seeking the face of his God rather than turning away from him in bitterness.

Our heavenly Father invites our honest, sincere, and even confused prayers! Pray honestly to God today, in the name of your Savior, Jesus Christ. Take him your struggles, your questions, and your suffering. And, by God's grace, ask him to help you comfort others in the right way!

When Good Things Happen to Bad People

It often seems that we live in a pretty upside-down culture, doesn't it? Rich and famous movie stars publicly do stupid and immoral things—and become more famous and rich because of it! Greedy and violent leaders become more powerful. In the midst of this, we see faithful Christians who get cancer, struggle, and die. We see followers of Jesus around the world suffering persecution and imprisonment because of their faith. We believe, because of God's word, that he has a perfect and good plan for all this, and we know that Jesus the great Judge will sort it all out. But it's difficult sometimes to wait, isn't it?

It's precisely this reality that Job uses to counter the continued speeches of his friends. Again and again, they have come back at Job with one recurring theme point: Job is suffering because he is wicked, or at least because he has done something very sinful. Wicked people, they argue, always get punished. Therefore, because Job is being punished, he must be wicked. Job finally, in exasperation, tells them to look around the world! Is it the case that wicked people always get punished and righteous people always have perfect lives? Absolutely not! "Why do the wicked live, reach old age, and grow mighty in power?" Job asks (21:7). Many of them, he adds, not only have success during their lifetimes, but are even remembered with great fondness and honor by their peers: "They spend their days in prosperity, and in peace they go down to Sheol" (21:13). Job is affirming, in other words, a fact that we know well from experience: some very *evil* people live very *comfortable* lives.

How often do we wonder, "How can God let *that* awful person have so much success and happiness?" Friend, God is up to something much bigger—much more eternal—than this life only. There will come a day when all is sorted out and when Jesus Christ the Judge divides the "sheep from the goats" (Matt. 25:32)—all who love him from all who have rejected his rule in their lives and hearts. Until then, God is working out his mysterious plan on this earth in ways that we will never fully understand until we are with him in his presence forever. It is our role to, like Job, trust God himself.

Ask God to help you trust his perfect plan, even when you see wicked people prospering now and godly people suffering now. Pray for an eternal perspective on these things, as you rest in Jesus Christ, the great Savior and Judge of all people.

A Life Lived Well

Job's friends are almost comically closed-minded; they insist, in stronger and stronger terms, that Job's suffering must be God's judgment on his sin. Job continues to affirm not his complete perfection but his life of *faithfulness* to God. We can feel his frustration as, even in the midst of his agony and suffering, he continues to be forced to disagree with his friends, who turn out to be pretty lousy comforters!

In this passage, Job makes his final appeal about his faithfulness in life to both God and others in God's name. He begins by affirming his sexual purity: "I have made a covenant with my eyes; how then could I gaze at a virgin?" (31:1). He describes his commitment to honest dealings in the world of business: "If I have walked with falsehood and my foot has hastened to deceit . . . then let me sow, and another eat, and let what grows for me be rooted out" (31:5–8). Job insists that he has done his best to treat his servants well at all times. He has done everything he can to help those who are poor and in need, and he has helped them because of a deep and reverent fear of God: "For I was in terror of calamity from God, and I could not have faced his majesty" (31:23). Job has not loved money in a sinful way, he says, and has even resisted the temptation to celebrate the downfall of his enemies (31:29). He ends with a final appeal to God, on the basis of a life lived well: "Here is my signature! Let the Almighty answer me!" (31:35).

Our first tendency, when we read a passage like this, is to think of Job as prideful. It is important to realize, though, that he is not arguing for his tremendous moral goodness for its own sake. He is merely affirming his life of faithfulness to his God and insisting that his suffering is not a direct result of personal rebellion against God. Job is no more perfect than any Christian will ever be; we who follow Jesus are all sinners saved by grace. Yet we, like Job, should be able to one day look back on a life lived well—a life lived in faithfulness to our God and his Son, Jesus Christ.

We are called to be people who are both saved by Jesus and then transformed more and more into our Savior's likeness by the power of his Holy Spirit in us. Pray today that your life would more and more reflect the character of Jesus, your Savior. Pray that every area of your mind, heart, and body would be marked by faithfulness to your Savior as he takes control of your life.

Knowledge Is Different Than Wisdom

Elihu is a young man; he has waited to speak until this point in the conversation out of respect for Job's three other friends, who are older than he. Yet he is not shy! We read that Elihu "burned with anger" at both Job and his three friends (32:3). He was angry at Job for insisting on his righteousness and faithfulness, and even angrier at the other three men for failing to give a clear and compelling answer for Job's suffering. As Elihu begins his speech, we wonder if he will indeed have a good answer for Job and his friends. Yet we find quickly that Elihu doesn't have any more wisdom to offer than Job's other three friends. He says some *true* things about God, but he applies them *wrongly* to Job's situation.

He begins by slightly misrepresenting the position of Job, claiming that Job has said, "It profits a man nothing that he should take delight in God" (34:9). Job never said that! He did suggest, as we read earlier, that wicked people do prosper sometimes and righteous people suffer. But Job never said that nothing good comes from fearing and following God! In verses 10–30 Elihu goes into a long justification of God's power, might, and justice. He points out many true things about God. God is incapable of evil and is in charge of the whole world. God is just, ultimately punishing the wicked and hearing the cry of people who are afflicted. These things are all true; Elihu says the right things about God's character!

As this chapter draws to a close, though, we see that even though Elihu has spoken true things about God, he will fail to apply them rightly to Job's situation. He—much like Job's other three friends—ultimately places Job in the camp of the wicked, those who are judged by God in his wrath. "Job speaks without knowledge," he says (34:35). "Would that Job were tried to the end, because he answers like wicked men" (34:36). This man knows a lot about God! Yet he doesn't *understand* him very well at all. Like Job's other three friends, Elihu lands in a shortsighted way on Job's sin and rebellion against God.

Pray today that God would fill you with knowledge of him; we do want to grow in his word and in our understanding of his ways. But pray too that God would help you grow in relationship with him through his Holy Spirit, so that you are able to rightly apply that knowledge of him and live in light of it.

God's Response

Who is right? God is. Job's friends have correctly affirmed God's holiness and judgment of sin, but they have falsely accused Job, who has lived faithfully. Job has rightly insisted that his circumstances do not necessarily imply God's judgment and wrath against him, but he has moved dangerously close to questioning God's motives and second-guessing God's plan. Now it's time for God to enter the conversation.

We can imagine God describing to Job the confrontation with Satan in heaven, after which God permitted Satan to strike Job with tragedy, loss, and sickness to prove the genuineness of his faith. But God doesn't do this! He doesn't explain his purposes to Job. Instead he hits him with a barrage of questions. God is not done working with Job; he still has much to teach him. Job has been faithful, but he has lost sight of God's sovereign plan and will. He has begun to question God's perfect purpose in his suffering. God needs to remind him of God's wisdom and Job's finite understanding.

God tells Job to "dress for action" and prepare to be questioned (38:3). He asks Job to explain the creation of the earth and the organization and management of the great oceans. He asks Job what control he has over the changing of days and the rising and setting of the sun. He asks Job how well he understands life and death—and what happens after death. In verse 21 he even pokes fun at the short time that Job has lived, compared with an eternal God. The point becomes obvious to Job quickly: God is the Creator. Job is the creature. God's wisdom is infinite; Job's is finite. There is a point when Job needs to stop asking God "why?" and start trusting God's perfect plan.

Before we think that God is being too hard on poor Job, remember that this entire discussion is an *answer* to Job! These are not the words of punishment, wrath, or judgment, but the words of a fatherly rebuke. "Job," God is saying, "remember who I am." God is graciously working in Job's life, helping his servant understand the right response of faith in a perfect and infinitely powerful God.

Pray today that you would—even as you pray honestly with God—ultimately rest in his sovereign care and plan for your life. Ask him to make you his humble servant—trusting that he is ultimately working out all things for the eternal good of those who love and follow Jesus!

Hand over Mouth

Finally, God shows up. But God doesn't answer Job's questions right away! In fact, he doesn't even say, "Sorry," or explain his purposes to him. Instead he descends on Job with a multitude of questions, all aimed at pointing Job to God's sovereignty and his own lack of infinite understanding. How would *you* respond to God at that point? Job's response shows us the heart of this faithful man of God.

The Lord concludes his first speech to Job by asking him, "Shall a fault-finder contend with the Almighty?" (40:2). Job does not come back at God with accusations, questions, or words of frustration. In the midst of his tragedy, suffering, and pain, Job acknowledges God's sovereign rule. He puts his hand over his mouth: "I have spoken once, and I will not answer; twice, but I will proceed no further" (40:5). In other words, Job says to God, "I'm done talking!" He's done verbally wrestling with God, done questioning his good purpose. Job has accepted the rebuke of the God of the universe. His suffering has not ended yet, but he is ready to completely submit himself to the will of his God—in everything. This is a response of faith; it is a response from which we have much to learn.

Still, God is not done speaking! After calling Job to again "dress for action like a man" (40:7), God presents his servant with another string of rhetorical questions. This time, his speech is centered on his perfect justice and power, since Job has called into question both his justice and power. God reminds Job that he judges proud people and brings wicked men down. Then he gives Job a picture of his power, telling him to look at the might and wonder of even a *creature* that God has made: the Behemoth. While scholars disagree on what creature God is talking about here (bull, hippo, elephant, etc.), God's point is clear: God's strength is evident even in the mighty creatures he has formed. God is far more powerful than they are, but they give us little glimpses of his great strength. In the midst of his suffering, Job listens to and accepts this rebuke from God. God is reminding Job of his power, justice, and infinite wisdom—because he loves him.

Pray today that God would help you respond to bad circumstances by keeping a correct vision of him, as the God whose good plan for you in Jesus Christ will not fail, even though you may suffer greatly. Ask God to help you put your hand over your mouth—and trust him completely.

Rebellion, Repentance, and Restoration

The past century in our world has been the bloodiest of all time; we've seen wars, great persecutions, plagues, natural disasters, genocides, and corrupt leaders all over the world. What is God's purpose in all this? The book of Job speaks to these contemporary questions; it is a book for believers today! It is helpful, not because it gives pat answers to difficult questions about evil but because it teaches us about God. God ultimately is after his *glory* and his people's *eternal good* in everything he does.

Just the same as in Job 40, God again chooses to not explain himself to Job! Job, as far as we know, never learns about the challenge from Satan to God that prompted the sufferings and tragedies that entered his life. The book of Job ends not with an explanation from God but with repentance from Job. Job has said too much; he admits this to God: "I had heard of you by the hearing of the ear, but now my eye sees you; therefore I despise myself, and repent in dust and ashes" (42:5–6). What Job needed—much more than God's explanation for his circumstances—was a heart that was even more submissive to the will of God.

God is not done. There is a stern rebuke for Job's friends, who "have not spoken of [God] what is right, as [his] servant Job has" (42:7). In an ironic twist, Job makes sacrifices on behalf of the very men who accused him of sin and rebellion against God! While Job has some repenting to do, much more repentance is needed from the false comforters, who insisted on putting God in a box by stubbornly linking Job's suffering to Job's sin. After this, God still is not done: he completely restores Job's fortunes—and then some! His family returns to him, and his wealth becomes greater than it was even before tragedy entered his life.

The story of Job is all about God's character: he is good, and he is after the eternal good of his people! The right response for us is not to try to understand perfectly the precise meaning of every single circumstance. The response for God's people—in every situation—is to remember God's character and trust that the infinitely wise and powerful Creator of the universe knows what is best for the people he loves dearly.

Our responsibility as followers of Jesus Christ is to rest in our good God. Pray today that we would all truly do that! Ask God to help you remember his character and to cling to his goodness and sovereignty even when you do not understand what he is doing.

His Delight Is in the Law of the Lord

The book of Psalms is, among other things, a kind of worship book for God's people. Many of the psalms that we read today were meant to be sung in worship together. They are poetic and rhythmic; some are even ancient acrostic poems. The book of Psalms is a kind of hymnal for God's people. But it is even more than that. The psalms, as they were sung, were intended to *teach* God's people more about God—about his character, salvation, and mighty works for his people. The book of Psalms is a worship book for God's people, which is designed to teach them how to wisely live in obedience to God's word.

With this theme for the book of Psalms in mind, it is easy to see why the book begins with this particular psalm. It is, in many ways, the theme psalm for the entire book! It captures the main idea, which will be repeated and elaborated on in many different ways in many other psalms: God's true people love and live by God's word.

The psalmist presents this important truth by giving us a blatant contrast in Psalm 1—a contrast between the righteous and the wicked. Look at verses 1 and 2 again. "Blessed is the man," the psalmist writes, who does not "walk," "stand," or "sit" with sinners, scoffers, or wicked people. In other words, the godly person is someone whose relationships are not wrapped up too deeply with people who do not love God or his word. The blessed man *delights* in God's word; he thinks about it all the time. This, the psalmist says, is the key to life—both now and forever. While wicked people will blow away like grass, the person who builds his or her life on God's word will be like a tree that is planted and rooted securely. The psalmist goes even further, pointing us forward to the final day of judgment, when the wicked will not stand before God or with God's people. The righteous, though, are known by God—and secure in him.

In six short verses, we have a clear introduction to the message of Psalms. God's people are to love, listen to, and live by God's word. Those who do this will find security *now* and eternal salvation *forever*.

Spend some time responding to Psalm 1 in prayer with God. Ask him to help you love his word—even delight in it. Pray that he would help you—through faith in Jesus—be established forever in him like a tree, not blown away like chaff with those who do not know him.

Kiss the Son

Much of the Old Testament—including the Psalms—is about historical Israel, but also so much more. So often, we are pointed forward to a future hope—a future King—that is much bigger than we suspect at first. Psalm 2 is a wonderful example of this.

The psalm begins with the raging of the nations against God and his people. In the historical setting of the psalm, this could have referred to the surrounding nations of Israel that threatened God's people and attacked them in battle. What is God's response? He *laughs*. The raging of the nations is humorous to the God who judges all things and holds the very world in his hands. But God doesn't just laugh. He will also judge all who oppose his rule, and he will judge them through his anointed King. "As for me," God says, "I have set my King on Zion, my holy hill" (2:6). To this King, God will give the nations as an inheritance. This King will judge God's enemies, and rule them with great might and power.

What is the only right response to the reign of this great King of God? It's to "*serve* the LORD with fear" and to "*kiss* the Son" (2:11, 12). "Kiss" refers to the payment of homage—bowing down in humble reverence and service. The only way to avoid the judgment of this mighty "Son King" of God is to bow before him and submit to his rule over the earth.

Now, in the immediate context, this psalm was written as a *royal psalm* to celebrate the rule of the house of King David over God's people. Yet this psalm quickly gets a lot bigger than merely human kingship. The actions described in these verses are too great—too cosmic—for any man (even David!) to perfectly fulfill. The psalmist seems to be moving past a merely human king to the great "Son of David"—the Messiah.

When we read Psalm 2, we can't help but look forward to Jesus Christ—the great Son of David. He is the only one who could fulfill all these actions of the king of God's people. God has made the nations Jesus's heritage. God has set him up as the eternal King. All who respond to his rule with submission and worship are blessed, because they have taken refuge in the only Savior for lost sinners.

What attitude toward Jesus does your life—your words, thoughts, and actions—reflect? God has placed Jesus on the throne; he will rule forever! Ask God today for strength and humility to live your life in submission to the rule of Jesus. Kiss the Son, and be blessed for taking refuge in him.

I Have No Good Apart from You

John Piper, an author from Minnesota and former pastor, has famously asked, "Would you want heaven *without* Jesus?"[1] In other words, would you be happy with all the blessings of heaven—seeing loved ones, feasting with friends, never being sick again—if Jesus himself were not there? It's a great question for all of us to ask ourselves, because it gets at the heart of our faith. Do we love God because of what we can get from him or because of God himself?

David, the author of Psalm 16, wants God for God's sake. He begins this psalm with a line that we would do well to pray often: "I say to the LORD, 'You are my Lord; I have no good apart from you'" (16:2). David does not mean that he does not have blessings in life; he is the king of God's people, fabulously wealthy and powerful. But when it comes to his relationship with God, his Savior outshines every blessing of life.

For David, this love for God has some implications. It means he loves to be with God's people: "They are the excellent ones, in whom is all my delight" (16:3). David takes delight in people who love God as much as he does. Also, David's love for God gives him a great hope for the future—for blessing, safety, joy, and eternal life. "My whole being rejoices," David writes, "for you will not abandon my soul to Sheol, or let your holy one see corruption" (16:9–10). David goes even further, boldly affirming that love for God is the path to the greatest pleasure. He says to God, "In your presence there is fullness of joy; at your right hand are pleasures forevermore" (16:11). David loves God for God's sake, yes, but that doesn't mean that God doesn't shower blessing on his people!

Don't be mistaken: to follow Jesus is to follow the path to eternal happiness—even though suffering may come in this life. Loving and serving God is the best thing for us! And yet the challenge to us today, as we read David's great prayer of praise to God, is to ask ourselves, "Do I love God, first, for who he is?" Do we seek Jesus for Jesus's sake—because we see *him* as our greatest prize?

We've looked at God as a heavenly Father who provides us with things. That is true in some sense; all good gifts do come from God! Yet God wants his people to love him. More than his blessings. Can you truly say to God, "I have no good apart from you?" Pray about these things today.

The Heavens Declare the Glory of God

"God, where are you? Why won't you just *talk* to me?" In Psalm 19, David, the author, gives a clear response to these kinds of questions. "God *has* spoken," David says. He has been talking to us, loudly and clearly. We just need to listen to him and respond in the right way.

According to David, the first way that God speaks to human beings is through the book of the world—through everything he has created. "The heavens declare the glory of God," David writes, "and the sky above proclaims his handiwork" (19:1). Those verbs David uses—*declare* and *proclaim*—are speaking verbs. He is saying that God's creation actually *speaks* to human beings in a significant way. God's very creation speaks to people, declaring that there is a mighty and glorious Creator.

But God doesn't stop talking at creation. God gets even more specific for his people in his communication to them. How? Through his law—his written word to his people. David moves on from the book of the world to the book of God's word. "The law of the Lord is perfect," he writes, "reviving the soul" (19:7). In verses 7–11, David rejoices in the gift of God's word to his people. His word is sure, right, and pure. In fact, because God's word tells people about God, David sees it as the most desirable thing in all the world. Why is God's word such a great gift? Because God has graciously moved past the majestic revelation of his glory shown through creation and has moved to specific instruction about how sinful people can be in a right relationship with their Creator.

What is David's response to God's word? "Declare me innocent from hidden faults" (19:12). David's response to God is essentially to beg God to find him blameless—to declare him innocent! David knows his sin; he knows he needs a Savior. Especially in light of God's revelation of who he is, David understands that he needs to be made blameless in the sight of this holy God, and he can't do it on his own. David's response to God's speaking should be our response—begging God to make us blameless in his holy sight. That's a response that God has answered—at the foot of the cross, where his Son bled and died for lost sinners.

Jesus himself—God's own Son—is the "Word made flesh," who came to save us. God has spoken to us. Thank God for speaking. Praise him for the wonders of the world he made. Thank him for the hope we find in the Bible. Ask him to help you listen better to his voice!

Why Have You Forsaken Me?

"My God, my God, why have you forsaken me?" (22:1). David is in a dark place! He can find no rest, despite his prayers to God. He is mocked by the people around him and jeered at because of his faith in God. He feels like he is absolutely surrounded by his enemies, as if they are strong bulls or dogs. Yet all the way through this psalm, David keeps returning to the reality of God's faithfulness to him and the certainty of God's ultimate rescue and victory, even in David's life. "Yet you are holy, enthroned on the praises of Israel," David writes, returning to the reality of God's character (22:3). He remembers God's hand in his life, even from the day of his birth.

David ends the psalm with an incredibly confident affirmation of God's victory and deliverance of him, basically shouting out in praise to God. Even in the midst of this terribly bad situation (we don't know what it is!), David remembers God's hand in his life and holds on to faith in God to work for David's good and for God's glory.

David pens this psalm from a very low place. He is feeling abandoned, persecuted, attacked, and utterly alone. Yet David goes to the right place; he cries out in prayer and petition to God. As in other messianic psalms, David seems to go beyond his own personal experience in this psalm.

Ultimately, this is a psalm whose words are only and finally fulfilled in the experience of Jesus Christ on the cross—where God forsook his own Son so that lost sinners might not be finally forsaken; where the Roman soldiers gathered around the cross, casting lots for Jesus's clothing as he suffered; where our Savior cried out for a drink, because he was so parched from heat and exhaustion. David's words describe the suffering of God's anointed for his people that is ultimately fulfilled at the cross of Jesus. Like Psalm 22, the story of Jesus's suffering ends with a song of victory. Jesus doesn't stay dead! He rises from the grave in victory, and people from all over the world will praise him and know God because of his work of salvation.

The words of this psalm bring us closer to the full agony that our Savior endured for us as he cried out to his own Father, "Why have you forsaken me?" Spend some time simply thanking Jesus that he was forsaken by God in our place. He bore God's wrath—utter spiritual agony—so that all who believe in his name would not have to!

You Are with Me

Think about someone you love and know well. Imagine that you spend all your time learning things about that person but not getting to know him or her better. That's so often the way that we relate to our God. We spend lots of time learning truths about him, and that's good and extremely important! But we sometimes don't seek to develop a personal relationship with him. Amazingly, that's what God wants with us, through his Son: a personal relationship. Psalm 23, a psalm of David, shows us a man who not only knows *about* God but who also *knows God personally.*

The psalm opens with the image of God as our shepherd. He is not just any shepherd; he cares for his sheep—his people—with intentionality and diligence. The sheep of this shepherd want for nothing and have green pastures in which to graze. God leads his sheep in the right paths, and even protects them against their darkest enemies—death and evil. David then switches the metaphor he uses to talk about God; God is not just his shepherd but his gracious host at a feast: "You prepare a table before me in the presence of my enemies . . . my cup overflows" (23:5). God is, for David, the one who takes care of David's every need, even caring for him in a way that mocks all the enemies who might have hoped to oppose him. The psalm ends with a declaration of hope in God's care and presence with David—forever.

Is God, for you, not just a set of true assertions but a person whom you know, love, and worship? David's prayer gives us a glimpse into a relationship with the holy Creator that is far from detached. The God of the universe wants to be *your* shepherd. He wants to guard you through life and bring you home one day into his glorious presence. The holy God who made you wants to be your host—to lay out a feast for you so that even Satan and death may be mocked because of it. God wants to do this for you, and he has made it possible through his Son. Cling to Jesus. Savor the relationship with your Creator that comes only through his Son.

As you pray to God today, ask him that you would not only know more about him but also know him more. Thank him for drawing near to you through the life, death, and resurrection of Jesus and making a relationship with him possible. Praise him for wanting to be your shepherd and your great host. Ask him to help you draw close to him every day in a relationship with your heavenly Father.

The God of Jacob Is Our Fortress

While many of the psalms are prayers *to* God, on a personal level, Psalm 46 is a song written *for* God's people *about* God. Psalm 46 is not written by David; it's by the sons of Korah, who most likely functioned as worship leaders for God's people. It's a song of God's faithfulness to his people who take refuge in him as their fortress.

Verse 1 gives us the main theme of this psalm: "God is our refuge and strength, a very present help in trouble." The image of God here is of a strong tower, a castle for his people. In contrast with God the refuge, though, is the raging that is happening all around them. God is a fortress, first, in the midst of the raging of nature. God's people will not fear, "though the earth gives way, though the mountains be moved into the heart of the sea, though its waters roar and foam" (46:2–3). God will serve as a refuge for his people, even though the physical world seems to go crazy sometimes; he is firmer even than the greatest mountains. Second, though, God is a fortress for his people in the midst of the raging of the nations. In a way that seems similar to nature, "the nations rage, the kingdoms totter" (46:6). God is not daunted by this either! In the face of political turmoil, great wars, and kings who mock God's name, "He utters his voice, the earth melts" (46:6). God is stronger than nature; he is the Creator. God rules the nations; he made them too!

The overwhelming theme that this psalm keeps emphasizing is the security of God's people in him, even in the midst of chaos and turmoil around them. There is no safer place—no sturdier rock—than the God of the universe. But there's another theme that emerges here as well: the ultimate and final silence of the nations. There are those who rage against God, but they will finally be silent before him. "He makes wars cease to the end of the earth," the psalmist writes (46:9). We even find a quotation from God in the next verse: "Be still, and know that I am God" (46:10). The English translation doesn't quite capture the power and force of God's words to the raging nations here; God is essentially telling them to shut up because he is God and he alone rules.

God alone is the place for true security. Pray today that you would find in him your greatest refuge. He is the God who made you—and who sent his Son to die for you. Ask God to give you faith to make him your fortress.

Renew a Right Spirit within Me

King David has sinned against God in a terrible way. After having an adulterous affair with a woman named Bathsheba, getting her pregnant, and arranging for the murder of her faithful husband, Uriah, David finally is confronted for his sin by a prophet named Nathan. David, who does love God, is finally filled with guilt and conviction because of what he has done. Psalm 51 is his prayer to God.

David doesn't waste time trying to justify his actions or explain why he did what he did. David brings to God a full acknowledgment of his sin. He holds nothing back, and he takes full responsibility. "I know my transgressions," David writes, "and my sin is ever before me" (51:3). Then David goes on to say something that surprises us. He says to God, "Against you, you only, have I sinned" (51:4). Excuse me? From our perspective, David has sinned against a bunch of people! He's sinned against Bathsheba by using his influence as the king to get her into his bed. He's sinned against Uriah by sleeping with his wife and then having him killed. David's sinned against the people of Israel by taking advantage of his royal position and doing something for which he would have any other Israelite put to death. Yet David's words to God remind us of an important aspect of sin and confession, one that we would all do well to remember: our sin is first and foremost vertical. In other words, our sin—before anything else—is an issue between us and God.

Yet David wants *more* than just forgiveness: "Create in me a clean heart, O God. . . . Restore to me the joy of your salvation" (51:10–12). David needs God's forgiveness; he knows that. But he also recognizes that his sinful actions have exposed more than just a one-time decision. David wants God to do work in his heart. He knows that he needs God to forgive him but also to *change* him more and more so that his desire for sin becomes less and less. Friend, we need God's forgiveness, and it is good to ask God for his mercy because of Jesus's death on the cross. But we also need to ask God to—more and more—change our hearts.

Spend some time today in prayer with your heavenly Father. Confess to him the ways that you fall short of obedience to his word, and ask him for his forgiveness on the basis of the cross of his Son. Then ask him to create a clean heart in you. Pray that he would, by his Holy Spirit, take away the love of sinning and fill you with joy in him.

Arise and Tell

God's people seem to have trouble remembering. Consider, for example, the incident with the golden calf in the wilderness. God had just brought his people out of slavery in Egypt in a totally miraculous way. Moses went up on the mountain for a few days and came back down to find the people bowing down in worship to a calf made out of gold—with Aaron the priest leading the way! How could they have forgotten so quickly, we wonder, the great things that the one true God had done for them? It's this failure to remember that is most likely the reason for the writing of Psalm 78. This is a *historical psalm*; it was written to help God's people remember all that he has done for them, so that they will rightly see his character and the response that God demands from them.

The psalm is written because there is a need to "arise and tell" the next generation about the works of God (78:6). The story of God's faithfulness and goodness to his people is one that must be told—again and again. Why? Because God's people *forget* so easily. The psalmist Asaph tells us that this is his reason for writing; he is desperate for the coming generations to "not forget the works of God" (78:7).

As this historical psalm goes on, we find that it is quite a circular story. Again and again God shows his faithfulness and saving power to his people, and again and again God's people demonstrate their forgetfulness and rebellion against him. God, for instance, demonstrates his goodness in the wilderness, and the people just keep on rebelling against him (78:10, 17, 32, 56).

Through it all, God was gracious; he "atoned for their iniquity and did not destroy them" (78:38). The psalmist ends his history lesson with David and the hope that God brings for his people through the reign of this king. The reign of David reminds us that God has not given up on his people despite their forgetfulness and outright rebellion. David points us to an even greater King—one who will reign forever over God's people and, through a cross, finally break the cycle of sin and bring both forgiveness and eternal life to sinners who so often forget their God.

Ask God to help you remember! We, like God's people in every age, need to actively remember God's goodness and grace to us. Pray that he would never let you forget who he is—and who you are because of his salvation through Jesus.

Teach Us to Number Our Days

It often takes a terrible tragedy to remind us of the fragility of human life. The death of a young person, for example, shakes us to the core. We are forced to remember that life is short, that death does come to every human being—sometimes at ten years old and sometimes at one hundred years old. And so the question for all of us in this life is this: So what? Where is our hope? What is our foundation, in light of the fragility of human life? Psalm 90 has an answer for us today: we must make sure that the eternal God is our dwelling place.

This is the only psalm attributed to Moses in the entire book. The theme of the psalm is clear even from the first verse: Moses wants God's people to consider the eternal dwelling place they have in God, in contrast with the brief and fragile lives of human beings. God, Moses reminds us, has reigned forever—from "everlasting to everlasting" he is God (90:2). Humans, however, are like grass. They grow, flourish, and live, but it is over so quickly! Even eighty years of life fly by in comparison with the eternal reign of a timeless God. So, where do we go from here?

Moses goes on to show us the right response to the contrast between our fragile lives and the eternal reign of God, our Maker. "Teach us to number our days," he writes, "that we may get a heart of wisdom" (90:12). Moses, in other words, is reminding us to view our lives rightly: to live in light of eternity, to put our deepest hope and trust not in our lives, bodies, health, or survival, but in the eternal God who is the only sure dwelling place for weak human beings. He is the one who showers us with steadfast love. He is the one who brings eternal meaning to brief earthly lives. He is the one who can help us actually accomplish things for his glory and his purposes in this life! And we know that he has gloriously and finally conquered death forever through the death and resurrection of his Son. With God as our dwelling place, death is not the end.

Psalm 90 reminds us that only in God do we find an eternal dwelling place. Only in him can we find meaning and hope in this short life that he has given to us. Only in Jesus can we find eternal life—the future glory of living forever in his presence. Pray the words of Psalm 90 to God.

How Can a Young Man Keep His Way Pure?

People write songs today celebrating lots of different things. Perhaps most commonly, pop songs are written to celebrate the loveliness of a significant other! But songs have also been written to celebrate the beauty of creation, a wedding, a fresh start to life, or the birth of a child. You probably would have to search for a long time, though, to find a contemporary song written to celebrate God's word. That's precisely what Psalm 119 is—a song for God's people in celebration of God's word.

You'll notice that this psalm is incredibly long—176 verses, to be exact! There are eight verses given for each letter of the Hebrew alphabet (Ps. 119:1–16 covers the first two: *aleph* and *beth*). If you read through the entire psalm, you'll feel strongly the writer's love for God's word and his thankfulness for this gift of God's communication to human beings.

In the first section of the psalm, we find that those who walk in the law of the Lord are the ones who are truly blessed. This is, really, the key idea for the entire psalm: those who build their lives on God's word receive his blessing. The psalmist then makes a personal commitment and prayer to God that he would be one of those blessed people. "Oh that my ways may be steadfast in keeping your statutes!" he prays (119:5), for then "I shall not be put to shame" (119:6). We are finding that, according to the psalmist, the surest path to blessing and joy is in a steadfast commitment to living under God's word.

In the second section (*beth*), we find that God's word is not only the key to blessing but also the key to purity. "How can a young man keep his way pure?" the psalmist asks. Only "by guarding it according to your word" (119:9). It is the storing up of God's word in the heart that the psalmist sees as the key to guarding his life against sin. Only by truly knowing, internalizing, and even delighting in God's word will God's people be able to resist sin's temptation and remain firmly committed to purity for Jesus's sake.

God's people ought to delight in his word. He has revealed himself to us; this is our path to life, joy, blessing, and purity. Pray today that this would be more and more your attitude to God's gracious gift of his word. Pray that he would make you love it more—and live by it—so that you would follow him in all purity and holiness.

My Help Comes from the Lord

As we read the Scriptures and know the Bible better, we learn more about our great God and all that he is to his people. He is the ruler, sustainer, comforter, and protector, just to name a few. In this psalm, however, the psalmist has one particular aspect of God in mind. He is focused on God as our *keeper*.

Psalm 121 is the first of the "Songs of Ascents"—a collection of psalms that were most likely sung by the people of God as they journeyed up to Jerusalem to worship God there. Given the geographical landscape of ancient Israel, it's not too surprising that the psalm begins the way it does: "I lift up my eyes to the hills" (121:1). The psalmist, in a moment of insecurity, looks for a place of security and comfort: "From where does my help come?" It may be that he is having a moment of temptation, feeling prompted to look to the "high places" of idol worship for his help. Or it may be a general phrase for "looking up" for help in a time of trouble. Either way, the answer that comes is clear: God alone is the helper and keeper for his beloved people.

God's people's truest help, the psalmist reminds them, is from God himself: "My help comes from the LORD, who made heaven and earth" (121:2). The psalm goes on to describe one central activity that God performs for his people: keeping them. The verb *keep* is used as an action of God six times in just eight verses; the psalmist obviously wants us to get the picture! The God who keeps us does not slumber; he is always awake and on watch for his people. God guards us night and day and even keeps those who love him from sin and evil. Best of all, this keeping is an eternal activity for God: "The LORD will keep your going out and your coming in from this time forth and forevermore" (121:8).

Rejoice in this today! God is our Savior and Creator, yes, but he is also our keeper. He has promised to keep all the people he has saved for himself through the death and resurrection of his Son, Jesus Christ.

Pray today to the God who is your keeper. Thank him for promising to keep your life—to protect your heart and soul and to be with you through every difficult circumstance. Ask him to keep you from sin and to guard you from temptations toward evil. Finally, pray that God would remind you to not look for help in difficult times in any other place than in him.

Dwell in Unity

These psalms are the last two of the Songs of Ascents. These two psalms, especially, give us glimpses into what was valued in the community of God in ancient Israel. We can see what we should value as God's people in the church today. We ought to pursue and celebrate *unity* among God's people. We ought to be enthusiastically committed to gathering to *bless* the name of the Lord together.

"How good and pleasant it is," the psalm begins, "when brothers dwell in unity" (133:1). Unity in the midst of the people of God is a beautiful thing. The two metaphors for unity that the psalmist used mean little to us today, and they even seem a bit strange. Unity among God's people, he writes, is like oil running down the beard of Aaron the priest. That sounds strange! But the picture is a symbol of holiness; unity in the midst of God's community is set apart and holy for God, like the priesthood of Aaron. The psalm also says this unity is like the dew of Hermon. Most likely, this is a picture of fruitfulness and life, like fresh dew that falls each morning on vegetation in nature. The point is this: nothing is more beautiful than unity in Christ among God's people.

The final psalm of these ascent songs changes gears a bit, as we are taken into an ancient worship service. Verses 1–2 contain a cry from the people to their religious leaders—their pastors, if you will. For those who stand by night in the house of the Lord, the call from the people is to bless the Lord and lift up their hands to him in worship. The people are calling their leaders to praise God and to lead them in worship. Verse 3 is the response from the religious leaders of God's people; they respond with words of blessing. "May the LORD bless you from Zion," they say to the people. This is a great picture of corporate worship in the community of God: God's people encouraging their leaders in their work and gathering with them in the worship of God; God's leaders blessing the people with God's word and God's blessing.

Pray today that God would, by his grace, help you dwell in unity with your brothers and sisters in Christ—forgiving them, bearing with them, and showing grace to them as Jesus Christ has shown to you. Ask him, also, to grow that unity through the corporate worship of your Savior together. Pray that God would make you even more excited about worshiping him and blessing his name together with other believers.

Search Me and Know Me

There isn't a man named Santa who knows and watches our every move, as the Christmas song "Santa Claus Is Coming to Town" implies. But we do have a Creator, who knows every inch of our lives and every inclination of our hearts.

David recognizes God's complete reign over his life. "O LORD, you have searched me and known me!" he writes. "You know when I sit down and when I rise up" (139:1–2). David admits that God even knows what David will say before he says it. Then, in verses 7–12, he moves on a bit; God not only knows all his thoughts, but he is always present with David, no matter where he goes. God's hand stretches everywhere! David's prayer is written to a God who *sees* and *knows* everything.

How does this make you feel? Trapped? Scared? Look at David's response to God's power, knowledge, and presence: "I praise you, for I am fearfully and wonderfully made. Wonderful are your works" (139:14). David's response to the God who knows and sees everything is . . . praise. Why? Because David recognizes that this omniscient Creator has taken the time to form and design *him*. "You knitted me together in my mother's womb," David exclaims with wonder (139:13). More than that, David is in a relationship with this all-knowing and all-seeing God; God's knowledge of David is no longer frightening but comforting. David's celebration of God's creation and intimate knowledge of human beings is filled with praise *because* of a close relationship with God through God's grace.

Verses 19–22 can catch us off guard. Yet these are part of David's prayer to God. He is asking his God—this God who sees all—to see the evil in the world and to do something about it. Part of David's worshipful response to God is loving what God loves and hating what God hates. And when God's people see evil and sin in this world, they are to do what David does: trust the God who sees all to act as the great righteous Judge.

God made you with precision, and he wants you to be in a relationship with him. Thank God for creating you according to his perfect purpose. Ask him to help you better understand his knowledge and power. Praise him for knowing you, making you, and providing a way for you to have a relationship with him through the death of his Son for your sins.

Everything That Has Breath

The final psalm of the book uses the word *praise* thirteen times. So the main theme is not a mystery: this is a psalm calling God's people to overwhelming, vibrant, joyful, praise for their Creator and Savior. While this theme is clear enough, however, sometimes applying a psalm like this is difficult for us. It can sound redundant when we're reading it, and we sometimes don't know what to make of it.

According to Psalm 150, God's people are to praise God in his sanctuary—or in the place where they have gathered to worship him. We should praise God because of his character and deeds—"according to his excellent greatness" (150:2). We should praise God in all kinds of different ways—with "trumpet sound" and "sounding cymbals" (150:3, 5). Finally, everyone everywhere should praise God—"everything that has breath" (150:6). There's one more call in this psalm that, while not mentioned specifically, is very evident in every verse. It's the call to praise God with exuberance and enthusiasm. The praise demanded here is vibrant, wholehearted, and intense. God's people are to praise him with everything they have—and all the time.

We need to understand a few things about praise, though, in order to rightly understand and apply Psalm 150. First, we need to know that God doesn't need his people's praise. God is completely self-sufficient and content in and of himself; he doesn't somehow become more God when we praise him. Second, we need to understand that while God doesn't need our praise, he does desire it. God loves to hear songs, prayers, praises, and blessings of his name from the lips of his people. Third, we need to know that our praise for God—desired, but not needed by him—is the *best thing* for our hearts and minds. It is good for us to praise God. So Psalm 150 is not a list of commands to make us give God what he wants! It is an encouragement for God's people to respond to his grace in the right way—through vibrant and overwhelming praise. And it is a call for God's people to do the very best thing for their hearts, souls, and lives.

Our posture in our minds and hearts toward a God who has poured out grace and forgiveness on us through Jesus should be one of praise: speaking about his goodness, thanking him for his mighty acts, singing, and worshiping him with his people. Spend some time in praise to God.

The Fear of God

You're probably familiar with some well-known examples of phrases that have become proverbs over the years. "Look before you leap." "The early bird gets the worm." "You can lead a horse to water, but you can't make him drink." Biblical proverbs, however, are more than just catchy sayings. The book of Proverbs—part of the Bible's wisdom literature—is composed of wise words that are given specifically for God's people. The proverbs contained in this book are *not* a path to salvation—a how-to book of sorts that tells people how to earn their way into favor with God. This book, as originally written, was meant to serve as wisdom for God's people as they lived godly lives in the midst of God's community.

In Proverbs 1:7, we find what we can safely label as the theme verse of the entire book, and possibly of all wisdom literature. True wisdom and knowledge begin with the fear of the Lord. Without the fear of God, none of these proverbs will do any good at all. It is the fear of God—a reverence and worship for him—that leads his true people to pay close attention to his word. Those who refuse to fear God also reject his wise word; they will suffer the consequences of foolishly choosing to "despise wisdom and instruction."

On the one hand, we hear the enticement of sinners, calling us to abandon God's way and live for pleasure and selfish pursuits. This is a call to violence—to "ambush the innocent without reason" (1:11). It is a temptation toward pursuing possessions and riches more than godliness: "We shall find all precious goods, we shall fill our houses with plunder" (1:13). But as enticing as this lifestyle can be, it will not end well; men who pursue violence, greed, and selfish pleasure "lie in wait for their own blood" (1:18). Obeying the call of sin ends in death. On the other hand, the steady and clear call of wisdom appeals to us to listen to God's word and live for him as his people. Wisdom "cries aloud in the street," looking for those who will humbly listen to God's good instruction (1:20). Those who listen to Wisdom—to the right word—will "dwell secure" (1:33).

Pray today that you would be quick to listen to the right word. Ask God to help you see the true end of sin, greed, and selfishness. Pray for his strength to resist temptation and to seek to follow your Savior in everything you do, think, and say.

God's Plan for Marriage

Our culture is crazy about sex: Magazine covers sell fashion and health tips to you with pictures of scantily clad bodies. Movies and television shows glamorize sexual affairs that are enjoyed without commitment or fidelity. Music celebrates lust. You can hardly walk out of your house without being bombarded by messages telling you that sex is great, good, and exciting. And the Bible doesn't disagree with that! Sex is created by God; it is indeed great, good, and often exciting. Of course, God created it for a specific context: marriage. Outside that context, it is a wildfire—burning and destroying those who engage in it without the proper boundaries and commitments.

Proverbs 5 is composed of words from Solomon to his son—words that particularly have to do with sexual temptation. It's clear in this chapter that sex is a good thing to be greatly enjoyed! "Drink water from your own cistern," Solomon writes (5:15). Married people can and should enjoy one another; "rejoice in the wife of your youth," the chapter tells us (5:18). The Bible is not shy about celebrating sexual love as a good gift from God, when enjoyed in the right context!

The big temptation—for us today and for Solomon's son back then—is to engage in sex sinfully and selfishly outside the context of marriage. "The lips of a forbidden woman drip honey," says Solomon, "and her speech is smoother than oil" (5:3). Sexual relationships outside God's intended context *look* good and *sound* good to us. Because God created sex to be enjoyed—it is connected to pleasure—our sinful desires always tug at our hearts in this area. But Solomon is clear: sinful sexual relationships never live up to their promise. "Her feet go down to death" (5:5). Sex outside marriage is a quick path to pain and destruction.

Solomon's instructions for his son—because of God's plan for marriage and the destructive power of sexual sin—can be boiled down to one simple phrase: *run* from sexual temptation. "Keep your way far from her," he urges, "and do not go near the door of her house" (5:8).

Pray that God would fill you with a love for Jesus, your Savior, which replaces a love for sin. Even if you are doing well in the area of sexual purity, ask God today to strengthen your commitment to his plan for sex—in the context of marriage. As you pursue Christ, pursue sexual purity in his name and for his glory!

A Matter of Life and Death

Two roads diverged in a wood, and I—
I took the one less travelled by,
and that has made all the difference.[2]

Those well-known words speak to the consequences of one simple choice. Here we find two different women—not two different paths. Lady Wisdom and Madame Folly both call to us, the personifications of the options that we have in life.

Lady Wisdom comes to us in this poetic chapter as a woman with a large, sturdy house. Seven pillars support it, and its table is loaded with a glorious feast. Her words too are appealing: "Leave your simple ways, and live, and walk in the way of insight" (9:6). This woman's call is away from the foolish life, away from sin, selfishness, and temporary pleasures. Her words direct us to the theme of all wisdom literature, which we've heard before: "The fear of the LORD is the beginning of wisdom, and the knowledge of the Holy One is insight" (9:10). This woman—personifying the right focus on God and his word—calls out to all who will listen. Her invitation is warm and kind, and the reward is real: *life*.

Madame Folly's invitation is appealing as well, however. She calls out with equal passion and fervor. While she shouts foolish things and knows nothing, she is nevertheless seductive and able to trap many people. She sells her lies, saying that "stolen water is sweet"—that sin is enjoyable and fun (9:17). Her words and ways, though, end in only one place: *death*.

Sometimes we need a picture to remind us of the clear choice that we all have. It's a choice between God and Satan! God's way—the way of wisdom—ends in life, and life abundantly. A life of sin and rejection of God's word—though often seductive—ends in destruction. With vivid images of these women and their words, Proverbs again reminds us that every human being must choose between God and Satan, life and death.

Thank God that, by his grace, you have listened to his words of wisdom. Thank him for salvation in Jesus. Then pray that you would see the world with a Proverbs-like clarity! Ask God to help you point other people to the one true source of life, salvation, and wisdom: Jesus Christ, God's Son.

Taking Every Thought Captive

We often look at the book of Proverbs a bit like we look at a book of quotations from a famous person, such as Winston Churchill or Benjamin Franklin. We treat it like a collection of sayings—random, disconnected, but entertaining. And, at first glance, Proverbs 16 does seem that way. There are proverbs in chapter 16 about kings, words, injustice, plans, attitude, honesty, and even gray hair! How do we interpret and apply a chapter of the Bible like Proverbs 16? Do we just enjoy the sayings and leave it at that?

While the chapter speaks to a lot of different subjects, the main point is this: God's people are to live wisely on earth below, in the sight of God above! We are to let the reign of God touch, influence, and shape every attitude, interaction, relationship, and pursuit in our lives. Consider just a few examples from this chapter. We are told that "the heart of man plans his way, but the LORD establishes his steps" (16:9). This speaks to our attitude toward *planning* in life; we plan, knowing that God is ultimately the one in charge of our lives. We are told also that "good sense is a fountain of life to him who has it, but the instruction of fools is folly" (16:22). We are learning from this verse about the foolishness of trying to get wisdom from fools! We need to go to God for guidance and good sense. Even the verse about hair has something to teach us about an attitude that is informed by the reign of God. When we read that "gray hair is a crown of glory" (16:31), we are being taught that growing old in the Lord is a blessing; aging can be a gracious thing, if a life has been lived well.

We could go on and on; this chapter in Proverbs has a lot to offer! But we'll end with these questions: Does God's reign touch every thought, attitude, relationship, action, and pursuit in your life? Are you living every part of your life in light of the reign of God? That is the message of this book of wisdom; wise living means living under God's rule—in *everything*.

Consider how often you consciously make decisions because of God's rule in the universe and in your heart and life. Then pray! Ask God to help you pursue honesty because of him. Ask him to help you be slow to anger because he has been merciful toward you. Pray that he would make you hungry for the wisdom of his word, which always points us to his Son.

True Beauty

Many sermons have been preached on this chapter, usually directed at women. While there are some wonderful applications for women here, there's a problem with teaching this chapter directly to women. What's that? The words in this passage were spoken by a woman to a man.

This passage is a stern and wise lecture from a mother to her run-around son. It's obvious that King Lemuel had a tendency to go after the wrong kind of women! Listen to the words from his mother: "What are you doing, my son? . . . Do not give your strength to women, your ways to those who destroy kings" (31:2–3). Lemuel's mother sees his tendency to chase the kind of women who destroy kings, not encourage them to fear the Lord. Her goal is to give him a vision of a godly woman—the right kind of wife, who will point him toward wisdom and toward God.

So that's the setup for 31:10–31—the portrait of an "excellent wife." Lemuel's mother tells him to pursue *this* kind of woman, because she is a gift of God to any man. What are her characteristics? She is trustworthy and does only good to her husband. She works hard. She contributes to the honor and growth of her husband, and she looks after her family and children with diligence and care. Ultimately, her greatest secret is that she fears the Lord; that is what makes her truly beautiful.

Men, what kind of young women do you pursue? Are they careless, silly, and flirty girls—the kind of girls our culture considers sexy? Or are you even now preparing your heart to lead you to a woman who is, above all else, godly? The only way you can train your heart to be attracted to that kind of woman is to be radically pursuing Jesus in your own heart and life.

Young women, while the picture of the excellent wife in Proverbs 31 is a somewhat idealized one, this should nevertheless be a good reminder of *how* to go about pursuing true beauty. It's through fearing the Lord and seeking him above all else. That pursuit will make you attractive to the kind of man you *want* to attract.

Pray about these things. Ask God to help you pursue him, above all else. Then pray that God will help you begin preparing now to be a godly husband or wife, if you are called to marriage someday.

Under the Sun

Have you ever struggled—I mean really *wrestled*—with the meaning of life? Or maybe you're pretty comfortable with life being all about loving, serving, and worshiping God, but you can't help being curious about what it would be like to experience all the pleasures this world has to offer. Whether you wrestle with questions about life's ultimate meaning, or wonder about tasting this world's greatest pleasures, you've found your way to the right book of the Bible: Ecclesiastes.

The man who brings these struggles together is this book's author, Solomon. He was, in short, the man who had everything: riches beyond our wildest dreams, one thousand women who each called herself Solomon's wife, wisdom that surpassed that of perhaps any ruler who has ever lived. Yet Solomon—this incredible king—struggled with life's meaning. In all his riches and success, he found little satisfaction. Ecclesiastes records the struggle of the man who had everything. It is an honest book; Solomon holds nothing back.

The repeated refrain of Ecclesiastes shows up in the second verse of the first chapter: "Vanity of vanities, says the Preacher, vanity of vanities! All is vanity." Everything is like a vapor. Riches, fame, success—all these pass away; you can't grab hold of them for satisfaction any more than you can seize a cloud and put it in your pocket. Solomon goes on to discuss the futility of pursuits that are done under the sun. He even dismisses his pursuit of wisdom; even great knowledge "is much vexation" and brings an increasing amount of sorrow (1:18). It's a sad first chapter!

Ecclesiastes lets us wrestle along with it; it leaves us with a lot of tension, even right up until the end of the book. Don't skip to the end! We need to acknowledge that this life is difficult and often confusing. For now, we'll end with just a hint of the answer. In verse 3, Solomon uses the phrase "under the sun." Friend, you will *never* complete your search for meaning if you search only "under the sun." You have to go *higher*. And when you do, you will find that this search *does* end somewhere.

Pray that you—if you are searching—would search with the goal of truly finding your answers. And pray in faith to the God who made you that he will help you see him clearly and know him personally.

Striving after Wind

Solomon was uniquely capable of pursuing pleasure to the greatest degree. He was a king of immeasurable power, influence, fame, and wisdom. He had riches beyond imagination. He had all the women he wanted—seven hundred wives and three hundred concubines. Solomon knew what the greatest pleasures of this world tasted like!

We find, in this chapter, that this pursuit of Solomon's was done very intentionally. In a search for life's meaning, he set himself toward this endeavor: "Come now, I will test you with pleasure; enjoy yourself" (2:1). What did the man who had everything ultimately discover? That even the greatest pleasures in this world come up empty; they are vanity—a "striving after wind" (2:11). Solomon tasted it all, and his witness to us is that there is no lasting satisfaction—no solid joy—in the pleasures that merely belong to this world.

Solomon didn't stop there. His search took him toward the pursuit of *wisdom* and of *toil*. Most likely, this wisdom that Solomon describes in Ecclesiastes 2 has to do more with great knowledge than with godly wisdom. The result of a life given to the pursuit of this kind of wisdom? Just as before, "all is vanity and a striving after wind" (2:17). Sometimes, in fact, greater knowledge brings even more sadness. So Solomon turns to toil, or work. He pursues projects and work, but he becomes disillusioned by the fact that these are all left to someone else after death. Ultimately, these pursuits and toils also prove to be like trying to catch the wind; he finds no lasting satisfaction here, either.

Solomon pursued all that the world had to offer—apart from God. And his witness is clear; it's like a vapor! As the chapter ends, we get a hint of where he is headed: "There is nothing better for a person than that he should eat and drink and find enjoyment in his toil. This also, I saw, is from the hand of God" (2:24). There are gifts from God, even in work and life. There is meaning in this life—a God who brings meaning to our toil and earthly pursuits. Solomon is going to point our eyes to him.

Earthly pleasures, without a love for God, do not satisfy. If you have come to Jesus and are living your life for him, you are in the right place! Pray that God would help you trust in him, even when the things of this world look so enticing. Ask him to give you hope in eternity and love for Jesus as your rock.

Joy in the Toil

Finally, Solomon's gaze begins to turn upward. While he hasn't gotten to the end of his search yet, he begins to speak of God in a more personal and real way. In this chapter especially, Solomon seems to land on respect and value for those who work hard all their days on earth—those who are not necessarily wealthy but have joy in the lives and work God has given them.

As the chapter begins, Solomon first looks toward the temple, the place of worship for God's people. His message here? Fear and respect God as you go into the temple to worship him. Solomon reminds us—with well-known words—that our words should be few in the presence of a holy God, because he is holy and infinitely *above us*. Again, Solomon is reminding us to take great care with our words and our behavior in the presence of an infinitely holy, just, and powerful God.

This chapter ends with some words about the lack of satisfaction that riches bring. Wealth does not bring peace; in fact, Solomon even suggests that people with less—who spend their days working hard at manual labor—find rest and sleep far easier than rich people. Not only do riches not satisfy, suggests Solomon, but they also can disappear! He describes great wealth lost in a foolish investment decision.

Solomon's conclusion begins to point us toward a life lived for God above all else. And yet he hasn't arrived in his search. What he does get to is this: *joy* in work and life is better than sadness and dissatisfaction. This is a good thing, according to Solomon: "To eat and drink and find enjoyment in all the toil with which one toils under the sun the few days of his life that God has given him, for this is his lot" (5:18). Those who work hard, stay busy, and thank God in heaven for the work and life he has given to them—these people seem to be on the right track, according to Solomon. The question remains: If *joy* is the right experience in life, what is the path to true joy?

The question today is this: Do you have joy in your life, work, and relationships? Joy, we find from other parts of the Bible, is not just an option for Christians; it is the necessary result of a relationship with Jesus. Pray today that as you pursue Jesus Christ above all else, you would begin to have true joy and real satisfaction in living for him, even as you serve him in the very ordinary details of life!

Death

"Death comes unexpectedly!" The pastor in the movie *Pollyanna* cries out this refrain over and over again.[3] Like that preacher in the movie, Solomon is consumed in Ecclesiastes 9 with the idea of death.

Death is the great equalizer: "The same event happens to the righteous and the wicked, to the good and the evil, to the clean and the unclean" (9:2). How often do we consider, with somber and clear vision, this inevitable march of death in this world? Most people are forgotten by history—a fact that Solomon points out as well. Solomon speaks about death more plainly than we often are comfortable with.

Solomon takes a breath of hope as he encourages people to eat and drink with joy under God's pleasure and to enjoy both family life and work. Then he turns somber again: "There is no work or thought or knowledge or wisdom in Sheol, to which you are going" (9:10).

He's still not done. First, Solomon goes into the seemingly random nature of both success in life and the timing of death. "Time and chance happen to them all. For man does not know his time" (9:11–12). He goes on to share a story of a poor man whose wisdom directly contributed to the survival of the city, only for him to be ultimately forgotten. The point seems to be this: life doesn't always work out the way we think it should! Good people seem to die suddenly, and evil people often live long, healthy, and successful lives.

We need to acknowledge that—at least on some level—Solomon is right. He's correct in his assessment of life—and death—in a world that is fallen, sinful, and under the curse of death. Death keeps coming. Friend, if our hope is only in this life, we would be right to be depressed. Of course, the book is not done, and neither is this discussion! God has given us the greatest answer to death—in the resurrection of his own Son.

Although God's children may be forgotten on earth, they are remembered by their Savior and dwell with him forever! Thank God for this, and ask him to remind you of the hope you have that extends beyond the grave.

The Fear of God

"Life is a journey, not a destination." Today, you're told that the search is what's important; you may never get to ultimate truth and the meaning of life, but there's value in being curious and in keeping an open mind. Ecclesiastes isn't about that. For Solomon, the search for meaning *ends* somewhere. In other words, in this chapter, the book of Ecclesiastes has landed. Solomon's search for meaning ultimately ends at the same place where we found the great theme of Proverbs and the great theme of wisdom literature in general: the fear of God.

Ecclesiastes 12 starts with a strong command from Solomon: "Remember also your Creator in the days of your youth" (12:1). In other words, Solomon tells young people—who are still at the dawning of their lives—that the best decision with the most meaning is to choose God *now*. In verses 2–8 he goes into an extremely artistic and poetic description of growing older, comparing an aging human body to a house that is breaking down, as well as various other pictures from nature. More than anything else, Solomon wants young people to give themselves to God now.

Solomon's final conclusion is along these same lines. "All has been heard," he says (12:13). There's been a lot of talk; Solomon has gone on and on about meaning and has extended his search in every direction. This well-qualified man has looked all around the world, in every direction, and has finally come to a conclusion: "Fear God and keep his commandments, for this is the whole duty of man" (12:13). What is life all about? It's about God—obeying God, living under his word. He is the one, Solomon reminds us, who will judge every human being and every secret thing as well. With God as both our Creator and eternal Judge, our search for meaning ends with him.

As we end our time in Ecclesiastes, we should be asking ourselves this question: *Has our search for meaning concluded?* Solomon's invitation—and the invitation of Jesus Christ himself—is to land with him: to find, in your Creator, your deepest meaning and your greatest belonging.

I encourage you to ask God to help you really believe that meaning, purpose, and satisfaction are only found in him. Pray that God would help you choose him now, in the days of your youth. He made you, and he will one day stand as the great judge of every human being. Ask him to help you live your life for him now, through faith in his Son, Jesus.

Love and Marriage

Probably no book in the Bible is so enthusiastically avoided by churches, pastors, and Bible study groups as Song of Solomon. It can be difficult, for both teens and adults, to understand why this book makes explicit mentions of certain body parts. For much of the church's history, the book was viewed as an allegory representing the love between Jesus Christ and the church. People couldn't imagine that such blatantly erotic language in Scripture could be referring to romantic *human* relationships!

While marriage does—throughout Scripture—represent the relationship between Christ and his church, the Song of Solomon was not primarily written to serve as an allegory. It really was written about human marriage. It vibrantly celebrates romantic human love within the context of marriage commitment. King Solomon (or someone very close to him) wrote this poetic book to express the beauty of sex, romance, and love when they are enjoyed as intended by the Creator God.

The first chapter of Song of Solomon is a romantic love scene with a cast of characters. The woman begins the book with words of love to the man who will be her husband: "Let him kiss me with the kisses of his mouth! For your love is better than wine" (1:2). These are the words of a woman deeply in love! Her words are both celebrated and supported by her friends in the community: "We will extol your love more than wine" (1:4). Before too long, the man speaks up in response. He calls her the "most beautiful among women" (1:8), then repeats this again: "Behold, you are beautiful, my love; behold, you are beautiful" (1:15). We have here a couple—and all their friends—who are caught up in the excitement of a romantic relationship between two people.

This chapter gives us a glimpse of God's great plan for human love and marriage. It is meant to be a beautiful, joyful thing! Romantic love, physical attraction, and intense affection are all gifts from God to human beings. These things are meant to be celebrated by his people and brought into the commitment of marriage.

Human love and marriage are gifts from God, and we are to enjoy them as we worship God even through them. Pray that this book would begin to shape your view of marriage. Ask God to show you his vision for it, and pray that he would guide you as you consider marriage in the future.

The Context for Intimacy

In Song of Solomon 7, we discover that physical and sexual love—and our bodies—can and should be celebrated and enjoyed secretly, privately, and in the context of committed love in marriage. There is no shame in sex. Intimacy between a man and a woman is a *good* thing; it's only made "dirty" and sinful when it is ripped out of God's context for it. The Christian response to the prevalence of sexual sin in our culture today is not to attach a feeling of shame to sex itself, but to bring sex back into the place where it is meant to be celebrated boldly and joyfully: marriage.

As the passage begins, we are introduced to a man who is crazy about his wife; he adores this woman. He is basically looking her up and down and telling her how much he likes what he sees! The comparisons are a bit strange for us today, it's true. We don't usually compare stomachs to heaps of wheat, or noses to towers of Lebanon. But in their day, these would have been compliments—believe it or not! These are the words of a man who is utterly and completely wrapped up in physical love and sexual desire for his wife.

Next, look at the brief words of the woman: "I am my beloved's and his desire is for me" (7:10). She is utterly and completely secure in her husband's love for her and only her. These are the words of a woman who knows for a fact that her man loves and wants her, to the exclusion of every other woman in the world. Her response is to save up her love only for him; she invites him to love her and is completely secure in giving herself to him.

Sex is created by God and meant to be enjoyed in the context of marriage commitment. This chapter shows us a man who is adoring his wife in the right way—obsessed with her alone. It shows us a woman who, in response to the exclusive love of her faithful husband, feels the security to give herself to him in love completely.

Even if you have failed in areas of sexual purity in the past, you can right now commit yourself in a fresh and new way to this vision that God has for human love, romance, sex, and marriage. That kind of marital love is the kind that points us to God—a God who loves his people with undivided and perfectly faithful love and invites their complete commitment to him in return. Ask God to help you commit to his grand plan for human marriage.

The Power of Love

A wildfire is so frightening and destructive because something that is good in the right context becomes terrible and dangerous when it is allowed to run rampant in the wrong context. Fire is a good thing! It helps us cook and stay warm, among other things. But a fire that runs wild creates havoc, fear, and sometimes death.

Sex can be like a fire. It is good in the right context, as Solomon seems to be suggesting—and celebrating! But in the wrong context sex can lead to destruction, despair, and great pain. In the midst of continuing to celebrate the beauty and passion of her married love with her husband, the woman gives out this warning to younger women: "I adjure you, O daughters of Jerusalem, that you not stir up or awaken love until it pleases" (8:4). Isn't that amazing? In the midst of enjoying married love, her impulse is to shout out to younger women, "Make sure you *wait* for this!" She understands how powerful love is; she'll go on to describe it in this way: "For love is strong as death. . . . Its flashes are flashes of fire, the very flame of the LORD" (8:6). Such a powerful gift of God must not be thrown around casually!

The book ends with some final words from the others on the same theme. They describe their younger sister, who is not yet ready for marriage. The language of "wall" and "door" has to do with chastity—protecting herself sexually until marriage. We see the idea that has been repeated throughout the book: sex and marriage are good and given by God, so we need to wait to enjoy them fully in the right context!

Song of Solomon shows us that the Bible is not shy about sex. Sexual and romantic love between a man and a woman is celebrated joyfully and without shame! The word for young people, though, is *wait*. Wait for the right time. Wait for the right, godly person. Then when you come to marriage, you will be able to fully engage in love, sex, and intimacy in the way God intended— a way that lifts him up as the loving Lord of his people.

Ask God for strength to support his plan for marriage even now. How can you do that? With his help, you can seek sexual purity in thought, word, and deed. By his Holy Spirit, ask God to help you live for that kind of purity. By this commitment, the world will know you are his, and you will be able to point others to salvation, life, and true hope in Jesus's name.

Words of Warning

When you hear the word *prophet* today, you probably think of someone who predicts the future. The main definition of a prophet in the Bible, though, is this: someone who speaks God's word to God's people. Prophets were God's mouthpieces to his people, who often spoke when the people had gone astray into sin. When we read the prophetic books of the Bible today, we should read them expecting to hear God's voice!

As we begin the book of Isaiah, we need to understand that we are going *backward* in history. The Bible has already included 1 and 2 Kings, 1 and 2 Chronicles, Ezra, and Nehemiah, so readers know that God's people go into exile because of their constant sin and rebellion. But as Isaiah begins, we are going *back* to before the exile. Isaiah begins with words of warning to God's people in Judah because of their sin.

First, Isaiah speaks of God's people as his *children*: "Hear, O heavens, and give ear, O earth; for the LORD has spoken: 'Children have I reared and brought up, but they have rebelled against me'" (1:2). Because of their sin, signs of judgment have already begun to come: "Your country lies desolate; your cities are burned with fire" (1:7). Even though the people bring sacrifices to God, they are not enough; God desires their love and obedience, not merely animals that they bring to him. God pleads with his people: "Wash yourselves; make yourselves clean; remove the evil of your deeds from before my eyes. . . . If you are willing and obedient, you shall eat the good of the land" (1:16–19). If God's people will simply turn back to him, he will respond with love, forgiveness, and blessing! If not, though, judgment will surely come.

After speaking about the Israelites as God's rebellious children, Isaiah changes metaphors: they are like an *unfaithful wife*. "How the faithful city has become a whore," Isaiah cries (1:21). This is a metaphor that you'll see all over the prophetic books. To God, his people are his bride; he loves them and cherishes them like a dear wife! When they rebel, it is like a wife who rejects the love of her husband and messes around with other men.

Let the words of Isaiah help you understand God's anger against sin—but also his deep love for you, his child. He hates sin, and he will judge it! But he is always ready to accept, forgive, and restore sinners who repent and turn back to him.

A Sinful, Not-So-Secret Handshake

In Isaiah 2, we get a peek into the future. "It shall come to pass in the latter days," Isaiah says, "that the mountain of the house of the LORD shall be established as the highest of the mountains, and shall be lifted up above the hills; and all the nations shall flow to it" (2:2). It's as if Isaiah pauses in the midst of his declarations of judgment and says, "This is what's coming later!" It's a picture of the mountain of the Lord—a place where people from all over the earth will join together to worship the one true God. The nations are depicted as flowing *up* to the mountain. This will be a miraculous work of God. One day, salvation will finally come, and God's people from all over the world will gather in the praise of his name.

But it's not time yet for all this. There is a significant obstacle to this grand plan of God for the world: the recurring sin of his people. God's people do not share God's grand vision for the worship of *him* alone. In fact, instead of worshiping God in a way that makes the nations flow to them, they are flowing to the other nations, with all their sin and idolatry! Isaiah says that "they are full of things from the east and of fortune-tellers like the Philistines, and they strike hands with the children of foreigners" (2:6). This striking of hands, unfortunately, is not to bring these other nations to the one true God. It means that God's people have compromised their worship and been influenced by the sins of these nations who do not fear God.

God has a glorious and perfect plan for his people—an end game. It's sin that keeps getting in the way. So we begin to realize that—in between Judah's sin now and the future glory of God reigning with his people—something will need to be done about their sin, something final. God will make his plan happen despite the sinfulness and rebellion of his people. It's to that act of salvation that Isaiah points us as the chapter ends. There will come a day, he says, when the Lord alone will be exalted. He will finally break down prideful people, deal with sin permanently, and his true people will put away all their idols forever.

God will accomplish the salvation of his people and deal finally with their sin. He'll do it through judgment—but not judgment on them. He will provide his only Son to take the judgment in his people's place, so that they can share in the glory of his presence forever. Thank God for your salvation and acknowledge to him that it is all his work.

Bearing Fruit as God's Vineyard

One of the roles of an Old Testament prophet was to get God's people to see things from God's perspective. That's what Isaiah is doing in the first few verses of Isaiah 5. He is singing a song on behalf of God, seeking to show the people God's perspective on their sin and rebellion.

Isaiah tells us that the song he has to sing is a love song, a song "for my beloved" (5:1). His beloved is God, and his song will be sung for God's people. The people are pictured as a vineyard, which God has planted for the purpose of growing grapes. The song that Isaiah sings speaks to the careful love and tenderness God gives to his people as he plants them and encourages them to grow. He prepares a place for the vineyard, clearing the area of stones. He builds a watchtower to protect it from intruders or any kind of damage. Yet despite everything God does for this vineyard, it doesn't do what it's supposed to do. It doesn't grow good grapes; it grows wild grapes. The fruit is inedible—worthless. Isaiah is painting a vivid picture of the sin of God's people.

By the time Isaiah gets to God's response, we understand where God is coming from. We'd be upset too if something we poured care, time, and love into didn't grow up like it should! God promises to take away his protection from his vineyard and allow it to be invaded. With God's wall gone, enemies will come to raid, conquer, and devour his people. Judgment is coming for God's sinful people who have continually refused to grow up the way God commands them.

This passage is for you and me as well! Jesus teaches that a good tree bears good fruit, and a bad tree bears bad fruit. We, believers in Jesus, are bought by the blood of Christ and now called to bear fruit for God our Father. While we're not saved by our fruit, it is nevertheless a good indication (according to Jesus) of the condition of our hearts, just as it was for God's people in ancient Israel. We, today, are God's vineyard, planted in Jesus Christ. He calls us to bear fruit in him, by the power of the Holy Spirit.

Pray to your Heavenly Father today that you would respond well to his gardening of your heart and soul. Ask him to enable you to grow well in him and to bear fruit for Jesus, your Savior.

Saved from Sin and Sent to Serve

In our reading of the Bible, one thing that's become abundantly clear is that God doesn't *need* people in order to accomplish his perfect purposes. Yet while God doesn't need people, he chooses to work through them as he works in this world. God can use anyone, but he delights to use people who love and cherish *him* as Lord and Savior.

What comes first is what *must* come first for anyone who truly puts his or her faith in God as Lord and Savior: a vision of God in all his holiness, glory, and splendor. Isaiah has a vision of God seated "upon a throne, high and lifted up" (6:1). He is surrounded by angels, who continually proclaim his perfect holiness and glory. God is so glorious and holy, in fact, that the earth shakes and smoke fills the space. For Isaiah—and for every true Christian—this is where salvation starts: with a vision of the holy, perfect, glorious God of the universe.

Next comes Isaiah's response—the right response of a sinful human being to the holiness of God. This response is all about humility and repentance. "Woe is me!" he cries. "For I am lost" (6:5). He admits that he has unclean lips; his sin makes him dirty in comparison to the holy God. Isaiah recognizes what we all need to see: apart from a miraculous act of God, we are infinitely separated from him because of our sin.

As one of the angels flies toward Isaiah, we are given a beautiful picture of atonement—God cleanses sinners and makes them clean. Isaiah's lips are touched with a burning coal from the altar, which is a picture of cleansing, ritual washing, and ultimately forgiveness. Isaiah—only by God's doing—has been made clean.

I think we too often stop here in our understanding of salvation. But this is not where Isaiah's encounter with God stops! He's had a true vision of God, repented of his sins, and been cleansed of his sin. Now God calls him into service for him. "Who will go for us?" God asks. Isaiah, now forgiven and set apart for God, immediately responds, "Here I am! Send me" (6:8). God saves his people by cleansing them of sin through Jesus, and then he sends them out to do his work in this world. That was the pattern for the prophet Isaiah; it is the pattern for every Christian as well.

Pray today that you would—with all God's people—rightly respond to God's salvation. Ask God to help you join his work in this world, which is all about knowing and worshiping Jesus and making him known to others.

Mighty God

Isaiah 6 looked at Isaiah's call from God. What was the message he was instructed to bring to God's people? One of judgment against sin—a message of God's wrath against the rebellion and stubborn idolatry of his people. That is exactly what we get as Isaiah 8 ends. "They will look to the earth," Isaiah says, "but behold, distress and darkness, the gloom of anguish" (8:22). Their sin is *that* bad, and God's holiness is *that* perfect!

Without looking back to Isaiah 8 like this, we don't appreciate and understand the way Isaiah 9 begins: "But there will be no gloom for her who was in anguish." If Isaiah 8 focuses on the gloom of God's judgment, Isaiah 9 is all about the end of that gloom! For God's people, there is still hope. Judgment is *not* the end of the story. How will this happen?

Isaiah introduces us to a figure—someone who brings light, hope, and peace: a king, but a king unlike any king before him. You've probably heard Isaiah's words at Christmas time: "The people who walked in darkness have seen a great light; those who dwelt in a land of deep darkness, on them has light shone" (9:2). How will God's people—ravaged by their own sin and humbled by God's judgment—ultimately stand again in hope, joy, and light? God will one day send them a child, a *Son*. And Isaiah doesn't hold back in describing the glory, power, and might of this child! He tells us, "The government shall be upon his shoulder, and his name shall be called Wonderful Counselor, Mighty God, Everlasting Father, Prince of Peace" (9:6).

Years later, at exactly the right time, a child was born—humbly, in a feeding trough in a barn. That child was God's Son, wrapped in human flesh. He was not the king God's people expected; he didn't defeat the Roman army and restore the earthly glories of Jerusalem and the Jewish nation. He came to die, to pay for the sins of God's people, and to rise from the dead to conquer death for them forever. Isaiah is pointing God's people forward to a great Savior—to Mighty God born in human flesh.

Pray today that you would see, understand, and praise God for the greatness of Jesus. Thank God that he addressed your deepest need—the darkness and gloom of your sin and separation from him—by providing his own Son, the great King, who laid down his life to save his people.

His Hand Is Stretched Out Still

What has gotten God so upset with his people? In this passage, Isaiah gets to the specifics of the sins of the Israelites. We see exactly what kinds of sins have made God so upset.

First, there is the sin of pride. What is this pride about? It has to do with their response to tragedy. Listen again to their words: "The bricks have fallen, but we will build with dressed stones" (9:10). When bad things happen, God's people are not responding as they should—by turning to God. They are proudly putting their faith in themselves and their ability to get things back to the way they were.

Second, there are bad leaders over the people. Isaiah says that "those who guide this people have been leading them astray" (9:16). The people are in trouble when those they are called to follow are leading them in a sinful direction!

Third, we come to a more general sin—an attitude of God's people. They are completely self-centered, and this leads to a total lack of satisfaction. Even though God's people have been living for their own purposes and appetites, they can't find lasting peace. "They slice meat on the right, but are still hungry, and they devour on the left, but are not satisfied" (9:20). This can become self-destructive, as Isaiah pictures the people devouring their own arms.

Fourth, and finally, Isaiah describes the sin of wealthy people who use their riches for greed and oppression. The prophet describes people who have wealth already, but who still insist on taking advantage of people with less. He cries woe on those who "turn aside the needy from justice and . . . rob the poor of my people of their right" (10:2).

For all these sins that have plagued the lives of God's people, Isaiah keeps repeating a refrain over and over: "For all this his anger has not turned away, and his hand is stretched out still" (9:12, 17, 21; 10:4). God's anger *will not* turn away from sin; his hand *will be* stretched out in judgment against evil.

The good news of the gospel is that while God's hand should be stretched out toward us in judgment, he chooses to stretch his hand out in judgment against his own Son instead. Take some time confessing sin to God; he loves it when his people turn back to him in repentance! Then thank him again for salvation in Jesus, the one who took our judgment.

Renewed Strength

While there are glimpses of future hope and salvation, Isaiah 1–39 do center on the theme of God's judgment against his sinful people. In Isaiah 40, a shift takes place. The prophecies begin to change from judgment to future salvation and hope. You can feel this change even in the first verse of Isaiah 40: "Comfort, comfort my people, says your God" (40:1). These words come to people who are experiencing God's judgment through exile. They are words that come to a sinful people whom God will, in his mercy, not completely destroy. Even this judgment—exile in a foreign land—is not the end of the story.

The chapter begins with a message of hope and ultimate forgiveness for the sins of God's people. "Speak tenderly to Jerusalem," Isaiah says, "and cry to her that her warfare is ended, that her iniquity is pardoned" (40:2). There will come a day, the prophet is saying, when God will finally pardon the sins of his people. He will not totally destroy them, but he will speak tenderly to them by forgiving and saving them.

What happens next is, really, a vision of God. He is, in himself, the ultimate answer to the problems of the people. The people need—more than anything else—to see God clearly in the midst of judgment. That's what the herald says to God's people: "Behold your God!" (40:9). He "comes with might," and yet he will "tend his flock like a shepherd" (40:10, 11). Man-made idols could never compare to this infinitely powerful and infinitely holy God, and nothing is hidden from his sight and knowledge. And with Isaiah's vision of the coming of God is *hope*. Hope for God's people in the midst of judgment. Hope in his ultimate salvation and forgiveness. Hope that the exile is not the end of God's plan for them. The chapter ends with a beautiful declaration of the strength of those who wait for God: "They who wait for the LORD shall renew their strength; they shall mount up with wings like eagles; they shall run and not be weary; they shall walk and not faint" (40:31). God's people need . . . God. Isaiah is reminding the people that God himself is their rock, their salvation, the almighty One, and their only true hope.

Confess your sin to the one who shows mercy to sinners through his own Son. Get your vision of God straight as you approach him in prayer, and thank him that he has graciously made a way for you to approach him—and even know him personally!

First Servant Song

When Isaiah speaks these words to God's people in the second part of this book, they are in exile, far from home, living under the discipline of God because of their continual sin, idolatry, and rebellion. Humanly speaking, their situation is a total mess. They've made it a mess because of their sin! God will make things right; we know that. But we haven't known exactly *how* God will do this. He will bring salvation and lasting joy to his people, not through an army, nation, or great city but through a person.

Here we come to the first of four Servant Songs in Isaiah. These songs point us to one person chosen by God to bring about his salvation for his people. These songs of the prophet begin, in their historical context, to develop a hope in the hearts of God's people for the Messiah who will one day come. This chosen one will be a great servant of God and a great leader for God's people. He will be the ultimate answer to their mess.

First, he is a chosen servant who will bring justice. In other words, he will be God's instrument to establish God's rightness in the world. Second, he will have a certain amount of kindness, mercy, and even gentleness. Listen to how Isaiah describes the work, ministry, and leadership of this servant: "A bruised reed he will not break, and a faintly burning wick he will not quench" (42:3). This servant will not be an oppressive ruler, but he will be kind and gentle with people who are weak, vulnerable, and oppressed. Third, this servant will be chosen, empowered, and sent by God himself; he will serve as God's covenant to God's people. Isaiah is saying that, in some way, this servant of God will *embody* God's covenant promises to his people.

It's not hard to see, even after reading just one of these four servant songs, that these promises and descriptions could never be fulfilled by a servant who is merely human. They describe a leader who is larger than life—divine, even. These are promises that we believe are only ultimately fulfilled in the great Messiah of God's people: Jesus Christ, God's Son.

We need to find our way to God's chosen servant: the Messiah. It's Jesus who will bring about God's perfect justice in this world. It's Jesus who will care for weak and broken people. It's Jesus who will embody God's promises of salvation to us. Find your hope—the solution to your mess of sin—in the right person. Thank God for the salvation and the eternal promise you have in him.

Brutal Babylonians

By this point in Isaiah, we've heard a lot about God's judgment and wrath against his own people. He is angry with them, frustrated by their continual sin and rebellion, and he has finally responded by allowing them to be captured by the Babylonians and taken into exile. But what about the Babylonians? God used them to punish and discipline his people, yes, but aren't they still guilty of violence, greed, and cruelty against God's people? In Isaiah 47, we find God's resounding answer to this question: *Yes!* God does use Babylon to judge his people, but that does not mean that Babylon is off the hook. They too will come under God's judgment because of their sin, even though they have functioned as part of God's infinitely wise plan for his people.

Isaiah begins the chapter with a call to Babylon: "Come down and sit in the dust, O virgin daughter of Babylon; sit on the ground without a throne" (47:1). This phrase speaks to a great humiliation; the nation that has been wealthy, powerful, and influential will be humbled to the dust by God's judgment on their sin. But there will be more humiliation than this: "Your nakedness shall be uncovered, and your disgrace shall be seen. I will take vengeance, and I will spare no one" (47:3). God's judgment on the nation of Babylon will be complete, brutal, and humiliating. Why? Because, despite their role in God's plan, God's people are still God's people! Listen to the basis that Isaiah gives for the coming judgment of God on Babylon: "I was angry with my people; I profaned my heritage; I gave them into your hand; you showed them no mercy" (47:6). Even though the exile was God's judgment on the sin of his people, he still holds the Babylonians responsible for their brutal treatment of the Israelites. While God's judgment didn't come on them right away, they were mistaken to feel secure in their wickedness!

Friend, this is a stern reminder to us today. God is not blind to sin. Even though he chose to use Babylon as part of his glorious purposes for the discipline of his people, that did not mean that the Babylonians were not responsible for their actions. God always judges sin; he is not blind.

Thank God that he provided a way for us to escape from his judgment, the judgment that we, like the Babylonians, so truly deserve. Pray that he would help you lean every day more on Jesus, our hope for salvation, who took God's judgment in our place!

Final Servant Song

When David approached Goliath in 1 Samuel 17, the giant Philistine was not at all impressed. In fact, Goliath "disdained [David], for he was but a youth" (1 Sam. 17:42). But despite his unimpressive appearance David turned out to be the right servant to defeat the threat.

The servant that Isaiah describes is similarly unimpressive, at least according to outward appearances. In this, the final of the four Servant Songs, he tells us that this chosen servant of God is *not* chosen because of his stature, good looks, or charisma. In fact, it's quite the opposite. Listen to how Isaiah describes the servant of God: "He was despised and rejected by men, a man of sorrows and acquainted with grief; and as one from whom men hide their faces he was despised, and we esteemed him not" (53:3). So what will this servant be all about, if not outward appearances?

First, Isaiah shows God's people that this servant will be about, ultimately, a kind of *substitution*. He will function as someone who will stand in the place of guilty sinners who deserve punishment from God for their sins. "But he was pierced for our transgressions," Isaiah writes, "he was crushed for our iniquities; upon him was the chastisement that brought us peace, and with his wounds we are healed" (53:5). Not only does this servant act as the substitute for God's people by bearing their sin; he also does this *willingly*. Isaiah tells us that "he opened not his mouth," as he is led away to slaughter on behalf of the people (53:7).

Second, Isaiah shows God's people that this substitutionary act of the servant is the main substance of God's plan to save many people through him. This is no small act from the servant; it will accomplish God's salvation for lots and lots of people! Here's what Isaiah says about what the servant's suffering will accomplish: "By his knowledge shall the righteous one, my servant, make many to be accounted righteous, and he shall bear their iniquities" (53:11).

This passage points us explicitly to the life and work of God's Son, Jesus Christ. Many other places hint at the fact that someone is coming; this passage tells us what that someone will do for God's people—*how* he will deliver them! It will happen through his sacrificial death.

Ask God to help you follow the suffering servant no matter what. Pray that he would help you treasure Jesus—his Son who suffered for your sins to make you righteous before God.

Ready to Be Found

How do you think about God? Sometimes, when we read passage after passage in an Old Testament book like Isaiah, focused on God's judgment, we can begin to get a skewed picture of God. We can begin to see him as the great "ogre in the sky," who takes pleasure in punishing his people. That could not be further from the truth! In this chapter—very near the end of the book of Isaiah—we are reminded of God's heart for his people. So, what does God want for the people he loves?

God wants them to experience his salvation and to be brought into a perfect relationship with him. Listen to Isaiah's record of God's words: "I was ready to be sought by those who did not ask for me; I was ready to be found by those who did not seek me. I said, 'Here I am, here I am,' to a nation that was not called by my name. I spread out my hands all the day to a rebellious people" (65:1–2). That is our God spreading out his hands to his people, always ready to be found by sinful people who will turn to him with hearts of genuine repentance. Yet sadly the response of even God's chosen people—the Israelites—was rebellion against God's word and God's love for them. They provoked God with their sin, disobeyed his commands, and continued in attitudes of pride and self-sufficiency. It is because of *this* that God's judgment comes.

Yet as the book of Isaiah draws to a close, the prophet again reminds us of God's ultimate grace and salvation for those who are truly his people. The good news of even this book, which is so full of judgment, is that God says that he will not destroy them all. God will not completely abandon his people—*ever*. He will ultimately find a way to accomplish lasting salvation for his true people, even as his judgment finally falls on those who reject him permanently. It's this future salvation that Isaiah sits on as the chapter ends. The prophet gives us a vision of the future glory of the mountain of the Lord—the place where God's people will gather together in worship and in perfect relationship with their God.

God has always been patient, merciful, and gentle with his people, and he has provided—in the death of his Son—the ultimate solution to their sin and a way for them to dwell forever with him in the new heaven and new earth. That is the God we serve. Pray to him. Thank him again for forgiveness of sins through Christ.

Faithful to the Word

Have you ever been asked to do something that was extremely difficult, particularly because of deeply personal implications? The call for Jeremiah is to stand against his people, on behalf of God, to declare to them God's anger with their sin. It's not surprising that Jeremiah's first response is to try to get out of this job! After all, he is quite young, and he tells God so: "I do not know how to speak, for I am only a youth" (1:6). But God won't let him off the hook so easily. Despite Jeremiah's age, God affirms that he has chosen Jeremiah specifically for this role: "I appointed you a prophet to the nations," God says, after reminding Jeremiah that he knew him—and formed him—before he was even born (1:5).

Like the prophet Isaiah, Jeremiah ministers to the people of God by speaking God's word to them during the reign of several different kings. His prophetic ministry continues up until the defeat of Jerusalem by Babylon; he is a preexilic prophet, who brings a message of warning to God's people, telling them about the impending judgment of God that is coming because of their sin against him.

As we mentioned, the message that God calls Jeremiah to bring to the people is not an easy or a popular one. It is a message of impending judgment. God tells Jeremiah that he, God, is busy calling the tribes of the kingdoms of the north to gather together in battle against Jerusalem, the capital city of Israel. Such a military force would mean sure defeat and destruction for God's people; they wouldn't stand a chance. Why is God prepared to do such a thing to his people? Because of their sin. "They have made offerings to other gods and worshiped the works of their own hands," declares God to his prophet Jeremiah (1:16). The idolatry, rebellion, and failure of God's people will finally catch up to them; that is Jeremiah's message.

While none of us today are like Jeremiah exactly, we are nonetheless all called by God to faithfully speak and live his word in difficult contexts, relationships, and situations. Age doesn't matter in this calling! If you belong to Christ, you can speak God's word to the people around you and live faithfully to the God who has called you to be his own.

Ask God to help you to be faithful to him and his word even when it's difficult or unpopular. Pray that he would help you to see loyalty to him as your first priority in life.

Once upon a Time

How many fairy tales begin with that well-worn phrase, "Once upon a time . . ."? In the first three verses of Jeremiah 2, the prophet reminds God's people what life was like once upon a time. He shares God's words with the people of Israel: "I remember the devotion of your youth, your love as a bride, how you followed me in the wilderness" (2:2). It's a picture of God's people going out from slavery in Egypt, chosen and holy.

But God's people repeatedly turned away from God, choosing other things to worship, love, and adore. Jeremiah uses metaphors that are far from flattering to describe God's sinful people and their rebellion:

- They have exchanged their glory for worthless things.
- They have rejected the true water of life and dug cisterns for themselves that hold no water.
- They have become like a wild vine that is good for nothing.
- They are so dirty from their sin that a good scrubbing with soap won't clean them!
- They are like a donkey or a camel that sniffs around in order to mate.

God's people have turned away from him and gone after everything *but* him. Jeremiah doesn't hold back from comparing them to stupid, lusting animals in their rejection of the one true God. The ironic twist comes in verses 26–28: when God's people get into trouble, *then* they cry out to God for help, even though they have rejected him again and again. God's response to this? Let the gods—the false, lifeless ones that the people have chosen over him—come to their rescue. He is fed up with the way the people keep turning to false gods and counterfeit saviors.

This chapter is a vivid and even harsh reminder to God's people—then and now—that the alternatives to the God of the universe are not good ones! It is so foolish to give our worship, allegiance, and adoration to anything or anyone other than the God who loves us and saves us through his Son. Yet you and I are tempted to do this!

We all need this reminder; we need Jeremiah's vivid picture of what sin and turning away from the one true God looks like. Ask God to keep you in the only right place: satisfied in worshiping him alone.

Refused to Repent

From the beginning of his dealings with his people, God has never demanded sinless perfection by their own strength. That's why Jesus, God's Son, finally comes—to provide the perfect forgiveness and righteousness that God's people desperately need! What *has* God always demanded from his people in every age? Repentance and faith in him.

It's precisely these things that God's people—in Jeremiah's context—are failing to show. No matter the warnings from God and his prophets, they continue to demonstrate an absolute refusal to repent of their sin and turn back to God in faith. Here's how the prophet Jeremiah puts it: "You have struck them down, but they felt no anguish; you have consumed them, but they refused to take correction. They have made their faces harder than rock; they have refused to repent" (5:3). Despite God's smaller judgments for his people's sin, they have continually refused to repent—to turn from their sins and turn back to their God.

It is not simply because of sin that God's judgment will come. Sin is the root cause, yes, but judgment comes specifically because God's people refuse to repent of their sin. It's this stubborn, hardened, calloused condition of the heart that finally brings God's judgment on his people. And it will be a fierce judgment. Just look at some of the ways Jeremiah describes God's hand of punishment on his people. Their crops will be destroyed. A foreign nation will come to destroy the land and make slaves of Israel. Terrible times are coming for God's unrepentant people, and Jeremiah is God's mouthpiece to declare all this to them.

This isn't a chapter where we expect to see a hint of God's grace, but that's exactly what we see next: the surprising mercy of God. Despite the terrible sins of God's people—and their failure to repent of them—God will not wipe them off the face of the earth. "Even in those days, declares the LORD, I will not make a full end of you" (5:18). God still wants to *teach* his people; he still desires their repentance and return to him!

What does God demand from you? The same thing he wanted from his people in Jeremiah's day: repentance from sin and faith in him. Take some time to repent again of your sin. Confess it to God, thank him for forgiveness through Jesus's death, and turn from your sin to him. Then pray that he would give you faith in him—faith that demonstrates itself by more and more obedience to him!

The Potter and His Clay

From time to time, certain dogs decide to test their owners to see if they are still in charge. Evidently, this is a characteristic of English boxers; they want to run the house, if at all possible! So when the dog gets in one of these moods, he'll charge and "attack" to see if he can get the best of his owners. Thankfully, it's not difficult for humans to remind the dog that—still—he is not the one in charge of the house! In Jeremiah 18, the perspective given to us by God's prophet serves as a similar reminder to God's sinful people about who is in charge. Jeremiah's picture? A potter and his clay.

As Jeremiah watches the potter mold his clay, ruining one batch and then remolding it the way he wants, God gives him the explanation of the image. "O house of Israel," God says, "can I not do with you as this potter has done?" (18:6). "I am the potter," God says! He is the one in control of his people. He, as the Creator of all things, has *infinite right* to do what he pleases with the people he has made. Amazingly, God allows his plans for the people he shapes to be influenced by their repentance and fear of him. If his people turn from their sins to him, he promises to deal with them gently and lovingly.

When we see God's role with his people in these terms—as a potter molding his clay—we begin to understand how completely foolish, stubborn, and stupid is the rebellion of the clay. The potter has infinite control over the clay; clay can't rise up and force the potter's hand into making it into whatever it wants! The role of the clay is to allow itself to be formed as the potter sees fit—to submit to the will of its maker. Rebellion by the clay is ridiculous!

Yet rebellion is precisely what God's people choose. God quotes back to them their attitude toward him: "We will follow our own plans, and will every one act according to the stubbornness of his evil heart" (18:12). Because of this ridiculously sinful attitude, God again promises judgment on his clay people who continue to choose sin rather than submission to his perfect word.

Thank God today for accepting you through Christ, even though you in your sin have rejected his perfect plans and rule in your life. Ask him to give you grace by his Holy Spirit to accept even more willingly and joyfully his forming and shaping of your life, according to his perfect will.

New Covenant

Duct tape can be used in many ways and can fix many problems, right? But some toys, sports equipment, and tools that are broken need something greater than duct tape to be fixed; they need a lasting solution. As wonderful as duct tape is, it will never get to the heart of the issue!

In Jeremiah 31, the prophet looks far ahead to a new day for God's people. There will come a day, he says, when—after judgment—God will bring a lasting solution to the problems, sin, and rebellion of his people. Someday, Jeremiah says, God will finally deal with his people's sin and enable them to live with and for him in a lasting way. No more duct tape; this will be final.

The way Jeremiah describes this future day is in terms of a new covenant. This new covenant will be similar to the old covenant with Abraham, but it will have a finality and a permanence to it. God will write his law on the hearts of the people. No longer will God's people need to tell and teach one another about God and his ways, because everyone will know him in the community of God's people. There will be final forgiveness for sin; God says he will remember their iniquities no more. We find too that this will be a final situation—rebellion, idolatry, or exile will never again turn God's people away from him. Jeremiah turns our eyes forward to a wonderful day—a day when God will deal with his people's sins forever, when people will have God's word on their hearts, not just in their ears!

You don't hear the words "new covenant" again for a while in the Bible. Then, years later, they jump off the page at us. In an upper room with his disciples, *Jesus* speaks those same words as he prepares to go to the cross to die. As he pours out wine for his disciples at the Last Supper, Jesus tells them that the cup is the "new covenant in [his] blood" (Luke 22:20). What will be the lasting solution for God's people? What will be the sacrifice that covers their sins forever and pays the penalty of death for them? The blood of Jesus.

We need to be daily returning to the basis and foundation of God's new covenant with us—sealed by the blood of his own Son, Jesus. In him we find forgiveness, salvation, eternal life, and lasting righteousness before a holy God. Thank God for the great promise we have in him—written in the blood of the very Son of God.

Gloom and Doom

Jeremiah's words—and those of other prophets—have been ignored. Repentance has not happened, and so God's judgment finally falls on his sinful, stubborn people. Yet even this dark chapter is not devoid of hope!

Jeremiah 52 begins with the rebellion of the king of Judah—Zedekiah—against the nation of Babylon, a great ruling power of the day. The king of Babylon responds with a swift and cruel invasion. The city is besieged, it falls before too long, and Nebuchadnezzar takes control. Zedekiah is dragged out, his sons are slaughtered while he watches, and—with his eyes gouged out—he is taken away as a slave to Babylon.

In the midst of this invasion of the Babylonians, the unthinkable happens: the temple of God is destroyed. The place of worship for God's people is ransacked by pagans who fear neither God nor his word. While the temple is destroyed with fire, the valuable objects used for worship are dragged off by the Babylonian forces.

Next, we see thousands of God's people taken into exile to Babylon. They are dragged off as slaves, forcibly removed from the land of promise that God gave to them so many years ago. So we are forced to ask this question as the book of Jeremiah ends: "What will become of God's kingdom?" God's judgment has rained down on his people; he has used an evil nation to uproot them from his place. But what about God's rule? And what about God's promises to Abraham, to Isaac, and to David?

As the book ends, we find in the last few verses a glimmer of hope. His people have been taken out of his place, but his *rule* is far from vanquished! In the midst of battle, brutality, and conquest, the king of Babylon mysteriously chooses to deal kindly with Jehoiachin, the king of Judah, during the thirty-seventh year of the exile. He gives him a seat at his table and preserves his life. God is preserving his people even there and allowing the line of David to survive. After all, it was to David that God had spoken of a "forever King" descended from him. And that great King is yet to come at this point in the story.

Confess to God the ways you have not taken your sin seriously enough; ask him to show you the depths of your need for him and his grace. Then spend some time praising him for his perfect plan—the plan that has its climax in the coming of the great Son of David, who is the final answer to the sin, exile, and rebellion of God's people.

Is This the End?

Whoever the author of Lamentations was, he had a front-row seat to the devastation of Jerusalem and the reality of the exile. Lamentations contains the weeping words of someone who loves God's people and God's place and mourns the ravages of sin that have finally swept over them.

The book of Lamentations can be confusing because it's hard to tell who's talking. Just in Lamentations 1 the writer switches back and forth between *describing* the devastation of Jerusalem and *speaking on behalf* of Jerusalem, as if the city itself has feelings and a voice. The total picture, though, is clear. The capital city of God's people has been devastated. This is cause for weeping, both from God's people and even, in a way, from the city itself.

We need to see—with sadness and tears—the awful horrors that come from stubborn sin and a lack of repentance. Sin brings devastation. The picture of Jerusalem—filthy and afflicted—is a picture of what sin will ultimately do to human lives apart from the grace of Jesus Christ. For the people of God in ancient Israel, it would have been unthinkable that Jerusalem could be conquered and burned to the ground. God would surely never let that happen to his special place! The book of Lamentations reminds us that this *really did* happen.

We need to see, though, that even a book like Lamentations is not without hope. The story of God's work in the lives of his people could end here, with the exile. But it doesn't. Even in the words of Jerusalem in the second half of the chapter, we begin to see the attitude that God has always desired from his people: repentance. The author puts these words in the mouth of the city: "The Lord is in the right, for I have rebelled against his word" (1:18). Finally, there will be hope for those who return to God in repentance, trusting in his perfect mercy. He is the one, after all, whose "mercies never come to an end" (3:22). And we know that is true, because the Bible doesn't end with Lamentations!

The exile to Babylon was not the end of the story for God's people, and our sin is not the end of the story for us, although God would be justified in wiping us all off the pages of history! But he gives grace in Jesus. Thank him for providing an answer to the great lament of sin and judgment. Ask him to help you to be a voice of hope in a fallen world—pointing people to his Son, the Savior.

The Holiness of God

A few basic facts will help you get an initial feel for the book of Ezekiel. First, Ezekiel has been in exile in Babylon for about five years by the time he starts prophesying. So he's speaking to people who have already begun to experience the judgment of God against their sin. Second, Ezekiel generally directs his words to three main areas: judgment on God's people, judgment on God's enemies, and the final future day of God's restoration and salvation for his people. Third, the *holiness* of God is a huge theme for Ezekiel.

After a few years of exile in Babylon, Ezekiel tells us that he sees visions of God. The vision of God's glory begins with a "stormy wind," a "great cloud," and a "fire flashing" (1:4). Out of this strange and glorious mass emerge four living creatures—angels of God. These angelic beings dart around quickly, Ezekiel says, like a "flash of lightning" (1:14). Next, Ezekiel sees a wheel—not just a wheel but a wheel within a wheel. This gyroscopic object moves along with the angelic beings, linked in some way to their movement. Finally, above a great expanse that sits above the creatures and the wheels, Ezekiel sees something like a throne, with a humanlike figure seated above it. This figure is full of fire, brightness, and rainbowlike splendor. No picture, movie, or illustration could ever do justice to what Ezekiel saw!

And that is the first point that needs to be made here: the glory of God is beyond the capacity of human speech or description. Ezekiel is using the best words he can to describe this appearance of God's glory, but he only has human words to recount what he sees! Our glorious God is gloriously *other*.

Well, even if Ezekiel can't do justice with his words to the vision of God that he sees, he gets the response to the glory of God exactly right. Confronted with this picture of God's infinite holiness, splendor, and glory, he falls on his face. And, as the chapter ends, we find that this glorious God—in his mercy—has something for Ezekiel. To this simple mortal, the God of glory begins to speak.

We must not forget the otherness of our God. We should run to him as our friend, yes, but we should also regularly fall on our faces before him. We ought to thank him with grateful hearts that, by the blood of Jesus, we can draw near to a holy God and love and know him personally.

A Scroll as Sweet as Honey

Ezekiel is called to go to the people of Israel—God's people—who have chosen a path of rebellion, stubbornness, and sin. God tells the prophet, "Son of man, I send you to the people of Israel, to nations of rebels, who have rebelled against me. They and their fathers have transgressed against me to this very day. The descendants also are impudent and stubborn: I send you to them" (2:3–4). Not a very flattering description of Ezekiel's audience! So, if this is Ezekiel's audience, what message will he bring? He will bring God's words of judgment to God's people. The imagery that we find for this passing of God's word from him to Ezekiel is striking; Ezekiel receives a scroll (representing God's word) and *eats it!*

The surprise in this part of the passage is the taste of God's words to Ezekiel. He describes it this way: "So I opened my mouth, and he gave me this scroll to eat. . . . I ate it, and it was in my mouth as sweet as honey" (3:2–3). Even though Ezekiel's words are words of judgment, they taste sweet to him, because they are God's true words for his people.

Like Ezekiel, we are called to digest God's word and then speak it to others! Here's the wonderful thing about this, which we learn from the first two chapters of Ezekiel: the holy and glorious God of the universe chooses to use human beings in his perfect plan. At the end of chapter 1, Ezekiel was flat on his face! Then God, in his grace and mercy, picks up this human being and begins to use him as part of his sovereign work in the world.

Yet following the call of God will not necessarily be easy. While the words of God given to Ezekiel are sweet, the work that he has in front of him is not fun work! This passage ends with a slightly downcast prophet: "The Spirit lifted me up and took me away, and I went in bitterness in the heat of my spirit, the hand of the LORD being strong upon me" (3:14). As Ezekiel makes his way toward God's exiled people, with a message of judgment for their rebellious hearts, he carries with him the weight of God's word. His message will not be a popular one!

Ask God to help you grow in your love for his word. Pray that, as you feed on it daily, you would—like Ezekiel—have his message to share with the people around you.

Gone from the Temple

Angelic beings and strange spinning wheels symbolize and accompany the magnificent presence of God. What is God's purpose in again showing Ezekiel this picture of his glory and holiness? It's to show the prophet that God is intimately, gloriously involved in the judgment of his people. God's command to his angel is this: "Fill your hands with burning coals from between the cherubim, and scatter them over the city" (10:2). Verses 6–8 also carry forward this picture of fire, held over the city by the angelic beings. It is a picture of judgment—fiery and sure.

If God is present with his people—especially in the temple where they meet for worship of him—is God essentially bringing judgment on himself? Is that even possible? Verses 9–22 answer these questions; they show us the removal of God's glorious presence from the temple. Here's the striking image that Ezekiel the prophet sees: "The glory of the LORD went out from the threshold of the house, and stood over the cherubim" (10:18). The glorious God of Israel is withdrawing his presence from the temple of his people, the meeting place for worship.

What would have been the great shock—and the great lesson—for God's people who heard this prophecy? They still would have been reeling from the fact that the *temple* had been destroyed. Had God been defeated? This chapter gives us the answer to that question: *No!* God has, at this point in history, voluntarily withdrawn his hand of protection from his people to judge their sin. Ezekiel shows us how this was even possible: God's presence retreats from the heart of the city—the temple—and allows his people to be defeated, humiliated, and taken away.

This passage reminds us to not make anything in our Christian lives into a lucky charm. God's people in Israel probably thought that no matter what they did, God wouldn't *actually* allow his temple to be destroyed. God chose to graciously meet with his people at temple worship, but he wasn't attached to the temple in some magical way. When his people's sin became so serious and rebellious, God removed himself from that connection to the temple and allowed them to suffer the consequences of their sins. God is serious about dealing with sin.

As you pray to an infinitely holy and glorious God, remember to thank him for bringing judgment to an end for you in Jesus. Ask him to help you cling to Christ, as your great temple, which God will never abandon.

The Story of an Unfaithful Wife

God is giving Ezekiel a story to tell to his people—a poignant illustration of their relationship with him and their rebellion against him. You see, it's one thing to keep on saying, "You have sinned against God." It's quite another to share a heart-wrenching story of an unfaithful wife, who throws every gift, kindness, and blessing back in the face of her faithful and loving husband.

As the story begins, we see the loving care of God for his people. First, he takes them in as a discarded, unwanted, bloody orphan. There Israel was, God says, birthed in the midst of a pagan world and wallowing in their own blood. God's words are beautiful: "I made you flourish like a plant of the field. And you grew up and became tall and arrived at full adornment" (16:7). God mercifully chose a people for himself, blessed them, cared for them, and helped them grow into full beauty.

Next, God shows covenant marriage love to his people. God, after playing the father to his people, now functions as a faithful husband. He now clothes and blesses his people—like a beautiful bride. "I adorned you with ornaments," God says (16:11). "And your renown went forth among the nations because of your beauty, for it was perfect through the splendor that I had bestowed on you" (16:14). This is a vivid picture of the blessing and splendor of the nation of Israel. God has been good to his bride; he has kept all his promises to her!

Finally, though, God's people abuse God's blessing and whore with the nations around them. From verses 15–34, Ezekiel goes on and on about the unfaithfulness—the whoring—of God's people through idolatry, pride, and even child sacrifice, like the pagan nations around them. It's because of this that judgment will come. God says that he will judge his people with the very nations that were so attractive to them. It's no small thing for God's people to turn against him! Their rebellion is like a beloved wife running after another man, spitting in the face of her faithful husband who has loved her so well.

As you pray, confess to God the ways that you have taken sin too lightly. Ask him for forgiveness for how—perhaps even this week—you have rebelled against his covenant love for you. Remember the depth of the forgiveness that is found in Jesus Christ, his Son, the head of God's church.

Not Off the Hook!

Even in the midst of your parents' discipline of you, you never *stopped* being their child! Your parents may have spanked you because you did something wrong, but they probably still fed you dinner and allowed you to keep living in the house. What we begin to find in Ezekiel 25 is a similar idea between God and his people. His words and actions of judgment toward them for their sin have been fierce and fiery (and rightly so!). But he is *still* not done with his people. We see his heart for them through his fierce judgment of the nations that have abused them.

This chapter begins a big shift in focus for the entire book of Ezekiel—from God's judgment on his own people to God's judgment on the pagan nations surrounding them. This new section begins with God's words of judgment on Israel's immediate neighbors, the four nations directly bordering them: Ammon, Moab, Edom, and Philistia. While God has clearly not been happy with the behavior of his own people, who have turned away from him like an unfaithful wife, he is also angry with the nations who have rejoiced in—and contributed to—the downfall of Israel. These nations will not get off the hook!

Why is God so angry with these nations? It has to do specifically with their treatment of his beloved people. Even as he judges his own people, he does not forget his protective care for them. Look, for example, at God's words to Ammon: "Because you said, 'Aha!' over my sanctuary when it was profaned, and over the land of Israel when it was made desolate, and over the house of Judah when they went into exile, therefore behold, I am handing you over to the people of the East" (25:3–4). Even as God judges his own people, he continues to act on their behalf through calling their enemies to account.

This chapter—though it comes out of a dark place in the story of God's people—can and should point us forward to the ultimate source of victory, protection, and even judgment that God provides for his people: Jesus Christ, his Son. *He* is God's ultimate protection for his people; he alone can conquer their greatest enemies, including their own sin.

What a faithful, patient, and loving God! That is our God: the God who did not stop working to save his people, the God who took human flesh and entered the story to take judgment on himself for his people's sake. Thank God for his amazing—even shocking—faithfulness to unfaithful people.

He Restores My Soul

After a well-explained punishment is over, what should happen between a parent and a child? *Restoration.* You actually see this often, especially when young children are disciplined by a loving parent. When the spanking or scolding is done, what often comes next? A big hug!

The book of Ezekiel began with judgment against God's *own people.* It brought them into judgment through exile—and that's where we found Ezekiel. Then Ezekiel's words moved toward judgment against the *enemies of God's people*—the surrounding nations who had abused God's people and contributed to their sin and destruction. Finally, Ezekiel begins to look forward, past the exile to a time of salvation, joy, and *restoration* for God's people. In Ezekiel 34, this restoration comes through God assuming the role as the shepherd for his people.

As we've seen before in other historical and prophetic books, the shepherds of God's people have failed to lead them well. The chapter begins with God calling out these bad shepherds. God says to them, "Should not the shepherds feed the sheep?" (34:2). Israel's leaders have been selfish, greedy, and uncaring toward the flock of God's people. So, what is God's *restorative* solution to this problem?

God promises that he himself will serve as the ultimate shepherd for his people: "Behold, I, I myself will search for my sheep. . . . I will rescue them from all places where they have been scattered" (34:11–12). God's people have been ruled by selfish and abusive shepherds; it's time for God to personally serve as the loving and caring shepherd of his flock. But there's one more piece to these words of restoration to God's people. God won't act alone in this shepherding role; there will be someone else involved. Who? God's servant David: "And I will set up over them one shepherd, my servant David, and he shall feed them. . . . And I, the LORD, will be their God, and my servant David shall be prince among them" (34:23–24). Just in case you forgot, King David is long dead at this point in the Bible story! And yet God is pointing his people to a perfect shepherd—in the line of King David—who will reign with God the Father over his people as a shepherd.

Pray today that you would rest in God and his great shepherd, Jesus, even in times of frustration, heartache, and struggle. Ask God to help you trust his loving care for you and his perfect plan for each day of your life.

Valley of Dry Bones

Ezekiel is brought by the Spirit of the Lord into a vision of a valley. The very fact that the valley is littered with bones gives us a big hint that the people to whom these bones belonged are dead. But Ezekiel goes out of his way to tell us that these were *very dry* bones. In other words, God shows the prophet a valley that is filled with the bones of people who are *very* dead. Then God gives Ezekiel a strange and almost silly command: "Prophesy over these bones" (37:4). As Ezekiel speaks, the bones begin to rise up, join together, and grow human flesh on them, until finally the entire valley is filled with a great army of very alive human beings.

Here's what God tells the prophet: "Son of Man, these bones are the whole house of Israel. Behold, they say, 'Our bones are dried up, and our hope is lost; we are indeed cut off.' . . . Behold, I will open your graves and raise you from your graves, O my people. And I will bring you into the land of Israel" (37:11–12). God is speaking again to his people about the *restoration* that will come, even after the judgment of the exile to Babylon. Even though God's people look at themselves and their nation as essentially dead, dried up, and hopeless, God promises through this vision to his prophet to one day restore them to their land.

While God is clearly talking about his people returning from the exile to the land, he hints at something eternal—and even more spiritual—about this vision. "I will put my Spirit within you, and you shall live," God tells his people (37:14). He seems to be hinting that something great is coming—some *change* that God will make to enable his Spirit to dwell in his people in a lasting and powerful way. Jesus, in fact, seems to think about this passage in Ezekiel that way. If you want to do a little extra reading, look at Jesus's interaction with Nicodemus in John 3. The words he uses to speak to Nicodemus about conversion and salvation—wind, spirit, flesh—seem to tell us that Jesus saw Ezekiel 37 as a picture of being "born again" (John 3:3), that is, born of the Spirit, not of the flesh. This is God's ultimate restoration for his people!

Thank God for this drastic and miraculous work he's done in your heart through his Spirit. Thank him that you know him eternally—that you live in newness of life. Let that reality motivate you as you live for him today.

Lions, Fires, and Prayers—Oh My!

When we come to the book of Daniel, we discover that we're still in the midst of the exile. The book of Daniel, though, homes in for us on what the exile meant for one man: the prophet Daniel. This book reminds us that the exile doesn't mean that God is done with his people. Far from it! There are three things to consider about this passage.

First, remember that the events of this passage unfold during a time of great trouble and suffering. Sometimes, the stories of the book of Daniel can become so familiar, childlike, and fun, that we forget the real fear and genuine hardship that came with them. The accounts of the lions' den and the fiery furnace are not just fun stories; they involved real danger and real deliverance for God's people from their enemies. In this passage, we also can't forget the situation of Daniel and his friends. The chapter ends well, yes, but they were still living in Babylon as exiles—ripped from their homes and families by the Babylonian armies.

Second, see that Daniel and his friends hold tightly to their identity as God's people—no matter what. The choice of Daniel and his friends wouldn't have been an easy one! As they—with many other young men—were trained and taught the ways of Babylon, the pressure to fit in and do well would have been immense! It's in that kind of context that they make their decision: "Daniel resolved that he would not defile himself with the king's food, or with the wine that he drank" (1:8). Daniel and his friends don't want to do *anything* that would compromise their distinctive identity as God's people.

Third, note from this passage that God's hand stretches even to Babylon. Just because his people have been taken out of their land doesn't mean that God can't still take care of them and bless them! In fact, God does much more than simply bless *them!* He blesses the king of Babylon through them; the king begins to rely on them as wise advisors, who are more equipped to help him than all the magicians and enchanters of his land. God is not just the God of the *land* of Israel!

Pray that your love for Jesus would motivate you to commit to him. Ask God to help you embrace your identity as his follower so that you can stand strong against pressure, temptation, and the attacks of the devil.

Revealer of Mysteries

Daniel 2 begins with a problem: Nebuchadnezzar, the king of Babylon, is tormented by troubling dreams. These dreams are so troubling, in fact, that he determines to discover their meaning. So he raises the stakes with his go-to magicians and wise men. Without revealing the dream to them, he asks them to not only interpret the dream to him but also to tell him the content of the dream. The request is ludicrous, and the wise men tell him so. This doesn't sit well with the king, who commands that all wise men in the country should be destroyed. Unfortunately for Daniel and his friends, "wise men" includes them!

Daniel goes to King Nebuchadnezzar to both *recount* and *interpret* the king's dream to him. By God's strength and wisdom, Daniel is able to miraculously perform this amazing task! He both identifies the events of the dream and interprets their meaning, which concerns the rise and fall of earthly kingdoms that will finally end with God's eternal kingdom being established forever. The passage ends with Daniel's exultation to a prominent place in the king's court. A happy ending, at least for now. Direct your attention to two statements—one from Nebuchadnezzar and one from Daniel.

First, look at Daniel's words to the king as he stands before him ready to reveal the meaning of his dream: "No wise men, enchanters, magicians, or astrologers can show to the king the mystery that the king has asked, but there is a God in heaven who reveals mysteries, and he has made known to King Nebuchadnezzar what will be in the latter days" (2:27–28). Daniel takes even this opportunity to give all glory to his great God.

Second, look at Nebuchadnezzar's words after witnessing Daniel's interpretation of his dream. After falling on his face, this wealthy, powerful king says, "Truly, your God is God of gods and Lord of kings, and a revealer of mysteries, for you have been able to reveal this mystery" (2:47). Amazingly, this story ends with a pagan king giving glory to God as the true ruler over all other gods and earthly powers. This is what God is all about—then and now. God wants to use his people to declare his glory and to lead others to sing his praises as well.

Ask God to make you committed to spreading the fame of his glorious name to everyone around you. He is a God of grace, love, truth, power, and goodness; people who know him want others to know about him too!

For the Praise of His Glorious Name

In Daniel 6, the main idea is this: God is for the good of his people and the glory of his name—even in Babylon. His work with his people is not done yet, and his work for the praise of his glorious name among the nations is not done either!

A Persian king, Darius, now sits on the throne of Babylon, having defeated a king named Belshazzar, whom Daniel also served. Daniel's wisdom and gifts are recognized by Darius as well. The chapter begins with Daniel being promoted to a position of great influence and power, even over the whole kingdom. Not surprisingly, his promotion breeds incredible envy in the other leaders of the nation. They devise a plan, playing on Darius's vanity to get him to sign an injunction stating that all people in the land should pray *only* to and through Darius. Daniel boldly continues praying to God—even publicly demonstrating this by placing himself by an open window in his house. As much as the turn of events disappoints Darius, he realizes that even he can't overturn the edict, and Daniel is faced with the penalty of disobedience: being thrown into a den of lions. As Darius waves goodbye to Daniel, he utters a halfhearted prayer that his God would deliver him, surely not believing that this could actually happen!

But it's time for God to show Darius, and all of Babylon, what kind of God he really is. God closes the mouths of the lions and delivers Daniel safely out of the den after spending an entire night with the ravenous beasts. The chapter ends with something that should shock and surprise us: the pagan Persian king of Babylon offering a decree and a song of praise to the God of Israel. This passage begins with a king who was quick to sign an edict commanding all people to pray directly to *him*; it ends with a prayer of praise by *that same king* to a God that he acknowledges as far higher than any human king. God has been completely committed to the good of his man Daniel—even in the midst of exile. And in that, he has been active in bringing glory to his perfect name—even from the lips of pagan rulers.

The greatest good that God gives to his people—salvation and forgiveness through Jesus—brings him the most glory because it shows the world his grace, mercy, and justice. Ask God to help you trust him more as you rest in his good and glorious plan for the world—and for your life.

Prophesying through Actions and Words

Hosea is different from other prophets in the way that his life is inextricably linked with his message. He is called to *live out* his message to God's people in a way that includes deep emotional anguish. How specifically does Hosea's life connect to his message? God calls him to marry an unfaithful woman so that his marriage can be a vivid picture of God's relationship with his unfaithful people.

As the passage begins, God calls Hosea to do something drastic: "Take to yourself a wife of whoredom and have children of whoredom, for the land commits great whoredom by forsaking the LORD" (1:2). This must have come as a shock to Hosea! God does not hide his purpose for this relationship; it is to mirror and reflect his relationship with a people who have spiritually prostituted themselves through idolatry, pride, greed, and other kinds of sin. Hosea obeys God's voice and allows his very marriage to demonstrate vividly for God's people the nature of their relationship with him. God even dictates the naming of Hosea's children—each named to point to the coming judgment on the sin of Israel, but the ultimate salvation for God's true people. Hosea becomes a prophet who painfully lives out the message of God to his people.

And when Hosea speaks, we hear a very familiar message: God's judgment for his people's sin. Hosea applies the Israelites' rebellion to the context of a marriage relationship with their God. Like an unfaithful wife, Israel has said, "I will go after my lovers, who give me my bread and my water, my wool and my flax, my oil and my drink" (2:5). Ultimately, God will give Israel up to the very nations they have unfaithfully pursued. They have envied the idolatry and sin of the people around them, so God will turn them over completely to those people.

Pray that God would give you more and more hatred for your own sin as you grow more mature in Christ Jesus. Ask him to show you the beauty of your redemption. Thank him that the blood of Jesus has brought you to God out of slavery to pride, sin, and spiritual wandering.

A Forever Marriage

In our country, we've all seen marriages fall apart. In this passage, though, you read about a marriage that God simply refuses to let fall apart! It's the marriage between him and his sinful, adulterous people. God simply won't let go of this relationship, even though he judges his people for their sin.

We find that God's judgment, while justified, is not God's final word for his people. Ultimately, God will "speak tenderly" to his people and bring them back into right relationship with him in a lasting way (2:14). And this marriage won't have the potential of falling apart again! Listen to God's promise to his bride for that coming day: "And I will betroth you to me forever. I will betroth you to me in righteousness and in justice, in steadfast love and in mercy. I will betroth you to me in faithfulness. And you shall know the Lord" (2:19–20). There will come a day, God is saying, when this relationship—this marriage—between him and his people will be established in a final, forever kind of way.

God then calls Hosea to live out this marriage promise to his people by doing something extremely painful: "Go again, love a woman who is loved by another man and is an adulteress, even as the Lord loves the children of Israel, though they turn to other gods and love cakes of raisins" (3:1). And so Hosea goes. He redeems (in this case, buys back) his wife from her life of sexual sin and adultery and brings her to live with him again. Hosea's life and marriage again serve as a vivid picture to God's people of his relationship of love and mercy toward them; God will take *them* back into marriage with him, just as Hosea redeemed his wife and brought her back.

So, how will God make this marriage hold together forever? Listen to Hosea's words about the day that will come in the future: "Afterward the children of Israel shall return and seek the Lord their God, and David their king" (3:5). The lasting answer to the sin of God's people and the key to their relationship with God will be a *king*, a king like David, but even greater—a king who will rule over God's people and keep them in right relationship with their God.

Are you trying to keep yourself in a right relationship with God by your own strength? As you pray today, ask God to help you trust in him alone for your right standing with him. Thank him that he took the initiative to redeem you out of your sin, rebellion, and spiritual adultery.

The Day of the Lord

We can't talk about the message of the prophet Joel without talking about his favorite phrase: the day of the Lord. While scholars debate the exact meaning of this phrase, it at least has to do—broadly—with God's judgment on sin and the final restoration of his people. And it seems that it can have a "right now" sense as well as a future sense to it. As God's people experience tastes of God's judgment because of their sin, they are pointed forward to an ultimate and final day of the Lord when God's final judgment will be poured out and only his true people will be saved.

Joel 2:1–17 captures well the two main parts of the prophet Joel's message: *judgment* at the day of the Lord and *hope of restoration* for God's people who truly repent and turn to him. Joel describes a "day of darkness and gloom," as God's people are attacked by "a great and powerful people" (2:2). Pictures of judgment and death accompany this great army—images of fire and burning flame. The surprise of this section is who is in charge of this invasion: God. "The LORD utters his voice before his army," Joel says, and "he who executes his word is powerful" (2:11). Whether this picture that Joel is giving us is of a literal army that invaded Israel, or just a figurative way to talk about a plague or natural disaster, the point he's making is clear: God is in charge of this, as he specifically judges the sin of his people.

Yet the passage turns to a hopeful note in verse 12: "'Yet even now,' declares the LORD, 'return to me with all your heart.'" Why should God's people return to the Lord, even in the midst of judgment? Because of who he is! Joel explains this to God's people: "Return to the LORD your God, for he is gracious and merciful, slow to anger, and abounding in steadfast love; and he relents over disaster" (2:13). In light of God's grace and mercy—the very core of his character—Joel calls God's people to drastic repentance with offerings, fasting, and corporate worship and prayer. When God's people respond to him in *that* way, there is always hope for restoration, forgiveness, and salvation.

There is time for men and women—even now—to turn to Jesus Christ in repentance and faith and be saved and forgiven. Make sure that you've done that personally! And if you have, ask God to help you make known to others his gracious and merciful character with more boldness, courage, and joy.

False Security

We can easily get tricked into thinking that when things are good, that means that God is pleased with us. *I'm passing tests, winning ball games, and making friends, so God must be very happy with me!* That kind of thinking is not always correct.

The prophet Amos writes to God's people during a time of prosperity. The economy is good; wealth has exploded. Because of this, God's people assume that God is pleased with them. Good times become, for them, a sign that God is happy with the way they're living their lives. So they begin looking forward to God's judgment on the nations around them.

Amos's prophecy starts in an expected way, at least for the people of God during his time. He begins by going from neighbor to neighbor, naming the pagan nations surrounding Israel and predicting the judgment for their sin that God will soon bring. "The LORD roars from Zion," Amos begins (1:2); his judgment will be fierce and violent. The judgment will come to Damascus, Gaza, Tyre, Edom, Moab, and the Ammonites. These are nations who have sinned against God and against his people; God will call them to account.

Then we find the big surprise of the prophecy of Amos. He turns to Judah and Israel next with fiery words of God's wrath. Amos declares God's words to his people: "I will not revoke the punishment, because they have rejected the law of the LORD, and have not kept his statutes" (2:4). Unlike the rest of the nations, God's people will be judged on the basis of God's law and their failure to live up to it. They have less excuse than these nations; they had God's law to guide them. Their prosperity hasn't been a sign that God has been pleased with their way of life! God will judge them along with their pagan neighbors, even with the same fire.

The surprise is that, while God will punish the enemies of his people, God's own people are guilty too. The answer for God's people will not only be judgment on their enemies; it will also involve God finding a way to deal with *their* own sin. The enemy is not just Edom, Moab, and Tyre; the enemy is God's own people because of their sin. The enemy is *us*.

Here is God's final solution for his sinful people: the death of his Son, which alone is sufficient to turn enemies into friends. Thank God that you, who were once his enemy, have been reconciled to him and saved from his judgment through the death of Jesus.

Grace Is for All People

While the word *grace* itself implies unearned favor, we can sometimes begin to think that we have *earned* our grace more than other people have! Deep down, do you sometimes believe that you are more deserving of God's grace than other people?

That was the prophet Jonah's problem! Jonah thought that God's grace was only for people with certain qualifications. In Jonah's case, this meant the Jewish people. Because of this attitude, when God comes to Jonah with a command to go to Nineveh with a message from him, Jonah runs in the other direction! Nineveh, you see, was a Gentile city, filled with people who did not fear God. Jonah wants no part of ministry to *those* people. God sends a storm to follow Jonah, as he has hopped on a ship going the opposite direction. Thrown overboard by the crew to save their lives, Jonah is swallowed by a great fish (sent by God) and spends three days inside it, praying to God. Finally back on dry land, Jonah is given the command by God that he received before. This time he goes!

Today you saw Jonah going to Nineveh and preaching a very short and simple message: "Yet forty days, and Nineveh shall be overthrown" (3:4). What happens next is shocking: Nineveh repents. From the greatest of them to the least of them—there is a complete turning from sin on the part of the citizens of this pagan city. Their king leads the way; he gets off his throne and covers himself in sackcloth—a sign of repentance and faith in God. God, seeing this repentance, responds according to his amazing mercy and grace: "God relented of the disaster that he had said he would do to them, and he did not do it" (3:10).

But Jonah isn't too happy about this: "That is why I made haste to flee to Tarshish; for I knew that you are a gracious God and merciful" (4:2). Jonah was happy receiving God's grace toward him as a "qualified" Israelite, but he didn't want God to show his mercy toward people whom he viewed as less deserving. Even by the end of the book, we're not sure that Jonah has learned his lesson. But what God is teaching is clear: his grace is for *all people*. No one is more qualified to receive grace than anyone else; that's what makes it *grace*.

Pray that your heart would line up with God's heart for lost sinners who need Jesus. Ask him to give you a desire that people everywhere would know his grace and salvation, found through Jesus Christ.

The Shepherd King

Like other prophets, Micah looks to a future day of restoration—after judgment—for all who are God's true people. This chapter, though, answers some important questions about this future restoration for God's people. How will this restoration come? Who will lead and rule God's people forever? Micah's words point us far forward from his time to one person who will accomplish all this for God's people: a shepherd king.

Micah describes the rise of a future king for God's people, a king who will come from the little town of Bethlehem and rule God's people with power, goodness, and truth. He will be a shepherd king—keeping the people secure and bringing peace to the nation. This king will also deliver God's people from all their enemies. But his influence will not end with Israel alone! The remnant of God's people who are led by this king will be "in the midst of many peoples"—lifted up in all the world "like a lion among the beasts of the forest" (5:7–8). Micah is saying that this king will lead God's people into a place of *prominence and glory*, even after judgment! And he goes on. Not only will this king bring security and prominence to God's people, but he will also completely abolish idolatry through his reign. This shepherd king will mean the *end of sin* for God's people and the final judgment on the nations; God says, "I will execute vengeance on the nations that did not obey" (5:15).

In Matthew 2, we find the familiar story of the wise men who traveled from afar to find the place where Jesus was born. King Herod, troubled by the birth of a king who might rival his rule, asks the scholars of his day where this king will be born. They quote back to him Micah 5! The prophet Micah is pointing God's people forward to a shepherd king, yes. But he won't be a human king. Rather, God's own Son will accomplish everything the prophet Micah talks about. Jesus will bring eternal security to God's people through his sacrificial death on the cross. He will establish a glorious people for himself through his salvation for them. And he will finally deal with sin and death through dying for us—and then rising up from the grave!

We need Jesus as our King to rule over our lives and to shepherd us perfectly. Thank God that he has given us a final solution to sin and judgment in Jesus. Turn to him in prayer for a few minutes today, thanking him for giving us such a great and loving King!

Walk Humbly with Your God

This is a very well-known passage and one that comes, therefore, with some danger. We can begin to think that Micah 6:8 is a verse that tells God's people how they can be saved, rather than how God's people are to respond to God's salvation.

Micah begins with an indictment—a legal declaration of guilt, spoken by God toward his sinful people. The rebellious Israelites are in trouble again! But look closely at how God grounds his indictment of his people. He reminds them of the saving acts that he has performed on their behalf: "I brought you up from the land of Egypt and redeemed you from the house of slavery" (6:4). God's appeal to his sinful people is *not* instructions on how they must be saved. He goes back through their history, in fact, to remind them that he already *has* saved them, delivered them from slavery, and brought them into his service. So how are God's people to respond to this salvation from God?

Too often, they tend toward mere religious ritual—at least, that's what it seems like from this chapter of Micah. And so, Micah brings these words to them: "Will the Lord be pleased with thousands of rams, with ten thousands of rivers of oil?" (6:7). In other words, is God really after animals, slaughtered before him on altars? That's what God's people are commanded to do in the Old Testament law, of course, but is that it? Micah even gets more extreme, asking if God will be pleased if his people offer up their own children as sacrifices. Is that the kind of response God is looking for from his people?

The answer is no. God has never been merely after sacrifices, Micah says. Religious ritual isn't enough. God wants his people *themselves*. That's where verse 8 comes in. What does God require from the people he has saved, redeemed, and delivered? He wants them to "do justice, and to love kindness, and to walk humbly" with him as their Savior and Lord. This is the right response of God's redeemed people. They are to live in total devotion to their glorious Savior.

God doesn't want mere signs of religious devotion; he wants our hearts! Confess the ways that you've trusted religious rituals—of any kind—to act as your offerings to God. Pray that he would enable you to give yourself more and more fully to the God who has made you, loves you, and has redeemed you through the work of his beloved Son.

God, the Great Judge

While God does bring judgment on the sin of his people, this judgment is not his final word to them; he will never fully abandon all his people forever. Salvation is the final word! In Nahum 3, we get a taste of this, as we see clearly that, since God is still for his people, judgment will come to those who have attacked, killed, and abused them.

The prophet Nahum speaks these words to Nineveh, the capital city of the ancient empire of Assyria. Roughly one hundred years earlier, Assyria had conquered and destroyed the northern part of the kingdom of God's people. Even though God clearly used Assyria to judge his people, that didn't excuse their evil behavior in the midst of their hardship. Nineveh, according to Nahum, has been a "bloody city, all full of lies and plunder" (3:1). It has been full of "whorings" and "charms," probably referring to a culture of idolatry and perversion (3:4). Nineveh was a nasty place full of an intentional commitment to all kinds of sin, violence, and perversion.

Nahum says clearly that, because of all this, God's judgment will come to Nineveh. God's words to this city are fierce: "I will throw filth at you and treat you with contempt and make you a spectacle" (3:6). The people of Nineveh will share the same fate as other nations who have spat in the face of both God and his people—Thebes, Cush, and Egypt.

We need to remember that Nahum is prophesying terrible judgment to a city that approximately one hundred years earlier had repented wholeheartedly at the preaching of Jonah. Remember that? Jonah, the reluctant prophet, preached to this city. And God relented of judgment because of their repentance. Now, two generations later, the city is completely retransformed back into its old ways of sin, idolatry, violence, pride, and perversion. That should shake us up a little bit; how quickly sin can take hold of an entire culture, much less one person! We also need to see, again, that our God is ultimately for his people to the end. God will not let the enemies of his people off the hook, even though he chose to use them to discipline his people! God, the great Judge, will in the end make all things right.

If you are a child of God through faith in Jesus and the grace he gives, then God is for you until the end. Do you believe that? Ask God to help you believe it even more! Rest in the fact that God will ultimately make all things right, even if it seems now that justice is nowhere to be found.

I Will Rejoice in the Lord

Have you ever wrestled with God? Have you ever wondered *why* God chooses to act in certain ways? The prophet Habakkuk is a man who knew what it was to wrestle with God and even to complain about the way God chose to do things.

We first find Habakkuk appealing to God about the sin of God's *own people*, which seems to go on unpunished and unnoticed by God. "Why do you make me see iniquity," Habakkuk asks God, "and why do you idly look at wrong?" (1:3). He feels—as we often do—that God is just *standing* there as his people continue to spit in his face and disregard his word completely. God tells his prophet that a response to his people's sin is coming—and it will be judgment at the hand of the Chaldeans (or Babylonians), a desperately wicked people. This makes Habakkuk even *more* confused and upset. How could a good God judge his own people through a far more wicked nation like Babylon?

This chapter marks the end of Habakkuk's story—his two-way debate with God. God's plan hasn't changed! But Habakkuk's heart has changed. While he accepts the fact that judgment will come—at least for a time—to God's people, Habakkuk also trusts that God ultimately will work for their good. He thinks back to God's great saving acts in history—the times when God "went out for the salvation" of his people and "crushed the head of the house of the wicked" (3:13). Even though the coming Babylonian invasion makes him tremble, Habakkuk decides to trust God and wait quietly for God to make all things right in the end.

The book of Habakkuk shows us a man whose *situation* has not changed, but whose *heart* has. He has wrestled with God and ultimately decided in faith to trust God and rest in his sovereign and good plan regardless of difficult circumstances. See how he wraps up his prayer: "Though the fig tree should not blossom, nor fruit be on the vines . . . yet . . . I will take joy in the God of my salvation" (3:17–18). How can Habakkuk rest in God regardless of circumstances? Because he knows him.

Read Habakkuk 3:17–19 one more time as you spend a few minutes in prayer. Can you truly speak those words today? Regardless of difficult circumstances, are you able to rejoice in God, knowing that he is your greatest joy? Pray that God would give you strength to treasure him above all things, so that you will stand firm in times of trouble.

Zechariah's Vision

The glory of the days of the great kings was long gone. Jerusalem was in ruins. God's people had to start all over! Many of them probably wondered if life would ever return to the way it had been in the previous years. It was hard to have great *hope* for the future.

The prophet Zechariah speaks to God's people in this very situation. He addresses their lack of hope by telling the people about his God-given visions of the future glory of God's people, God's place, and God's rule through the promised Messiah.

Zechariah looks, and sees a vision of a man with a measuring line, intent on measuring the city of Jerusalem. As Zechariah talks to this man—who turns out to be an angel—another angel comes up with an exciting message for the prophet: "Jerusalem shall be inhabited as villages without walls, because of the multitude of people and livestock in it" (2:4). Even though it seems so weak, small, and fragile as God's people return from exile, there is a bright future for this city of God; it will again be vibrant and full of life. God's people will again flourish in God's place.

The angel tells Zechariah God's words concerning Jerusalem: "I will be to her a wall of fire all around . . . and I will be the glory in her midst" (2:5). God says to Zechariah that *he himself* will be the wall around his people. He will be their security. More than that, God promises to live—in all his glory—in the midst of his people: "And many nations shall join themselves to the LORD in that day, and shall be my people. And I will dwell in your midst" (2:11). Zechariah's vision, in other words, points to a future day when God's people will be gathered from all nations to dwell in the presence of God forever.

Zechariah's vision is not merely about physical Jerusalem; it points us forward to the ultimate and final hope for all God's people. Through faith in God's Messiah—Jesus Christ—we, along with God's people from every tribe and nation, will dwell in the presence of our glorious God forever.

God accomplishes his salvation through Jesus, who came as the great Messiah to die for our sins and secure our eternal salvation as we put our faith in him. Is your hope in anything less than this today? Pray that God would help you to keep looking up to his eternal, glorious plan for his people—and find hope in that!

The Sun of Righteousness

It had been about one hundred years since the decree of Cyrus that sent a good portion of the Israelites back to the land. The temple, while rebuilt, couldn't begin to compare to its past glory. The culture of Israel was in disarray, along with its worship. In some ways, it seems that even after a century back in the land, God's people are still adjusting to life out of exile. It's into this situation that the prophet Malachi speaks.

Malachi points God's people forward to a great future day of God's glory—through both judgment and salvation. "The day is coming," says Malachi, "when all the arrogant and all evildoers will be stubble" (4:1). But this day won't bring judgment only: "For you who fear my name, the sun of righteousness shall rise with healing in its wings" (4:2). For God's people, this great day will bring healing—salvation! God is not finished with his great plan for the world, both in judgment and in salvation.

Malachi also points God's people to a *sign* of this coming day: a powerful prophet of God who will come before it. He says this: "Behold, I will send you Elijah the prophet before the great and awesome day of the LORD comes" (4:5). This prophet's ministry will be a sign that this day is approaching, a hint that the "sun of righteousness" is about to dawn on God's people. The book of Malachi ends, and then . . . silence. For four hundred years. No prophets address God's people. They are left waiting and hoping, looking for the coming day of the Lord, wondering when this great promised Messiah will come.

Then, in the Gospel of Luke, we hear echoes of Malachi's words, spoken by a faithful priest named Zechariah about his son: "For you will go before the Lord to prepare his ways, to give knowledge of salvation to his people in the forgiveness of their sins, because of the tender mercy of our God, whereby the *sunrise shall visit us from on high*" (Luke 1:76–78). This sun of righteousness is coming, says Zechariah! And so John the Baptist—a great prophet—comes into the picture, pointing God's people to the one who will be able to finally save them eternally.

This is our story too. We enter much later, but we enter the same story. God's people—after the coming of the Messiah—seek to live in faith and obedience to him. Praise God that he did not let his people wait forever. Thank him for sending his only Son. And thank him that, through the work of Jesus Christ, you too can be part of his people forever.

ACT 5

Jesus to the End

King Jesus

Thousands of people gather in the streets of the city, looking up toward a grand stone balcony. Suddenly, there is the sound of trumpets blasting an energetic tune. Whom do you expect to see at the end of that scene? What kind of person? A king, of course!

In the first few verses of the book, Matthew sends one message loudly and clearly: this is the king! In Matthew's day, ordinary people wouldn't have had recorded genealogies. But if you were a king, your genealogy would be central to your reign. Far from a boring list of names, this is an obvious sign that the gospel Matthew writes is about someone extremely important; it will be about a king. Let's look at just a few aspects of this genealogy today.

First, notice that Matthew doesn't go to great effort to hide the sins of God's people who have had prominent parts in this history. Look at how he identifies King Solomon: "And David was the father of Solomon by the wife of Uriah" (1:6). What does this little detail tell us? It reminds us that the genealogy of Jesus is full of imperfect and sinful people, like David, who murdered Uriah and stole his wife! Jesus's coming will need to deal with the greatest problem of all God's people, even the kings: their sin.

Second, notice that Ruth—a Moabite, a Gentile woman of faith—is mentioned by name in Matthew's genealogy. It's not just a list of a bunch of Jewish people; it's not even just a list of men! God used all kinds of people to accomplish his purpose; even in the Old Testament, Matthew reminds us, favor with God depended on faith in him, not ethnicity.

Third, you'll see that Matthew has Jesus's genealogy broken up into three fourteen-generation parts: from Abraham to David, from David to the exile, and from the exile to Jesus. What's missing from this genealogy? Well, the lineage from Adam (the first man) to Abraham is missing, as well as the line from Jesus to *us*! Matthew is presenting Jesus as the King who initiates the final act of the history of the world. Friend, we are living in the last act! There is nothing more that needs to happen as part of God's plan for the world—other than the second coming of Jesus.

Ask God to renew your faith, hope, and belief in his Son. As you pray today, bow before Jesus with your heart and your words. Thank him for being the gracious King who came to save us.

The Birth of the King

I'm sure you know about Jesus's humble birth in a manger. But we don't find that part of the story in Matthew's account. This is because Matthew focuses on presenting Jesus Christ as the great King of God's people—the promised Messiah.

Matthew shows us that this King is miraculously conceived by the power of the Holy Spirit. Jesus is human, yes, but he is the only human being in history to ever *not* be born from a man and a woman coming together in some way. Joseph, Mary's husband-to-be, finds out she's pregnant before their marriage. But his plan to walk away from their approaching marriage is broken by a visit from the angel of the Lord, who tells him something amazing: the child that Mary carries is from the Holy Spirit. The very birth of this King is a miracle of the Holy Spirit!

Matthew also shows us that this King will fulfill God's Old Testament promises to his people. The angel tells Joseph to call Mary's son Jesus, for "he will save his people from their sins" (1:21). This theme—salvation from sins—was one promised in many of the messages of the prophets. Matthew then quotes Isaiah's prophecy about a virgin conceiving and bearing a son—pointing to the miracle of Jesus's birth from Mary as the fulfillment of that promise. As Matthew 2 begins and wise men from the east search for Jesus, the scribes and priests point to Micah—accurately—as prophesying the place of the Messiah's birth. Matthew's message is clear: God's promises to his people through the prophets are all coming together in this one person!

Matthew sets up a stark contrast between the different ways people will respond to the coming of this King. Some—like the wise men from the east—will journey far to fall down and worship him, offering him great treasures and gifts. Some—like Herod, the Jewish king—will see King Jesus as a threat to their power and position and will plot against him to kill him. Not everyone will want to follow this King Jesus!

The right response to Jesus is demonstrated for us by Matthew in the actions of the wise men. God wants us to fall at his feet with great joy and offer him everything. Have you responded to Jesus in that way? Ask God to help you respond joyfully to King Jesus—the King who came to save God's people from their sins.

Repent!

Something big was happening in the land of Israel. A prophet had emerged, a strangely dressed man who spent his days in the wilderness eating locusts and wild honey. He had created quite a stir; Matthew tells us, "Jerusalem and all Judea and all the region about the Jordan were going out to him" (3:5). John the Baptist, the prophet who points to the Messiah, has finally come. In fact, Matthew makes it clear that John fulfills a great promise of the Old Testament prophet Malachi that there would be a voice crying in the wilderness to prepare the way of the chosen one of God. John's message is not complex, but it is powerful and urgent: "Repent, for the kingdom of heaven is at hand" (3:2). In light of the coming of the great Messiah, John's call to people in Israel is to repent—to change their minds and hearts—and to get ready for his coming.

The question for the Jewish people, though, would have been this: Who *is* this man, really? Will he be the Messiah? After all, John's ministry had created a huge stir in the land of Israel; people were flocking to him from all over! John is absolutely clear, though, that he is not the Messiah. His role is to point God's people to Jesus, the true Messiah. He makes this clear: "I baptize you with water for repentance, but he who is coming after me is mightier than I, whose sandals I am not worthy to carry. He will baptize you with the Holy Spirit and fire" (3:11). There is someone coming who is even greater than this John the Baptist!

The surprise about Jesus—when he shows up—is what happens. It's something, in fact, that is even surprising to John! Jesus has John baptize him. Jesus doesn't need to repent and get ready for the kingdom; he *is* the King! What is he doing? First, he is affirming the ministry of John. He is saying, very publicly, that this is a true prophet of God. Second, he is identifying himself with the sinful people he comes to save. Jesus doesn't need to repent or be washed clean of sin; he's the perfect Son of God! But he is taking an intentional step to say that he has come to identify with God's lost and sinful people.

Have you repented? Not just said "I'm sorry" to God, but completely turned from your sin to follow Jesus completely? If so, pray to God today that you would keep following the glorious Savior who came for you. And pray that you would—like John—always be pointing others to him!

Jesus, the Perfect and True Israel

In the Old Testament, the wilderness wanderings led to temptation and sin for God's people, as they often grumbled against God's rule and his word. When we open up Matthew 4 and find Jesus is being "led up by the Spirit into the wilderness" (4:1), we see him continuing in the pattern of God's people: going out into the wilderness with temptation coming.

Satan, also called "the tempter" (4:3), comes to Jesus in the wilderness. First comes a temptation geared at exploiting Jesus's frail physical state, as Satan tempts him in his hunger to turn stones into loaves of bread. But Jesus will not allow Satan to tempt him to use his power and glory for his own comfort or allow his human frailty to make him weak spiritually. Jesus reminds Satan of his true source of strength: the word of God. Next, Satan urges Jesus to throw himself down from a high point of the temple—a temptation to put God to the test. Jesus again stands strong against this plan. Finally, Satan brings out the biggest temptation of all: "Fall down and worship me" (4:9), he says, and the kingdoms of the world will belong to Jesus. Satan is tempting Jesus to abandon his path to suffering and death, in exchange for earthly rule, glory, and power. Jesus again stands strong against Satan's advances, declaring his allegiance to God alone.

Matthew is showing us that Jesus is completely faithful, in every respect, where God's people have failed. The Israelites went into the wilderness; Jesus went into the wilderness. God's people were tempted toward sin; Jesus was tempted toward sin. The Israelites fell into temptation; Jesus *stood strong* in purity and holiness in every respect! Jesus is, in this way, the perfect and true Israel. He is the perfect representative for God's people—having faced incredible temptation at his weakest physical point without breaking.

It's not inappropriate to learn from Jesus's resistance of temptation, even though we're obviously not Jesus! How does Jesus respond? He counters Satan's advances, every time, with the word of God. Friend, when we are tempted, is our first impulse to speak God's word into the situation? That is how Jesus, our Lord, responded to temptation.

Pray that your response to temptation would be to bring God's word into the picture and let its light shine. Ask God to help you do this more!

Jesus Is the Standard

Before we get into the meaning of Jesus's teaching in this setting, we need to be clear on his intended audience. There are huge crowds of people surrounding Jesus as he speaks, so we might assume that Jesus is talking *to* the crowds. But what does Matthew tell us? "Seeing the crowds, he went up on the mountain, and when he sat down, his *disciples* came to him" (5:1). The Sermon on the Mount was given by Jesus to his *disciples*, to people who had already chosen to follow him. That is very significant!

Next, notice how Jesus sets up his teaching: "Do not think that I have come to abolish the Law or the Prophets; I have not come to abolish them but to fulfill them" (5:17). A lot of times we think that Jesus is anti-law—that he comes to somehow relax the requirements of holiness for God's people. Actually, Jesus makes the surprising statement that his disciples' righteousness needs to be *greater* than the righteousness of the Pharisees, who were the strictest and most committed group of religious leaders of the day. Jesus is not relaxing anything; he seems to be upping the ante regarding holiness, righteousness, and obedience for God's people!

Finally, notice Jesus's repeated refrain as he gets into the main teaching part of this sermon. Again and again, his favorite phrase is, "You have heard that it was said . . . but I say to you . . ." (see 5:21–22, 27–28, 31–32). This would have been shocking to any teachers of the law who happened to be listening to Jesus! Why? Because Jesus is placing on himself the authority and responsibility for interpreting and applying God's law to God's people. He's placing weight on *his own* words; what Jesus says is what is most important for us.

This leads us to what seems to be the main point of this sermon: it's all about the person of Jesus. Jesus perfectly fulfills the law of God. Jesus is the only one who can authoritatively teach and apply the law. The standard of holiness for God's people is no longer the letter of the law; the standard is Jesus himself. Jesus, speaking primarily to his disciples, is telling them what following him will look like. It will be nothing less than following—and becoming like—the Lord Jesus Christ in every way.

Pray that God would help you look to Jesus as your standard of holiness. Thank him for salvation and righteousness in his name. Ask him to help you pursue obedience as the Holy Spirit makes you more like your Savior.

Total Authority & Complete Commitment

Authority is a major theme as Matthew writes about Jesus the Messiah. Jesus has all authority; he is the Son of God and the great forever King of God's people. Matthew presents Jesus as the one with all authority to teach and interpret God's law to God's people. In fact, this is how Matthew sums up Jesus's teaching on the mount: "The crowds were astonished at his teaching, for he was teaching them as one who had authority, and not as their scribes" (7:28–29).

In Matthew 8, we see that Jesus's authority doesn't stop at interpreting God's word; it extends to every part of creation. First, Jesus heals a man who has leprosy—an infectious, painful skin disease. Next, Jesus heals the servant of a Roman centurion, and does so from a great distance. Next, Jesus shows his authority over the forces of creation as he calms a storm in the presence of his disciples. This miraculous act leaves the men amazed and asking, "What sort of man is this, that even winds and sea obey him?" (8:27). The chapter concludes with a showdown between Jesus and a man possessed by demons. The demons cower at the power of Jesus the Son of God and beg him to send them into some nearby pigs. Jesus demonstrates his total authority over not only diseases and the forces of creation but over the demonic realm as well.

Wedged in the middle of these miracles, we find two confrontations that Jesus has with people who are clearly intrigued by him. But each person comes to Jesus with a worldly distraction that prohibits immediate and total commitment. One man seems to not understand the difficulty of following Jesus; Jesus reminds him that "the Son of Man has nowhere to lay his head" (8:20). Another man mentions wanting to bury his father first, probably meaning that he needs to wait (possibly years) until his father dies, and *then* he will follow Jesus completely. Jesus's response to this man again implies the kind of commitment that his authority demands from his followers: *complete* commitment.

What is the right response to Jesus? It's to drop everything and follow him! The right response to the Son of God—the Messiah—who has all the authority in the world, is to follow him with complete and utter devotion.

Pray today that you would respond to the call of this authoritative Lord and Savior. He laid down his life to redeem you, a lost sinner. The only right response is to lay down your life and follow him.

Fruitful Hearing

For those of us who have accepted the message of the gospel—Jesus Christ as the Son of God and the Savior of lost sinners—it can sometimes be hard to understand why anyone wouldn't want to accept him! Jesus's words here help us with this confusion. He gives his disciples—and us—this parable to explain the various responses to the word of truth.

Jesus tells a story of a sower who sows seed, which he hopes will grow. The seed falls in four different environments: a hard path, rocky ground, thorny soil, and good soil. The seed on the hard path gets eaten up by birds right away. The seed that falls on rocky ground can't find a good place to grow; it seems to flourish at first, but dies because of a lack of firm roots. The seed amongst the thorns gets choked out by those thorns. It's the seed that falls on good soil that grows, flourishes, and bears incredible fruit.

Jesus explains to his disciples that he speaks in parables not to make things clearer but to *hide things* from some people. He quotes from the prophet Isaiah, telling his disciples that he teaches in this way in order to fulfill the prophecy: "You will indeed hear but never understand, and you will indeed see but never perceive" (13:14). This leads to the first lesson that we get from this passage: God is the one who ultimately determines who receives his word in the right way.

As Jesus goes into a longer explanation of the parable, though, we see what each different part means. The different kinds of soil represent different kinds of people—and their different responses to the word of the kingdom. Some people are like hard paths; the gospel word doesn't even dent their hearts and minds. Other people like the idea of the gospel; real faith and repentance just don't take root. Others want Jesus, but they want to keep going after sin, selfishness, and pleasure—the thorns of the world. True believers, though, are those who respond to the message of the gospel by hearing it, understanding it, and bearing fruit in it. Not everyone will accept the message about Jesus! The ones who truly belong to Jesus, though, will be marked by their true hearing.

Ask God that he would protect you from all the things that so easily can distract us from being good hearers of the word—sin, worry, doubts. Pray that he would help you live as someone who has truly embraced the message of the gospel of Jesus Christ.

Miracles

People who *make* the rules are the ones who can sometimes *break* the rules. In Matthew 14:13–33, Jesus essentially breaks the rules of nature: turning a small amount of bread into a huge amount of bread and walking on top of water. Both actions are—naturally speaking—impossible!

Jesus withdraws to a desolate place in order to be alone, but crowds of people follow him there. Jesus has compassion on the crowds, healing many of them and spending time with them. Since they're out in the middle of nowhere, though, there's no food to give all the people. Taking just five loaves of bread and two fish, Jesus miraculously multiplies this into food that is enough for five thousand men, along with women and children. This miracle—the only miracle recorded by every Gospel writer—shows us that Jesus is the divine provider for God's people; he can bring food and sustenance out of nothing!

After the miraculous feeding, Jesus sends the disciples away on a boat, while he stays behind to dismiss the crowds and pray. After he is finished, with the boat already far from shore, Jesus does something amazing: he walks out on the water toward his disciples in the boat. There is no way this miracle can be explained away! Jesus is doing something that is, according to all the rules of nature, absolutely *impossible*. Only God himself could have this kind of total command of the world, ordering even water to hold the weight of a human being. Jesus even invites Peter to come out to him on the water, enabling him to walk for a while, until Peter's faith wavers. Jesus lifts Peter up out of the water as he himself continues to stand firm in the midst of the waves!

It's no accident that this section of Matthew's gospel ends with worship. The disciples, remember, have just witnessed both of these miracles of Jesus—the miraculous feeding and the walking on water. How do they respond? "And those in the boat worshiped him, saying, 'Truly you are the Son of God'" (14:33). Jesus's disciples proclaim his true identity; he is the very Son of the one true God, who made all creation. They respond in the only appropriate way to the one who is God: they worship him right there in the boat.

Pray today that God would help you live a life that is filled with the worship of Jesus Christ in every area. He is the one who can multiply bread and walk on water. And he is the only one who can save us.

The Cost of Following Jesus

When Alex came to college as a freshman, he was excited about being a member of the basketball team. Being part of the team, he got free gear to wear proudly around campus, and people looked at him differently. And then . . . practice started in October. It was tough! Three hours every day. Defensive drills—over and over again. Sore muscles. It was a big wake-up call! He had gotten excited about his *identity* as a college basketball player. But he hadn't understood the *purpose* of being on the basketball team—it meant hard work to prepare for games.

At first, it seems that Peter really gets who Jesus is. It's Peter who blurts out a beautiful, faith-filled confession: "You are the Christ, the Son of the living God" (16:16). He recognizes who Jesus is—the promised Messiah for God's people, the Son of God himself. Jesus affirms Peter's faith, telling him that he will build his church through Peter's ministry and leadership. It seems that Jesus's disciples are beginning to understand his *identity*. But they still don't understand his *purpose*.

The very next account Matthew gives us records an interaction between Peter and Jesus as Jesus begins to set his eyes toward Jerusalem, where he will go to die. In fact, Jesus has started openly talking about his death and resurrection. Peter—who has just affirmed Jesus's identity as the Christ—takes Jesus aside to rebuke him for this kind of talk! He does not understand that the primary purpose of Jesus's coming is to secure salvation for sinners through his death and resurrection. The *cross* is the key to Jesus's ministry; Peter does not understand that this suffering will be central to the purpose of the Christ.

The chapter ends with Jesus, after his rebuke of Peter, turning to the disciples to teach them that his path of suffering will mean hardship and sacrifice for all who want to follow him. "If anyone would come after me, let him deny himself and take up his cross and follow me. For whoever would save his life will lose it, but whoever loses his life for my sake will find it" (16:24–25). The path of the Messiah was not one of earthly fame and glory! His path was to the cross—the place where the Son of God suffered and died in the place of lost sinners like you and me.

Pray today that God's Holy Spirit would enable you to love Jesus more than anything else. Ask God to help you take up your cross—denying self, sin, and pride—in order to follow Jesus and gain him forever.

The Transfiguration

In the classic fairy tale "Beauty and the Beast," a selfish young prince is visited by a beautiful enchantress who shows up at his door disguised as an old beggar woman. Disgusted, the prince sends the old woman away, only to find her instantaneously transformed before his eyes; the enchantress stands before him, and he realizes that the entire encounter has been a test! In this passage from Matthew 17, you saw the curtain pulled back from Jesus. For a few brief moments, his three core disciples are exposed to a clear vision of his identity as he is revealed to them in his heavenly glory.

The very fact that Jesus leads Peter and James and John up to a *mountain* clues us in to the fact that something big is about to happen. They gather around Jesus, and all of a sudden he is joined by the great prophets of God: Moses and Elijah. They are talking with him as he stands with face shining and clothes dazzling bright. This is one instance where the words of the text probably can't even begin to describe to us the dazzling glory, beauty, and splendor of what the disciples saw on the mountain that day.

Matthew is showing us the *divine glory* of Jesus. He's reminding us that this Jesus is not just the lowly suffering Savior of lost sinners—he is also the eternal, glorious, *authoritative judge* of the world. This Jesus is the heavenly King; Jesus is showing his disciples his true identity.

As he so often does, Peter begins to blabber! Then a voice comes from heaven—God's voice: "This is my beloved Son, with whom I am well pleased; listen to him" (17:5). It is the public, divine declaration of God's stamp of approval on Jesus Christ, his Son. God is pleased with him. He is the great King—chosen of God—for his people. And this leads us to our right response to Jesus, which we get from this passage. We are to listen to Jesus. That's what God wants his people to do—listen to his Son! And Peter and the other disciples finally get the other part of the response to Jesus correct: they fall on their faces before the glorious Messiah.

Spend some time thinking about your view of Jesus. Do you see him as the powerful and glorious Judge of the world? You must! Do you see him as your gentle Savior, who laid down his life for you and leads you by his word? You should! Thank God for the Savior he has sent. Listen to him, and worship him today in your prayers, words, and actions.

The King Has Come—to Be Killed

Jesus's ride into the city of Jerusalem is no ordinary one! After securing a donkey colt, Jesus rides in and is met by screaming crowds who welcome him. The people spread their cloaks on the road and cut branches from trees that they wave before Jesus—symbols of Jewish pride and victory. The people greet Jesus with shouts of victory as well: "Hosanna to the Son of David," they cry (21:9). They obviously think their true King has come! They see Jesus as the promised one—the King who comes in the line of David to rule over God's people. While we know that they don't understand what *kind* of kingdom Jesus has come to rule, and *how* he will build that kingdom, they are at least partially correct: they are welcoming God's authoritative King to Jerusalem.

The first activity in Jerusalem that Matthew shows us is Jesus's visit to the temple—the central place of worship, sacrifice, and word teaching for God's people. What he finds there is not genuine worship but corruption; money-changers and merchants have transformed the outer courts of the temple into places of business. Most likely, they were trying to make money off people who had traveled from a distance to worship God and needed animals for sacrifices. Jesus's words are harsh: "'My house shall be called a house of prayer,'" he says, "but you make it a den of robbers" (21:13). His actions are even harsher: he turns over the tables of the merchants and drives them all out. This is not the gentle, meek, and mild Jesus that we so often picture! Jesus again asserts his authority as God's King not only over Jerusalem but also over the temple of God.

Are we there yet? Has the reign of the King in Jerusalem begun? His disciples—as we know from other places in the Gospels—may have thought this. Yet we see in the next few verses a hint of what is coming for Jesus. The chief priests and the scribes, seeing all that Jesus has done and the way that the people are flocking around him, begin to get angry. You see, Jesus is the King with all authority; we get a glimpse of this in Matthew 21 as he enters Jerusalem. But he will be a different kind of king than God's people have ever seen before. He has marched triumphantly into Jerusalem—not to be enthroned but to be killed.

Spend some time praying to your great King. Remember who Jesus is! And thank him that he is a King who, first, will die for his people—and then reign over them forever.

All Alone

From Jesus's entry into Jerusalem, everything is headed toward the cross. And as Jesus's journey speeds toward the climax of the cross, he very openly continues to teach his disciples about his death. Jesus speaks openly about his impending crucifixion. He speaks of his anointing with perfume as a kind of preparation for his upcoming burial. He even predicts the betrayal that will come at the hands of one of his own disciples. Jesus does everything that should be required to prepare his disciples for his trial, death, and resurrection; they should be ready to stand with him in this difficult process!

And so, even when Judas turns against Jesus, we keep waiting for the other disciples to step up and defend Jesus. We can tell that Judas is a bad apple—evil to the core. He's been captured by a love of money, making a deal with the chief priests to turn Jesus over to them secretly for the price of thirty pieces of silver. Even when the betrayal in the garden actually happens, you might think that Jesus's disciples will stand up for their Lord.

Then comes the surprise. It's *not only Judas* who betrays Jesus! Yes, he is the one to actually sell Jesus into the hands of his enemies, but—when all is said and done—Jesus's other disciples don't come off much better than Judas. Look again at verse 56. The crowd is ready to seize Jesus. Jesus speaks to them; they close in. And his disciples run away. Here's how Matthew puts it: "Then all the disciples left him and fled" (26:56). As Jesus approaches his death, he stands alone, abandoned by those closest to him, left to walk the path to his death—a death that he will die for the salvation of even those very disciples who ran away from him.

Friend, this is *us*! *We* are the ones who—in our sin—have abandoned and turned our backs on Jesus Christ, the Son of God. We are no better than his cowardly disciples; in fact, we would have probably done the same thing! Jesus went alone to the cross—alone to die a death that would pay the penalty for our sin.

Pray that God would help you stand up boldly each day for the King who went to the cross—alone—to take your sin in your place. Ask him to give you courage to live, speak, think, and act completely for him.

Only One Hero

This passage is in the midst of the last stages of the Gospel of Matthew. The Son of God is headed toward the cross in order to accomplish salvation for God's people. We see varied responses from different people to Jesus as he walks this path to the cross. Think about the different people that we read about today in this passage.

First, we see the religious leaders—the chief priests and the council. These men falsely accuse Jesus of blasphemy and mock him mercilessly. Then we come to Peter—Jesus's most loyal follower. Peter blatantly denies Jesus, abandoning his Lord in the hour of his greatest need. Next, there is Judas, the one who sold Jesus out to his enemies. His end is tragic; he commits suicide, overcome by grief and bitter with despair, guilt, and remorse. Then, of course, there's the crowd. They don't do very well either; in a wild frenzy, they choose a murderer to be released instead of Jesus. Matthew then shows us Pilate, who—in cowardly fashion—figuratively washes his hands of the whole situation. And this passage ends with the crowds jeering as the soldiers torture Jesus mercilessly before leading him away to be crucified. Varied responses, yes. But they're not too different in their substance, are they? Matthew is giving us an overall picture of the total rejection of Jesus by every single human being in the story.

Here's the point: there is only one hero in this story. It's Jesus. He does not stop marching toward the cross, even though he has been rejected by everyone in the world—including his own disciples. He knows that he is going to die for *their sins* as well. These chapters in Matthew give us pictures of what human beings have been doing throughout all of history: rejecting the God who made them and loves them. There is only one hero of the Bible story as well. It's God—a just God, who is also infinitely gracious and merciful, a God who will not stop his plan to save sinful people, even if it means sending his only Son to stand completely alone, and to go alone to the cross.

The amazing thing about the gospel story is that Jesus—completely alone—still walks on toward the cross. He dies for the very people who reject him, mock him, and spit on him. Thank Jesus—with all your heart—that while you were still a sinner, he died for you. Thank him for paying for your sins when you, dead in your sins, didn't deserve it at all.

The Agony of the Cross

Jesus endured intense physical agony as he died. When Matthew writes, "They had crucified him," he doesn't offer many details (27:35). But his original readers would have known what it meant. Crucifixion, they knew, was the manner of execution that had been designed by the Romans to deliver the maximum amount of pain and suffering. Nails were driven through both hands and feet, and the victim was forced to pull himself upward by those nails in order to breathe. Death, which sometimes took hours, finally came through total exhaustion, as the person crucified was unable to pull up to breathe any longer.

But Matthew shows us more: Jesus endured far more spiritual suffering than physical suffering. The physical pain was brutal. But the true punishment that Jesus received on the cross is demonstrated in his desperate words to God the Father: "My God, my God, why have you forsaken me?" (27:46). Jesus endured the agony of feeling God the Father treat him like a sinner by turning his back on him in wrath. The broken communion with the Father was far worse than the nails.

Matthew—and all the other Gospels—is absolutely clear: Jesus really died. After a loud cry, Jesus "yielded up his spirit" (27:50). After that, he was dead. There was no mistaking it. A man named Joseph took Jesus's body and buried it. People would have noticed if Jesus had not been completely dead! Think about this. The Son of God *really* died. He paid the penalty for our sin fully—all the way to the very end.

Finally, Matthew tells us that Jesus's death is an event with cosmic significance. Look at everything that happens in the moments after Jesus's death. The curtain of the temple is torn from top to bottom; dead people come out of their tombs and walk around the city. An earthquake shakes the place. This was not the death of any ordinary man! The earth shakes, the curtain is torn, people are raised—because Jesus's death means something. The perfect Lamb has been killed so that all who look to his substitution in their place can escape the wrath of God.

On the cross Jesus accomplished what we could never accomplish on our own. He experienced the full power of God's wrath against sin, so that all who put their trust in him will never have to. Thank Jesus again for going to the cross for you. Remember what he accomplished for you there.

The Risen King

The first thing that Matthew shows us in his account of the resurrection of Jesus is the response of his followers who see him. Mary Magdalene and the other Mary have gone early to the tomb of Jesus. They are met by an angel, whose appearance is terrifying to these women. As they go quickly from the tomb to tell the good news of the resurrection to Jesus's disciples, Jesus himself meets them. What is their immediate response to seeing their risen Lord? Matthew tells us: "And they came up and took hold of his feet and worshiped him" (28:9). In the presence of the Son of God, risen from the dead, there is only one right response: worship.

Some people—amazingly—still insist on stubbornly denying the power and lordship of Jesus. Matthew tells us of the plot, initiated by the chief priests, to bribe the soldiers who guarded the tomb of Jesus. They are paid to tell people that Jesus's disciples have stolen his body. It's amazing, isn't it? Even with all the evidence pointing to the miraculous resurrection of Jesus, the chief priests still insist on denying both Jesus's identity and power. Some people will not believe—even after the resurrection. Sadly, this still happens today.

As we come now to the very end of the book of Matthew, we find ourselves focusing on the same theme that was there at the beginning: the ultimate authority of Jesus the King. Matthew began with a genealogy, which he used to point us to Jesus's identity as the King—the promised Messiah of God's people. This great King, now risen from the dead, sends his disciples out to bear witness about him. Listen to how this great commission begins: "All authority in heaven and on earth has been given to me. Go therefore . . ." (28:18–19). Jesus's sending out of his disciples comes with a claim of total authority. This great King has died for the sins of God's people; he has made the final sacrifice. The King has risen from the dead; he has broken the power of death for all who belong to him through faith. His call to his disciples— and to us today—is to spread the message of his loving rule to all the world.

Pray that you would obey this command that Jesus gives to his disciples. Ask God to help you focus—by his strength—on making disciples and teaching others about Jesus. He is the Savior and the risen Lord, and he is worth knowing!

The Fast-Paced Gospel

Imagine that you're at school and something big is happening that you want your friends to know about. You sprint down the hall to your friends, who are on the other side of the building. You need to get the facts out quickly. And you need to inspire action very quickly—you must ignite a response! That's exactly the sense we get when we read Mark's Gospel. It's fast-paced and fact-driven; you could even call it breathless.

Mark begins with these words: "The beginning of the gospel of Jesus Christ, the Son of God" (1:1). Mark's goal is to tell the good news about the Son of God who has come. After quoting from the prophet Isaiah, who describes the messenger who comes before the Lord, Mark hurls us immediately into the story. John the Baptist comes, fulfilling the Old Testament prophecy. John comes with a simple message—"a baptism of repentance for the forgiveness of sins"—and points the people forward to one who will come after him.

Then, before we know it, Jesus appears. Do you see how quickly Mark is moving? He includes a brief summary of Jesus's baptism by John the Baptist, and—like Matthew—he tells us about the voice that comes from heaven: "You are my beloved Son; with you I am well pleased" (1:11). After this, we see Mark's favorite word show up: *immediately*. Jesus is driven by the Spirit into the wilderness, and Mark gives us only a general summary of his temptation there by Satan.

It seems that Mark has some basic, and very important, facts that he wants to communicate about Jesus. He begins, in verse 1, by identifying Jesus as the "Son of God." He wants his readers to understand, without any confusion, who this Jesus is. By quoting Isaiah at the outset, as well, Mark wants us to get that Jesus fulfills God's promises to his people. Finally, listen to how Mark summarizes Jesus's message when his ministry begins: "The time is fulfilled, and the kingdom of God is at hand; repent and believe in the gospel" (1:15). Because Jesus is the Son of God, and because he fulfills the promises of God and ushers in God's kingdom, Jesus calls people to repent and believe the gospel.

Thank God again for sending his own Son into this world to fulfill all his promises to his people. If you're not sure that you've repented, do that today! Confess your sins to Jesus, the Son of God. Tell him that you want to believe the good news about him and live for him from now on.

Scarier Than Storms

We're tempted to impose our situations—our "storms of life"—onto the story of Jesus and his disciples. Jesus will "calm our storms," or at least, that's what we've been taught. The problem is that the passage isn't primarily about our storms. So what is it all about?

As the passage unfolds, we discover that Jesus's disciples find themselves in a desperate situation! While they are crossing over the Sea of Galilee in a boat with Jesus, "a great windstorm arose, and the waves were breaking into the boat" (4:37). At least three of these men are fishermen, familiar with this sea. They have seen their share of storms! This storm, though, is one that they *know* they can't survive. They wake Jesus, who is sleeping in the storm, with these desperate words: "Teacher, do you not care that we are perishing?" (4:38). Jesus calmly steps up, speaks, and the storm is *immediately calm*. This is a stunning miracle. So, what is this story teaching?

There's one big indication that this story isn't necessarily about Jesus calming all the various storms of our lives, or taking away all our fears, problems, and troubles. Look closely again at verses 40–41. What happens to the disciples after Jesus takes away the storm that was threatening their very lives? They are more afraid of Jesus than they were of the storm! In fact, Mark never even says that the disciples were scared by the storm (although they probably were, at least to some extent). What freaks them out is the power and authority of the man who's in the boat with them. Being in the presence of that kind of divine power is far more terrifying to the disciples than any wind, rain, thunder, or lightning. Jesus's miracle in the boat didn't *solve* the disciples' life problems; it gave them a bigger problem. Now they had to figure out what to do with Jesus. And Jesus was scarier to them even than the prospect of death!

So, what is Mark's main point in telling us this story? It's all about Jesus's identity. Mark wants us to ask—along with Jesus's disciples—"*Who* is this guy?" They don't get it at this point in Mark's Gospel. But we need to get it. He's the Son of God, the ruler of all creation, the one with infinite authority, power, and control.

Ask God to help you see clearly who Jesus Christ is. Pray that he would help you answer the disciples' question ("Who then is this . . . ?" 4:41) with confidence, joy, and faith, declaring: "He is the Son of God—my Savior!"

Changed by Mighty Jesus

After Jesus's calming of the storm, the disciples are left asking serious questions about Jesus's identity: "Who is this?" They are beginning to wonder if there is anything that this Jesus *can't* do. Is there any part of creation over which this man does not have authority?

In typical Mark fashion, he doesn't give us much time to think before he answers that question. Jesus and his disciples exit the boat and are hit with another situation. "Immediately there met [Jesus] out of the tombs a man with an unclean spirit" (5:2). The story moves right along; Mark doesn't let us catch our breath!

The man whom Jesus and his disciples met would have been almost as terrifying as the storm they had just faced. Possessed by demons for years, he was like something out of a horror film. "He lived among the tombs" (5:3), which is scary by itself. On top of that, his demonic possession seemed to have given him supernatural strength. Mark tells us, "He had often been bound with shackles and chains, but he wrenched the chains apart, and he broke the shackles in pieces" (5:4). This man—under the grip of Satan—had become a wandering freak show. And *this* man was about to meet Jesus.

When the demons that possess this man see Jesus, they ironically know exactly whom they're dealing with—unlike Jesus's disciples in the last passage. They cry out, "What have you to do with me, Jesus, Son of the Most High God?" (5:7). Jesus calmly asks the man his name, and the many demons speak for him, telling Jesus that there are many of them. Then something very important happens. The demons start pleading with Jesus. Jesus has complete authority; Satan's minions are begging for their lives at the feet of this man. So Jesus sends them into a herd of pigs, and their true destructive, hell-bent nature is demonstrated by the response of the pigs: they run straight for the sea, dive in, and die! Meanwhile, the man—formerly a monster—stands before Jesus healed and sane, much to the amazement of everyone who used to know him! He's been changed by Jesus, the Son of God who rules wind and sea, and before whom the forces of Satan cower in submission.

Ask God to help you remember just how mighty Jesus is. Pray that your worship and reverence for your Savior would increase, and that you would—like the healed demoniac—be desperate to follow him!

Honoring Jesus with Our Whole Heart

Susie's mother made cleaning her room a prerequisite for doing a fun activity with friends. And so, Susie would "clean" her room. That meant shoving everything in sight under her bed, and whatever didn't fit under the bed got shoved into her closet! She had obeyed the "letter of the law" when it came to her mom's instructions, but she hadn't fulfilled the "heart" of what she had been asked to do.

This brief story illustrates Mark 7:1–23, in which the Pharisees—according to Jesus—have the wrong focus. They are concerned with the letter of the law, the specific obligations and details of God's word. But in their obsession with rituals, details, and special regulations, they have missed the true *heart* of God's law in all kinds of significant ways.

Jesus's disciples aren't following the Pharisees' extra rituals when it comes to their premeal washing. The Pharisees confront Jesus on this point: "Why do your disciples not walk according to the tradition of the elders, but eat with defiled hands?" (7:5). They think they've got Jesus trapped; they've just proved that their righteousness is greater than his! Jesus's response, though, is devastating, as he cuts right to the heart of the issue. He quotes Isaiah, who takes issue with people who honor God with their lips and not with their hearts. Then Jesus accuses the Pharisees of making their traditions more important than the actual word of God! His point is clear: the Pharisees are guilty of missing the very heart of God's word, by becoming obsessed with the details of religious ritual.

After this showdown is over, Jesus calls his disciples to explain what has just happened. He explains to them: "There is nothing outside a person that by going into him can defile him, but the things that come out of a person are what defile him" (7:15). Jesus, as he always does, cuts right to the heart of the matter. Following and loving God is not about dirty hands at a meal! It's about hearts that are completely given over to him—every thought, inclination, hope, and passion.

We have to remember that God is ultimately after our hearts; he wants holy behavior that emerges as genuine fruit of hearts that are given wholly in faith and repentance to Jesus. Pray that God would enable you to live for him in holiness in every way, because you truly worship Jesus as Savior and Lord.

Humble, Childlike Faith

Mark shows us a tender scene: people are bringing young children to Jesus so that he can touch them. His disciples get angry, probably because they think the children are crowding Jesus or wasting his time. Jesus's response, though, is quite different. Rebuking his disciples, he teaches them an important lesson: "Truly, I say to you, whoever does not receive the kingdom of God like a child shall not enter it" (10:15). There is something about the *attitude* and *approach* of a child that Jesus seems to desire from those who would follow him.

Second, Mark shows us a striking scene between Jesus and a man who is described, primarily, as being rich. He seems to want to follow Jesus; he runs up to him, asking, "What must I do to inherit eternal life?" (10:17). This very question betrays an assumption that this man has about eternal life! "What must *I do*?" he asks Jesus. Salvation, at least in his mind, depends in some way on his merit; he thinks he can earn it!

Jesus responds by reciting several commandments related to interaction with other human beings: honoring father and mother, not committing adultery, not committing murder, and so on. The man enthusiastically affirms that he's kept these commandments! It's time for Jesus to once again cut to the heart. "Go," he tells the man, "sell all that you have and give to the poor, and you will have treasure in heaven; and come, follow me" (10:21). The man goes away sad, because of the wealth he's been asked to give away. Jesus has demonstrated the man's failure to keep the first commandment—to have no other gods before the one true God. The man has made his money his god.

Those who follow Jesus must come to him with humble and childlike faith. How does a child come to an adult for help? He or she brings nothing. That is how we are to come to Jesus! Not asking what we can do to earn our salvation, like the rich man. Not holding on to idols that we love more than God, like the rich man. We are to come to Jesus humbly, holding nothing in our hands, hoping in him alone for salvation, forgiveness, and eternal life.

Pray that you would come to Jesus in the right way! Ask him to give you humble, childlike faith, as you look only to him for salvation. And pray that he would show you your idols, knock them down, and help you to worship and love him alone.

Be Ready!

It can sometimes seem like this world will continue going on as it does now—forever. But that's not what Jesus says. "Heaven and earth will pass away," he tells his disciples (13:31). Everything in this world is rushing forward to an ultimate *end*.

The whole segment of teaching in Mark 13 is touched off by the disciples' admiration of the temple. Looking at the grand building, they exclaim, "Look, Teacher, what wonderful stones and what wonderful buildings!" (13:1). Jesus doesn't exactly join in their admiration, but he instead tells them that, one day, every stone that they see will be torn down! As the disciples try to process this comment from Jesus, four of them privately ask Jesus this question: "When will these things be, and what will be the sign when all these things are about to be accomplished?" (13:4). It's that question that Jesus answers in the rest of the chapter.

We can't go into all the different potential interpretations of everything Jesus says in this chapter. But we will note a few things. First, we see that the final days of this earth will be preceded by obvious signs that point to the coming judgment. Wars, natural disasters, unrest—all these things are meant to warn us that this world will not last forever. Second, we see that Jesus teaches that tough times are coming for God's people. Salvation is ultimately the great hope for all who follow Jesus, but persecution, suffering, and even physical death could come with it. Third, it seems that an antichrist—or antichrists—will come before Jesus returns to earth to judge the world in glory. There will be some who will attempt to deceive people concerning where they should put their trust and hope; Jesus is warning us against this. So what do we do about all this?

There's only one response that we see Jesus calling for, as he teaches his disciples: "Be on guard, keep awake" (13:33). No one knows when all these things will happen, Jesus says! In fact, Jesus says that during his days on earth, only the Father knows the exact timing of this entire plan for the judgment of the world and the final victory of the Son. What are followers of Jesus called to do? Be ready.

Pray that God would help you "stay awake" as you follow Jesus. Ask him to give you, by his Holy Spirit, more love for your Savior and more faith in his word, which Jesus tells us, will never pass away.

You've Got the Whole Word in Your Hands

Have you ever thought to yourself, "I wish I just could have been there to see the life of Jesus"? Wouldn't that sort out all our doubts that sometimes plague our faith? Friend, Mark would answer that question, "Absolutely not!" He would want us to see that, actually, we are in the much better position to believe in Jesus. According to Mark's Gospel, it was actually very *difficult* for the eyewitnesses to understand what Jesus was all about.

Now Jesus has been speaking very openly not only about his death but his resurrection as well. His disciples—and even the women who followed him—should have been ready for all this, right? Wrong. Look at the actions and attitudes of Mary Magdalene, Mary the mother of James, and their friend Salome, as they come together to visit Jesus's tomb on the first day of the week. They bring spices to anoint him. Do they expect Jesus to be alive—risen? No. They come to anoint a dead body. Even more surprising is their response to the visit of the angel, who gives them the good news about Jesus's resurrection. The angel tells them explicitly to go and tell his disciples the good news. What do the women do? They run away, terrified, and don't tell anyone because of their fear! What is Mark's point? It seems that he is showing us that it will take some time before even Jesus's disciples and other eyewitnesses to his resurrection understand what has happened and what it all means.

So what does this all mean for *us*? It means that we sit in a very privileged spot. We get to, from a distance, learn about the death and resurrection of Jesus, the Son of God, and we have the witness of the New Testament to help us make sense of all of it. We are *so* blessed! We have the clear teachings of Scripture that *explain* to us what this all meant. The word of God means that we have it *better* than the people who were actually there. There is only one right way to respond to this witness about Jesus: it's to put all our trust and hope in the Son of God!

Spend some time thanking God that you live in a time of clarity, with the whole witness of Scripture at your fingertips. Ask him to help you put your faith more and more in his inspired word, which points with clarity to the salvation that is found only through his Son!

Our Reasonable Faith

It doesn't take too long to realize that Luke writes his gospel from a slightly different perspective—and with a slightly different intent—from either Matthew or Mark. He begins by addressing his book to someone named Theophilus. According to Luke, it's written so that this Theophilus would have "certainty concerning the things" that he's heard about Jesus (1:4). With that end in mind, Luke tells Theophilus that he has tried to compose an "orderly account" of the life of Jesus (1:3). Luke is trying to show how *reasonable* it is to believe in Jesus. And Luke has made his end goal clear for Theophilus and for us: that we would have certainty about all that we've been taught about Jesus Christ.

If it weren't for Luke, we wouldn't have many of the well-known accounts of the events surrounding the birth of Jesus Christ. But Luke begins even earlier than the birth of Jesus; he starts with the events leading up to the birth of John the Baptist. The Gospel of Luke begins in a temple, with a priest named Zechariah, whose wife is barren. While serving in the temple, Zechariah is visited by an angel, who tells him about a son who will be born miraculously to his wife, Elizabeth. His son will be the promised prophet who will come before the Messiah; the angel tells him, "And he will go before him in the spirit and power of Elijah, to turn the hearts of the fathers to the children, and the disobedient to the wisdom of the just, to make ready for the Lord a people prepared" (1:17).

But even a priest like Zechariah can get cynical and can struggle to keep faith in God. He doesn't believe the angel. After all, the facts are pretty clear: "I am an old man, and my wife is advanced in years" (1:18). Physically, Zechariah and his wife are way past the years of childbearing. But God isn't going to let this get in the way of his plan for his people. Remember, God has done miracles like this before!

Zechariah is disciplined for his lack of faith; he is unable to speak until this child is born. And yet God is gracious. His plan will continue, even though Zechariah doubts it. The passage ends with Elizabeth conceiving. The child to be born will point the way to the Messiah. God's salvation plan is in motion, and it begins with a miracle!

Pray that you would be fully convinced of the truth of the good news of salvation through Jesus Christ. Ask God to give you faith in him—the God who keeps his promises to sinful people.

A Faith-Filled Teenager

Everything is changing for the people of God. For four hundred years—the time in between the Old Testament and the New Testament—God has been silent. Now, all of a sudden, the time has come! God is moving; he is finally starting to fulfill his promises to his people, through the coming of John the Baptist first and then Jesus Christ the Messiah.

Luke tells us that God's angel Gabriel comes to Mary, a young girl who is betrothed to a man named Joseph. Gabriel's message is huge: "And behold, you will conceive in your womb and bear a son, and you shall call his name Jesus. He will be great and will be called the Son of the Most High" (1:31–32). This teenage girl is visited by an angel, who tells her that she will give birth to the Son of God! When Mary innocently asks how exactly this will happen, the message of the angel gets even more surprising: "The Holy Spirit will come upon you, and the power of the Most High will overshadow you; therefore the child to be born will be called holy—the Son of God" (1:35). What's the answer to Mary's question? It's that this birth will be *a miracle*—something God will supernaturally make possible. What a shocking day for a teenage girl!

Mary's words to the angel strike me every time I read them. They are faith-filled words, words of trust in God: "Behold, I am the servant of the Lord; let it be to me according to your word" (1:38). Mary basically says to God, "Whatever you want; I'm yours." What a response of faith! Even Zechariah the priest, remember, had trouble believing that God could miraculously give a son to his aging wife. Mary—confronted with the promise of a far greater miracle than John the Baptist's birth—takes God at his word.

We see, though, as the chapter goes on, that Mary's faith-filled response isn't totally blind. She visits her relative Elizabeth, whose baby leaps inside her when he senses the presence of the Son of God inside Mary. Mary's great Magnificat, the song that she sings in response to this leaping, shows us that Mary knew the word of God and his promises to his people. And she's excited that she gets to be a part of God's plan!

Are you submitting yourself to God's word and his will in your life? Make Mary's prayer your prayer. Commit yourself to living as God's servant. Ask him to help you live—in every way—according to his word.

A King for Shepherds and Princes

This is how the *King* comes? That's the question that should be in your mind as you read this account. In fact, almost everything about the way Jesus comes should strike us as very unkingly. First, there is the place and manner of his birth. His humble parents—away from home for a census—have no place to stay. Bethlehem doesn't exactly roll out the red carpet for the Messiah! Luke tells us that Mary "gave birth to her firstborn son and wrapped him in swaddling cloths and laid him in a manger, because there was no place for them in the inn" (2:7). There, among the animals, laid in a feeding trough, the Savior and King is born. It's hard to imagine a less royal beginning to life—in the midst of the filth and stench of barnyard animals!

Next, Jesus's birth is announced not in the royal courts, or even in the temple, but to a group of shepherds in the fields. You haven't known too many shepherds, so you may think that they were kind, gentle, good-looking, respectable men with well-kept beards and nice tunics. They weren't. The shepherds were the blue-collar workers of Jesus's day. They were out all night in the fields, protecting valuable flocks of sheep from fierce wild animals. And the angels of heaven come to these men with the good news of the birth of the Messiah! Here's how Luke describes this visit from the angels: "And suddenly there was with the angel a multitude of the heavenly host praising God and saying, 'Glory to God in the highest, and on earth peace among those with whom he is pleased!'" (2:13–14). At Jesus's birth, heaven's angels sing—not to kings, not to priests, not to the Pharisees—to *shepherds*. God chooses to announce the birth of the Savior of the world—first—to a group of very ordinary men.

What is Luke telling us, and what is *God* showing us about his Son, the Savior? We're learning that Jesus, the Messiah, will be the Savior of all people. He won't show up in a royal court; he is no merely political ruler. He won't come first to the upper-crust folks; he is a king for shepherds *and* for princes. Jesus will come as the humble Savior. Even his birth is a sign that his rule will not ultimately be from an earthly throne but from a humble cross.

Pray that your response to Jesus would be to glorify and praise God like the shepherds. Thank him, right now, for the gracious and humble coming of his Son—your Savior!

Jesus's Bold Move

Luke's goal is to put together an orderly account of the life of Jesus so that his audience—Theophilus—will have certainty about the things he's heard about Jesus. But Luke also seems to have a certain focus throughout this account on the *least of these*: the misfits, Gentiles, people who are ritually unclean. Luke seems to go out of his way to emphasize that Jesus—the Messiah—comes for these people, as well as the "clean" people.

At the very beginning of Jesus's public ministry, he heads back to Nazareth, his hometown. Jesus is called upon to read Scripture, and he chooses to read from the prophet Isaiah, who speaks of good news coming to the poor, and the "year of the Lord's favor" (4:19). Jesus boldly affirms that this prophecy is being fulfilled *through him*. It's a bold move indeed! And it's no wonder that the people from Nazareth, who have watched him grow up, begin to grumble. They evidently don't see anything special about this hometown boy who now is making declarations about himself!

What happens next, though, really ignites the fire. Jesus, in light of the rejection he receives from the people of Nazareth, takes them back to a couple of stories from the Old Testament. He mentions the widow of Zarephath, to whom Elijah was sent to minister. He talks about Naaman, the Syrian general who was healed by Elisha. What did Naaman and this widow have in common? They were Gentiles, not part of "God's people." Yet in the Old Testament, they both received God's blessing as they put their faith in the God of Israel through the ministry of God's prophets.

Jesus has, in the Jews' minds, far overstepped his bounds. He's identified himself with the great prophets of God and reminded them that God will not hesitate to send his prophets even to Gentiles—people who were probably seen as dirty to these Jews. Jesus is telling these people that he—God's great prophet—has come for everyone who will accept him—both Jew and Gentile. It's not about ethnicity; it's about faith. What Jesus is saying makes these people so angry that they form a mob and drag him to the top of a hill, hoping to throw him off to his death!

We need to be reminded that we—apart from Christ—are wretched, lost sinners. We need God's grace, and we should rejoice that God's grace in Christ is available to truly everyone who genuinely repents and puts his or her faith in him. Pray that God would help you do that.

The Cross

In Luke 23, indeed, we have come to the very center of the entire Bible: the death of Jesus Christ, God's Son. It's important to get clear on that point! This is the *climax* of the entire biblical narrative—the point that the whole story is moving toward. So, what is the gospel writer Luke telling us that the cross of Jesus is all about?

First, Luke shows us that, at the cross, Jesus stands alone as the innocent Son of God, in the midst of hopelessly sinful people. Jesus is crucified, obviously, mainly because of the attacks of the Jewish leaders. The rulers scoff at him, mocking him for his supposed inability to save himself from death. The Roman soldiers make fun of Jesus and make a game out of dividing up his clothes as souvenirs. Even a criminal in unthinkable pain on a cross next to Jesus finds strength to make nasty remarks to him. At the end of Jesus's life, he hangs on a cross alone.

Second, Luke shows us that, at the cross, Jesus makes possible the justification of hopelessly sinful people. In an exchange that we only get in the Gospel of Luke, we find the conversion of a criminal who hangs on a cross next to Jesus. This man rebukes the other criminal, who has joined the soldiers and rulers in mockery of Jesus. He then turns to Jesus and offers him one simple phrase: "Jesus, remember me when you come into your kingdom" (23:42). Without a moment of hesitation, Jesus gives him a clear answer: "Truly, I say to you, today you will be with me in paradise" (23:43). Remember, this is not a man who has "lived his life for the Lord"! Yet Jesus justifies this sinner who utters one simple word of faith. He is made right before an infinitely holy God, in an instant.

Finally, Luke is showing us that, at the cross, there is only one right response for hopelessly sinful people. What is that response? It's that of the criminal we've just been discussing: repentance, faith, and total reliance on the grace of Jesus to wash away sin and offer us gracious acceptance by his mercy alone. There was no leaning on good works for that criminal; he probably hadn't done *any*! He trusted in Jesus *alone* and gained heaven eternally for it.

Make this your prayer: "Jesus, remember me, by your mercy, and because of your death on the cross for my sins!" Thank God that, because of the death of his Son, you will be one day with him forever.

In the Beginning Was the Word

We introduce ourselves in very different ways, depending entirely upon the situation, don't we? If I were to go to speak to a group of young men at a basketball camp, I might begin by saying, "My name is Jon. I love basketball, and I played competitively for years." Speaking to someone who I know is reading Homer's *Odyssey*, I might tell him or her that I was an English literature major in college. This is true of the gospel writers as well. Remember Matthew? He wants to emphasize the kingly authority of Jesus as the promised Messiah; he starts his Gospel with a genealogy. Mark just wants to tell the basic facts of the good news of Jesus, the Son of God; he dives right into the story. Luke sets out to write an orderly account of the life of Jesus; Luke introduces Jesus by paying close attention to the historical facts. John writes, it seems, for the entire world; his Gospel doesn't seem to be limited at all in its audience. John is concerned only with people's *belief* in Jesus Christ, as we'll see from the passages we read. It makes sense that John starts his Gospel not with a genealogy or historical details, but *theology*.

So who is Jesus according to John? Jesus is the eternally existing, all-powerful Word of God made flesh. John begins with these well-known words about Jesus: "In the beginning was the Word, and the Word was with God, and the Word was God. He was in the beginning with God" (1:1–2). Jesus, John is explaining, has always existed. He is fully God, and he has always been fully God. That means that Jesus was active in creation; John tells us that "without him was not any thing made that was made" (1:3). Who is this Jesus? He is God! Then comes the beautiful surprise.

John tells us that the eternally existing, all-powerful Word of God becomes flesh. He "dwelt among us," John explains (1:14). Literally, the word for *dwelt* could be translated *tabernacled*. In other words, the full glory of God has come to be with human beings—not in a tent, as during the days of Moses and the Israelites in the wilderness, but in the person of Jesus Christ. He is the full revelation of God to us. Jesus is God coming near to his people in the fullest way possible.

Spend some time thanking God for this amazing salvation plan. Praise him for the amazing good news that, in Jesus, God has come near to lost sinners like you and me. Ask him to open your eyes in a new way to Jesus as you read passages from the Gospel of John.

Water into Wine

It's the gospel writer John who helps us understand the true meaning and purpose behind the miracles of Jesus. He does this simply by referring to them not as miracles but as signs. What does a sign do? It points us to something that it only *represents*. That is what Jesus's miracles do! They point us to a deeper reality that the miracles signify. In John 2:1–12, John tells us about the first of Jesus's signs: the miraculous changing of water into wine.

Jesus, his mother, and his disciples are all at a wedding together. There is a problem; the wedding hosts have run out of wine. This would have been a terrible embarrassment to the hosts, and so Jesus's mother appeals to Jesus to do something about it. Jesus instructs the servants who are working at the wedding, and they bring jars of water to the master of the feast. Along the way, the water has turned into wine. The master of the feast tastes it and congratulates the bridegroom for bringing out the best wine at the end of the party! So what is this first sign of Jesus showing us?

It's amazing how much we learn about Jesus through this sign. First, we see that he has complete control over even the laws of nature; Jesus has the power to change the molecular makeup of water into a different substance. This is a true miracle; it defies the laws of science. Second, we see that Jesus cares deeply about people by providing for their immediate needs. Jesus could have brushed off this opportunity as an unimportant, trivial matter, but he doesn't! He provides for the simple needs of the bridegroom at this small-town wedding, showing that he is anything but disconnected from the details of the lives of the people he comes to serve.

What do Jesus's disciples do about this first sign? Look again at verse 11: Jesus manifests his glory through this sign, and "his disciples believed in him." That is the intended result of this first sign—and of all Jesus's signs. John, remember, is all about helping people come to believe in Jesus as the glorious Son of God.

Our response to the Son of God should be the same as that of his first disciples: total belief. Ask God for strength and faith to believe in Jesus, your Savior, with even more confidence. He is the one who can turn water into wine—and so much more! Pray that your faith would rest firmly on Jesus Christ, God's glorious Son.

Born Again

Nicodemus knew the Old Testament Scriptures; as a Pharisee, he had devoted his life to studying them! Now he is faced with a dilemma: the person of Jesus Christ. What was going on with this man? John wants to show us through this secret, middle-of-the-night conversation that some of the Jewish leaders in Jesus's day had read Scripture for years and missed a very important point: the entire Old Testament points to a final salvation that comes through Jesus Christ, God's Son.

Jesus's answer to Nicodemus's first question is really about salvation: "Truly, truly, I say to you, unless one is born again he cannot see the kingdom of God" (3:3). This confuses Nicodemus; he begins thinking about literal birth and how it's impossible for a human being to literally be born all over again. Jesus goes on to explain that salvation, ultimately, is about a spiritual birth that comes by a work of the Holy Spirit. He does this by going back to a passage that Nicodemus would have known well: Ezekiel 36 and the valley of dry bones in Ezekiel 37. This vision probably signified for Nicodemus a hope for the future of God's people, Israel. Jesus, though, is telling him something new about this prophecy: it's all about the salvation he brings. New life—this miraculous spiritual birth—is what is required for God's people to truly be saved. And it all comes through Jesus. But how?

It becomes clear as Jesus goes on. Jesus must be "lifted up" as the Savior of all people: "As Moses lifted up the serpent in the wilderness, so must the Son of Man be lifted up, that whoever believes in him may have eternal life. For God so loved the world, that he gave his only Son, that whoever believes in him should not perish but have eternal life" (3:14–16). These verses are familiar to us, but they would have been *revolutionary* to a man who thought he had the Scriptures figured out! Ezekiel's vision of dry bones coming to life was all about spiritual birth—salvation. And that salvation would be accomplished by the man standing right in front of Nicodemus—Jesus, God's own Son.

It seems that Nicodemus got it. He embraced Jesus as God's Son and followed him even to the cross—and beyond—for we later see him helping to bury Jesus's body. Pray that God would help you see more and more how Jesus is the ultimate answer for lost sinners. Ask him to help you read your Bible with his Son at the center of it!

Jesus and the Pharisees

You've probably noticed that, throughout all the Gospels, the Pharisees serve as a kind of foil for Jesus. In this passage, we find an extended dialogue between Jesus and the Pharisees (and some other Jews) that John records for us. So what can we learn from this back-and-forth interaction?

First, we are learning that some people are blinded to the reality of Jesus's true identity. Verses 22 and 27 give us two clear examples of how some of the Jews Jesus talked with were on a totally different wavelength than he was. At one point, they think Jesus is talking about killing himself. At another point, they can't figure out that he's talking about God the Father—a fact that seems obvious to us. John is trying to show us that, for some people, "getting" Jesus just doesn't come easily. When it comes to the identity and teaching of Jesus, they're blind and deaf.

Second, John is showing us that, ultimately, the point on which everything hinges—for the Pharisees during Jesus's time and for us today—is the identity of Jesus Christ. Jesus blatantly affirms that he is God; he even uses the well-known "I AM" identifier of Yahweh from the Old Testament. This makes the Jews furious; they try to kill him immediately! John is showing us that there is one ultimate question that we all have to answer: Is Jesus God? If he is God, it really does mean that faith—salvation—is all about him. It's not about being Jewish (literal ethnic children of Abraham). It's not about keeping the law only. It all centers around the man who is *God*. At the end of all things, there will be a line drawn in the middle of all humanity, between those who affirm that Jesus is Lord and those who fight that truth with stones—or with their very lives.

Finally, we are learning that—to some—God does give the miraculous gift of belief. Verse 30 reminds us of this gracious good news. Some people do believe in Jesus; in fact, John says *many* people believe in him. This is a miracle, and we need to remember that! Faith is a gracious gift of God, who alone can open the blind eyes and soften the hard hearts of lost and sinful human beings.

It's a grace that we believe in Jesus and that we joyfully affirm that he really is God. Thank God today for allowing you to see Jesus as he truly is. He has been gracious to you!

The Resurrection and the Life

As you think back over John 11:1–44, let this miracle hit you again with all its weight. Jesus brought Lazarus back to life. Lazarus was a man—just like any other man—and he had really, truly, physically died. Jesus, whose powerful hand had created the universe, spoke just three words—"Lazarus, come out" (11:43)—and the power of death was broken. Death reversed itself at the words of Jesus.

Jesus is, again, revealing something about himself: he is showing us his divine power over life and death. That's what this sign is meant to signify. This Jesus—God in human flesh—holds complete command over every part of creation.

But we're learning something else from this account as well. Jesus reveals his identity for the good of people who love him. The difficult thing for us to grasp (though not quite so difficult as it was at first for Mary and Martha!) is that Jesus's allowing of Lazarus's death is a key part of his far bigger plan to reveal his glory and power to his followers. Look carefully at how John describes Jesus's decision to stay away when he heard that Lazarus was ill: "Now Jesus loved Martha and her sister and Lazarus. So, when he heard that Lazarus was ill, he stayed two days longer in the place where he was" (11:5–6). Did you catch it? The word *so*. Jesus stayed away and allowed Lazarus to die *because* he loved him and Martha and Mary so much! He loves them so much, in fact, that he wants to show them his glory.

Why is this? Why would Jesus go so far as to even allow the death of his beloved friend in order for his glory to be revealed? Because to see the glory of the Son of God—and to believe in him—is the best thing that fallen, sinful human beings like you and me can ever do. That is the only way for them to never die. Jesus is after something much, much bigger than an earthly kingdom. He is building an eternal kingdom, filled with people who believe that he is the resurrection and the life!

As you apply this passage to your life, you shouldn't need to go anywhere other than Jesus's pointed question to Martha after declaring himself to be the resurrection and the life; he asks her, "Do you believe this?" (11:26). Pray that Martha's answer would be the resounding response that wells up from your own heart. Ask God to strengthen your faith in Jesus, his Son, in whom alone is eternal life and resurrection power!

We Serve Because He Served

This is a passage that we tend to read and then jump immediately into application. Jesus is serving his disciples, we notice, and he is doing it in the most humble and servant-like way possible. So we take this as an example for us; Jesus is showing us how we are to serve the people around us. We need to humbly kneel before brothers and sisters in Christ and serve them. We need to put their needs and comfort before our own. We need to honor Jesus by accepting even humble tasks that are done in the service of others. We need to be more like Jesus! And all those things are true. But they're not the main point of this passage.

Look again at how John begins: he tells us that Jesus, "having loved his own who were in the world, he loved them to the end" (13:1). This activity will be a part of the way that Jesus loves his disciples to the end—all the way to the cross. Then comes Jesus's interaction with Peter during this foot-washing event. Peter doesn't want any part of this! He knows that he—a sinful man—should be the one washing Jesus's feet, and not the other way around. Jesus's answer is telling: "If I do not wash you, you have no share with me" (13:8). Now, Jesus does go on to tell his disciples that this act of humble service is an example for them; they are to act toward others with the same attitude of loving service. But not until Jesus has first done it for them. In other words, not until Jesus has made them clean. Jesus needs to first serve them before they can go out and serve others.

This foot washing is not disconnected from Jesus's death—some random example of humble service that Jesus throws the disciples' way. It is a picture of Jesus's death, which will make them perfectly clean from sin. What is the point of this passage? It's John's way of telling us that we need to be *saved* by Jesus before we can *serve* him. He needs to serve us on the cross by dying for our sins. Only then will we be truly able to follow his example and lay down our lives sacrificially for others.

You can serve others humbly only because Jesus once-and-for-all humbly served you by dying for your sins and conquering death forever. Thank God that Jesus has served you—and saved you. Ask him to help you humbly serve and love the people around you every day, because of the cross.

The Way, the Truth, and the Life

The disciples are troubled. Why? Because Jesus has been talking about going away. His disciples can't bear the thought of losing Jesus, if he really does go away! When we understand this, we begin to realize that Jesus's words in John 14 are all about *comfort*. So how does Jesus comfort his troubled disciples?

First, Jesus comforts his disciples by pointing them to a place—a place to which, he says, they will go too. "In my Father's house are many rooms," Jesus says. "If it were not so, would I have told you that I go to prepare a place for you?" (14:2). This is Jesus's first word of comfort to troubled people—that his departure will mean the beginning of preparations for a place for God's people in the presence of God forever. It's a promise of heaven eternally for all who love and follow him.

Jesus's disciples seem to think he's still talking about a place located somewhere on the earth; Thomas points out, "Lord, we do not know where you are going. How can we know the way?" (14:5). Jesus answers this question with one of the clearest articulations of the way to salvation for human beings. How can sinful people find their way to the Father? Only through a person: Jesus Christ himself. "I am the way, and the truth, and the life," Jesus says. "No one comes to the Father except through me" (14:6). The only way to God's place is through God's chosen person—his Son.

Jesus has told them about a glorious place, and he's reminded them that that place is only accessible through one person. Now he gives them one great promise in the meantime: "And I will ask the Father, and he will give you another Helper, to be with you forever, even the Spirit of truth" (14:16–17). Even though the disciples know Jesus—the right person—they will have to wait for a while until they are with him in God's place. While they wait, though, they will receive the gift of God's Holy Spirit—to guide them, help them, and lead them to Jesus.

What is the greatest comfort for Christians who are troubled? It's the hope of a place—that one day, they will be at home with God himself. It's the hope of a person—Jesus, the only Savior of sinners and the only way to God. And it's the hope of Jesus's great promise—that all who belong to him have the presence of the Holy Spirit with them to guide them every step of the way. Pray to your heavenly Father, asking him to help you hold on to this greatest hope in times of trouble.

Abide in Jesus

One question that high school pastors hear a lot is "How can I tell if my friend is really a follower of Jesus?" The slightly different version of the same question was "How do I know for sure that *I* am really a Christian?" In John 15, Jesus gives his disciples a clear picture of what it looks like for people who truly follow him. The picture is of branches connected to a vine.

Jesus's big point is this: real branches bear fruit. In fact, branches that don't bear fruit aren't true branches; these branches he takes away. If a branch is a branch, it will do what a branch is supposed to do! If you belong to Jesus Christ, your life, actions, thoughts, and words will demonstrate that clearly. This is something that we cannot fake! Good fruit—fruit that represents Jesus—will come off people who truly follow him.

But Jesus also wants to be clear about something very important: no human being can create good fruit on his or her own. "Whoever abides in me and I in him, he it is that bears much fruit, for apart from me you can do nothing," Jesus says (15:5). The only way a branch can bear any fruit is by staying connected to the vine—by abiding in Jesus. That's why Jesus uses this organic metaphor for his relationship to his people. Growth and fruit will *only* come from a relationship with him. When the relationship is there, this will happen *naturally*. We can't make our own fruit. It happens as we go after Jesus with all our hearts.

How do we abide in Jesus? How do we begin to bear fruit? How do we pursue a relationship with him? It starts as we listen to—and live by—his word. Jesus tells his disciples, "If you keep my commandments, you will abide in my love" (15:10). Abiding in Jesus is about paying attention to his word—everything that he has instructed his disciples. It's through the word of Jesus—the good news about salvation—that we come to him. And, as we abide in our Savior, fruit begins to appear in our lives!

We should—through a real relationship with Jesus Christ—begin to see real, natural growth and fruit. Pray that God would help you abide in Jesus. Ask him to make you more ready to listen to his word and obey it. Pray that he would make you a branch that is truly connected to the vine!

The High Priestly Prayer

If you have read any plays by William Shakespeare, you know that he often makes use of something called a soliloquy. In a soliloquy, a character steps away from the action and makes a speech designed to show the audience his or her inner monologue. In John 17, we come closest to getting a soliloquy from Jesus. John has recorded for us Jesus's great prayer to God—sometimes called the high priestly prayer. So how does Jesus pray to God the Father?

First, Jesus prays for himself—that he would be glorified. This is not a selfish prayer! In fact, what Jesus asks God for is a kind of *mutual* glorification: "Father, the hour has come; glorify your Son that the Son may glorify you" (17:1). Jesus is coming to the end of his work on earth; he is moving toward the final chapter: the cross. His prayer, at this point, is that through his death he would be glorified—lifted up. That will be for the eternal life and salvation of lost sinners and for the eternal praise of God's name.

Next, Jesus prays for his disciples—that they would be kept and sanctified by God. Jesus asks God to "keep them in your name" (17:11). He prays that they would be kept and guarded from the evil one. Ultimately, Jesus's prayer for his disciples is that God would sanctify them—make them holy—by the power of his word of truth. Jesus commits his chosen disciples to the infinite, perfect care of God the Father to *keep* them from sin and to *guard* their hearts and souls to the end.

Finally, Jesus prays for all believers in him in the future—that they would have unity in their belief in him. Friend, Jesus is praying for *you and me* at this point in the prayer. Isn't that amazing? Jesus, just hours from his death, looks forward to all the people who will come to faith in him in future years and asks God to give them unity in their belief in him as Lord and Savior. What is the purpose of this unity? It's that "the world may know that you sent me and loved them even as you loved me" (17:23). Jesus wants his people to be unified so that more people will know him as the loving Savior of the world.

Pray that your unity with other Christians would be grounded in the true identity of Jesus. Ask God to help you be one with other Christians—in your church and community—who truly affirm Jesus as the only Savior of lost sinners. Pray that God would use that unity to bring more people to Jesus!

Pontius Pilate

The man Pontius Pilate was a Roman governor who had been appointed by Rome to rule over the area of Judea. He ruled the Jews in this area, since Rome held ultimate power during the time of Jesus, having conquered Jerusalem years earlier. He enters the picture in John 18, because executions had to be done with Roman authority behind them. So the Jewish leaders have to bring Jesus to Pilate. Pilate, at first, shows no sign of wanting to be involved: "Take him yourselves and judge him by your own law," he tells the Jews (18:31). The people insist, however, that Pilate take a close look at Jesus in order to support their charges against him.

Pilate can't figure out who this Jesus is or what his intentions are. And he's intrigued by Jesus. "So you are a king?" he asks him (18:37). Jesus has already explained to Pilate that his kingdom is not of this world; in verse 37 he goes on to tell Pilate that his *voice* is the key to human beings finding truth. Pilate's answer to Jesus shows us his heart: "What is truth?" (18:38). Pilate is a man who has lost hope in discovering truth. He is a cynic, captured by money, power, and politics, and he is far from a relationship with the God of the universe.

Something about Jesus, though, seems to fascinate Pilate and even attract him to him. He slowly tries to release Jesus; he knows that, at the very least, Jesus is not a dangerous criminal! Unable to reason with the screaming Jewish crowd, Pilate finally turns to Jesus and, with frustration, almost begs him to answer the charges against him. Jesus calmly tells Pilate that any authority he has over Jesus is only given from above. John tells us that from then on, Pilate tries to release Jesus. But in the end, his fear of the crowd (and his fear of losing favor with Caesar, the Roman emperor) leads him to give the word. Pilate turns an innocent man over to be crucified. He's an intriguing figure, this Pilate. He's fascinated by Jesus, but won't follow him, defend him, or believe in him.

There is only one right response to Jesus, and it's the response that Pilate just could not get to. It's belief. Belief that Jesus is the Son of God—the one with total authority. Belief that Jesus's words are the only way to ultimate truth. Belief that leads to the submission of self to the rule of Jesus in our lives. Have you gotten there? Pray that your relationship with Jesus would go past intrigue and fascination, to worship, submission, love, and obedience!

John's Perspective of the Crucifixion

The Gospels offer four different perspectives on the crucifixion and death of Jesus Christ. Each gospel writer describes the same event. The basic details are the same, and yet we've noticed already that each man has a slightly different focus. So, what does John want his readers to focus on as he describes the death of Jesus Christ?

First, it seems that John focuses on the way that Jesus's death fulfills key parts of Old Testament Scripture. The soldiers, casting lots for Jesus's clothes, are fulfilling the words of David in Psalm 22. John points out that Jesus's statement—"I thirst"—is also in fulfillment of Scripture (19:28). Even the way that Jesus is pierced in the side by the soldiers, rather than having his bones broken like the other crucified men, is a clear fulfillment—for John—of the witness of the Old Testament. John goes out of his way to show us that the death of Jesus, in every part, is in fulfillment of God's word. In other words, this is all according to plan. It's according to the plan of God, who remains completely in control, even as his Son is put to death on a cross.

Second, though, it seems that John wants to show us that—even in the midst of the horror and brutality of the crucifixion—some people believed in Jesus as the Son of God. John himself believes in Jesus, of course. But other people start showing up in his account as well. Joseph of Arimathea—a prominent Jewish ruler—shows up to take Jesus's body. He's been following Jesus secretly, but he really believes in him. Nicodemus comes forward as well; you may remember him from John 3. It seems that he too has decided to believe in Jesus. And, ultimately, that is what John wants for us—his readers—as well. He makes a rather obvious insertion of his own voice in verse 35: "He who saw it has borne witness—his testimony is true, and he knows that he is telling the truth—that you also may believe." John wants us to *believe* in this crucified Lord and put all our faith in him.

Ask God to strengthen your belief in Jesus, the Son of God, who died to fulfill all God's promises to God's people. Pray that you would see more and more the wonder of his sacrificial death for you, as you follow him as your Lord.

Undeniable Evidence

Every gospel writer emphasizes the fact that Jesus's disciples had trouble understanding that Jesus was actually going to rise from the dead. John explains to us, even in this chapter, that the disciples "as yet . . . did not understand the Scripture, that he must rise from the dead" (20:9). In this passage, though, we begin to see the beauty of belief, as Jesus's followers begin to understand the crowning act of Jesus's saving work. John, in chapter 20 of his Gospel, is confronting us with the reality of the bodily resurrection of Jesus Christ.

Mary Magdalene, Peter, and John begin to realize that something has happened. But it hasn't all come together in their minds by verse 10: "The disciples went back to their homes." They don't know what to do! Waiting by the tomb, Mary gets the first glance at their resurrected Lord. Jesus himself stands in front of her with words of comfort and hope. Mary runs and tells the other disciples that she has seen Jesus!

Finally, Jesus visits the entire group of disciples, who are huddling together in the safety of a locked house because they are afraid of the Jewish leaders. He demonstrates that it's really him by showing them his wounded hands and side. But there's one who still doesn't believe. It's Thomas. Sometimes known as "doubting Thomas," he declares—rather loudly, it seems—that he will not believe that Jesus has risen from the dead unless he sees Jesus with his own eyes and touches his hands and feet. Jesus even gently strengthens the faith of this doubting disciple by allowing him to touch him—and believe.

In this account, John shows us how person after person—when confronted with the reality of Jesus's resurrection—turned from confusion, doubt, or fear to belief in Jesus. These were not people who would have been naturally inclined to believe that people could just reverse death! But for Mary Magdalene, Thomas, and the rest of Jesus's disciples, the evidence for Jesus's resurrection was undeniable. He stood in front of them, talking to them and eating with them. Jesus had truly beaten death, and there was no other option but to believe in him.

Do you believe in the resurrection of Jesus Christ? Are you confident that you have life in his name? Do you rest for your salvation only on your hope in the death of the Christ, the Son of God, on the cross for your sins? Answer those questions today as you spend some time in prayer with God.

More Than Forgiveness

No matter how badly you've messed up, there was a certain disciple who messed up far worse than you. His name was Peter. A brash, strong, outspoken fisherman, he had boldly stepped out in faith to follow Jesus, leaving his old life behind. He had sworn to remain faithful to his Lord, even if it meant suffering, imprisonment, or even death! But when the big moment came, Peter blew it. He denied Jesus—not just once but three times in a row, and the last time with a few curses thrown in for good measure. Peter turned his back on Jesus when it mattered the most. You haven't blown it as badly as Peter, no matter what you think!

And that's what makes John 21 so amazing and so moving. Jesus Christ, now risen victoriously from the dead, does not abandon this man who failed him so terribly. Jesus, with true compassion and grace, restores Peter with his words and sends him out to do great work for him in the world. This isn't without a subtle reminder of Peter's failure. Jesus asks Peter *three* times if he really loves him. After the third time, Peter becomes offended; he knows that Jesus is patterning these questions after his threefold denial of him. Jesus is not trying to hurt Peter, but he is reminding him of his failure in order to show his own full forgiveness and grace. And Jesus offers Peter more than forgiveness; he gives him a high calling. Peter will be called to feed the sheep of Jesus, the Lord. It won't be without suffering, but it will be for the service of the King.

Do you see the encouraging news of John 21? Peter's worst day—his utter failure to remain faithful to Jesus—is not the end. He has fallen, yes. But Jesus now picks him up, forgives him, and puts him to work. Peter, as we know from the rest of the story of the New Testament, will go on to become a great apostle and a key leader in the foundation of the early church. The Gospel of John ends with a story of grace to a man who had fallen and who is now forgiven and lifted up by Jesus. Friend, this can be your story too!

Have you fallen? Have you blown it, even this week? Jesus Christ, the risen Savior of sinners, is waiting to forgive you, pick you up, and restore you. He wants to put you to work for his glorious cause! Messing up does not have to be the end of the story. Turn to Jesus today. Ask for his forgiveness and grace.

Mission Made Possible by God

The movie is about to end—and then something happens. You find out that the villain is not actually dead! The story is not over. You've been set up for a sequel. Luke's Gospel is only part one of a larger story about the work, ministry, and gospel of Jesus Christ. The book of Acts—written by Luke—is continuing Luke's account of the story of Jesus Christ. So, what will this sequel be all about?

First, it's about a mission. The disciples, long confused about Jesus's ultimate purpose and long-term plan, will now finally get some clarity about the meaning of his death and resurrection and what that implies for their role as Jesus's disciples. Jesus is going away, and this means that their work as witnesses to Jesus has just begun! Jesus's words to them are clear: "You will be my witnesses in Jerusalem and in all Judea and Samaria, and to the end of the earth" (1:8).

Second, it's about a mission that is empowered by the Holy Spirit. Jesus's departure is not a happy time for his disciples; they don't want him to go! But as he has told them before, his departure means a new gift: the coming of the Holy Spirit, the third person of the Godhead. He says, "But you will receive power when the Holy Spirit has come upon you" (1:8). Earlier, he's spoken about their being baptized with the Holy Spirit. Here's the point: the disciples will not be on their own in this mission of witnessing to Jesus. The Holy Spirit—the third person of the Trinity—will be with them with his powerful presence.

Third, this is a mission initiated by God himself. We need to make sure we don't miss how Jesus is using language that is specifically reserved for Yahweh himself. Turn in your Bible to Isaiah 43:10–12. There you'll find God the Father calling his people—the Israelites—to be his witnesses among the nations. Jesus now uses the same language for *himself*. This is a huge claim! He is declaring himself to be equal with God. The disciples are called to be witnesses to and for the glorious Lord of all.

The good news of Jesus Christ—because of this mission he gave to his disciples—has made it all the way to you—in the twenty-first century, in a nation of Gentiles. Thank God that Jesus gave this mission to his disciples and that their work of witness meant that you now know how to find salvation in Jesus.

Jesus Sends the Holy Spirit

The disciples were waiting—because that's what Jesus had told them to do. He had told them "not to depart from Jerusalem, but to wait for the promise of the Father," the coming of the mighty Holy Spirit (1:4). This was a big promise that Jesus had given to his disciples, one that would make all the difference in their witness and work for him.

Finally, it happens. At the feast of Pentecost, all the followers of Jesus are together in a house. Suddenly, a "mighty rushing wind" fills the place, and the appearance of tongues of fire rests on each of them (2:2–3). The Holy Spirit has come; Jesus's promise is coming true! The disciples begin to move out from the house, speaking about Jesus in other languages—miraculously—as they are led by the Holy Spirit. People begin to gather around them, because this is truly a phenomenon. Foreigners are hearing the good news about Jesus in their own languages, which is amazing, because these men are mostly Jewish. Some people mock the disciples, but most people are astounded at this amazing thing that is happening. So, what does it all mean?

Think about the state of Christianity after the death and resurrection of Jesus: A few disciples. Some women. Some other followers of Jesus who are hanging around. They're huddled in a house together in Jerusalem. Waiting. Now think about the state of Christianity today: people around the world worshiping the resurrected Lord Jesus Christ as their beloved Savior. Churches in dozens and dozens of different countries. The power of the gospel—changing thousands of lives around the world every day. What happened? What changed? Acts 2 happened. Jesus sent the Holy Spirit to empower his little band of followers to begin preaching the gospel everywhere. The rest of the book of Acts will give us the story of how this began to happen in the first century. The gospel began to grow. The message of Jesus the Savior began to miraculously grip hearts and changes lives.

Thank God that, by his Holy Spirit, you too know and understand the good news about Jesus Christ. That is a miracle! God entrusted his message of salvation to a ragtag band of people hiding out in a house and—empowered by his Holy Spirit—sent it around the world and across the centuries. Thank God today that you know about Jesus, the Savior of sinners. And ask him for boldness to step out and share him with others.

Peter Points to Jesus at Pentecost

I'm not sure how you feel about sermons; hopefully, you see them as helpful expositions of passages of God's word. In this passage, you read the account of the very first post-resurrection sermon. We see God beginning to use powerful, Christ-centered preaching to accomplish his saving purposes in people's lives!

Think about how amazing it is that *Peter* gives this sermon. He's a few weeks separated from his denial of Jesus. Restored by the Lord and entrusted with a great mission, Peter has received power and direction from the Holy Spirit to preach powerfully about Jesus Christ. This should point us toward hope for forgiveness, restoration, and even powerful ministry in our own lives.

Most importantly, notice Peter's main point: Jesus Christ is the fulfillment of all God's promises to his people—for all time! First, Peter responds to the criticism that followed the coming of the Holy Spirit at Pentecost when some people thought that the disciples were drunk! Peter points out that what is happening is the fulfillment of the prophetic words of Joel, who speaks of God pouring out his Spirit "on all flesh" (2:17). This time, Peter says, is a time of Joel's words coming true, as God's people are proclaiming Jesus Christ with Spirit-empowered means. Second, Peter points to the resurrection of Jesus as the ultimate sign that Jesus is the Christ—the great Messiah of God and the King of God's people. He's far greater than King David, who died and stayed dead! He is the risen Lord—God's own Son. Peter is putting the Bible together for all the people who hear this sermon; he is claiming that Jesus is the point of it all!

Finally, Peter reminds the people that this Jesus—this divine Messiah—is the man that they crucified and rejected. What happens next is what should happen to everyone who is truly confronted with both the ultimate and infinite lordship of Jesus and the depth of our sin: repentance of sin and belief in the name of Jesus. And three thousand people joined God's kingdom that day!

Wonder at Jesus. Sorrow at sin. Pray that those two responses would characterize your response to God's word and God's truth every single day of your life. Ask God to help you see his Son as more beautiful and glorious, even as you understand more and more the wonder of your own forgiveness through his cross.

The Early Church

Your church may look different from other churches. Hopefully, though, you're part of a church that is faithful to the gospel and consistently teaching God's word. Acts 2:42–47 describes the life of the early church when it was in its first stages of development. These verses aren't meant to show us what every church should look like today! But they teach us how God's Spirit worked in these early years to grow his church and to gather a people together who had been changed by Jesus Christ. So what can we learn from what was happening?

This church was excited about worship. The new believers "devoted themselves to the apostles' teaching" (2:42). They were all about learning more about Jesus Christ and the salvation and new life that are found in him. They also loved to meet together, joining corporately in people's homes for worship. Remember, no one was making them do these things! Their conversion to Jesus created a hunger for biblical teaching and worship with God's people. Is that true in your heart and life?

Second, this was a church of people who loved each other with incredible generosity. The sharing and having "all things in common" that is described in verses 44–45 is not some kind of weird communistic arrangement! These verses simply describe a commitment to one another in Christ that led to generosity and sharing—of time, money, and possessions. God's people were excited about worshiping him together; they were also excited about caring for one another in Jesus's name.

Ultimately, this is a church that grew by God's power, not human strength. The final verse of this passage leaves no room for confusion regarding the source of this church's growth: *God* was the one adding to their number. It wasn't about church growth strategies, a certain program, or even the excellence of the preaching (although it certainly was excellent!). *God* was doing a work in these days—growing this church of people who loved and worshiped Jesus Christ as Savior and Lord.

Friend, this is our heritage! While our churches look different from those in these early days, they should be built on the same principles: the teaching of the apostles about Jesus Christ, worship together, vibrant generosity. Thank God that you are a part of the church that began to grow by his power after Jesus's resurrection. Ask him to help you love worshiping, meeting, and serving with your brothers and sisters in Christ.

From the Inside Out

We all get obsessed with appearances. It's hard not to! As human beings, the first thing we often notice is the way a person looks; we can't immediately see his or her true motives or heart. This chilling account from the book of Acts reminds us that outward appearances are not all that important. God, ultimately, is after the heart. He wants people who are holy from the inside out, and he is never fooled by simple appearances.

The story that you read in this passage happens in the context of great generosity. The early church is excited about Jesus and excited about giving to others in his name. A man and a woman named Ananias and Sapphira want to be a part of it. So they *do* give generously, selling a piece of property so that they can give to the church. But they give under false pretense. They pretend that they give all the money they received for their sale, when, in reality, they keep some of it for themselves. God's response to this deceit is fiercely decisive, to say the least. What do we learn about God from this passage?

Friend, God is passionate about the purity of his church. People who say that the "God of the Old Testament" is a God of wrath and the "God of the New Testament" is a God of grace need to take another look at this passage. God is passionate about holiness; he is holy, and his people must be holy and pure before him. We see—as the Old Testament shows—that God's holiness is more important than human life. God really does hate sin, and he really does want the people of his church to fight the deceitfulness of sin in every way.

Remember that you can't fool God! God sees all our inward motives, and he will one day judge all of us based on the true attitude of our hearts. Are we giving off merely the *appearance* of following, loving, and serving Jesus, or have we *truly* repented of sin and put our faith in him?

Take a good look at your heart! Are you building up a good outward appearance of holiness, obedience, and love for Jesus, without truly worshiping him in your heart and mind? If that's the case, remember that God sees it all! Ananias and Sapphira couldn't hide their hearts from the God who made them, and neither can we. Confess to God the ways that you make your outward appearance as a Christian more important than your inward attitude of worship and love for Jesus. Ask him to make you his holy child—from the inside out!

Stephen's Speech

Stephen is in danger—grave danger. He has been performing wonders and signs, along with bearing witness verbally to the saving work of Jesus Christ the Messiah. Unable to counter his wisdom, the Jewish leaders in Jerusalem finally resort to the same dirty tactics they found useful with Jesus: they gather false witnesses to accuse Stephen of blasphemy. Brought before the council of Jewish leaders, Stephen is asked to give an answer for his behavior—and his supposed blasphemy. That's where the passage picks up, with Stephen's very life hanging in the balance.

Invited to give his defense, Stephen tells the story of God's people. He covers the call of Abraham, the story of Joseph in Egypt, and the leadership of Moses over God's rebellious people in the wilderness. At this point, however, Stephen's story takes a major turn. He points out that God never actually lived in the tabernacle in the wilderness, or even in the glorious temple of King Solomon. In fact, he says, God never wanted or needed a house made by human hands! Stephen is pointing out the absolute incompleteness of the Old Testament story. No tent or temple could ever fully contain the God of the universe or offer lasting salvation to sinful people. The next point, though, is what really gets him in trouble. He tells the Jewish leaders that what brings completion to the Old Testament Scriptures is not a new temple or a new law; it's a *person*: Jesus Christ, the Messiah. And it's this Jesus that he accuses the Jewish leaders of rejecting and putting to death.

The sticking point here is Jesus. If Jesus is who he said he is (and who Stephen says he is), then the Jewish leaders have missed the point of the entire witness of Scripture. They understand the implications of this. If Jesus is God's Messiah—the "Righteous One," as Stephen refers to him in verse 52—then they are guilty of claiming Abraham, Joseph, Moses, and David but rejecting the very Son of God. The council can't bear this thought, and they are furious at Stephen for even suggesting that they have missed the central figure in God's plan for humanity. So they turn to fury—and murder. They grab stones and kill this faithful follower of Jesus Christ.

Would you stake your life on the claims of Jesus? Would you die affirming that he is God's Son come in the flesh? Pray that God would test your heart and strengthen your belief in his Son. Ask him to give you strength to stand up for the truth about Jesus Christ—at any cost.

Saul Scatters the Gospel

Acts 7 ended with a mysterious man named Saul lurking in the background. Stephen—that faithful servant of Jesus—has been put to death, and Saul stands there, giving implicit approval to this stoning. As Acts 8 begins, we find out what this Saul is after; he helps to launch a huge persecution against all followers of Jesus Christ. It begins with the murder of Stephen. Saul begins "ravaging the church" as he "drag[s] off men and women and commit[s] them to prison" for claiming the name of Jesus (8:3). Stephen was only the beginning; Saul was just getting started in his violent persecution of Christians.

A beautiful irony here teaches us a lot about our God. In his sovereignty, God uses this persecution to spread the gospel all over Judea and Samaria. The violent opposition of Saul and others *helps* the good news of Jesus make its way to more and more people. As God's people are scattered because of persecution, the gospel is scattered too, and it grows wherever it goes! Saul has unwittingly contributed to a gospel explosion.

Luke, the author of Acts, gives one example of this gospel scattering through the ministry of Philip. First, Philip goes to Samaria, where he confronts the false teaching and demonic influence of a magician who has great sway in the region. Then, as he continues to follow God's leading, Philip has an incredible interaction with an Ethiopian eunuch in the middle of the desert road that runs from Jerusalem to Gaza. This man—a Gentile—believes in Jesus as Philip explains that Christ fulfills the words of the prophet Isaiah about the suffering servant. After performing a spontaneous desert baptism, Philip is whisked away by the Spirit, and he goes on preaching the gospel in every town he visits.

Friend, there will be even more glorious irony in the story of Acts. Yes, God used a scattering persecution to make the gospel flourish in new regions. But now God is about to do something even more surprising. He's about to go after the leading persecutor of Christians himself: Saul.

God will not let the gospel message be defeated, though many will try to fight it. He does this because he loves his people, and he does this because he loves sinners like you. Spend some time praising God that his sovereign hand allowed the good news about Jesus to spread across Judea and Samaria during these days. Thank him that he was so committed to making his grace and salvation known!

No Lost Causes

From our limited human perspective, some people just seem to be lost causes. We simply can't imagine them ever turning to Jesus Christ, repenting of their sin, and trusting him as Lord and Savior. Acts 9:1–22 should stop us from ever thinking—or talking—this way! It's the story of a man who was one of the great lost causes in history. He not only rejected Jesus but also killed and persecuted his followers. He not only disagreed with the message of the gospel but also made a living of opposing it! Saul is the most unlikely convert to Jesus Christ. Yet the power of the gospel captures even him.

As we think back on this amazing account, let's consider a few important points briefly. First, we need to notice that Saul is confronted by the risen Jesus Christ himself. Jesus appears to Saul on the road to Damascus! Listen to his words: "I am Jesus, whom you are persecuting" (9:5). Saul, later called Paul, is a man who has seen and interacted with Jesus Christ. This fact is vital to his being considered an apostle (one who has seen the risen Christ and been commissioned by him).

Second, notice that Saul's conversion to Christ is linked to a specific call to gospel ministry. Those two go hand in hand! Here's what Jesus says to Ananias about Saul: "He is a chosen instrument of mine to carry my name before the Gentiles and kings and the children of Israel" (9:15). In all Paul's writings, we find him going back to this powerful conversion as the foundation for both his relationship with Christ *and* his preaching and church-planting work. For Paul, to follow Jesus meant to spend his life proclaiming Jesus.

Finally, as we consider the reality of this dynamic conversion, we need to realize that the power of the gospel can transform any life and any heart. Paul was the least likely convert; friend, there are no lost causes who are beyond the powerful reach of Jesus Christ, the Savior of sinners! We need to keep praying for people who do not know Jesus. God is able to reach down and powerfully save even the most unlikely people!

Consider your relationship with Christ. You—a sinner—have been reconciled to God through the powerful work of Jesus Christ. Thank God for this. Then consider the way you pray for people who don't know Jesus. Pray for at least one person—trusting God that he can do a miracle in that person's life and bring him or her to repentance and faith in Jesus.

Full Inclusion for Gentiles

Acts 10 begins with two visions. Two men who don't know each other both receive visions from God. Cornelius, a Gentile centurion, is told to visit Peter. Peter's vision is more complex. While resting on the roof of a house, he sees a sheet come down from heaven filled with all kinds of animals, reptiles, and birds that, according to Old Testament law, are unclean for Jewish people to eat. A voice from heaven commands Peter to eat these animals. As a good Jew, he resists this command until the vision is taken away.

It isn't until his visit from Cornelius that Peter begins to understand the meaning of this vision. It wasn't about food; it was about people. God was telling Peter that his people were expanding; Gentiles like Cornelius were going to get into God's community by faith in Jesus Christ. Peter ultimately receives this with joy, and the chapter ends with the baptism of Cornelius and the people with him, as they are—like the Jewish believers—filled with God's Holy Spirit.

This passage has huge implications for the rest of the book of Acts and the rest of the New Testament. God is showing Peter—and all his people—that Gentiles can have full inclusion in the people of God through faith in Jesus Christ. The same Holy Spirit falls on them, just as he had come to the Jewish believers in Jerusalem at Pentecost. We are learning that Jews and Gentiles together will make up the new people of God. Why? Because it's about faith in Jesus Christ—not about rituals, animal sacrifices, or a certain ethnicity.

We shouldn't take this for granted! We should see ourselves—joyfully—with Cornelius, who was brought in to God's people through faith in Jesus Christ and the gift of the Holy Spirit. We are outsiders too, and we graciously get in by faith in Jesus. We become part of a beautiful, diverse picture of God's people—Jew and Gentile—who will one day sing praises to our Lord and Savior before his throne.

Acts 10 is showing us that God's heart is for Gentiles to get into the community of his people. He has paved the way for them—for us—through the once-and-for-all sacrificial death of his Son Jesus Christ. So today thank God that Cornelius, and you, will be praising Jesus in heaven one day along with Abraham, Moses, and David. Praise your Savior for redeeming you from your sin, and including you with his people!

First Gospel Missionaries

If you've been around the Christian community, you've probably gotten to know some overseas missionaries. In this passage, you read about the first days of the New Testament missionary movement. This is where it all began! Back at the beginning of Acts 13, the Holy Spirit had instructed God's people to send out Paul and Barnabas: the first gospel missionaries!

As they come to a place called Antioch in Pisidia, they are invited to speak in the synagogue, the Jewish place of worship. Speaking to an audience of mostly Jews, Paul begins to tell the history of God's people, but when he gets to David, he jumps from there right to Jesus! Just after mentioning King David, Paul says this: "Of this man's offspring God has brought to Israel a Savior, Jesus, as he promised" (13:23). By heading straight to Jesus from David, Paul is making an important point to the Jews in Antioch; he's telling them that Jesus Christ is the key to understanding Scripture and all the promises of God to his people. He quotes David's words in the Psalms, telling the people that they all point forward to Jesus Christ, God's own Son, come in the flesh.

Why is the coming of Jesus so wonderful for sinners? The reason is this: the great King David died, but Jesus, God's Son, rose from the dead to reign forever. Paul concludes his sermon with these words: "Let it be known to you therefore, brothers, that through this man forgiveness of sins is proclaimed to you, and by him everyone who believes is freed from everything from which you could not be freed by the law of Moses" (13:38–39). What is so great about this Son of David? Through him, and because of his death, God's people can find ultimate forgiveness.

As usual, the message that Paul and Barnabas preach is met with mixed responses. Some want to hear more. Some believe their message. The Gentiles, in particular, rejoice at the message of Paul and Barnabas, because it means that they—through faith in Jesus Christ—can be a part of the people of God! But some Jews are jealous. They round up a mob and drive Paul and Barnabas out of town. Yet the gospel continues to grow, and these men continue to preach it.

Pray that God would give you a new enthusiasm for the gospel message—the message of hope and salvation for lost sinners. Pray that he would remind you—through the book of Acts—of the life-changing power of knowing Jesus Christ, the great Savior of all God's people.

Faith Alone in Christ Alone

Even the best, most healthy churches sometimes go through disagreements, struggles, and tough times. The early church—although growing tremendously and in exciting ways—had problems too. As the gospel began to spread across the ancient world, many Jews put their faith in Jesus Christ as the promised Messiah of God's people. Many Gentiles also trusted Jesus as Savior and Lord, even though they didn't have Jewish backgrounds. This dynamic led to some problems in the early church, which many of the New Testament epistles spend lots of time trying to work out!

At this point in Acts we're not far removed from the time when God's activity was primarily (although never completely) focused on those who are part of the ethnically Jewish community. It's not too surprising that there were some issues as God's community expanded to include Gentiles.

In Acts 15, we find that some Jewish leaders in Jerusalem are busy teaching Gentile Christians that they need to be circumcised to be saved. They are urging these Gentiles to become fully Jewish to be accepted into God's people. In other words, they are telling them that they need more than Jesus to be "in" with God. Peter and Barnabas and Paul quickly shut this down! They tell stories of the way that God's Holy Spirit has come to Gentiles. They defend the simplicity and purity of the gospel, which comes to people who respond in faith to Jesus *alone*—not to an entire set of Jewish customs and ritual laws. They settle on an agreement by the end of the passage; they will *not* force Gentile Christians to be circumcised but will ask them to pursue sexual purity and not eat meat that has been sacrificed to idols.

Why was this issue so important to Peter, Paul, and Barnabas? Because there was a tendency in those days for Jewish Christians to put forward the idea to Gentile believers that they needed Jesus plus something else in order to be accepted by God—that, in some way, faith in Jesus was not sufficient for them to be truly part of God's people. We can have that same tendency today. We can begin to think that we need Jesus *plus* something else. And that is *never* true—and is even dangerous!

In the early church, Gentiles who came to Jesus with no Jewish heritage still had a full share in salvation through faith in Christ alone. Jesus is truly enough. Ask God to remind you of this glorious reality! Jesus is all you need; lean on him fully, for your salvation, hope, and peace.

Paul in Athens

New York City is a global city and a cultural center—a place where you expect to see pop stars and celebrities. Have this picture in your minds when you read about Paul going to Athens; it also was a global city and a cultural center. But in those days, the celebrities were philosophers, poets, and religious thinkers. Lectures and philosophical speculation ruled the day. In fact, in verse 21, we find that people in Athens "would spend their time in nothing except telling or hearing something new." In this context Paul preaches his next public sermon in the Areopagus, where everyone comes to lecture, debate, and argue.

Notice that Paul adjusts his methods and his starting point based on his context. Paul starts his sermon in a different place with these Gentile people than he did with the Jews. Where did Paul begin when he shared about Jesus to Jewish people? With Abraham and the story of God's work in the nation of Israel. To these Gentiles in Athens, though, that kind of presentation wouldn't make much sense! They have no background in the Old Testament. So Paul takes a different approach.

Paul finds a way in to the gospel from their lives and their context. Looking around the city, Paul comments on the religiosity of the Athenians, noting that they even have an altar to "the unknown god" (17:23). Paul then begins to tell them about the God of the universe who is *unknown* to them. He begins with the creation of the world by God and moves toward the coming judgment that will happen through his Son, Jesus Christ. In light of this, Paul calls for the response of repentance from the Athenians now that they have heard this message.

It's important for us to realize that even the great apostle Paul's gospel presentation in this great global city is met with mixed results. Some people are interested. Some people laugh. And a few people do come to faith in Jesus Christ. The gospel *can and will* bear fruit, even in totally pagan contexts like Athens! We, like Paul, need to be always thinking about how to creatively and faithfully keep on sharing the good news about Jesus in every context today.

Pray that God would make you passionate about the truth of the gospel so that you are more committed to sharing it. Ask him to help you, like Paul, be creative in meeting people where they are with the truth of the gospel, even as you trust God completely with the results of your witness.

Rooted and Bearing Fruit

You may have had the experience of saying goodbye to a grandparent or some other loved one. You will not soon forget the last conversation you had with that person. In Acts 20, we find Paul's final charge to the elders of the church in Ephesus, just one of the towns where he helped establish a local body of believers. It's the last time that they will see Paul; you can bet that they wouldn't have too quickly forgotten his final message to them!

The first thing that Paul does is remind the Ephesians of his greatest passion, which was evident to them: the gospel. Paul reminds them that, when he was with them, he "did not shrink from declaring" anything to them that was "profitable," as he bore faithful witness to the need for "repentance toward God and of faith in our Lord Jesus Christ" (20:20–21). Later in this goodbye speech, Paul says that his faithful declaration of the gospel in their midst makes him innocent regarding them. In other words, since he has taught them "the whole counsel of God," he has fulfilled his responsibility to them as a gospel preacher (20:27). Paul's final words to the Ephesians are all about the gospel.

Paul's second area of focus, though, can take us by surprise. He's talked about the gospel; we expected that! But next he gives them a word about generosity. Paul reminds them that, when he was in Ephesus, he didn't covet any of their silver or gold, and he was mindful of helping those around him. He wraps up his speech with a call to them—a call to help the weak and follow the words of Jesus regarding giving. Why does he end with this?

It seems that generosity is one important and tangible way that the gospel bears fruit in people's lives. That is the connection in Paul's mind as he says goodbye to his Ephesian friends. He wants them to hold on to the truth of the gospel as he has! And Paul wants the gospel to bear fruit in the Ephesian church in lives that selflessly and generously give themselves to others.

Is the gospel of Jesus Christ central in your life and heart? Is your belief in Jesus bearing fruit in generosity—even now, while you're young? Pray that God would make you a person who does not shrink from telling others about Jesus. Ask him to help you give generously to others, because you know that your greatest treasure is in Jesus Christ himself.

The Whole Gospel Brings Radical Change

Paul is in court, standing before a king named Agrippa, and he is making his own defense. This part of the book of Acts is teaching us a very important truth: the true gospel will always be opposed. In Paul's case, as recorded for us by Luke in the book of Acts, this meant opposition from the Jewish leaders. In Acts 25 they even go so far as to hatch a plot to ambush Paul on the way to his trial in Jerusalem. What is it about Paul's gospel that makes them so furious, even to the point where they would try to have him killed?

In short, it comes down to the person of Jesus Christ. You see, the Jewish leaders who have not accepted Jesus as the Messiah recognize what their acceptance of him would mean. It would mean a complete change in their lives: the end of their religious system and a new focus on worshiping Jesus as God's glorious Son, a shift away from their good works and a different emphasis on the unearned grace of God through Jesus's death on the cross for sinners. The Jewish leaders know that they have everything to lose if Paul's gospel takes off.

Isn't that the case today as well? People who oppose the gospel—perhaps even people you know—oppose it because, deep down, they know that their acceptance of Christ would mean radical change to the way they live their lives. And, friend, people don't want to change the way they live their lives! This is why we need to keep preaching the true gospel, the gospel that declares Jesus Christ as the crucified Savior and the risen Lord, the gospel that calls for *repentance* from sin—and also *faith* in Jesus Christ for salvation.

We see today that Paul is true to this gospel even when he's in court. He faithfully proclaims the gospel to King Agrippa, and Festus as well, even trying to convert him as he gives his own defense! It's the resurrection of Jesus that finally makes Festus scream out, "Paul, you are out of your mind" (26:24). Agrippa can't quite believe the message Paul preaches, and in this way, he is no different from the Jewish leaders who persecute Paul.

Are you telling people the whole gospel like Paul? The gospel message that is full of God's grace but that also demands total repentance and complete surrender to the lordship of Jesus Christ? When people truly accept that gospel, their lives will change as they follow Jesus. Pray today that you would not proclaim anything less!

The End of Acts

At the beginning of Acts, Jesus had risen from the dead and left his disciples with a promise that the Holy Spirit would come to them and that they would be his witnesses everywhere. It wasn't a very impressive bunch! There were perhaps one hundred twenty people huddled together secretly in Jerusalem, waiting for the fulfillment of Jesus's promise. And now, by Acts 28? The gospel has exploded. It has spread, multiplied, and taken root through the faithful preaching of Peter, Stephen, Barnabas, Silas, and of course, Paul, to name a few. Yet we saw too that gospel ministry will never be without opposition. We find Paul today in chains.

When Paul arrives in Rome, he finds himself in a fairly good situation. He quickly locates some other believers in Jesus Christ and is allowed to stay by himself, guarded by a Roman soldier. What happens next shouldn't surprise us: Paul begins to share the gospel even in Rome! He begins with the local Jewish leaders, whom he invites to come to him. Paul, in the midst of his imprisonment, shares with them all about Jesus, "testifying to the kingdom of God and trying to convince them about Jesus both from the Law of Moses and from the Prophets" (28:23).

But this ministry to the Jewish leaders isn't the end of Paul's ministry! In Rome for two whole years, he "welcomed all who came to him, proclaiming the kingdom of God and teaching about the Lord Jesus Christ with all boldness and without hindrance" (28:30–31). Paul's visitors would have included both Jews and Gentiles. Do you see what God is doing here? He is using even Paul's imprisonment to make the good news known to people in the great city of Rome.

And so the book of Acts concludes. It is the story of God's gospel—the good news about Jesus the Savior—exploding, expanding, and spreading across the ancient world. As that gospel spread, churches were founded in towns everywhere. The epistles coming next are ancient letters from the apostles *to* these early churches, and we'll learn much from them!

May your faith in the true gospel be strengthened as you reflect on how a fragile group of believers in Jesus multiplied into thousands of Christians by the power of the Holy Spirit. And may you be challenged by the fact that you too can and must be a witness to the good news about Jesus the Savior. Pray that God would strengthen your belief in his Son and your commitment to bear witness to him.

Not Ashamed of the Gospel

Are you tempted to be ashamed of your faith in Jesus Christ and your commitment to him? If you are, some of the reason for this is that you have forgotten the power and glory of the gospel of Jesus Christ. Romans is just the book to remind you how great our gospel hope is! This is an epistle of Paul, written to early believers in Rome—Jews and Gentiles—who certainly felt out of place at times. His audience, like us, needed to be reminded about the *essence* of the gospel and also about the *need* to boldly spread it to every person everywhere.

What is the gospel, according to Paul's introduction to Romans? The gospel is the good news that was promised by the prophets and by the entire Old Testament. It's the continuing story of God's work of redemption in the world—and the fulfillment of his promises to his people for all time. Second, the gospel is about Jesus; Paul says this gospel is "concerning his Son" (1:3). This may seem obvious, but when we talk about the gospel, we are talking about the person and work of Jesus! Third, the gospel is about Jesus, who is fully man and fully God. Paul reminds the Roman believers of this fact by mentioning both Jesus's lineage through King David and also his resurrection from the dead. Fourth, it's a gospel that is meant to "bring about *the obedience of faith*" (1:5). The right response to this gospel is faith! Finally, the gospel—according to Paul—is meant to go to all the nations. This is not just a Jewish gospel; Paul will make that abundantly clear in this epistle. It's the gospel of Jesus Christ for every human being who has ever lived.

Then he reminds his readers of the right attitude about this gospel in the midst of a world that is mostly against Jesus: unashamed proclamation of the good news about Jesus Christ. "For I am not ashamed of the gospel," says Paul (1:16). Why? Because it is the power for the salvation of every human being ever created by God. The gospel also actually shows us God's righteousness—an idea that Paul will explain even more clearly in Romans 3. It's this word of the gospel—this good news—to which Paul is entirely committed, without any shame.

Ask God to remind you that the gospel is the only way to salvation for every single one of your friends. Pray that he would help you understand that more deeply. Ask him to give you strength, boldness, and courage to speak out about the salvation that comes through Jesus Christ alone.

The Wrath of God

You're waiting in an exam room when the doctor walks in. Without saying a word or even looking at you, he hands you a prescription for an extremely powerful medication. What would you say? You'd probably say, "Wait a minute! What's wrong with me?" It wouldn't make sense for a doctor to give you a prescription for medication without first giving you a diagnosis of your disease. In the book of Romans, Paul recognizes that people need to understand the *problem* with human beings before they talk about the great *solution* of the gospel. So what's the problem, according to Paul, for which the gospel is the ultimate solution? In a word, it's *wrath.*

Paul tells us that the entire world is under God's wrath because of human sin: "For the wrath of God is revealed from heaven against all ungodliness and unrighteousness of men" (1:18). Paul then shows us both the extent of the sin of the world and its perverted development in people's lives. Even though the world itself points to a loving and glorious Creator, we as human beings have become fools, choosing to worship things other than God. Then, when the cycle of sin begins, that sin leads to more sin, which leads to more sin, and so on. Lust leads to other kinds of impurity. Sexual impurity leads to other kinds of perversions, including homosexual behavior. And, in case we are in danger of not seeing ourselves in this chapter, Paul gives us a list of the other ways that sin has taken over the world—and our lives and hearts. Because of the way that the entire world is under sin, Paul writes, human beings deserve to die.

This passage shows us our biggest, most deadly problem as fallen human beings: God himself. We are *all* in the same position before a holy God. We are under his wrath, deserving death because of our sin. The first and most important thing we must do in life is figure out how to deal with this problem.

Paul wants us to see that we are under God's just wrath because of sin. Unless we truly understand this, we will not understand the glory and grace of the gospel message. If you don't understand the depth of the problem, you will not understand the miraculous solution through the cross of Jesus Christ. Pray that God would help you understand your own sinfulness and his infinite holiness. Ask him to give you a new grasp of the infinite chasm that we would not be able to cross apart from Christ!

The Righteousness of God

Romans has been telling us about a problem. A *big* problem. It's the problem that every single human being shares just because we're human. We are under sin and under God's wrath. Paul reminds us of that problem in Romans 3, making this all-encompassing statement: "All, both Jews and Greeks, are under sin" (3:9). Paul wants his audience—both Jews and Gentiles in Rome—to know that they're all in the same boat: under sin, under God's wrath, in need of a solution. So, what is the great solution?

The cross. The solution is the righteousness of God—his perfect justice and goodness—that is revealed ultimately in the gospel. In the original Greek, Romans 3:21–26 is actually one sentence. One Bible scholar has called it "the most important paragraph in the Bible."[4] Why? Because here Paul shows us (probably in the clearest way in all Scripture) how sinners can be saved and how they can be saved in a way that is still faithful to God's perfectly just character.

First, how are sinners saved? They're saved because of what Jesus did on the cross. The word that Paul uses for this is *redemption*. We have all sinned, as that well-known verse 23 reminds us, and have fallen short of God's infinite glory. But at the cross Jesus redeems us from our sin. That word means that he buys us back from sin; he pays the ultimate price for us. Sinners can be saved because Jesus has accomplished redemption for us!

But Paul's legalistic opponents would have brought up a challenging point to this gospel of grace to sinners: How could a just God declare sinners righteous? That wouldn't be fair, would it? Again, the cross is Paul's answer. And the key word here is *propitiation*. What does *propitiation* mean? It means the removal of wrath. Jesus's death absorbs all God's wrath against human sin—all the wrath that Romans has been talking about! God doesn't randomly wave his hand and say of our sin, "It's OK." God justly punishes sin; he just punishes Jesus in our place.

Spend some time thanking God for the gospel. Thank him that, at the cross, Jesus redeemed you from your sin and became the propitiation for all God's wrath against you! The only right response to this glorious gospel is humility, worship, and complete surrender to the Savior who died for you.

Jesus, the New and Better Adam

The Bible is not a collection of disconnected stories. It is one big story—a story about God's redemption of lost sinners through his Son, Jesus Christ. It can be easy to lose sight of that as we make our way through the laws of Leviticus, the stories of Judges, or even the parables of Jesus in the Gospels. But passages like this one keep reminding us of the *unity* of the Bible. All Scripture tells one story, which begins in Genesis and goes on forever!

Paul has been talking about the salvation that is accomplished on the cross for sinners through the sacrificial death of God's Son, Jesus Christ. Then, all of a sudden, he mentions a character from the Bible story who has been dead for a few thousand years: Adam. Why in the world does Paul bring up the very first man God created, especially at this point in his letter to the Romans?

Paul is making a contrast between two representatives for human beings. Adam had been a representative figure for every man and woman who followed him. In the garden, Adam and Eve sinned. Because of Adam's sin, "death spread to all men," and Paul even says that "death reigned" in the world after the fall (5:12, 14). You and I—and every other human—enter the world under the representative headship of Adam. We are under the curse of sin, hopelessly fallen. We are born into sin and into a world filled with sin.

But the gospel tells us that we can—by faith—have a new representative. Just as Adam served as a representative of *death* to many people, Jesus serves as a representative of *life* because of his saving work on the cross. Like Adam, he is a representative for humanity—not for sin and death but for justification and life! Paul is helping us put our Bibles together, even in the way he explains the gospel to us. Jesus is not just a random Savior. He is the *new Adam*, the better—perfect—representative for all who will turn from sin to faith in him.

Make sure that you have the right representative for your heart and soul! Through faith and repentance, make sure that you look to the new Adam for life, forgiveness, and salvation. Thank God for sending Jesus to finally break the bond of sin and death that held us fast!

A License to Sin?

Think about a person whom you love very much—a family member or a dear friend. Then imagine that you have hurt or wronged that person in some terrible way. Later, when you come back to that person, he or she looks at you with a smile and says, "I love you, and I forgive you for what you did." Would that person's forgiveness make you want to hurt him or her again in the same way? No! Such forgiveness would make you grateful; it would make you want to treat that person with love and respect. Strangely enough, the opponents of the apostle Paul made a very different argument. It seems that they suggested that the gospel of grace and forgiveness that Paul preached would lead people into more and more sin.

Paul asks the question that his opponents are asking: "Are we to continue in sin that grace may abound?" (6:1). His answer is even stronger in Greek than it is in English: "By no means!" (6:2). There is *no way*, according to Paul, that the gospel of God's grace through Jesus Christ should lead people into more sin! In fact, he tells us that repentance of sin and faith in Jesus Christ must have a very different effect on our lives. Why? Because, through faith in Jesus Christ, believers have died to sin. Faith in Jesus Christ means sharing in his resurrection *and* sharing in his death. When God's Spirit enables us to trust in Jesus, our old sinful self is nailed to the cross with Jesus—never to rise up again. Grace is not just a get-out-of-jail-free card for sinners. A true experience of God's grace means a total change in our nature.

Do you ever look to the cross of Jesus as a kind of "forgiveness protection" for the way that you live? If so, you may be misunderstanding grace—and the cross! God's grace in Christ doesn't give us a license to sin; it sets us free from being slaves to sin. Any gospel that makes people feel better about sin is, according to Paul, a false gospel. It's cheap grace, not the costly sacrifice of the Son of God on the cross. Those who truly get the gospel are dead to sin; they begin living more like their Savior.

Ask God today to forgive you for times when you have made his grace in Jesus cheap in some way. Pray that he would help you never take sin lightly, because it was paid for on a cross by his Son. Ask God to give you strength by his Spirit to live truly as if you are dead to sin through faith in Christ.

The Law That Sets You Free

In Romans 6, Paul considered the attitudes and criticisms that he received from his opponents. Paul's gospel of grace, in their minds, would become a license for sin. Paul's answer to this critique was fierce. Seeing grace as a license for sin will *never* be the response of a Christian who has truly experienced God's grace through Jesus. In Romans 8:1–11, though, Paul goes deeper into this concept. How, exactly, is it possible for Christians to live as though they are dead to sin and alive to their Savior? The answer is the Holy Spirit.

Paul first clarifies that the law is incapable of doing what the Holy Spirit can do. The law was not a bad thing! It taught God's people about God's holy character, showed them how to live in God's community, and exposed their sin and need for God's grace. Yet obedience to the law could never bring about heart change. The law—by itself—had no power to transform people so that they would hate sin and love God's ways. That's what Paul means when he says that, through the gospel, "God has done what the law, weakened by the flesh, could not do" (8:3). What could the law never do? It couldn't, on its own, get to the root problem of human sinfulness.

But, Paul teaches, where the law fails, God's *Spirit* gives life! He even calls the rule of the Holy Spirit in the Christian's life a different kind of law: "The law of the Spirit of life has set you free in Christ Jesus from the law of sin and death" (8:2). Those who put their faith in Christ are ruled by a greater law than the law of Moses. It's greater because it's not a written law; it's a person. The presence of the Holy Spirit in our hearts and lives gets to the root of our sin problem. Through God's Spirit, we are able to do what is right.

Friend, if you have put your faith in Jesus Christ as your Savior and Lord, you are dead to sin and alive by the Spirit—really. This means that the Holy Spirit—the third person of the Trinity—indwells you and enables you to say no to sin and yes to obedience to God's word.

Thank God that your conversion to Christ was not simply about affirming a set of truths (although that was a part of it!). Thank him that, when you put your faith in Christ, you received the powerful indwelling of his Holy Spirit. Then ask him to help you—by his Spirit that dwells in you—to say no to sin today.

Faith and Election

Paul has spent eight chapters explaining the glorious gospel of Jesus Christ. It's a gospel of amazing, surprising grace to sinners—sinners who are ethnically Jewish and ethnically Gentiles. Yet Paul is a Jew! It's obvious from the first few verses of Romans 9 that Paul's heart breaks for Jews who have not accepted Jesus Christ as the Messiah from God. Yet he continues to make the point that Jewishness is not enough for saving acceptance with God. Why is this?

First, it's because all Israel is not *true* Israel. Israel has always been about those who have faith in God, not just those who have a certain ethnicity. Paul reminds his Jewish listeners of this fact by calling to their minds one of the sons of their patriarch Isaac: Esau. He was Abraham's grandson, and he wasn't a true spiritual child of Abraham through faith.

Second, we find that God is the one responsible for choosing where his saving mercy falls. It's not about ethnic heritage; it's about God's sovereign choice. Paul quotes God himself, who says to Moses, "I will have mercy on whom I have mercy, and I will have compassion on whom I have compassion" (9:15). He mentions Pharaoh, whose heart God chose to harden as part of his gracious and sovereign purposes for his people. The Bible does not teach us that we are robots, incapable of making real choices. But the Bible does clearly teach that God is ultimately the one who sovereignly designs salvation and elects certain people to spend eternity in his presence.

Paul closes this passage by anticipating some of our confused responses to God when we hear about his election of some and not others. The right response is not to question God but to fall on our knees, understanding that we are recipients of an utterly miraculous grace. We know Jesus Christ; we have received mercy. In other words, the shocking reality is that *some* sinners are saved. That is the mercy and grace of God—that he lovingly and graciously preserves a remnant of people to be in eternal relationship with him. If you believe in Jesus as your Savior and Lord, then you are part of that remnant. Give thanks to God, and do so with great humility!

Praise God that he has brought you to a saving faith in his Son, Jesus. Ask him to help you grasp more and more the wonder of your salvation, so that you are more and more committed to sharing the gospel hope.

Jesus Wants All of You

Have you ever listened to a long speech or lecture and sat back and thought to yourself, "So what?" If you've asked that question of the book of Romans thus far, then this passage is Paul's resounding answer to your question. Romans 12:1–2 is the "so what" of everything that comes before it. Paul tells us what we must do in response to the gospel of grace he has just proclaimed. He will get practical as he tells Christians how they must live in the church, the community, and in relation to their government.

The *therefore* that begins these verses points us back to the previous eleven chapters. The next phrase—"by the mercies of God"—reminds us that Paul's appeal comes on the basis of the amazing gospel of God's grace and mercy that he has just explained. Paul is appealing to the readers of his letter about how they should respond to the gospel. What should they do?

They should "present [their] bodies as a living sacrifice" to God (12:1). That is the right response of someone who understands the death of the Son of God for sinners. The phrase is Paul's way of talking about total and utter commitment and surrender to Jesus. It is a call to offer Jesus everything—our hearts, souls, and even our bodies—in worship and praise to him. What does Jesus, the Savior, want from you? He wants *you*! And he wants *all* of you.

Paul goes on to explain that someone who surrenders himself or herself to Jesus must not be "conformed to this world" but "transformed" (12:2). Part of the way that we know whether or not we've given ourselves to Jesus is by seeing if we get sucked in by the world and all kinds of sinful ways of acting and thinking, or if we are totally changed by Jesus and the Holy Spirit. In other words, the gospel changes people completely. If we have not experienced transformation—and are not experiencing gospel change in our hearts and lives continually—then we may need to ask ourselves whether we have truly believed it.

Are you totally surrendered to God in worship—in thought, word, and deed? Do you conform to the world in significant (that is, sinful) ways, or are you truly allowing the truth of the gospel to transform and change you to be more like Jesus? Talk to God honestly about this, and ask him to help you respond to Jesus in the way that this passage lays out.

Church Disunity

If you're a sports fan, you know the excitement—and the frustrations—that can come when your team gets an extremely talented rookie. Expectations are high. The player's talent and potential are off the charts! But talent isn't everything. Maturity comes as players gain more experience in competing at the highest level and playing a long, grueling schedule. This rookie idea should help you get a picture of the nature of the church in the ancient city of Corinth. Paul had planted this church on one of his missionary journeys, and it was a vibrant and growing church. It was also an extremely gifted church. This is why Paul begins his letter to them by giving thanks to God for them. But the Corinthian church was not a mature church.

One of the main issues in this gifted but not mature church was disunity. The congregation was split—in multiple directions, it seems. Paul attacks this disunity right away: "I appeal to you . . . that all of you agree, and that there be no divisions among you" (1:10). The heart of the issue was that some people identified with certain Christian leaders more than others; "I follow Cephas," for example (1:12). Some, it seems, tried to act more spiritual than the rest, simply identifying themselves (in a haughty way) as belonging only to Christ. This is always a big sign of spiritual immaturity!

What is Paul's solution to their disunity? What does he call them to remember? In short, he calls them to remember the gospel that he preached to them. One gospel. About one Christ. "Is Christ divided?" he asks (1:13). Paul reminds the Corinthians that he preached "Christ crucified" to them (1:23)—that is the message that they should focus on. *That* gospel should bring unity, not disunity, to believers in Jesus. This is a lengthy letter, and Paul will need to remind them of the gospel multiple times along the way, because the church at Corinth has multiple issues! We can learn from this church because many of us are gifted but need to grow to more maturity in Christ.

Far too often, our gifts and abilities make us proud and arrogant. Pray that God would expose areas in your life—maybe areas that are similar to those of the believers in Corinth—that demonstrate spiritual immaturity. Ask God to help you grow up more in Christ, your Savior—in every way!

Our Firm Foundation

Some of the greatest musical groups in history have run into a problem that has nothing to do with their talent, musical creativity, or popularity. Sports teams too can be plagued by this issue, which can rip them apart and make them ineffective, despite tremendous athletic ability. What problem am I talking about? The problem of disunity, when competing opinions and competing egos lead to divisions and strife. Sadly, this is exactly what was happening in the church at Corinth when Paul wrote 1 Corinthians.

This kind of disunity is, for Paul, nothing other than a deep sign of spiritual immaturity. He uses some language that borders on insult, calling the Corinthians "infants in Christ" (3:1). In the church in Corinth, the divisions are about what particular Christian leader different people have chosen to identify with. Paul reminds them that these leaders are all *nothing* compared to Christ. The Corinthians' unity comes from a share in Christ, not in a particular preacher of the gospel of Jesus Christ. These people preached, yes. But Paul reminds the Corinthians that "God gave the growth" (3:6).

In our churches today, we need to watch out for this same tendency, which can divide believers who agree on the core truth of the gospel. Even in Christian circles, we sometimes buy into a celebrity culture, where we identify ourselves by the pastor of our church or by our favorite well-known preacher of the day. We all would do well to remember that, for Christians, the only real foundation is Jesus Christ.

But there is a wider application here as well. We, as followers of Jesus Christ, need to remember that significant divisions and hatred toward Christians in our communities who hold to the core of the gospel are signs of spiritual immaturity. When we act like that, says Paul, we are behaving in a merely "human way," rather than as God's spiritual people (3:3).

It's easy for us to get consumed with which Christian leader we like the most, rather than Christ the Savior himself. For the Corinthians, these obsessions led to disunity and quarreling. Pray that God would not let you go there! Ask him to help you stay focused on your Savior, much more than any human who proclaims him to you, no matter how great and wise he or she may be. Stay focused on Jesus; that will lead to unity with others who follow him.

Mourning over Sin

There isn't just one sin plaguing the church at Corinth. But evidently one particularly disgusting one has become quite public. Paul has received the report that "a man has his father's wife" (5:1). Amazingly, this sexual perversion is not the worst part. "And you are arrogant," writes Paul (5:2). Evidently the church at Corinth saw this relationship as acceptable—perhaps even cutting edge. We're getting into a bit of speculation here, but it could be that as a church they wore this relationship as a demonstration of how up-to-date and accepting they could be of alternative lifestyle choices. For Paul, though, this is nonsense. The relationship is sinful and has no place in the church of Jesus Christ. So what should their response have been?

First, the church at Corinth should have mourned over this sin. That's what Paul says in verse 2. Such blatant sexual sin should make followers of Jesus sad, not arrogant. But Paul goes further than that: "I am writing to you not to associate with anyone who bears the name of brother if he is guilty of sexual immorality or greed, or is an idolater, reviler, drunkard, or swindler—not even to eat with such a one" (5:11). This is a hard verse, and we need to work hard to understand it.

Paul is speaking of people who call themselves followers of Jesus Christ but who continue boldly in unrepentant, sinful ways. This is a very specific designation! Paul *doesn't* mean that we should distance ourselves from Christians who are struggling with sin but asking for forgiveness and seeking help. He's also made clear that he doesn't mean alienating unbelievers who live sinful lives; we can't hold them accountable to live like Christians! But for people who claim the name of Christ and arrogantly continue in blatantly sinful ways, there is a time to say, "Enough!" That attitude and approach to life means that something is terribly wrong with a person's heart, and confrontation by Christians may be just what God will use to point him or her back to repentance—and back to Christ.

Paul says that we ought to mourn sin. Do you do that? Are you grieved by sin—especially sin that you see in your church and in your own heart? Ask God to help you mourn over sin and better understand the beauty of the salvation we share through Jesus Christ, who died on a cross to set us free from grievous sin.

Many Gifts, One God

Have you ever broken a bone? Even breaking your pinky finger causes a sharp pain, maybe even needing the attention of a doctor, who can reset the finger by putting it in a splint. Such pain—and from such a little finger! If you've had a similar experience—even a toothache—you know how crucial it is to have every part of your body working correctly. This is exactly what Paul says about the church, which is the "body of Christ" (12:27). Every little part is important!

The Corinthian church was a gifted church; they were good at many things. But it seems that some gifted people thought that their gifts were better and more important than the gifts of other people. This was just one more cause for the divisions that threatened to rip this early church apart! Paul's answer to this issue is clear and strong: "There are varieties of gifts, but the same Spirit; and there are varieties of service, but the same Lord" (12:4–5). Gifts are different, says Paul. But the God who gives the gifts is the same!

Going on, Paul gives one of the clearest, most vivid pictures of what the church of Jesus Christ is meant to look like. It's like a human body. And, just like with a human body, every part is important. For one person in the church to look at another person as unimportant is as ridiculous as a human hand wanting to get rid of the human head! God has designed the different parts and gifts of the church to work together beautifully to encourage the body and to lift up the name of Jesus. In fact, some parts that we are tempted to look at as unimportant are actually "indispensable" (12:22). No part of Christ's body is to be dismissed! This passage calls us to unity, as we value every part—every person—in God's church.

Pray today that God would help you to see your church like this! We tend to think of some people in our church as more valuable or more important than others. But that is not God's perspective; there are "many parts, yet one body" (12:20). Pray that you would love and value every brother and sister in Christ as integral and important parts of God's community. Ask God to give you love for all his people, not just the ones who stand out the most.

A Stern Rebuke

Imagine that you've done something wrong (crashed the car, stayed out past your curfew, lied about something, etc.), and you are in the middle of a stern lecture from your father. Then, right in the middle of a sentence, your father breaks into song—singing a quiet love song from the 1960s! That would be utterly surprising, right? Yet that is not far from the way that we often read 1 Corinthians 13! We hear it preached at weddings, and we hang it as a nice poem on the walls of our houses. So what's the problem with that?

The problem is that Paul (in case you haven't noticed) writes this chapter in the midst of a letter that is filled with rebuke! This church has all kinds of problems—disunity, sexual immorality, conflict—that Paul calls signs of immaturity. It wouldn't make any sense for him to randomly shift gears and include a nice poem about love. That would be totally out of context. So how should we read this part of Paul's letter?

First, we need to understand that this chapter comes as part of Paul's discussion about spiritual gifts. Look at 1 Corinthians 12 and 14; they are both chapters about gifts. Paul writes this love chapter to show the Corinthians what love is supposed to look like in the Christian church. More than that, he wants to show them that love is more important and central than any particular gift. He would rather the Corinthians love each other than speak in tongues, prophesy, or even perform miracles!

How would the Corinthian believers have heard this part of Paul's letter? Well, in 1 Corinthians 5, he reminded them that they were arrogant about their sin. Here he tells them that love is "not arrogant" (13:4). Back in 1 Corinthians 1 and 2, he confronted these believers about their divisions and selfish competition. Here he tells them that love "does not insist on its own way" (13:5). How would the Corinthians have heard this chapter? As a stern rebuke. Paul is showing them what true Christian love looks like, and they are seeing that they don't look very much like this picture of love!

True Christian maturity is demonstrated by the way that we love other believers in Jesus Christ. Pray today that your faith in Jesus Christ as your Savior—and your experience of his ultimate love for you—would bear fruit in true love for the believers in your community.

What Is the Gospel?

We talk a lot today about the gospel. We talk about preaching the gospel. We encourage people to share the gospel. We talk about having gospel-centered ministry, programs, and youth groups. But with all the use of the word *gospel*, we can forget to actively define it. We need to remember what we're talking about when we say "the gospel." What is it?

That's the question that Paul answers for the Corinthians—and us—in the beginning verses of 1 Corinthians 15. He's said a lot of things by this point, and he hasn't taken it easy on the Corinthian believers! But here he takes a moment to remind them of the core of the gospel that he preached to them. This is the gospel that is "of first importance"—it is the central and most crucial thing that Paul taught them (15:3)! What is the substance of this all-important gospel?

First, it is the news that Jesus Christ died for our sins. At the core of the gospel message is the cross of Christ as the place where the Son of God died as a substitute for sinners. Paul starts with this; so must we. Connected to this is the idea that Jesus was buried. In other words, Jesus *really died*. His was a real death; the God-man really died as the final sacrifice for sinners who deserve God's wrath.

Second, this gospel is that Jesus was "raised on the third day" (15:4). It's about Jesus's death for sins but also about Jesus's resurrection from the dead. The gospel message tells us that sin is paid for on the cross and that death is defeated forever through the resurrection of Jesus Christ.

There's one more part, though, to Paul's definition of the gospel. Did you see that phrase attached to every sentence? It's this: "In accordance with the Scriptures." The gospel, Paul says, fulfills God's word and all his promises to his people for all time. It's not a separate story from the Old Testament; the death and resurrection of Jesus is in accord with Old Testament Scripture. The story of the gospel is the same story that began in Genesis 1! It's this gospel that we receive by faith as we understand the salvation that *God* has finally accomplished for his people through his Son.

Do you treasure the hope and truth of the gospel more than any other earthly treasure? Do you share this good news with others—any chance you get? Pray today that God would help you never get tired of his glorious gospel.

Real Suffering and Real Comfort

The book of 2 Corinthians contains a theme that is impossible to avoid: suffering. Now, we're not always sure how to define and apply the Bible's teaching about suffering to our lives. But suffering was a big part of Paul's life and ministry. And his suffering will play a big part of his writing in this second letter to the church at Corinth. It comes up even in the first few verses of the book. What is Paul's suffering as an apostle of Jesus Christ all about?

Ultimately, Paul's suffering is all about sharing with Christ, the Savior, who also suffered. That's Paul's most basic understanding of his suffering for the gospel. He writes this: "As we share abundantly in Christ's sufferings, so through Christ we share abundantly in comfort too" (1:5). Suffering for the gospel is about being linked with Christ.

But there's another way Paul talks about his suffering and hardship. It is suffering that is motivated by his gospel ministry to people like the Corinthians. That's what motivates Paul through hardship, imprisonment, beatings, and all kinds of struggles! Here's how he puts it: "If we are afflicted, it is for your comfort and salvation" (1:6). Paul is willing to endure suffering so that the Corinthians will get the gospel and grow in Christ.

Finally, Paul wants to point out that suffering for Christ is always suffering that is comforted by God. This theme comes up again and again in these verses; God is the God of all comfort and the one who "will deliver us again" (1:10). This book later speaks to how that suffering can actually be an opportunity for the genuineness of Paul's ministry to be proved. Paul's work has received opposition, and this should be expected for anyone who holds true to the gospel. But for Paul, suffering has been more than worth it in serving Jesus and preaching the gospel. The church in Corinth is just one result of his faithful ministry!

Suffering—when it is done for Jesus—is a way in which God graciously allows us to share with our Savior. All suffering—even the suffering of saying no to sin each day—should be understood in this way. We share with Christ in suffering, and we will one day share with him in his glory. Pray that God would help you remember this when you suffer hardship.

Don't Lose Heart

Any of us can battle discouragement and even depression at times. Yet few of us have experienced the kind of hardships that the apostle Paul faced in his ministry: beatings, shipwrecks, long stays in multiple prisons, verbal abuse, riots. It was not an easy road for him! Yet Paul begins this chapter with these bold—and somewhat shocking—words: "We do not lose heart" (4:1). *How, Paul? How do you not lose heart in the midst of your struggles?*

Paul won't lose heart, first, because he knows that God ultimately controls who believes the gospel and who rejects the message. Whether or not people have saving faith isn't up to those to whom the apostles preach; it's finally in God's hands. The gospel, writes Paul, is only hidden "to those who are perishing" (4:3). For some, the god of this world—Satan—has such a strong hold that the gospel simply won't get through. That is God's business! Paul will keep on preaching and trusting God for the results.

Second, Paul won't lose heart because his weakness gives more glory to God. God delights to spread the gospel through "jars of clay" like Paul, because this won't allow people to mistake where the real "surpassing power" comes from (4:7)! As Paul looks at his weakness and suffering, he doesn't see failure; he sees an opportunity for God to get even more glory as the one responsible for the triumph of the gospel and the faith of people who do turn to Jesus.

Finally, and most wonderfully, Paul will not lose heart because he knows that there is a future glory coming that will blow this earthly life out of the water! This life includes suffering, hardship, and weakness; Paul knows that well. But for those who remain faithful to Jesus and his glorious gospel, an "eternal weight of glory beyond all comparison" waits at the end of this life (4:17). If you are a Christian, this is your hope too! You will one day share in the eternal glories of Christ your Savior.

Ask God to remind you that your greatest good comes when he is glorified in your life and your witness to Jesus. Pray that he would help you hope in the unseen things—the future glory that you will share for all eternity with Christ your Savior. Ask your heavenly Father to give you strength by his Holy Spirit to enable you to not lose heart.

Ambassador for the Gospel

This passage gives several great summaries of the gospel. In verse 17, we find the well-known declaration of the drastic change that faith in Jesus brings to a person's life; the "old has passed away" and the "new has come." In verse 21, we find an explanation of Jesus's work on the cross for sinners like us: the Son of God, who had no sin, nevertheless became sin for us that "we might become the righteousness of God." That is the greatest trade in history! But another theme weaves its way through this passage. It's the way the gospel's work in our lives and hearts naturally makes us witnesses to the gospel that has changed our lives. People who are saved through the great gospel become witnesses to that great gospel. That was true for Paul, and it should be true for all of us.

The gospel leads us to see people from God's perspective. "From now on," Paul says, "we regard no one according to the flesh" (5:16). Those who have put their faith in Jesus Christ are new creations. Paul wants to be an ambassador for the gospel to the rest. Think about your perspective on the people around you with whom you cross paths every day. Do you see fellow Christians as new creations, sinners reconciled to God along with you? Do you see yourself as an ambassador to those who have not yet put their faith in Jesus?

For Paul too, the very gospel work in his own heart and life is precisely what makes him want to bear witness to what has happened to him. God has reconciled us to himself through the death and resurrection of Jesus. But that's not all! He has also entrusted to us "the message of reconciliation" (5:19). The God who saves us is now actually "making his appeal" to other people through us, Paul says (5:20). We have been reconciled to God through Christ; we now get to tell others about the great reconciliation that can happen between sinners and God through the cross of Jesus!

Are you motivated to tell others about the reconciliation they can have through Christ because you are so excited about the reconciliation you have with your Creator through the cross? Ask God to make you courageous and bold as an ambassador for the gospel. Pray that he would help you bear witness to what has so changed your life.

Thorn in the Flesh

Have you ever heard someone talk about a person, thing, or circumstance as his or her "thorn in the flesh"? Most likely that person was very annoyed and frustrated with a reoccurring problem or friend. Well, this phrase comes from this passage! It's an expression used by Paul, and we can learn much from his response to this thorn.

We need to point out that we don't know what this thorn is. Very intelligent people have speculated endlessly about what it could have been. A temptation Paul had toward a certain sin? A physical handicap or deformity? Some have argued that it was a specific demon sent to torment Paul, since he calls this thorn a "messenger of Satan." We simply don't know.

Why don't we know? Because Paul doesn't tell us what this thorn is. And he could have! It seems like this would have been a great opportunity for Paul to be "totally authentic" or even "deeply vulnerable" with the people to whom he writes. But Paul doesn't do this, probably because he doesn't want the Corinthians to focus on what this thorn is. He wants them to focus on God's response to his repeated prayers about it. What was God teaching Paul through this thorn in his flesh?

God wanted to show Paul this simple fact: "My grace is sufficient for you, for my power is made perfect in weakness" (12:9). God was using this thorn, as painful as it was for Paul, to show Paul—and us—the marvelous power of his grace. God's power, in fact, often becomes even clearer in the midst of human weakness. Paul ends this passage by boasting in his weakness, knowing that his imperfections can show Christ's glory and power even more clearly.

Are you sometimes discouraged by your weakness? Maybe you feel that you're not being very effective for the gospel or that you are not strong, good-looking, popular, or powerful. Paul tells us that he boasted in his weaknesses, because they were opportunities for God to look big through his life and ministry. Ask that God would be glorified through your weaknesses. This is not an excuse for sin; that is not what is meant by weakness! Pray that God would use even parts of your personality and life that seem weak to point others to the life-giving gospel of Jesus your Savior!

"Jesus Plus" Christianity

One of the biggest dangers that you may face in your walk with Christ is a subtle one. It's difficult to detect because it doesn't tempt you to reject Jesus directly. In fact, it embraces Jesus as the Savior and uses lots of good "Christian" language. What danger am I talking about? That of buying into a "Jesus plus" kind of Christianity—a belief that we need Jesus *plus* something else to please God and live as truly spiritual people. This thinking affirms Jesus as the *Savior* of sinners but not the true *Sustainer* of our faith in God and of our lives of obedience. This *plus* aspect to faith can take many forms; probably most commonly, it looks like legalism. We start out believing that we are saved by grace, but we begin thinking that we stay in God's favor by earning our way through good works, church attendance, or devotions. That is "Jesus plus" Christianity, not biblical faith in Christ alone!

A version of this "Jesus plus" Christianity proved to be a great threat to the lives of believers in the ancient city of Galatia. It came from the Jews who urged their Gentile brothers and sisters to embrace Jesus *plus* Jewish customs, rituals, and ceremonial laws in order to secure their salvation. Jesus was necessary for salvation, they taught, but Jewish customs were still required in order to attain salvation completely.

Paul shoots down this "Jesus plus" teaching with great intensity! Devastated that Gentile Christians have bought into this destructive teaching, he asks the rhetorical question, "Having begun by the Spirit, are you now being perfected by the flesh?" (3:3). "Jesus plus" teaching tempts Christians—who begin a relationship with God through faith in Christ alone and salvation by grace alone—to begin relying on their own power, goodness, and strength to continue and to grow in their relationship with God. This gets Paul as fired up as he ever is in his epistles. Why? Because the very gospel of *grace alone* is at stake here.

Do you feel yourself being tempted toward embracing a "Jesus plus" mentality? We all do sometimes! As you pray, ask God to remind you of the amazing grace by which you're saved and by which you live for God in obedience and faithfulness. Ask God to give you strength to trust Jesus for salvation—and then to keep trusting him every day to help you live for him!

Jesus Saves Completely

In Galatians 5, Paul again speaks to the deadly danger of adding legalism, rules, and regulations to the sufficient gospel of Jesus Christ. The main problem in the Galatian church was the teaching of Jewish people who tried to convince Gentile believers that they needed Jesus *plus* other things—Jewish rituals, regulations, and circumcision. For Paul, this teaching was to be battled at any cost. For the Christian, it's Christ and only Christ.

"But we're just adding to Jesus; that's a good thing!" That's probably what the opponents of Paul were saying. "We're not rejecting Jesus," you can hear them arguing. "We're just saying that you can be even *more* holy and righteous before God if you keep Jewish regulations and laws like circumcision." For Paul, though, people who go back to circumcision and legalistic rule-keeping to earn salvation have been "severed from Christ" (5:4). They have "fallen away from grace" (5:4). The legalism that was preached to the Galatian believers was far from a helpful add-on to faith in Jesus Christ; it was directly opposed to the gospel of grace through faith in Jesus Christ. Attempting to use rules and regulations to attain or further secure justification before a holy God is rejecting the total power of Christ Jesus to save *completely* people who put their faith in him.

Yet Paul, as in other places in his writings, wants to be absolutely clear about the moral results of a life that has been changed by the gospel of grace. We're saved for freedom—that is what we have been called to in Jesus rather than slavery to a set of rules. But that freedom is not license to engage in sin, because that's actually not true freedom! The freedom of the gospel is freedom to walk by the Spirit rather than walking in slavery to the sin nature. The gospel of grace sets us free to do what God wants us to do. People who try to bring legalism back into the lives of gospel people have missed the power of the Holy Spirit, who now rules the lives of believers, allowing them to live in true freedom.

Pray that God would help you rest in Jesus as your Savior, who completely paid for your sins and made you righteous in God's sight. Pray that God would help you rest in Jesus as your sustainer, who will help you to live by the Spirit and remain faithful and obedient to God until Christ returns again.

Every Spiritual Blessing

If your family is like most American families, at Thanksgiving you probably share what you're thankful for. Aunts, uncles, brothers, sisters, and grandparents probably talk about the blessings of health, family, food, and friends. And this is all good! It is right that we remember our blessings. But when was the last time that you thought deeply about the immense spiritual blessings that you have in Christ Jesus? It's with *these* blessings in mind that Paul begins his letter to the ancient church at Ephesus. What are the blessings of Christ Jesus all about?

First, we are blessed through God's sovereign choice to save us. This is probably one of the places where the Bible most clearly teaches the doctrine called *election* or *predestination*. Paul says that Christians are blessed because God "predestined [them] for adoption" (1:5), and this is something that God decided to do "before the foundation of the world" (1:4). If you have trusted in Jesus as your Lord and Savior, that means that God chose you long before you were born to be *his* child. That is a great blessing!

Second, we are blessed through redemption and forgiveness through the cross of Jesus Christ. Remember, friend: your redemption comes through the blood of Jesus! Your salvation was not cheap; it was bought through the work of Jesus. This work was God's lavishing his grace upon sinners like you and me.

Third, we are blessed with a future inheritance in Jesus that will last forever. Since we belong to Jesus, we are going somewhere! We share a future home with our great Savior and Lord. That's not all; God has given his Holy Spirit to dwell in us and act as the guarantee of our future inheritance with Jesus. Heaven is coming, and the Spirit's presence in our hearts and lives is God's promise to us that we will get there!

There are many small blessings to thank God for—and we should thank him for blessings great and small! But make sure that you are most thankful for the eternal, infinite blessings that you have through faith in Jesus Christ, the Son of God. Thank God for his sovereign choice of you. Praise God for the gracious work of redemption. Ask God to help you trust his Holy Spirit's presence as the guarantee of your future life with Jesus forever!

A Miracle of Grace

Imagine a toddler at a public pool. She walks away from her parents and falls into the water. No one notices for a couple of moments, then someone yells out, and people spring into action. Adults jump in and save the little girl—thankfully she is completely fine.

While that is a wonderful example of being saved in some way, it is *not* a good illustration of our eternal salvation, which has been secured through the work of Jesus on the cross. Paul describes the Ephesians' situation *before* Jesus saved them: "You were dead in the trespasses and sins in which you once walked" (2:1–2). Where were we when Jesus found us? Treading water? No! We were dead in our sins—lifeless at the bottom of the ocean.

Far too often we have the wrong picture of our salvation. We know that we need saving. But many times we think the saving we need is more like help from Jesus. We're drowning on our own; we need Jesus to help us swim. Friend, that is not the message of Scripture regarding our salvation.

There was no good thing in us when Jesus saved us. We weren't drowning—we were dead. Paul tells us that we were "by nature children of wrath, like the rest of mankind" (2:3). We are not basically good apart from Jesus. We are in danger of experiencing God's full wrath because of our sin. We don't need a little bit of help; we need a miracle of grace!

Then in verse 4 comes what some have called the most beautiful conjunction in all Scripture: "*But* God . . ." God—who is rich in mercy—makes sinners alive through the death and resurrection of Jesus, his Son. The gospel of Jesus Christ is not a message of help for good people who need to get a bit better. It is the message that miraculous life and complete forgiveness can come to people who are hopelessly sinful, under God's wrath, and spiritually dead. That is why Paul stops midsentence to exclaim, "By grace you have been saved" (2:5)!

If you grew up in a Christian home and attend church, chances are that you need to be reminded (maybe often!) about what you are apart from the grace of God in Christ Jesus. You were by nature a child of wrath and dead in your sins. But not anymore! You are made alive with Jesus Christ and are completely forgiven through the cross. Praise God for this message of grace!

To Live Is Christ

Paul's tone in 1 Corinthians was a tone of rebuke. The church at Corinth was in shambles—filled with sin and stricken by relational issues and divisions. As Paul begins his letter to the church at Philippi, we learn quickly that this church is not like the Corinthian church. Paul gushes about the Philippian church: "I thank my God in all my remembrance of you, always in every prayer of mine for you all making my prayer with joy" (1:3–4). He begins with a *joyful* tone; this is a healthy church, and they have proved this to Paul through their generous and faithful partnership with him in the gospel.

The church at Philippi, however, while a healthy church, is susceptible in a couple of specific areas, which Paul will call out in this letter. In this passage, we see that this church is in danger of losing gospel joy. The Philippian believers have the tendency—as we do—to allow their joy to go up and down based on changing circumstances, rather than anchoring their joy in the advance of the gospel of Jesus Christ in the world. Paul attacks this tendency head on. First, he talks about his imprisonment in Rome. (He is most likely writing this letter from a Roman jail.) What is Paul's attitude in the midst of this? He's joyful. Why? Because his being in prison has "served to advance the gospel" (1:12). Some have heard the gospel because of Paul's chains, and others have been made more bold to speak about Jesus Christ. Paul won't even allow himself to be bothered by some of his opponents who have used his imprisonment to bash him and lift themselves up as gospel rivals. Paul shows the Philippians that he has anchored his joy to the advance of the gospel of Jesus Christ.

In this context, Paul writes some of his most well-known words—words about his perspective on life and death. The pinnacle of this section is Paul's summary of his position: "To me to live is Christ, and to die is gain" (1:21). Life, for Paul, means service to Christ and proclamation of the gospel. Death is far better, for it means being in the very presence of the Savior. We would do well to adopt this perspective!

What dictates your joy? Ask God to help you to anchor your joy firmly to Jesus Christ himself. Don't put it anywhere else.

The Mind of Christ

Today, especially in the US, people are comfortable talking about one aspect of the person of Jesus: his example. Even atheists point to him as a great example of a humble man who suffered, healed people, and loved others in remarkable ways. While Christians know that Jesus offers much more than an example, we need to acknowledge that he doesn't offer *less* than this either! It is true that Jesus is our King, Savior, and Lord, but he should also be a shining example to us of how we should humbly suffer and put others first. Paul teaches exactly this in Philippians 2:1–11.

Here we find another problem plaguing this church: disunity and conflict. Later in the book, two of the offending individuals are called out by name—you can imagine how red their faces turned when this letter was read out loud to the church! Paul's call to unity is clear: "Complete my joy by being of the same mind, having the same love, being in full accord and of one mind. Do nothing from selfish ambition or conceit, but in humility count others more significant than yourselves" (2:2–3). Paul wants this problem to stop! Gospel people, he urges, must have unity in Christ. They must put others first, rather than their own concerns and comforts. But how does Paul call the Philippians to this?

Paul presents Jesus Christ, their Savior, to them as the ultimate example of one who counted others more significant than himself. Beginning in verse 5, Paul recounts the radical descent of Jesus Christ from the right hand of God to incarnation on earth as a human being. And that wasn't even the extent of his humiliation! Jesus "humbled himself by becoming obedient to the point of death, even death on a cross" (2:8). Jesus Christ had the right to continue ruling in all glory as the God of the universe. But Jesus humbled himself to bring sinners to God. Because of this, Paul writes, Jesus will be exalted forever, and every knee will one day bow and confess that he is the Lord of all. *This mind*—the mind of Christ Jesus—is the key for unity among the believers in Philippi.

Pray that you would have the mind of Christ as you deal with other believers. Pray that, because of the gospel, you would be able to look to the interests of others, just as Jesus looked to your eternal interests when he died for you.

The Supremacy and Sufficiency of Jesus

Jesus is Lord, and Jesus is enough. You could probably sum up the message of the book of Colossians with that simple sentence. To put it in more technical terms, Colossians argues for the *supremacy* and the *sufficiency* of Jesus Christ. Jesus is supreme—the infinitely holy, wise, and powerful God of all creation. Jesus is sufficient—more than enough to not only save and forgive people but also to sustain and empower them for the Christian life. Paul's goal in the letter to the church at Colossae is to lift Jesus high—to exalt him as the glorious Lord who is more than enough for his people. But why does Paul feel the need to send *this* message to *this* church?

It seems that as this church grew, certain people who were opponents of the true gospel of grace began to creep into the community. This happens a lot in the New Testament churches; that should be a lesson for us today! While the essence of the "Colossian heresy" is debated, it seems most likely that it was some kind of Jewish-related mysticism—a strange spirituality that promised deeper holiness, truer knowledge, and a more advanced level of spiritual development. Paul's goal in this letter is to counter this heresy by showing that nothing more than Jesus is needed—either for salvation or for the Christian life.

In this glorious passage, you saw Paul lifting up Jesus as, first, the Creator of the world. Jesus—the eternally existent second person of the Trinity—was active in creation. We must not forget that! Next, Paul points us to the primacy that Jesus has in relation to the church of God. "And he is the head of the body, the church," writes Paul; he is also the "firstborn from the dead" (1:18). More than all this, Jesus is the one who brings eternal salvation, peace, and forgiveness through his work on the cross. It is in Christ that we are reconciled to God, because of the "blood of his cross" (1:20). Jesus—Creator, head of the church, bearer of the cross. It's as if Paul is shouting, "Why would you want or need anything else?"

Do you really—practically—believe that Jesus is enough? Enough to say no to sin? Enough to fill you with ultimate joy, satisfaction, and peace? Paul tells us to believe that Jesus is sufficient for us in every way. Pray that you would believe this. Ask God to help you rest in your Savior even more!

Christian Clothing

Our culture is crazy about clothes, isn't it? We spend tons of money on them; designer blue jeans can cost several hundred dollars! Many people have bought into the idea that our clothes are tied to our identity. How we dress—we are taught to think—sends a message about who we are. Well, that's exactly the point Paul is making in Colossians 3:1-17! But he's not talking about clothes made out of cotton or denim. He's talking about the clothing of our lives—our behavior, speech, and thoughts. Those things, Paul says, demonstrate our true identity.

The commands that Paul gives in this passage all hinge on one big *if*. "*If* then you have been raised with Christ,*"* he begins (3:1). Everything that he will have to say about how to dress ourselves will ride on the answer to this question: Have we really been raised with Christ? Well, have *you*? Have you come to Jesus with repentance and sorrow over your sin and turned to him in total faith, belief, and surrender? In other words, have you truly experienced Christian conversion? If so, Paul's words are for you. So what are they?

The first word for people who have been raised with Christ is this: put sin to death. People who have been forgiven by Christ's work on the cross are called to violently rid themselves of the sin for which he died. Paul's phrase—"put to death" (3:5)—can't be misunderstood. Sin in the lives of Christians is to be killed! We who follow Jesus are to "put off the old self" like dirty clothes that are so filthy that you decide to just throw them in the garbage (3:9)! So, what are we to put *on*, then?

Christians are to put on the clothing and characteristics of their Savior. What does this look like? Compassionate hearts. Kindness. Humility. Forgiveness. Love. Peace. In short, God's people are supposed to begin looking more like Jesus. That is the clothing we are supposed to wear!

If it is true that your spiritual clothing points to your identity, take a moment and evaluate how you are dressed today. Are you putting sin to death daily? Are you clothing yourself with Christlikeness? Pray today that your faith in Jesus would show itself more and more in your character, words, and thoughts. Ask God to help you put sin violently to death as you get dressed more and more with the character of your Savior.

A Living Hope

First Thessalonians 4:13–5:11 homes in on one of the main themes of the book. It's the theme of the second coming of Jesus Christ. This was an idea that was evidently giving the Thessalonian believers a very hard time. They didn't quite understand how the second coming of Jesus would work, and it even seems that some of them had begun to doubt that it would even happen! Have you ever had doubts about Jesus's second coming? Do you struggle to believe that it will *really* happen? If so, you need Paul's words today too.

Paul's first word to the church at Thessalonica on this subject, really, is a word of *hope*. People have been dying in their church, and it seems that the congregation has started to become very discouraged by this. Paul, though, steps in with this word: "For since we believe that Jesus died and rose again, even so, through Jesus, God will bring with him those who have fallen asleep" (4:14). The resurrection of God's people will *really happen*, says Paul! It's this glorious truth that allows Christians to grieve with hope for loved ones who die. It's OK to grieve, says Paul. But don't grieve without resurrection hope!

But in the midst of hoping for the return of Christ and the resurrection from the dead, Paul wants the Thessalonians to avoid one thing: detailed speculation about when exactly this all will happen. They don't need to worry about exactly when Jesus will come back; in fact, Paul reminds them that the one thing we *do* know about the return of Jesus is that it will come *unexpectedly*, like a thief in the night. If that is the case, what is the right response for a believer to the future coming of Jesus? It's to just live for God! It's to "keep awake and be sober" (5:6), which simply means being ready for Jesus's return through belief in him and obedience to his word.

Jesus will return. The dead will be raised. We don't know exactly when all this will happen. Those are the truths that Paul is teaching the Thessalonian believers in this passage. Pray that you would believe in and expect the return of Jesus Christ. Ask God to make you ready for your Savior's return through faith and obedience to him.

A Contradiction in Terms

In its early days, the Christian church was a radical community—a place where people worshiped Jesus Christ as Lord, affirmed the resurrection from the dead, and loved one another with grace and forgiveness. It was a countercultural community, and many of the Thessalonian believers surely discovered that the church was their true home in a difficult world. Yet it seems that something bad started happening in the church at Thessalonica. Perhaps because they thought Jesus was going to return any minute or because people were kind and generous, some members of the church became extremely lazy. They stopped working, content to depend on the kindness of other people in the church.

Lazy Christian is not a phrase that makes sense to Paul. A follower of Jesus should *never* use his or her faith, the church, or the love of God's community as excuses to refrain from hard work and discipline. Paul points the Thessalonians to his example: "You yourselves know how you ought to imitate us, because we were not idle when we were with you, nor did we eat anyone's bread without paying for it, but with toil and labor we worked night and day" (3:7–8). Paul worked *hard*. He never used Christianity as an excuse to take it easy—his faith made him work even harder! Paul gives this stern command: believers in Jesus should work hard.

Do you see the Thessalonian tendency toward laziness in your own life? Do you sometimes use Christian lingo to justify a failure to work hard— at school, in your job, in sports, or in your family life? If you know Jesus, his grace should inspire you to work even harder than people who don't know him. Of course, you're not working to earn God's favor; his grace has already been poured out on you in Jesus. But your love for God and your experience of this grace should push you to hard work for the glory of your Savior!

Ask God to show you areas in your life where you might be guilty of laziness. It's not an area that we often bring to God in confession, is it? But pray about it today! Ask God to show you where you are being idle in your spiritual life. Ask him to help you work hard in school, sports, music, and your job (if you have one). Pray that he would help you respond to Jesus's grace with energy, joy, and diligence in everything you do!

Spiritual Mentors

Have you ever had anyone in your life whom you considered a mentor? Someone who took you under his or her wing to train you and teach you the ropes? Perhaps this was a coach, teacher, or music instructor. If you've had someone like this in your life, you'll always remember many things that he or she taught you. You will be forever marked by this mentor's influence. A good mentor in your life can help you, train you, challenge you, and point you to Christ!

Paul was Timothy's mentor. He even calls Timothy his "child in the faith" (1:2). Timothy, a young pastor in Ephesus, has been trained by Paul; now he is experiencing some of the hardships of serving and leading a church full of difficult and sinful people! The letter of 1 Timothy is the first of what we call the Pastoral Epistles—letters from Paul regarding how early church leaders should guard and shepherd Christ's flock. What is it that Paul will begin with for Timothy, his child in the faith?

Paul wants Timothy to hold on to the true gospel. That is the core of Paul's message to Timothy in both of his letters to him. He wants Timothy to believe the gospel, preach the gospel, live the gospel, and guard the purity of the gospel. The true gospel of Jesus—his death for sins and resurrection from the dead—will always be opposed! And so, Paul begins this letter to the young man he has trained with these words: "Remain at Ephesus so that you may charge certain persons not to teach any different doctrine" (1:3). Timothy, Paul's protégé, has received his charge: don't let *anyone* teach anything other than the true gospel of Jesus Christ!

Teaching matters. That's what we are learning as the book of 1 Timothy begins. Paul does not want anyone to teach a different doctrine than the true one—the gospel of Jesus Christ. Are you putting yourself in places where you will hear good biblical teaching? Are you tempted to listen to messages in your world that are opposing the truth of the gospel? Pray that you will devote yourself—like Timothy—to guarding the truth of the Bible's message of salvation through Jesus Christ alone. Ask God to make you a faithful witness to his Son!

Godly Leaders

The Bible's big story started with God's creation of the world—and of human beings, who fell into sin. Then, God graciously formed a people for himself, starting with Abraham, to whom he gave a great promise of blessing. God's people became a great kingdom, which peaked during the reigns of David and Solomon. Even through sin and exile, God remained faithful to his people, giving them prophets who pointed them to the coming Messiah. Jesus broke onto the scene; his death and resurrection was the climax of the story. He ascended into heaven, promising to return again and leaving his people to grow, worship him, and spread the gospel as members of God's church. That's where 1 Timothy and the other epistles come in. Paul is training a young man, Timothy, to lead God's church well. But how will the church stay faithful and focused? Godly elders are necessary.

This passage is not meant as a description of Christian perfection. Aware that no human being will achieve perfect holiness until heaven, Paul is giving Timothy a picture of godly character and Christlike integrity that must be represented in the lives of men who will lead God's church. Leaders in the church must be godly and faithful; their character will determine the direction and holiness of the congregation! The kind of man who should lead God's people should be "above reproach, the husband of one wife, sober-minded, self-controlled, respectable, hospitable, able to teach, not a drunkard, not violent but gentle, not quarrelsome, not a lover of money" (3:2–3). This is a high calling!

Did you see the one difference between the qualifications for elders and the qualifications for deacons? Elders must be able to teach. It seems that the elder role that Paul is describing here includes both elders *and* pastors; deacon is a separate category. Those two roles—elders and pastors—are part of the same category for Paul. The term *overseer* describes men who lead the church with integrity and godly character and are also capable of faithfully and accurately teaching the Bible to God's people.

You may not be an elder or deacon! But you can strive—with Jesus's help—for more self-control, gentleness, and hospitality. Pray today that God would help you grow in Christlike character so that you can serve his people well.

Only One Way

There are lots of ways to fail a test in school. You can skip class on the day the test is given or sleep through the period. You can write all the right answers in the wrong spaces. You can get caught cheating. There is only *one way* to pass a test: you have to get the right answers. There are lots of ways to mess up; there's only one way to succeed.

This is the idea that Paul wants to leave with Timothy as he ends this first letter to him. Paul wants this young pastor to know that in the days to come, people will start believing and teaching all sorts of things—even the "teachings of demons" (4:1). Timothy will come across all kinds of crazy cults, spiritual abuses, and weird teachings that contradict Scripture. In other words, there are lots of ways that people will depart from the true gospel of Jesus Christ! So what is Timothy to do? Is he to study up on every false teaching? Become extremely familiar with every demonic teaching and legalistic impulse that threatens to enter the church? Absolutely not.

Timothy, Paul says, is to hold tightly to the "good doctrine" that he has already followed (4:6). He is to keep on preaching the gospel! People who train to detect counterfeit money don't waste their time becoming acquainted with the counterfeits; they study the real thing so that they can tell a fake bill immediately. In the same way, Timothy is to stick closely to the gospel teaching he has received from Paul. Paul wants him to devote himself to reading the Bible publicly and to exhortation and teaching. The answer to false teaching is not to chase down every one of those teachings and try to interact with them! In fact, Paul tells Timothy to have nothing to do with much of it. The answer to false teaching is always God's word—going back to the core truths of the gospel. Timothy, Paul's child in the faith, is charged to keep proclaiming Jesus Christ as the Son of God and the Savior of sinners. That is the message with God's power behind it.

Pray today that your preparation for life in this world—and all the strange teachings and beliefs that you will hear—will be to ground yourself in the one true gospel of Jesus Christ. Ask God to give you a greater conviction of the truth of his word. Ask him to help you commit to speaking his truth to others no matter what.

Hold Fast to the Gospel

While the exact date of the writing of the letter of 2 Timothy is not certain, Paul wrote it near the end of his life. He writes from a Roman prison, where he is most likely awaiting his death. Paul knows the end is coming, and as he prepares, he pens one final letter to his young protégé, Timothy. You can imagine how seriously Timothy would have taken these final words from his beloved mentor!

Paul begins by reminding Timothy of his wonderful family legacy of faith. Timothy's "sincere faith," says Paul, came about—at least in part—because of the influence of the godly women he had in his life: his grandmother, Lois, and his mother, Eunice (1:5). Timothy has had the privilege—like many of you—of growing up surrounded by people who knew Jesus and who have taught him the good news of the gospel. He has believed in Jesus personally as well and has now become a teacher and a preacher of the gospel.

It's because of Timothy's legacy and gospel faith that Paul issues the next command: "I remind you to fan into flame the gift of God, which is in you through the laying on of my hands" (1:6). This verse is much debated, but the meaning, really, is quite simple. Paul is encouraging Timothy to grow in his ability and confidence to preach and teach the gospel as a servant of Christ Jesus. The laying on of hands refers to Timothy's ordination as a pastor; Paul is telling him to grow as a preacher of God's word!

Paul will stay on this point for most of the rest of this letter to Timothy. He will issue a call for firm endurance in the gospel. He will urge Timothy to stick closely to the truth of God's word against all kinds of opposition. He will charge Timothy to *preach* God's word no matter what.

Even if you didn't grow up in a Christian home, you have a legacy of faith that is given to you by God. People have invested in you spiritually, and you are called to carry on that gospel legacy! Thank God for the people who have pointed you to Jesus. Ask him to help you carry on a legacy of the gospel as you point others to the Savior as well.

The Gift of Good Pastors

If you've been around the church for a while, you've probably heard this passage quoted by a church leader at some point. It's one of the favorite passages of pastors who believe in biblical preaching! But as you read Paul's charge to Timothy to preach the word, you might have struggled to connect. Maybe you've never imagined yourself as a preacher and aren't interested in full-time ministry, much less pastoral ministry. How does this charge from a dying pastor to a young pastor apply to your life?

First, this charge should guide you in finding the right church. If you love Jesus and believe God's word, then you want to be a part of a community that values biblical preaching! You want to be in a place that has reproof, rebuke, and exhortation—all done with the authority and truth of the Bible behind them. You should want to be under a pastor who takes these words of the apostle Paul as his personal charge in pastoral ministry.

Second, this passage should help you know how to encourage your pastor. Paul is clear that people won't always want to hear biblical preaching; in fact, most of the time they will prefer teachers and teachings that "suit their own passions" and tickle their "itching ears" with what they want to hear (4:3). You can encourage your pastor by listening to his biblical (excellent *or* ordinary) and faithful preaching and thanking him for it. He is seeking to fulfill the ministry that God has given to him, rather than seeking to tickle the ears of people who don't want anything to do with God's word.

Third, this charge should remind you that God's word is what God's people need the most! That's why Paul charges Timothy to commit himself to preaching it faithfully. It's God's word that has the power to convict, change hearts, open eyes, and point sinners to salvation in Jesus Christ. You need biblical preaching whether you know it or not!

Although you are young, you can start to make commitments about what kind of church community you want to join, serve, and even possibly lead. Ask God today that he would lead you to a church in the coming years that is committed to faithfully preaching his word. Ask him to help you find a pastor who has committed himself to saying what God says, not what he thinks people want to hear. That is where we all need to be.

Spiritual Training

How do you think about your church? What core activities come to mind? Maybe it's singing; the church is the place where believers gather together to sing praises to their God. Maybe it's preaching; your church has a strong commitment to biblical preaching, week after week. Maybe it's fellowship; your church has a huge emphasis on believers gathering together regularly for encouragement and support. All these things are good! But it seems that in Titus 2, Paul has a very specific idea in his mind when he writes to Titus about the church. He sees the church as a place of *training*.

After giving instructions for how the older men in the church are to conduct themselves, Paul turns to the older women in the church. What are they to do? They are to "teach what is good, and so train the young women to love their husbands and children, to be self-controlled, pure, working at home, kind" (2:3–5). Paul then turns back to Titus, the pastor, and tells him how he should be training the young men. Paul is telling this pastor that the church is supposed to be a place of training—God's people training and teaching each other to live out gospel faith. Paul wants older men training younger men and older women training younger women. Do you attend a church that has members of all different ages? According to Paul, that is a huge blessing! Take advantage of relationships with older and more mature believers, and learn from them about life in Jesus.

As the chapter ends, Paul reminds Titus that, ultimately, training in godly living happens as we experience the grace of God. It is this grace that has appeared to us in Jesus, and this grace trains us to say no to sin as we wait for our great future hope: "the appearing of the glory of our great God and Savior Jesus Christ" (2:13). For Paul, the church is meant to be a place where believers are trained to live for Jesus Christ. This happens through relationships with older believers, and it happens through a true experience of God's saving grace in Jesus Christ.

Pray that God would help you see your church not as a place you go once a week to check it off your list. Ask him to help you see your church body as a place of spiritual training. Start pursuing relationships with believers who are older, wiser, more godly, and mature. Ask God to train you—by his grace—to live for him until Jesus returns.

Countercultural Reconciliation

Philemon is a short letter from Paul to a man named, of course, Philemon. It seems that Philemon was a wealthy man who owned a slave named Onesimus. Onesimus had run away from Philemon and had probably also stolen from Philemon when he ran. But the runaway slave ran into Paul—and he repented of his sin and put his faith in Jesus Christ. He became a dear friend to Paul, who was in prison in Rome.

This puts Onesimus in an interesting position. He is on the run from his earthly master, whom he has seriously wronged. But now he is a Christian; he shares a common faith in Jesus with his former owner. This is where Paul comes in. He tells Onesimus that he needs to make things right with Philemon. But Paul makes an appeal to Philemon as well. Reconciliation with God implies reconciliation with God's people. That's what Paul says to Philemon in the letter that Onesimus carries back to his master.

While Paul stops short of *commanding* Philemon to forgive Onesimus and accept him back, he urges him on the basis of the gospel to do so. Paul wants Philemon to take Onesimus in "as a beloved brother . . . both in the flesh and in the Lord" (v. 16). Paul tells Philemon that he will cover whatever debt Onesimus owes Philemon and urges him to take Onesimus into his house as an equal. Paul is not afraid to twist Philemon's arm a bit!

Why does Paul urge his friend Philemon to do this? This would have been a countercultural move. Runaway slaves could be legally beaten—or even killed. But, as Paul argues, gospel people do things differently. Onesimus's reconciliation with God through Christ must lead to forgiveness and reconciliation with Philemon. Philemon must show grace to his brother in Christ—just as Christ has shown grace to him. Their relationship has changed forever. These two men are brothers in Christ—saved by the blood of the same Savior.

Are you harboring hatred toward someone, or does someone have something against you that is not resolved? If you are reconciled to God through repentance and faith in Christ, then you must be reconciled to your brother or sister in Christ. Ask God to help you take the first step toward confession, forgiveness, and reconciliation today.

Jesus Is Better!

Probably no New Testament book does a better and more thorough job than Hebrews of showing us how Jesus fulfills all God's promises to his people throughout the Old Testament. While we don't know who the author of this book was, we know that he understood how *every* part of God's law and *every* promise of God's prophets rushed forward until the day when Jesus, the Son of God, appeared on the earth—to live, die, and rise again. You could sum up the message of the entire book with a simple phrase: *Jesus is better!* He's better than the sacrificial system. He's better than any human priest. He's better than any human king. Jesus is the *best*. Hebrews shows us that Jesus is the climax to the whole Bible story.

In Hebrews 1, this theme becomes immediately apparent. The author tells us that "at many times and in many ways, God spoke to our fathers by the prophets, but in these last days he has spoken to us by his Son" (1:1–2). Jesus is God's final and perfect Word to the world. It is in Jesus that God's people see his salvation perfected and the mystery of his plan of redemption unlocked. Jesus is the glorious God—the radiance of his glory, in fact—and he has finally made "purification for sins" through his death on the cross (1:3).

Specifically, in this chapter, the point is this: Jesus is greater and more glorious than angels. This might not be something that you wonder about, but it would have been on the minds of the original audience of this book. Jesus, God's Son, is set apart from every other spiritual being. He "upholds the universe" by his very word; no angel does that (1:3). God has called him his Son. In fact, angels are commanded to bow down and worship Jesus! The writer goes to several other Old Testament passages to keep hammering home the same point: Jesus is far superior to all the angelic beings. He is God's Son—not created, but eternally existent. He is God's final word to the world. And he is to be worshiped.

Ask God to remind you that he holds the universe by his word. Ask him to help you worship his Son and accept him as the great Lord of your life. Thank him for sending his Son at the right time to fulfill all his promises to sinful people who need salvation!

Jesus, Our Perfect Priest

Jesus is better. That is the main point of the book of Hebrews. The author is concerned with showing us how Jesus Christ, God's Son, is the perfect fulfillment of all God's promises to his people for all time. He is the better reality, to which all the shadows, pictures, and signs of the Old Testament point. And Hebrews 4:14–5:10 focuses on Jesus as the better priest for God's people. So how does Jesus perfect priesthood for us?

First, Jesus is a priest who is also God. In the Old Testament, the priests were mediators for God's people—go-betweens for sinners who offered sacrifices and led them in worship and through teaching. The problem was that these human priests were sinners too! Not so with Jesus. We have a high priest—a mediator between us and God—who "has passed through the heavens, Jesus, the Son of God" (4:14). Our go-between is God himself; there is no better mediator for sinners!

Second, Jesus is a priest who is fully human. His divinity does not mean that he doesn't understand what we go through and how we are tempted. Jesus became human; he knows our situations. Here's how the writer of Hebrews puts it: "For we do not have a high priest who is unable to sympathize with our weaknesses, but one who in every respect has been tempted as we are, yet without sin" (4:15). Jesus has "been there"—on this earth, in our shoes. He can sympathize with broken sinners like you and me!

Finally, Jesus is a priest who is himself the sacrifice for sin. Human priests had to sacrifice animals, according to the law of Moses. Jesus, though, gives himself as the final, perfect, sacrifice for sin to bring eternal salvation to lost sinners. Jesus, appointed by God as the Savior, "became the source of eternal salvation to all who obey him" through his death on the cross (5:9). We do not need any other priest. Jesus is the *perfect* high priest for us!

Spend some time thinking about Jesus as your perfect priest. Praise him as the one who is God Most High—the Creator of the world. Thank him as the one who took human flesh and came near to this sinful world. Trust him as the one whose sacrificial death paid the final penalty for your sin against an infinitely holy God. Ask him to help you cling to him only as your mediator and advocate before God's throne!

Blood Sacrifice

All of the Bible is God's word. This means that, if you are serious about hearing God's word to you, you have to work hard on understanding the Old Testament! The good news is that New Testament books like Hebrews help us understand the Old Testament. Hebrews 8 can help you better "put your Bible together" in your mind.

From Hebrews, we understand that the laws and rituals of the Old Testament were *copies* and *shadows* of heavenly things. Goat and sheep blood cannot *actually* take away sin against a holy God. The sacrificed animals had very little to do with sin and the punishment sin deserves! The Old Testament priests—and their customs and rituals in accordance with God's law—pointed God's people to the heavenly realities that these things represented. Something real lay behind the "copy" of animal sacrifice: the blood sacrifice that would one day be paid with the blood of God's own Son.

Second, we need to understand that the Old Testament prophets, laws, and rituals always pointed forward to the new covenant promises of God in Jesus Christ. This is behind the author of Hebrews' decision to quote in verses 8–12 an extended passage from Jeremiah. It comes from the point in the book of Jeremiah where the prophet looks forward to a new covenant that God will make with his people. This covenant will be different from the covenant with Moses. It will have at its heart the potential and intention of heart transformation. The blood and saving work of Jesus Christ *alone* can bring about such lasting change!

God's people were always called to look to the reality behind the copy and shadow. Even during the days of the covenant of Moses with the law, true believers in God were saved as they trusted not their good deeds or ritual-keeping but the mercy of a gracious God who would provide forgiveness, mercy, and salvation for sinful people. When Jesus broke onto the scene, God's plan became fully evident. But the way to salvation had not changed. It had always been by grace through faith.

As you read these passages, I hope you're seeing Jesus as the glorious center of God's big plan of redemption for his people—and for the whole world he created. Thank God that, through the sacrifice of his own Son, rebels can be justified and sinful hearts can truly be changed.

Once for All

Hebrews is such a powerful book—and such a helpful book for "putting our Bibles together." As you read through it, you may have asked questions like: Why is Jesus better? What is it, precisely, about Jesus that makes him the great high priest? It's these questions that the author of Hebrews goes even deeper to answer in Hebrews 9. Why is Jesus better? He's better because he is the Son of God.

Because he is the Son of God, his blood secures an eternal redemption. Every human high priest of God's people had to enter the holy places of the tabernacle "by means of the blood of goats and calves" (9:12). Every human high priest was sinful; they needed sacrifices for their sins too, and the best they could do was to offer animal sacrifices again and again for God's people, in accordance with the law. Jesus, though, offers his own blood. This sacrifice brings not momentary redemption but *eternal* redemption.

Because Jesus is the Son of God, his sacrifice was *a once-for-all sacrifice* (9:12, 26). The author of Hebrews describes the animal sacrifices being made again and again, year after year, to keep up with the sins of God's people. Jesus doesn't need to "offer himself repeatedly" as a sacrifice (9:25)! The Son of God died *once*—as an ultimate sacrifice for sin. If we belong to Jesus, our sins were paid for completely—through his ultimate sacrifice. The eternal Son of God took *all* the sins of God's people—all at once!

Because Jesus is the Son of God, his death purifies our consciences. What does this difficult phrase mean? It means that Jesus's saving work can actually change sinful people from the inside out. Animal sacrifices, while part of God's plan for a time, could not—in themselves—bring internal change. Jesus's sacrifice, by the power of the Holy Spirit, can bring internal change! If you belong to Jesus Christ today through faith, your conscience can be purified. You can "serve the living God" (9:14). You can say no to dead works and have victory over sin!

You serve Jesus Christ, the great high priest! If you are struggling with sin, ask God to give you strength to overcome it. If you are wondering whether you are truly forgiven, ask God to help you look again at the cross where the Son of God shed his blood for you as a once-for-all sacrifice.

The Hall of Faith

Hebrews 11 is one of the most well-known passages in all of Scripture. You've probably heard Hebrews 11 referred to as "The Hall of Faith." Only the greatest saints in history get mentioned here; it's the place where great followers of God are remembered. It's a fun chapter to read, because it calls to mind so many of the great stories of the Old Testament. But what is this chapter in the book of Hebrews really telling us? What is it all about?

This faith chapter shows us the mark of God's people in every age. What is that true mark? Faith. Faith in God. Trust in him alone as Savior, Creator, and Lord. God's people—in every point in the history of this world—have found favor with their Creator through faith alone.

But also this faith chapter reminds us that God's grace is big enough to save even people who are far from perfect. Look again at the names that are mentioned in this chapter: Rahab, the prostitute from Jericho who joined God's people; Jephthah, the judge who made a terribly foolish and tragic vow; Samson, the immature and slightly out-of-control hulk of a man. These people are not necessarily all ones you would expect to see here! But, by God's grace, they are listed here in this summary of faithful people. God's grace is amazing; it is big enough for sinners like you and me.

Finally, we need to see that this chapter is clear that faithfulness to God will have different earthly results. Some people achieve great victory and accomplishment. Others suffer tremendously! God's promise is not that faith will lead to comfort on this earth. In fact, for some, faith in Jesus is what leads to terrible pain and anguish on earth. But ultimately the hope for all of God's true people is in the city and the kingdom to come: an eternity in the presence of Jesus, the great King and Savior.

Ask God that you would be numbered with his people throughout all the ages who have been marked by their faith in him. Ask him for strength to believe his promises. Ask him for courage to live by his word. Pray that he would enable you to trust in Christ alone as your Savior. And, by his grace, look forward to the day when you will praise his name forever as you stand with David, Abraham, Moses, and the rest of God's redeemed people.

Responding to Jesus

The book of Hebrews shows that Jesus Christ is the better and perfect fulfillment of all God's Old Testament promises to his people. He is the better priest—the final sacrifice for sin. Hebrews 12:1–2 is in some ways the conclusion of the entire book of Hebrews. How should we respond to Jesus?

The writer tells us that, first, we need to put sin away. That is the right response to seeing Jesus as the Savior who removes our sin and forgives us. If this life is like a race, then sin is like a weight—a heavy backpack or metal chains—that weighs us down as we try to run for the glory of God. The call to redeemed people is to "lay aside every weight, and sin which clings so closely" (12:1). Are you still struggling with sin today? Maybe you're not even *struggling* with it; you're just continuing to do it! If that is the case, the call to you is clear: If you belong to Jesus, you must lay aside the sin for which your Savior died. Trust him to forgive you, and ask him to help you put away the weight of sin in your life as you live for him.

But the Christian life isn't just about putting sin away, as important as that commitment is. The Christian life is ultimately about looking at Jesus! How do we run the race that God has called us to run? How do we find strength to say no to temptation and the enticing pleasures of sin? By "looking to Jesus, the founder and perfecter of our faith" (12:2). He is the one who endured the cross for our forgiveness and salvation. He is the one who is now seated at the right hand of the throne of God, waiting to return and judge this world in power, glory, and holiness. It is a *focus on Jesus Christ*—his salvation and his future judgment—that will keep us living well for God's glory on this earth.

Is there sin in your life that you need to put aside? If so, talk to God about it. Ask him to give you strength to confess that sin to him and others and to fight it by the power of the Holy Spirit. If you're not sure about the answer to that question, ask God to continually reveal areas and attitudes of sin that you need to put aside more and more as you follow Jesus; we all have these!

Faith That Works

James tends to be a difficult book for Christians to get a handle on. Even the great theologian Martin Luther struggled with understanding and applying it; he was said to have referred to James as the "epistle of straw."[5] Why is it so difficult? Because Christians who believe in salvation by *grace alone* struggle with the firm teaching of James on the importance of good works and obedience in the lives of Christians. Is James preaching a different gospel from Paul's? Is he saying that we are saved not by grace alone but by our good works? The answer to these questions is, "Absolutely not!"

James shows us that true faith in Jesus Christ will lead to good works. He is not saying that good works save anybody; he is saying that anybody who truly has faith will *demonstrate* that faith by the way he or she lives. Here's how James puts it: "So also faith by itself, if it does not have works, is dead" (2:17). A faith that doesn't bear fruit in a changed life is a dead faith; that's what James is saying. That kind of faith can't save a person, because that kind of a faith isn't true faith at all!

James also shows us that true faith is more than mental assent to a set of truths about God. Even the demons, says James, believe in God; they even shudder with fear at God because they know his power so clearly! Belief— in the sense that belief describes mental assent to a certain reality—is not the same as saving faith. Saving faith is *active faith*; it is building one's life on the object of that faith. James uses both Abraham and Rahab to demonstrate his point. These Old Testament believers both had saving faith in God—faith that was demonstrated by their actions. In this sense, they were justified by what they did—not declared righteous because of the actions themselves, but the actions were effective in *proving* the genuineness of their faith.

Here's the point: true faith *works*. We are saved by faith alone, but faith is never *alone* (that is, never independent of a changed life that leads to obedience and good works).

If your faith in Jesus is genuine, it will bear fruit in obedience and good works. Ask God to grow good fruit in your life by the power of his Holy Spirit. Ask him to make your faith living, active, and effective!

More Dangerous Than Sticks and Stones

You have been hurt by words. At some point in your life, someone has said something that stung you with a pain that is altogether different from physical discomfort. Friend, you know the power of words. You know how they can hurt—especially when they are flung carelessly and cruelly by someone you love. You also know that you can hurt other people with your words as well—and perhaps you have learned this the hard way! James knows this too. And he wants us to know that our relationship with Christ must impact the way we speak.

The human tongue is dangerous and powerful. That's the first thing James points out in this passage. The tongue is like a small bridle, which controls a huge and powerful horse. It's like a rudder, which can steer a massive ship in the ocean. It's like a small fire, which can set a huge forest ablaze. Much damage has been done throughout history with sinful human words. Because of this, James says that getting control of one's tongue essentially proves that one can have self-control in every area. Do you have control of your tongue today? Do you measure every word and use all your speech to glorify Jesus and encourage other people?

If your speech is an area of your life over which you have little control, James has another word for you today: "From the same mouth come blessing and cursing. My brothers, these things ought not to be so" (3:10). Just as fresh springs can't shoot out both salty and clean water, so a person led by Jesus should not spout out both praises to Jesus and words that are dirty, unkind, or untrue. Our speech must line up with the call of our Savior. It's not right to claim to follow Jesus and accept a habit of cursing, gossip, or filthy talk. It just doesn't fit!

Pray specifically about your words today. Think about the things you've said, even in the past few days. Is your tongue held captive to Jesus, your Savior? Or is your speech out of control—capable of lighting up a forest with angry words, gossip, or dirty talk? Pray to your Savior and ask him to let your life line up with his holy character at every level. Give him your speech today, and ask him to take it over for his glory!

Hope and Holiness amid Exile

Think about how many things we do every day that are motivated by wanting to fit in. Think about the clothes you wear or the way you talk. The way Peter begins this letter should come as a surprise to us, then; he writes to "elect exiles" (1:1), people who are not at home, people who don't belong where they are. Most likely, Peter has a strictly *spiritual* meaning in mind here. He writes to people who are exiles—social misfits and outcasts—because of a relationship with Jesus Christ. They may not be literal exiles, but spiritually speaking they are far from their true home. This world has become an uncomfortable, foreign place for them because of their faith in Christ; they no longer fit in here! What does Peter have to say to these elect exiles?

Peter calls these suffering people to lives of holiness. Suffering for Jesus does not imply a laid-back approach to obedience! The spiritual exiles to whom Peter writes seem to need encouragement to keep on pursuing holy lives in Jesus, their Savior. See what he writes to them: "Do not be conformed to the passions of your former ignorance, but as he who called you is holy, you also be holy in all your conduct" (1:14–15). The call to holiness for believers in Jesus Christ is unavoidable! Think about your life. Are you passionate about pursuing holiness—set apart, obedient living—for the glory of your Savior, even in hard times?

Second, Peter calls these exiles to a great eternal hope. While the call to holiness is a kick-in-the-pants kind of call—an *exhortation*—this call will ultimately be measured by a great source of hope, about which Peter reminds his audience. What's the hope that spiritual exiles have, even in the midst of suffering? It's the "living hope" (1:3) that we have through faith in Jesus Christ—the "inheritance that is imperishable, undefiled, and unfading, kept in heaven" for us (1:4). The call to follow Jesus is a call to suffer with him, but it is a call to glorious eternal hope as well. Peter wants suffering people to pursue holiness without losing this great hope!

Ask God today to make you even more passionate about pursuing holiness, obedience, and faithfulness to his word—not with legalistic motivation (to earn favor with him) but as the right response to his saving grace. Pray that he would help you keep your hope firmly fixed on the future reward, with Jesus, even in the midst of struggle.

Christian Suffering

It doesn't take long, when reading 1 Peter, to realize that you have to deal with the theme of suffering in order to understand this letter! Peter is writing to elect exiles—spiritual misfits who face suffering because of their relationship with Jesus Christ. What kind of suffering, specifically? It seems that Peter's audience faces verbal abuse, insults, and social marginalization because they follow Jesus and don't engage in the world's sinful practices. Life in Christ has given them great hope for an eternal future, but it has made everyday life extremely difficult! What does Peter have to say to us about specifically Christian suffering?

First, Peter wants us to be ready for it. "Do not be surprised," he writes, "at the fiery trial when it comes upon you to test you" (4:12). Christians shouldn't be shocked when suffering comes! This is difficult for us—our culture trains us to expect comfort, not suffering. Peter's message, though, is clear: your Savior suffered, so you should be ready to suffer too, if you belong to him.

Second, Peter wants us to rejoice in suffering. Why and how can we do this? We can do it because, in suffering, we are being linked (by God, and even by the people who persecute us) with Jesus Christ himself. In suffering for following Jesus, we can have great joy; we "share Christ's sufferings" (4:13). Like the apostles in Acts who rejoiced that they were "counted worthy to suffer" for Jesus's name (Acts 5:41), we too should even be honored to be treated with abuse along with our Savior.

Finally, Peter wants us to see that we should be ready to be purified by suffering. While 1 Peter 4:17–18 is a difficult passage, Peter's point is that the persecution that comes to the church of Jesus Christ is God's purifying judgment that comes, first, on his own people. It foreshadows the final judgment of the world on all who "do not obey the gospel of God" (4:17). For the church, the purpose is purification; it will reveal true believers and expose fake Christians. As you get ready for suffering, the best preparation is to get close to Jesus, your Savior!

No matter our situation, Peter's words to us are to get ready for suffering, rejoice as we share in Christ's sufferings, and be purified by it as believers in Jesus. Talk to God about these things. Draw close to your Savior in prayer!

Make Every Effort

Imagine that you are hiking and get lost in the woods. It's just you, your backpack, and a big wilderness. You wonder how you will make it through the night! Then you remember something. You take off your backpack, which has attached to it a small tent and a sleeping bag. Inside the pack are a flashlight, matches, and enough food to last at least two days. You have everything you need to survive overnight in the wilderness. You breathe a sigh of relief; you'll be fine, and you'll find your way home in the morning.

As Peter begins this letter, he wants to be clear about one important point for followers of Jesus Christ: we have everything we need to live lives of obedience, holiness, and faithfulness to our Lord and Savior. Our spiritual backpack is fully packed, and we are ready to go! Here's how Peter puts it: "His divine power has granted to us all things that pertain to life and godliness" (1:3). God's power in us—his indwelling Holy Spirit—has made us capable of living for him in this sinful and fallen world. We can say no to the sin that used to rule over us, and we have "escaped from the corruption" that plagues those who do not know Jesus (1:4). If we have everything we need to live for Jesus through faith in him, what should we do?

Peter's answer is simple: work hard on your faith. That sounds like it might be legalistic; it's not! Peter believes what the rest of the Bible teaches—we are saved completely by God's grace, through faith, because of Jesus's work on the cross for us. In fact, Peter knew that well; he had failed Jesus on more than one occasion. He was not one to trust his own effort as his means of salvation! Yet Peter calls us to "make every effort to supplement [our] faith" with Christian virtues—good signs of obedience to Jesus Christ (1:5). It is this kind of effort—this kind of intense pursuit of holiness by the power of the Holy Spirit—that Peter says will keep us from being "ineffective or unfruitful" in our relationship with our Savior (1:8).

Do you really believe that you have everything you need to live a holy life for Jesus in this world? If you are a real Christian, then Peter says that you do! Ask God today to help you put forth effort as you walk with him. Seek to obey him—by the strength the Holy Spirit gives—so that you will be effective and fruitful as you follow your Savior.

Eyewitness and a Better Witness

The basketball game was tied with just three seconds remaining on the clock, and the home team had the ball. Just before the final buzzer sounded, one of the players—fading away from the basket—threw a final shot. *Swish!* The fans rushed onto the court; it was a fantastic, buzzer-beating win for the hometown team. The next day, a still-elated fan was asked about the game by several of his friends who had not been able to attend. As he recounted the final seconds to them, they listened and trusted his description. Why? Because he had been there. He was an eyewitness!

How can we know that Jesus is the Son of God—the divine ruler who will one day judge the earth in glory? Peter reminds us that he was there. He saw Jesus on the Mount of Transfiguration, changed before the eyes of his disciples and glorified in their presence. Peter remembers the words that God the Father spoke on that day about his Son: "This is my beloved Son, with whom I am well pleased" (1:17). "I was there!" Peter reminds his readers. "We were with him on the holy mountain" (1:18). Peter knows from firsthand, eyewitness experience that Jesus Christ was who he claimed to be: God's Son, the glorious King, the divine Judge of the entire earth. Then comes the surprise.

Peter says something is more sure than even his own personal experience that confirms that Jesus is God's Son—the infinitely powerful King, Ruler, and Judge of all the earth. What could it be? It is the witness of Scripture. More sure than eyewitness experience, more certain than Peter, James, and John's hearing God's voice speaking from heaven, *God's word* is the surest indication that Jesus is the almighty ruler and Judge! Peter writes, "We have the prophetic word more fully confirmed, to which you will do well to pay attention" (1:19). God's word—the Old Testament Scripture, in this instance—verifies who Jesus is. That is a better witness than even people who saw him face-to-face!

Talk to God about your attitude toward his word. Measure it against Peter's attitude: Peter trusted the witness of God's word more than his own personal experience! Ask God to help you believe his word and trust its witness that Jesus Christ is who he claimed to be—the Son of God, come in the flesh, who will one day return as the glorious King and Judge of all the earth.

It's Not Science Fiction

A series of television commercials for the United States Air Force shows scenes that look like they come straight from futuristic, science fiction movies. We see shots from outer space and amazing, weird technology. Then comes the tagline: "It's not science fiction." The shot morphs into a battle scene or a man in a control tower. What seems like science fiction is actually reality; our Air Force is doing amazing things with technology and military advancements. It's an effective ad campaign.

Peter makes a similar point as he turns to the topic of the return of the Lord Jesus Christ. It seems that some people had begun to question the reality of our Savior's return to this earth. "Where is the promise of his coming?" some were asking (3:4). This was dangerous talk, and it seems to have the potential to distract true Christians from reality. Peter's response is like that Air Force commercial: "It's not science fiction; Jesus really is coming back!" His exact words are, "The day of the Lord will come like a thief, and then the heavens will pass away with a roar, and the heavenly bodies will be burned up and dissolved, and the earth and the works that are done on it will be exposed" (3:10). The day of the Lord is coming—it's not science fiction. When Jesus, the great Judge, does return, it will mean the destruction, judgment, and exposure of this sinful world before his glory and holiness. What do we do about it?

Peter's call to his audience in light of this coming return is actually intensely practical. Jesus is coming back. The earth is going to be dissolved by fire. What should we do? We should live holy and obedient lives in Jesus Christ, our Savior. In this kind of living, we serve to hasten the coming of Jesus as we wait expectantly for our Savior to come. Do you believe Jesus is coming back to judge this earth? Are you *living* like you believe that?

Ask God to make you more conscious of the return of his Son, Jesus Christ, to this world. Pray that he would help you believe that Jesus is coming back—it's not science fiction! Then ask God to help you live in a way that is mindful of this fact. Pray that he would give you strength to pursue holiness and godliness as you follow your gracious Savior every day.

Walk in the Light

There is a popular sentiment today that what really matters is not what we *do*; it's the fact that our heart was in the right place. Amazingly, people in our culture today have the ability to somehow separate morality and goodness from the actual way they are living their lives. We learn from the book of 1 John that this tendency is far from new. During the days of the apostle John, people who claimed the name of Jesus Christ sought to separate *knowledge* about Jesus from *lives of holiness and obedience* lived for him. John tells us very clearly: our actions matter.

Here is how John begins to make this point in this passage: "God is light, and in him is no darkness at all. If we say we have fellowship with him while we walk in darkness, we lie and do not practice the truth" (1:5–6). John could not be clearer as he makes this point—a point that he will continue to make throughout this letter. "Christians" who continue to sin intentionally and habitually are demonstrating that they do not truly belong to Jesus. Their knowledge or good intentions are irrelevant; ultimately, they prove who they are by how they live. Friend, are you walking in the light today?

In case you think John is some kind of legalist or someone pushing a "salvation by works" agenda, listen to what he says right after the verse we read: "If we say we have no sin, we deceive ourselves, and the truth is not in us. If we confess our sins, he is faithful and just to forgive us our sins and to cleanse us from all unrighteousness" (1:8–9). John is not teaching that Christians must be perfect, or that they ever will be until heaven! Rather, this verse helps us discover what kind of sin does not fit into the life of a follower of Jesus: *unconfessed, intentional, habitual sin.* There is grace and forgiveness and cleansing for all who repent of sin! People who truly experience that, though, will not live intentionally in their sin any more.

Spend a few minutes thanking God for his forgiveness and the cleansing we receive through the sacrificial death of Jesus Christ in our place. Then ask God to help you walk in the light, not in the darkness. Pray that he would make your life reflect Jesus!

How Do I Know That I Am Saved?

A young man sat in his youth pastor's office, head in his hands. The pastor had known him for a long time; the young man was a prominent part of the youth ministry at church, and the pastor was excited about his life, leadership at church, and gospel ministry at school. Yet the young man had asked to meet because he was struggling with serious doubts about his salvation. "How do I know, for sure, that I am really saved?" he asked, sincere concern in his eyes.

Have you been there? Have you wondered how you can know if you truly belong to Jesus forever? Wouldn't it be nice if there were a checklist that you could work through to make sure? Well, the apostle John doesn't give us a checklist, but he does help us boil this question down to two important marks of a true Christian.

First, a true Christian has genuine love for other believers in Jesus. That's a repeated theme in John's letter, and it is a major theme in 1 John 3:11–24. John says that the simple command to love one another is one that has been there "from the beginning" (3:11). In other words, this has always been a marker of God's true people! John even clarifies, helpfully, what kind of love we are to have for other Christians. It's love like that of Jesus, who "laid down his life for us" (3:16). That is how we know what love is! It's radically sacrificial love for other believers in Jesus. Does that characterize your life and heart today?

Second, a true Christian affirms that Jesus Christ is God's Son, come in the flesh as a human being. This is a concept that has shown up more strongly in other parts of John's letter, but he mentions it again briefly in this passage, as he summarizes the two marks of a real Christian: "This is his commandment, that we believe in the name of his Son Jesus Christ and love one another, just as he has commanded us" (3:23). Real Christians love God's people, and they believe in Jesus Christ as God's Son in the flesh.

Are those marks of a true Christian evident in your life today? I hope they are! I hope that you find yourself loving God's people more and more, despite the many imperfections of the church today. I hope that you boldly affirm—in every situation—the divinity and humanity of Jesus, God's Son. Pray that these characteristics would mark you strongly as you follow Jesus!

Deceivers and True Believers

You've probably noticed that there is a lot in the New Testament—and especially in the Epistles—about people who are labeled "deceivers" (v. 7). Paul is worried about these kinds of people; the apostle John is as well. But we don't always know what deceivers look like in today's church context. What does a deceiver look like today? More importantly, how do we know that we are not being deceived as we follow Jesus Christ?

John's answer to these questions will have very little to do with the deceivers themselves and much more to do with how we live out our faith as Christians. While he does mention these deceivers, who "have gone out into the world," he doesn't spend any time identifying them or giving us key ways to expose them (v. 7). John focuses only on what our lives should look like as followers of Jesus. The genuine Christian life, John is saying, is the key to resisting these deceivers. What does he tell us to do?

Well, it is a very familiar message—one found also in 1 John. First, we continue to love one another as we follow Jesus together. True Christians love one another—it's the same commandment that has been given to us "from the beginning" (v. 6). As followers of Jesus truly love one another with the sacrificial love of Jesus, the gospel is bearing fruit in their lives in the right way! Second, we believe that Jesus Christ came to this earth as a human being. The first command had to do with our love—our lives with other believers. This command has to do with our belief. Deceivers, it seems, will question the reality of the incarnation of Jesus Christ—that he really came to earth as a human being and was fully God and fully human. True believers will commit themselves to continually affirming this wonderful—and mysterious—reality. It is so important because this is the core of our understanding of salvation!

How do you know if you are being deceived today? One way will be to look at your relationships with other followers of Jesus. Are you loving other Christians and making sacrifices to serve them? Another way will be to look at what you believe about Jesus and tell to other people about him. Are you resting in him as the Savior—fully God and fully man—who alone is the only way to peace with God? Talk to God about these things today. Ask him to protect you from being deceived!

Gaius and Diotrephes

There is a good chance that 1, 2, and 3 John were all written by the apostle at one time and carried together in a packet to be delivered. If this is true, then one of the three letters in this bundle was this letter—a more personal letter, to a man named Gaius. It's a short letter, which maybe you've never read before or given much thought to at all! What does this little letter, written to Gaius long ago, have to say to us today as twenty-first-century followers of Jesus Christ?

This letter reminds us, first, that God is pleased when we support and encourage his people. That's what the apostle John commends Gaius for as this letter begins. While we know nothing about Gaius outside of what is in this letter, John makes it clear in verses 5–8 that this man helps the brothers, loves the local church of Jesus, and supports the work of people who are preaching and teaching the gospel. We probably won't know until we meet Gaius in heaven exactly *how* he helped, supported, and encouraged these gospel workers, but because of John, we know that he did. And God is pleased with this man who encouraged his people as they sought to make Jesus known in the ancient world.

But another character shows up in this letter—a fellow named Diotrephes. John is not too happy with this man. Why? Because he "likes to put himself first" and does not recognize the authority of the apostles of Jesus Christ and their teaching (v. 9). This man has evidently spoken evil and untrue words about John, and possibly other apostles, and does the exact opposite of Gaius: "He refuses to welcome the brothers, and also stops those who want to and puts them out of the church" (v. 10). Diotrephes opposes the gospel of the apostles and fails to support and encourage God's people. God is not pleased with him, and neither is John! He tells Gaius that he will deal with this man when he comes.

While 3 John is a short letter, its message is clear: God's people, in every age, support gospel ministry and those who engage in it. How about you? How do you treat God's people? Do you pray for—and support—people who seek to share the good news about Jesus in your country and around the world? Ask God to make you like Gaius—a man who loved God's people and supported God's work.

Stay in the Love of God

Some books in the Bible require serious work in order to discover the author's purpose in writing. Jude is not one of those books! Jude tells his audience exactly why he is writing. He had hoped to write to encourage them, but he felt compelled to adjust his purpose in light of the situation of his audience. Jude's adjusted purpose is to encourage them "to contend for the faith that was once for all delivered to the saints" (v. 3). The believers to whom Jude writes are in a dangerous situation. Opponents of the gospel have crept into their midst and are threatening them with false teaching and sinful living. So how will Jude encourage these believers to contend for their faith?

First, he will remind them of God's judgment on sin throughout the ages. The middle part of the letter of Jude confuses people, but it's not that complex! Jude refers to several Old Testament examples—the Israelites who didn't have faith in God, the cities of Sodom and Gomorrah, and others—that all show God's righteous judgment against sin. Jude is reminding his audience that this kind of judgment waits for the false teachers who are plaguing God's people, as well as all who follow them.

Second, he will urge them to make an effort as they follow God; he tells them to "keep [them]selves in the love of God" as they wait for Jesus to finish their salvation (v. 21). This spiritual effort will not be individually focused only; Jude calls these believers to show mercy to people and to try to bring people back who have been deceived by false teachers!

Finally, Jude will remind them that the only way they can truly contend for the faith is if they are kept by God's powerful hand. Jude ends with one of the most beautiful benedictions in the entire Bible. He commits these believers to the God who is able to "keep [us] from stumbling" and to ultimately "present [us] blameless" on the last day (v. 24). Ultimately, how do believers contend for the faith? They are kept—perfectly—by a powerful and loving God!

There are false teachers today—even in your context! You will always be confronted with teaching that denies the gospel, the truth about salvation in Jesus Christ. Ask God to give you strength to keep yourself in his love as you contend for the faith that you know is true. And, as you do that, remember that God ultimately is the one who will keep you until the end. Trust him to do that for you!

The Beginning of the End

A frightening beast, giant scorpions, ghostly riders on horses—these are just a few of the features of the book of Revelation that can tempt us to think of it as science fiction rather than reality. Full of unfamiliar visions, great battles, and cosmic events, it is a book that intrigues us but often leaves us confused. Some Christians give up on it completely. "Jesus wins," they say, "that's all I need to know." But it's better to dig in to it and get serious about trying to understand Revelation! God has put Revelation in our Bible on purpose for us—for our encouragement and for our spiritual health. Therefore, dig in to this book!

The book of Revelation, as we find in the opening verses, is a grand vision that God gave to the apostle John, which he wrote down for the benefit of God's people in his day and in ours. This revelation was given to him so that God could "show to his servants the things that must soon take place" (1:1). So there is a future-oriented focus to this book; that's probably not surprising to you! Revelation tells us where this world is going and how this grand story will ultimately end. This is the ending to the story that began way back in Genesis 1 with God's creation of the world. It is the story that will finally be completed with Christ's return to judge the world and to perfectly redeem and reward all his true people. Friend, Revelation tells us about the final chapter of *our story*.

Meditate for a few moments on the final phrase of today's passage. John tells us that "the time is near" (1:3). We do not know exactly how soon; the Bible makes clear that Jesus's return will be unexpected. But we need to understand that—in the perspective of John and of the Bible—we are living in the last days. The time is near. Jesus will return to judge the world. This earth will end, and the new heavens and new earth will be established, with God reigning over his people forever. Are you ready for that?

Ask God to make you ready for Jesus to return and excited about the coming judgment and reign of your Savior. Pray that God would help you dig in to this great book and be challenged to believe its words—and to respond with true repentance and genuine faith!

Jesus Speaks

Of all the various parts, sections, and scenes of the book of Revelation, the first three chapters are probably the easiest to understand. In fact, what we find in these chapters is not unlike what we see in many other New Testament books: letters to ancient Christian churches. But there is something especially powerful about these seven letters: Jesus Christ himself dictates them to John. The risen and glorified Lord Jesus spoke these words to those ancient churches. We need to hear these today, and we should pay close attention!

Let's back up for a moment. John tells us that he was on the island of Patmos—exiled there as a criminal because of his faith in Jesus Christ and for preaching the gospel. John is old by this time and quite possibly discouraged. Yet it is on this island that John receives this astounding vision from God. This vision will be a grand, cosmic vision for the entire world. The book of Revelation shows us the end of the grand story of God's redemption! But we see in this passage that John's vision had another purpose as well. It was written—originally—for churches that were enduring persecution for the sake of Jesus Christ.

What is the first thing that Jesus wants to make sure these churches understand? It's that he is utterly in control—reigning as the risen and sovereign King over all creation. Listen again to what Jesus says to John as the apostle lies prostrate before him: "Fear not, I am the first and the last, and the living one. I died, and behold I am alive forevermore, and I have the keys of Death and Hades" (1:17–18). Jesus comes to John—and these seven ancient churches—first with a reminder of his resurrection and his power. Jesus is reigning. Even their persecution hasn't changed that! And it will be this glorious Savior and King who will speak powerful, encouraging, and challenging words to these seven churches. They will be words that we need to hear today as well!

As you think about this passage, remember that Jesus himself appeared to John in order to speak these words to these seven churches. Ask God to prepare your heart to listen to Jesus in the book of Revelation! Pray that your vision of Jesus, as you hear his words, would be the right one—a vision of the reigning and sovereign King of the entire earth.

Great in Jesus's Eyes

In this passage, Jesus speaks to two churches—the church at Sardis and the church at Philadelphia. You'll begin to notice that for every church, the message from Jesus is slightly different. Most have a mixture of encouragement and challenge, but usually the message is overwhelmingly either a rebuke or a comfort. As you consider the words to these two churches, think about what Jesus might say to your local church community.

Sardis, it seems, is a church whose faith has become dry, lifeless, and fake. They have the "reputation of being alive" (3:1)—this is a well-known and well-respected church! Yet Jesus finds fault with them. What is the solution to this deadness and lack of genuine faith-filled life? It is *repentance*. "Wake up," Jesus tells them (3:3). This is a group of people that started out strong, but they have lost their joy, their life, and the true foundation of their faith. Sin has crept into their community, and it has led to dry and inauthentic worship. It is time for Sardis to repent, wake up, and remember the word of the gospel that was at the beginning of their faith.

The tone of Jesus's words to Philadelphia (not to be confused with the American city!) is completely different. This is a different kind of church from Sardis; rather than a great reputation, Philadelphia has "but little power" (3:8). Yet they receive one of the greatest compliments Jesus can give: "You have kept my word and have not denied my name" (3:8). This little church— weak in the eyes of the world—has stood strong for Jesus in the midst of persecution and suffering. They have held fast to "patient endurance" and have not let go of the gospel (3:10). For this church, Jesus has nothing but words of encouragement. He points them forward to a day when they will be with him forever in the "city of my God" (3:12). The little church at Philadelphia has proved more faithful than the church with the great reputation. And it's Jesus's opinion that matters most!

Do you need to hear the voice of Jesus saying to you today, "Wake up!"? If so, listen to him! If there's repentance of sin that you need to do, do it right now, before God. If you need to be reminded of the gospel, spend some more time in God's word today. Let Jesus's words to these churches speak directly to your heart and life!

A Strong, Fierce Jesus

There's a famous painting by William Holman Hunt (perhaps you've seen it!) of a gentle, mild-looking Jesus knocking on the door of someone's heart. He's pleading to enter in to have fellowship with this person. But there's a catch: the door only has a handle on the inside! The person must open the door of the heart to Jesus and allow him to come in.

That was one artist's take on this passage of Scripture—this letter from Jesus to the church at Laodicea. Certainly, Jesus is knocking on the door of this church, asking them to let him in so that he can eat with them. This artist—and many others—took this passage to be an evangelistic invitation from a gentle and mild Jesus. Though many other passages of Scripture do call us to evangelism and show us a kind and gentle Jesus, this passage is *not* one of them. What is this passage all about?

First, this is a letter to a church! It is not a letter to people who have not heard the gospel, nor is it designed as an evangelistic invitation. Jesus speaks here to people who are part of the church of God—people who have heard the gospel and professed faith but are living in pride, sin, and self-sufficiency. The Laodiceans' words are words of spiritual pride not of humble faith: "I am rich, I have prospered, and I need nothing" (3:17). These people have completely forgotten the grace of Jesus that saves sinners. This church has lost the gospel; they think they can do it all on their own.

Second, this letter is a rebuke from a strong, fierce Jesus. Look again at the phrase that comes before Jesus's knocking: "Those whom I love, I reprove and discipline, so be zealous and repent" (3:19). This is not a gentle tapping on the door! This is Jesus pounding on the door of his church and demanding repentance from people who have forgotten the gospel. Today, let this passage speak to your own heart. Let it warn you to not forget the gospel and the grace that you need from Jesus. Without him, we are all "wretched, pitiable, poor, blind, and naked" (3:17).

Spend a few minutes talking to God about this passage. Ask him to help you always remember the gracious gift of salvation, which comes only through faith in Jesus Christ. Pray that he would protect you from spiritual pride and would help you to be always dependent on Jesus the Savior.

Into the Throne Room of God

You may not like the word *theology*. It may frighten you a bit, or it may sound like a word for serious scholars who have done much more studying and writing than you'll ever do! Theology, you may think, has no place in the life of a normal, everyday Christian. But the reality is, we all do theology. Theology—meaning, literally, "God talk" but understood as "the study of God"—is something that we can't help but do every time we read the Bible, pray, or have a conversation with someone about our faith. *You* do theology if you have ever thought or talked about God!

You can have opinions on lots of things that don't matter. You can argue about which NFL team is the best or about what movie is the greatest of all time. But your thoughts about God matter. The way you think about and understand the God of the universe matters. What is your vision of God?

Revelation 4 takes us directly into the throne room of God in heaven and gives us just a small glimpse of a vision of God. The first aspect of this vision that strikes us is the worship and praise of this great God. It goes on continually! The throne of God is surrounded by other thrones, with elders, spirits, and angelic living creatures. These living creatures—the final angelic beings mentioned—spend their time praising God: "Day and night they never cease to say, 'Holy, holy, holy, is the Lord God Almighty, who was and is and is to come!'" (4:8). God receives unceasing praise and worship from his angelic servants.

But the living creatures aren't the only ones who worship and praise this great God. The elders—probably a different kind of angelic being—continually fall down before the throne, cast their crowns before God, and declare God's worthiness. They praise him for being the Creator of all things, the one who is deserving of all praise and honor. This is the God who is completely worthy of all praise from every creature he has created.

What is your response to this passage—this praise scene from the throne room of heaven? Is this your vision of God? More importantly, do you want to join in this praise? This chapter of Scripture shows us a God who is completely worthy of all praise and glory. His true servants love joining in with the angels to glorify the God who is the glorious and worthy Creator!

A Great Multitude

Many intelligent people have debated the meaning of this text! The main source of debate is the large number of people who are gathered—144,000 "from every tribe of the sons of Israel" (7:4). Is this a literal number, identifying the exact number of ethnically Jewish people who will be saved at the last day? Is this a figurative number, meant to symbolize the fullness of God's people who are saved? Here, we'll focus on what seems to be central in the apostle John's view as he writes this part of the book of Revelation. Regardless of what or whom the 144,000 represent, a big group of people shows up soon after, and this group will be of interest to anyone who knows Jesus as Lord and Savior!

John wants us to know that God's redeemed people will be a mixed multitude of people from all over the world: "A great multitude that no one could number, from every nation, from all tribes and peoples and languages" (7:9). This is a snapshot of the people of God, who will gather in praise to their great King forever. This is where *you* are headed, if you belong to Jesus Christ through faith—part of *this very multitude*, singing with people from all history and all parts of the world, who have tasted the great salvation of God through Jesus Christ. These verses should encourage you to keep sharing the gospel and to keep hoping for this future day of joy.

John wants us to understand how God's redeemed people become God's redeemed people. One of the elders before the throne of God tells us the answer to this question: "These are the ones coming out of the great tribulation. They have washed their robes and made them white in the blood of the Lamb" (7:14). What do all these people from all over the world have in common? They have been saved, forgiven, and redeemed by the blood of Jesus, shed for sinners. This is what, ultimately, brings diverse people together; it is the only lasting source of true unity for different nations and peoples. It is the saving work of Jesus Christ on the cross!

Ask God to help you look forward to the day when you will gather with his redeemed people to sing praises to him for his salvation. Pray that he would help you remember that it is the blood of Jesus alone that can unify this great multitude, and ask him to help you share the gospel hope with others!

Jesus Will Win

This passage seems almost mythical, doesn't it? Like something you might see in a science fiction movie or *The Lord of the Rings*! And, while there are many different views on the precise meaning (and timing) of the events in this passage, almost everyone agrees that there are at least *some* figurative parts and descriptions going on here. While we don't have time to tackle every interpretation of what happens in this passage (and *when* it happens), we will identify two major truths that we see here. First, we see that God's Son will reign over God's people and will never be defeated by evil. John sees a vision of a "woman clothed with the sun, with the moon under her feet, and on her head a crown of twelve stars" (12:1). Most scholars agree that this woman represents God's people, Israel. The woman's Son then is the promised Messiah—Jesus Christ himself. The dragon, Satan, attempts to devour the child, but the child is "caught up to God and to his throne" (12:5). The point here is clear: this Son—Jesus—is God's protected and promised King for his people. Satan's efforts against him will *never* succeed; God's purposes through Jesus will surely come to pass!

Second, we see that Satan will continue to make war on God's people until he himself is finally destroyed. While God's protection of the Messiah and his plan through him is clear from this passage, it is also clear that the battle isn't completely over yet. Satan will keep on going after all who follow this Messiah—for as long as he can! Here is what John sees: "Then the dragon became furious with the woman and went off to make war on the rest of her offspring" (12:17). The final verdict is secure: Jesus *will* win in the end. But until then Satan will attack God's people out of his hatred and spite.

Be encouraged by this chapter in Revelation. Thank God that his purpose in Jesus—for you—is secure. Jesus will win in the end, and if you belong to him, you will one day reign with him! But also be warned by this chapter. Satan's days are numbered, but he still has fury left to unleash on all who follow Jesus. There may be difficult times ahead for you; ask God to keep you safe and secure in your Savior!

The Only Categories That Matter

We divide and categorize people in lots of different ways, don't we? In your school, students are divided by grades—freshman to senior. Economically, we sometimes divide people into three basic categories: lower class, middle class, and upper class. We could go on. Yet passages like Revelation 14 remind us of the one great divide at the end of this world. At the last day, there will be only two categories for every human being who has ever lived. What are they?

First, we see the redeemed people of God. What does John's vision tell us about this group? Their seal of salvation is secure, unbreakable, and eternal. This group of 144,000—most likely a figurative number representing the complete group of God's people—is set apart as those who have the name of the Lamb written on their foreheads. They are singing joyfully before the throne of God as they stand blameless before a holy God, because of the redemption they have in Jesus Christ, his Son. If you belong to Jesus, through repentance and faith, this is *you*. You will stand with all God's redeemed people on the last day and sing praises to your Savior.

Second, we see another group: all people who follow and worship "the beast and its image" (14:9). This group of people receives God's wrath, poured out in judgment on all who reject his Son. Here is the terrible description of the judgment that this group receives: they "will be tormented with fire and sulfur in the presence of the holy angels and in the presence of the Lamb" (14:10). The chapter ends with the vivid picture of God's wrath poured out on the earth, depicted by harvest imagery. Jesus himself comes as the great Judge, and he swings his sickle to harvest the earth.

This is the great divide at the end of time, when Jesus Christ returns to judge this world. These two categories—redeemed and judged—will be the only categories that matter—the *final* categories. Every human being who has ever lived will one day stand before Jesus as one of the redeemed or be judged under God's wrath for rejecting the great King and Savior.

Pray today that God would make you expectant, hopeful, and ready for the return of your Savior, Jesus Christ. Then ask God to make you even more excited to share the good news of the salvation that can be found in Jesus, so that others will join the crowd of the redeemed!

The End of Sin

This passage is grotesque, at least as it concludes. It is meant to be that way! This passage shows us the two meals that will conclude history—one meal that you want to be a part of and one meal that you want nothing to do with. If the imagery is vivid, it is because God wants his people to see the ugly end of sin and the great banquet that awaits all those who belong to Jesus.

The first meal that we read about in this passage is a glorious one—the marriage supper of the Lamb. Whether or not this is a literal meal that will happen some day for all God's people, the point of John's vision is clear: all God's redeemed people will feast joyfully in the presence of Jesus, their Savior! Those who will take part in this meal are called blessed—they are part of God's people, the bride, and they will share in celebration and worship forever. For those who belong to Jesus, this is the source of great hope. A day of feasting, celebration, and joy is coming. We will get to sit and dine with our Savior!

The second meal, though, is not so happy. John tells us that not everyone will be invited to this marriage supper of the Lamb. All who reject the rule of God over them will experience the "great supper of God" (19:17). What is this supper all about? It is about God's judgment on all who make war against him and his Son. While Jesus does sit and feast joyfully with his people, he is also the fierce judge of all the world—the one who will one day make war in righteousness and "fury" (19:15). As Jesus conquers and judges his enemies, John hears an angel cry out to the birds flying overhead: "Come, gather for the great supper of God" (19:17). Here is the second meal of the passage. This is no joyful feast; these birds will devour the flesh of God's enemies as God's righteous judgment falls upon them through Jesus.

Remember that this is meant to be, for us, a vivid reminder of the end of sin—the final result of all who reject Jesus Christ. They will be judged for failing to come under the rule of God's great King. Ask God to give you hope, in Jesus, that you will one day share in the marriage supper of the Lamb. Ask him to remind you of these two meals, so that you will live your life with eternal perspective.

Lake of Fire and Book of Life

Revelation 20 describes three of the most important events that will ever occur in all human history. Friend, we are coming to the end of this story. Many people believe that these things haven't happened yet—but they will. God, because he loves us, has told us what is coming! So, what are these events?

First, John tells us that Satan will be bound, and Christ will reign with his people on earth for a period of one thousand years. Depending on your church and theological tradition, you may believe that this is a symbolic period of time—actually taking place now—during which Satan is bound and the gospel is able to grow in the world. Or you may believe that this speaks of a future period of time when the reign of Christ and his people will be much more open, forceful, and obvious. Either way, this is a *temporary* situation, which comes *before* the final judgment of Satan and of all people.

Second, we find that Satan and all his forces will be defeated and punished forever. After the period of Satan's binding, the great enemy of God's people will emerge one more time to "deceive the nations" and "gather them for battle" against Jesus and his people (20:8). It won't be much of a contest, though! Fire will come down from heaven and this army of sin and death will be finally destroyed, with Satan cast into the lake of fire forever. This is the last we hear from Satan!

Finally, this passage tells us that there will be a final judgment for every human being who has ever lived. After Satan is defeated and punished, the books will be thrown open. John describes a great multitude of people "standing before the throne" to be judged (20:12). Those whose names are found in the book of life will be saved, to live forever in the presence of Jesus the King. Those whose names are not there are thrown into the same place as Satan—the lake of fire.

We will stand before the throne of Jesus someday to be judged. On what grounds do you hope to survive that judgment? On what basis do you expect to escape the lake of fire, where Satan and all who follow him will be punished? Ask God to help you stand firm on faith in Christ alone. It is Jesus—only Jesus—whose death and resurrection can secure our place in the book of life. Trust him today!

Will You Be There?

You've probably seen cartoons of angels on clouds holding harps! If we're not careful, we can embrace a skewed vision of heaven that is anything but biblical. In fact, many of us (if we're honest) have wondered if heaven will be boring. An eternal church service? No, thank you!

The vision of eternity with Jesus that we see in Revelation 21 is anything but boring. And, as the chapter begins, our first mistaken way of thinking about eternity is corrected. We think about heaven as an ethereal, spiritual, and perhaps even *weird* place. That's not what is in store for followers of Jesus Christ. Listen to what John says: "Then I saw a new heaven and a new earth, for the first heaven and the first earth had passed away" (21:1). Heaven is not *just* heaven; it is a new heaven and a new *earth*. A physical place. A marvelous, glorious, perfect place where human beings will live, dwell, work, and worship forever. This will be beyond our imagination—far greater than the best experiences we have ever had in this fallen world. There will be nothing boring about God's new creation for his people!

Yet while the place itself is amazing, John's focus is not merely on the place. He calls our attention to God's people. There they are—there *we* are—presented finally and perfected as the "bride adorned for her husband" (21:2). We are reminded that this marvelous place—this new heaven and earth—has been prepared by God for his beloved people. All those redeemed by Jesus, God's Son, get to share in this eternal joyful existence.

So here we are—at the end of the story. It is yet to come, but this ending is secure and safe, because God has determined and planned it. This wonderful day will come! God's people will be forever in God's place, under his perfect rule. The only question that remains—for you and every other person on earth—is: Will *you* be there?

Spend some time looking forward to the ending of God's story. John glimpsed it far into the future. It is coming more quickly than you or I can imagine. Are you ready? Are you excited about being with your Savior forever? Is this ending your great hope, the motivation for your daily life? Talk to God about this. Ask him to establish you securely in your faith in his Son, so that you will look forward to this great day with joyful expectation!

Amen!

If you have any doubt about the Bible being one big story of God's redemptive work in the world he created, look at how the final chapter of the Bible begins. What do we see there? It's a familiar object—one that showed up at the very beginning of this story in the book of Genesis. It is the tree of life. This same tree, which Adam and Eve were barred from after their sin, is now central to the eternal city of God. It bears fruit for all God's people, and they have full access to the eternal life that God gives. This is the glorious ending to the big story of the Bible. The great fall has been dealt with, sin is conquered through Jesus, and God's redeemed people partake forever in *life*.

In the midst of the final descriptions of this great eternal city of God, there is one central idea that John—and Jesus—want us to get. What is it? Jesus, the Savior and Judge, is coming soon to complete this world's story. Jesus keeps repeating this, doesn't he? He says, "Behold, I am coming soon" (22:7). And again: "Behold, I am coming soon" (22:12). And finally: "Surely I am coming soon" (22:20). John even adds a comment, to make sure we don't miss what Jesus is saying: "The time is near" (22:10). Friend, Jesus *is* returning to this earth *soon*. It may not be tomorrow, but it will happen. Jesus wants us to know this, and he wants us to be ready!

After the final repetition of this theme by Jesus, John responds to his quickly approaching return with words of faith—words that all true Christians should echo in their hearts. John says, "Amen. Come, Lord Jesus!" (22:20). Is *that* the prayer of your heart today? Do your heart and soul echo a great "amen!" to Jesus, who promises to return, judge, and reign *soon*? Are you eager to meet your Savior and worship him for all eternity? Believe this glorious word, and wait expectantly for this story's ending. For, if you are in Christ, you have an infinitely glorious future that awaits you.

Spend some time today expanding on that response of John: "Amen. Come, Lord Jesus!" Think about how you can better prepare to meet him face-to-face. Ask God to make you a bold witness to the only one who can save, forgive, and completely justify lost sinners!

The Gospel

To conclude, we are going to look at three key passages that remind us of the central message of the Bible story: the gospel. We will look at the gospel *promised* (Gen. 3:14–15). We will see the gospel *explained* (1 Cor. 15:1–4). And we will see Jesus's call to all of us for the gospel to be *proclaimed* (Matt. 28:16–20).

GENESIS 3:14-15

The Genesis passage reminds us that the gospel was not an afterthought in God's plan, some kind of sideshow endeavor, or a plan B for his sinful, stubborn people. The gospel was God's plan for saving lost people from the very beginning. How amazing is it that even in Genesis 3, at the darkest and lowest point of human history, we hear the first promise of the gospel in Scripture. Adam and Eve have just blatantly disregarded God's word and rebelled against his rule. They both ate the forbidden fruit and rejected God as their King. God would have been completely justified in being *done* with humanity at this point—in throwing them away and starting over. But God didn't do that. He made a promise, even as he punished sin. He pointed far into the future when a human seed of Eve would bruise the head of Satan and have complete and final victory over sin.

This promise of God, often called the *protoevangelium* (or "first gospel") gives us a way to understand the entire drama of the Bible from Genesis to the Gospels. The events are not random! God is sovereignly laying the groundwork for the fulfillment of this first gospel promise that he made to his people. In fact, the whole story of the Bible is rushing forward to the ultimate culmination of all God's promises in Jesus Christ—his incarnation, sacrificial death, and glorious resurrection from the dead. Friend, remember the kind of God you serve and worship! He is the God who—at the darkest moment for humanity—made a promise of life, forgiveness, and salvation, which would cost his Son his very life. What an amazing, gracious, saving God!

Think back to that day in the garden of Eden, after the fall. Feel the shame, guilt, and devastation of Adam and Eve after their rejection of God's perfect rule. Then remember the gospel promise that our God made, even back then: a promise of final victory and salvation that would be achieved by the seed of Adam and Eve. Thank God for Jesus, who fulfills this great gospel promise!

1 CORINTHIANS 15:1-4

The 1 Corinthians passage summarizes the substance of the gospel, which was promised long before. It is, really, the gospel *explained*. So if someone asks you at some point, "What is the gospel?" you can take him or her to this passage. How does this passage explain the gospel to us?

First, it tells us that the gospel is about Jesus's sacrificial death. Paul begins by reminding the Corinthians about the gospel—the things "of first importance"—when he writes: "That Christ died for our sins" (15:3). We need to remember this! Any description of the gospel that does not include Jesus's death for our sins hasn't done the job. The gospel tells us how Jesus's death dealt finally with the sin of God's people—a sacrificial death *for* sin. Above all, this is what the cross of Jesus accomplishes; Jesus makes atonement for the sins of all God's true people, who will repent of sin and trust in him as Savior and Lord.

Second, this passage tells us that the gospel is about Jesus's resurrection from the dead. His death on the cross paid the price for our sins, but it was his resurrection that conquered death forever for all his people. The gospel is about Jesus's death *and* his resurrection from the dead. Jesus doesn't stay dead; his resurrection is God's proof that this work on the cross was acceptable and effective for lost sinners. Christians serve and follow a risen Savior and Lord; their hope for eternal life is anchored in his resurrection!

Finally, this passage tells us that the gospel is also anchored in God's word. Did you notice the phrase that is repeated after each part of Paul's gospel summary? It's the phrase, "in accordance with the Scriptures." Paul wants to be clear—everything about the gospel is *in line* with God's word and all his promises to his people. Christ's death for sin and his resurrection from the dead fulfill God's word—including that first gospel promise in the garden of Eden!

Thank God for this gospel! Thank him for the good news that Jesus died for your sin and rose from the dead to secure your resurrection and eternal life. Ask God to help you hold on to this gospel with all your strength. It is of first importance!

MATTHEW 28:16-20

We will end with the final words that Jesus spoke to his disciples before his ascension. These words—famous ones, to say the least—call *all* followers of Jesus Christ to bear witness to the gospel everywhere!

The call from Jesus is clear; his disciples are to go everywhere and teach everything that they have learned from him. This gospel—promised by God long ago and delivered gloriously in the person of Jesus Christ—is good news for all the world. It is meant to be shared! Then Jesus goes even further. His disciples are not just to preach the good news; they are to make disciples of people who believe. Friend, people who *believe* the gospel are to *share and teach* the gospel. They are to multiply and to spread the good news of Jesus everywhere!

As you end this year of Bible reading, I leave you with this challenge: if you truly believe the gospel that the Bible proclaims, share it boldly! Tell others about Jesus. Become a true disciple of your Savior and begin making disciples of others. The Bible is the great story of God's salvation, and it is a story that must be shared with the world!

Thank God for his glorious word. Thank him that he is a God who speaks to his people—who makes the news of his salvation accessible and understandable to us. Ask him to make you a witness to the gospel, so that others will know Jesus because of your life!

Notes

1. A paraphrase of John Piper, *God Is the Gospel: Meditations on God's Love as the Gift of Himself* (Wheaton, IL: Crossway, 2005), 15.
2. Robert Frost, "The Road Not Taken," *Mountain Interval* (New York: Henry Holt and Company, 1916), 9.
3. *Pollyanna*, directed by David Swift (1960; Burbank, CA: Walt Disney Studios Home Entertainment, 2002).
4. Andy Naselli, "The Most Important Paragraph in the Bible," Andy Naselli website, November 19, 2009, http://andynaselli.com.
5. Martin Luther, quoted in Philip Schaff, *Modern Christianity: The German Reformation*, vol. 7 of *History of the Christian Church*, 8 vols. (1888; Christian Classics Ethereal Library, 2005), 289, http://www.ccel.org/ccel/schaff/hcc7.pdf.

Scripture Index

Bold text indicates devotional passages.

Also Available from Jon Nielson

In *Knowing God's Truth*, Jon Nielson provides a clear, meaningful, and practical approach to the basics of systematic theology, including Scripture, man, sin, church, and more. For further study, the attributing workbook and video study explore each chapter of the book, summarize the main points, and give biblical application.

For more information, visit **crossway.org**.